SAS/C™ Compiler, Student Edition

Release 1.0

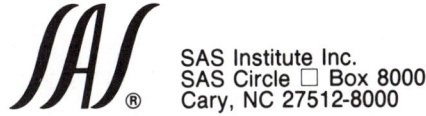

SAS®
SAS Institute Inc.
SAS Circle □ Box 8000
Cary, NC 27512-8000

The correct bibliographic citation for this manual is as follows: SAS Institute Inc. *SAS/C™ Compiler, Student Edition*, Cary, NC: SAS Institute Inc., 1988. 656 pp.

SAS/C™ Compiler, Student Edition

Copyright © 1988 by SAS Institute Inc., Cary, NC, USA.
ISBN 1-55544-301-X

All rights reserved. Printed in the United States of America. No part of this publication may be reproduced, stored in a retrieval system, or transmitted, in any form or by any means, electronic, mechanical, photocopying, or otherwise, without the prior written permission of the publisher, SAS Institute Inc.

89   88   4   3   2   1

Base SAS® software, the foundation of the SAS System, provides data retrieval and management, programming, statistical, and reporting capabilities. Also in the SAS System are SAS/GRAPH,® SAS/FSP,® SAS/ETS,® SAS/IMS-DL/I,® SAS/OR,® SAS/AF,® SAS/REPLAY-CICS,® SAS/DMI,® SAS/QC,® SAS/SHARE,® SAS/IML,® SAS/STAT,™ SAS/DB2,™ SAS/SQL-DS,™ and SAS/ACCESS™ software. Other products include SYSTEM 2000® Data Management Software, with basic SYSTEM 2000,® QueX,™ Multi-User,™ Screen Writer,™ CREATE,™ and CICS interface software; SAS/RTERM® software; and SAS/C™ and SAS/CX™ compilers. *SAS Communications,*® *SAS Training,*® *SAS Views,*® and SASware Ballot® are published by SAS Institute Inc. The Institute is a private company devoted to the support and further development of the software and related services.

SAS, SAS/OR, SAS/AF, SAS/FSP, SAS/GRAPH, SAS/ETS, SAS/IMS-DL/I, SAS/REPLAY-CICS, SAS/DMI, SAS/RTERM, SAS/QC, SAS/SHARE, SAS/IML, SYSTEM 2000, *SAS Communications*, *SAS Views*, *SAS Training*, and SASware Ballot are registered trademarks of SAS Institute Inc., Cary, NC, USA. SAS/STAT, SAS/DB2, SAS/SQL-DS, SAS/ACCESS, SAS/C, SAS/CX, QueX, Multi-User, Screen Writer, and CREATE are trademarks of SAS Institute Inc. A footnote should accompany the first use of each registered trademark or trademark and should state that the referenced trademark is used to identify products or services of SAS Institute Inc.

Contents

List of Illustrations ix

List of Tables xiii

Credits xv

How to Use This Book xvii

Part I C Language Tutorial 1

Chapter 1 An Introduction to Using C 3
Introduction 5
Tutorial Purpose 5
Tutorial Organization and Conventions 6
Using the Tutorial with Your Computer 7
Introduction to the Learning Modules 11
Module 1: Program Structure and the main() Function 11
Chapter Summary 17

Chapter 2 Data: Bits, Numbers, and Variables 19
Introduction 21
Module 2: Storage Concepts 21
Module 3: Identifying Data Items in C 27
Module 4: The Declaration Statement 33
Chapter Summary 40

Chapter 3 Operators and C 41
Introduction 43
Module 5: Operators—a First Look 43
Module 6: Introducing the C if Statement 49
Module 7: Writing Expressions in C 51
Chapter Summary 60

Chapter 4 Program Flow - Control and Repetition 61
Introduction 63
Module 8: More Control - the C switch Statement 63
Module 9: Looping with Control 68
Chapter Summary 87

Chapter 5 Introduction to Reading and Writing Data in C 89
Introduction 91
Module 10: Understanding Input and Output Operations .. 91
Module 11: How to Use the Basic C Input and Output Functions 95
Module 12: Using the C Preprocessor 105
Creating a Simple Menu 109
Chapter Summary 113

Chapter 6 Introduction to Functions in C 115
Introduction 117
Module 13: Function Basics in C 117
Module 14: Function Structure 120
A Function for Fun - The Shell Game 133
Chapter Summary 145

Chapter 7 Introduction to Arrays and Pointers 147
Introduction 149
Module 15: Working with Arrays in C 149
Module 16: An Introduction to Pointers 158
Converting Units of Measure 171
Chapter Summary 178

Chapter 8 Expanding the Basics: More on Operators and Types **179**

    Introduction **181**

    Module 17: More Operators - Working with Bits **181**

    Module 18:   More About Expressions **187**

    Module 19: An Introduction to Advanced Data Types **191**

    Chapter Summary **214**

Chapter 9 More on Expressions and the C Preprocessor **217**

    Introduction **219**

    Module 20: Storage Classes and Scope **219**

    Module 21: More on the C Preprocessor **228**

    Language for Fun - An Example Using the Preprocessor ... **239**

    Chapter Summary **248**

Chapter 10 Working with Data: Files, Structures, and Storage **249**

    Introduction **251**

    Module 22: More on I/O - Working with Files in C **251**

    Module 23: An Introduction to Data Structures **259**

    Chapter Summary **303**

Chapter 11 Helpful Hints **305**

    Introduction **307**

    Correcting C Code - Common Mistakes **307**

Part II User's Guide for the SAS/C™ Compiler, Student Edition 317

Chapter 12 Introduction to the User's Guide for the SAS/C™ Compiler, Student Edition 319
Introduction 321
Using the Student Compiler User's Guide 321
Your Program and the Student Compiler 323

Chapter 13 Installing the Student Compiler 327
Introduction 329
Recommended Computer Systems 329
Copying and Installing the Student Compiler 330
Creating a Path to Your SC Directory 333
Running the "Hello.C" Program 334
Chapter Summary 335

Chapter 14 Using the Student Compiler and Editor ... 337
Introduction 341
Using the Editing Screen and the Program Screen 341
Getting Started: Creating and Editing Programs 350
Compiling and Running Programs 370
Using the C Language Templates 383
Chapter Summary 388

Chapter 15 Programming Environment for the Student Compiler 389
Introduction 391
How the Student Compiler Uses Memory 391
Handling DOS Error Messages 394
The #include Files 396
Chapter Summary 398

Chapter 16 Standard Function Library for the Student Compiler 399

Chapter 17 Graphics and Screen Management Functions for the Student Compiler 527
Introduction 529
Introduction to Graphics on the Student Compiler 529
Screen Interface 529
Screen Management and Graphics Functions 537

Chapter 18 Source-Level Debugger for the Student Compiler 567
Introduction 569
The Student Compiler Debugger 569
The User Interface 571
Chapter Summary 584

Appendix 1 Error Messages for the Student Compiler 585
Overview 587
Compiler Operational Errors 587
Debugger Operational Errors 590
Compiler Syntax Errors and Warnings 590
Compiler Internal Errors 598

Appendix 2 ASCII Character Set 601

Part III Glossary and References 609

Glossary **611**

References **633**
   Compiler and C Programming References **635**
   PC DOS and MS-DOS References **635**
   iAPX86 References **636**

Function Index 637

Index 643

Illustrations

Figures

1.1	The Tutorial and Your Computer	8
1.2	Compile and Execute	10
1.3	Compile, Link, and Execute	10
2.1	Bit Positions in a Byte	22
4.1	Program Loops	70
4.2	The `for` Loop	73
4.3	The `while` Loop	78
4.4	The `do-while` Loop	82
5.1	Input and Output of Data	92
5.2	I/O Communication Process	92
5.3	Stream of Characters	93
5.4	Diagram of `getchar`	97
6.1	Sample Program Structure: `main()` and Three Other Functions	118
6.2	Shell Game Program Structure	119
6.3	Calling a Function with Formal Parameters	125
6.4	Basic Definition of a Function	131
7.1	The Ten Elements in the Array `numbers`	150
7.2	Array `numbers` with 4-byte Elements	150
7.3	Contents of Array `numbers`	151
7.4	An Array of Pointers	170
8.1	C Types	192
8.2	Using the Dot Operator	196
8.3	Using the Structure Pointer Operator	197
8.4	Space Requirements of a Union Versus a Structure	199

x Illustrations

8.5	Program Flow Using the Add Option	204
9.1	Definition of an External Variable	223
10.1	Relationship Between Data, Data File, and Data Base	260
10.2	A Data Base Entry	262
10.3	A Simple Linked List	267
10.4	The Components of a Simple Binary Tree	268
10.5	A More Extensive Binary Tree	268
10.6	Construction of the Linked List	270
10.7	Construction of the Binary Tree	271
10.8	The Data Base Operations	275
10.9	Sorting a List into a Tree	291
12.1	Translating Your Program	324
15.1	Model of the Student Compiler's Memory Organization	392
17.1	Character Boxes for an Uppercase A and Lowercase Q	531
17.2	Attribute Byte for a Character Box	535
18.1	Debugging Process	570

Screens

13.1	Installing the Student Compiler on a Hard Disk System	331
14.1	Editing Screen	343
14.2	Display of the SC Default Menu	346
14.3	The Edit Menu	352
14.4	The Block Menu	356
14.5	The Search Menu	364

14.6	Searching for a String	**365**
14.7	Program Screen	**367**
14.8	The File Menu	**371**
14.9	Help Window Display	**372**
14.10	Help Window—Function Display	**373**
14.11	Executing a Program	**377**
14.12	Program Screen While Debugging	**381**
14.13	The Templates Menu	**384**
18.1	Debugger Screen	**572**
18.2	Session Menu	**575**
18.3	Display Menu	**576**
18.4	Where Command	**579**
18.5	Break Menu	**580**
18.6	Execute Menu	**582**

Tables

2.1	Typical Ranges for C Variables on a PC (Machine Dependent)	30
3.1	Relational Operators	46
3.2	Logical Operators, Use and Meaning	47
3.3	Order of Evaluation for Operators—Highest to Lowest	53
5.1	Character I/O Functions	96
5.2	String Input/Output Functions	100
5.3	ASCII Character Manipulation Macros in `ctype.h`	107
8.1	General Rules for Arithmetic and Implicit Type Conversions	202
8.2	C Operators	214
9.1	Availability and Duration of C Storage Classes	220
9.2	Storage Class Keywords and the Use of Definitions	221
9.3	When to Use the Keyword `extern`	224
10.1	File Modes in C	254
13.1	Creating an AUTOEXEC.BAT File	333
14.1	Summary of Commands in Each SC Menu	344
14.2	Selecting a Menu	347
14.3	Executing a Command Within a Menu	348
14.4	Fast Path Method of Executing Commands	349
14.5	Student Compiler Key Combinations	382
15.1	Student Compiler's Data Type Characteristics	394
15.2	`errno` Codes and Their Definitions	395
17.1	Text Display Modes	532
17.2	Graphics Display Modes	533

xiv Tables

17.3	Background Colors and Blinking Characteristic for Text Display Modes	536
17.4	Colors for Graphics and Text Display Modes	536
17.5	Foreground Intensity and Text Appearance	537
17.6	Display Modes and Constants	540
17.7	Color Palette	555
18.1	Summary of Commands in Each Debugger Menu	574

Credits

Publication Credits

Composition	Gail Freeman, Cindy Hopkins, Blanche Phillips, Craig Sampson, David Tyree
Graphic Design	Jesse Chavis, Ginny Matsey
Proofreading	Gina Eatmon, Bruce Brown, Rick Cornell, Reid Hardin, Michael Smith, Helen Weeks
Technical Review	Kevin Bond, Mark Gass, Joe Hutchinson, Richard Krueger, Gary Merrill, Holly Whittle
Testing	Eric Brinsfield, Betsy Corning, Anne Corrigan, Ottis Cowper, Carolyn Dean, John Gough, Ann Lehman, Carol Linden, Toni Sherrill, Judy Whatley, Curtis Yeo
Writing and Editing	Susan Johnston, Gary Merrill, Dee Stribling, Harriet Watts, Curtis Yeo

Software Credits

Product Design and Integration	Richard Krueger
Editor	Richard Krueger
Compiler	Glen Musial, Gary Merrill, Richard Krueger
Debugger	Richard Krueger, Russell Gonsalves, Edmund Burnette
Help Feature	Gary Merrill
Window/Menu Interface	Edmund Burnette
Examples	Kevin Bond, Gary Merrill
Testing	Mark Gass, Twilah Blevins
Language Features and Environments Manager	Gary Merrill
Division Director	Oliver Bradley

How to Use This Book

Introduction

This book combines two books into one: a C language tutorial and a user's guide to the SAS/C Compiler, Student Edition. The Tutorial teaches you how to write programs in the C language and provides many examples and samples to work with. The User's Guide describes the SAS/C Compiler, Student Edition Software, which includes a C compiler, editor, source-level debugger, and sample programs.

This section explains how you can best use this combined book. Each part of the book is described here so that you know where to go for information based on your level of knowledge of programming or of the C language. The organization of this book is as follows:

- Part I: C Language Tutorial
- Part II: User's Guide for the SAS/C Compiler, Student Edition
- Part III: Glossary and References
- SAS/C Compiler, Student Edition software for an IBM personal computer (or its compatible equivalents).

Part I: C Language Tutorial

The Tutorial introduces you to the C programming language. The first half of the Tutorial presents basic C language concepts and features to help you build a good C programming foundation. The second half introduces you to more advanced features and programming techniques. The first half of the Tutorial assumes that you have no knowledge of programming or of the C language. Users already familiar with C may want to review the first half and then concentrate on the second half of the Tutorial.

In each chapter of the Tutorial, you are given examples and programs to write. These involve specific tasks that you will use in building larger C programs in Part II. As you work through the Tutorial, read over the examples in each chapter and try them out. The more you try and experiment, the more you will learn about C.

The C Tutorial is not written with a particular C compiler or computer system in mind. The description of the C language in the Tutorial notes some areas where there may be differences between various compilers and the Draft ANSI Standard. These differences are often due to the computer or operating system under which your programs run.

Using this Tutorial, you can learn C whether you have a mainframe computer, mini- or microcomputer, or any one of a number of operating systems. The differences between these computers and systems are noted and explained when they occur. The Tutorial assumes only that you have enough experience to log on to your own computer and operating system. In other words, you do not need any formal programming background to use the first half of the Tutorial.

xviii How to Use This Book

The Tutorial is divided into two parts so that you can start programming in C as quickly as possible. The first half includes seven chapters on the following topics:

Chapter 1   "An Introduction to Using C"
provides an overview of the C language and of the Tutorial. It also gives you a first look at a C program.

Chapter 2   "Data: Bits, Numbers, and Variables"
explains how the computer stores and represents numbers and characters, and how you create and declare variables.

Chapter 3   "Operators and C"
describes the basic operators in C, introduces the conditional **if** statement, and shows you how to write simple expressions.

Chapter 4   "Program Flow—Control and Repetition"
introduces statements that provide program control, such as the **switch** statement. Program loops (**for**, **while**, **do-while**) are described, with suggestions on when to use each loop structure.

Chapter 5   "Introduction to Reading and Writing Data in C"
explains simple ways to read and write data (known as input/output operations) and describes a standard set of files that C uses to handle data. A basic set of I/O functions and the C preprocessor, which preprocesses C code before the compiler handles it, are also introduced.

Chapter 6   "Introduction to Functions in C"
shows you how to write functions, which are independent units of C code that accomplish a specific task. The structure of C functions and how to use them in your programs is also explained.

Chapter 7   "Introduction to Arrays and Pointers"
describes how to handle multiple data values using arrays and how to use memory addresses to manipulate data via pointers.

The second half of the Tutorial expands on the material presented in the first half, providing you with a more complete background in C and C programming techniques. The second half includes four chapters on the following topics:

Chapter 8   "Expanding the Basics: More on Operators and Types"
completes the description of operators with bitwise and conditional operators. Types are covered in more detail, including enumerated types, structures, and unions. Type conversions (casts) are also explained.

Chapter 9 "More on Expressions and the C Preprocessor"
describes the C storage classes and the concept of scope. The information on C preprocessor commands is expanded, showing more uses for macro definitions.

Chapter 10 "Working with Data: Files, Structures, and Storage"
provides more information on input/output (I/O) operations and compares some of the standard and nonstandard I/O functions. This chapter also covers storage allocation and introduces the concept of data structures, linked lists, trees, and shows you how to put these advanced concepts to use by building a simple data base.

Chapter 11 "Helpful Hints"
describes common C programming errors and provides helpful programming hints.

As you can see, the Tutorial takes you beyond the basics of C and teaches you some of the more advanced concepts in C programming. The Tutorial is structured to make this an enjoyable experience, and you have the added benefit of several useful C programs when you have completed the Tutorial.

Part II: User's Guide for the SAS/C Compiler, Student Edition

The User's Guide for the SAS/C Compiler, Student Edition, describes a compiler product that you can use on an IBM personal computer (PC). The User's Guide shows you how to create a file and write a C program, and then how to compile, execute, and debug your program. The software for the **Student Compiler** (as it is usually called in Part II) is included on two diskettes in the back of the book. You can start using it immediately if you have an IBM PC or a compatible computer.

The User's Guide can be used along with the C Tutorial to write and run your programs. It assumes you have access to a PC with a hard disk or double-floppy disk system, and that you know PC DOS or MS-DOS well enough to install the compiler, given detailed installation instructions. Part II explains the processes of editing, running, and debugging a program, but it does not teach you how to program in C. For that, you should read the Tutorial.

This User's Guide is divided into seven chapters and two appendices, as described below.

Chapter 12 "Introduction to the User's Guide for the SAS/C Compiler, Student Edition"

xx How to Use This Book

explains how the User's Guide is organized and where to go for help if you need it.

Chapter 13 "Installing the Student Compiler"
describes everything you do to prepare the Student Compiler to work on your personal computer.

Chapter 14 "Using the Student Compiler and Editor"
teaches you to use the compiler and editor so you can develop and run your own C language programs.

Chapter 15 "Programming Environment for the Student Compiler"
explains the compiler's programming environment. Here you can learn more about what goes on "behind the scenes" when you compile and execute your program.

Chapter 16 "Standard Function Library for the Student Compiler"
describes the standard functions provided with this compiler.

Chapter 17 "Graphics and Screen Management Functions for the Student Compiler"
explains the background information you need to set the characteristics of your display screen and to create simple line drawings. It then describes a set of screen management and graphics functions

Chapter 18 "Source-Level Debugger for the Student Compiler"
describes the source-level debugger provided with this compiler.

Appendix 1 "Error Messages for the Student Compiler"
lists the error messages that you may receive while compiling your program.

Appendix 2 "ASCII Character Set"
includes a table of the ASCII character set, which is the character set most frequently used with C language implementations.

If you are new to programming and the C language, you should read the C Tutorial in Part I of this book. If you are familiar with C but new to the SAS/C Compiler, Student Edition, see Chapter 13 to install the compiler, Chapters 14 and 15 to get you going, and Chapters 16 and 17 as references for the function libraries.

Part III: Glossary and References

This part contains a glossary and bibliographic references for Parts I and II. The Glossary defines programming terms and some C language terms that have been introduced and used in the Tutorial and User's Guide. References lists other C language books and personal computer and operating systems manuals that you may find helpful.

Part III also contains an index for the entire book and a function index that lists the graphics, screen management, and standard functions.

Key and Typeface Conventions

This section describes the typeface and key conventions used throughout this book. Whenever specific terms, names, or concepts need to be emphasized in the text, the following conventions are used:

    <enter>   sends a line to be processed. On some keyboards, the ENTER or RETURN key is represented by an arrow symbol that points down and to the left.

    CTRL-D   sends a control character sequence to be processed. Hold down the key labeled Control (or CTRL) and press the key for the letter or symbol shown, in this case, "d".

    boldface   indicates an important word or concept.

    `code`   means that the item is specific to the C language or a C program.

Part I: C Language Tutorial

Chapter 1
An Introduction to Using C

Chapter 1

CONTENTS

Introduction	5
Tutorial Purpose	5
Tutorial Organization and Conventions	6
Organization	6
Key and Type Conventions	7
Using the Tutorial with Your Computer	7
Using an Editor	8
Compiling Your Program	9
Producing an Executable File	9
A Note on Computers	11
Introduction to the Learning Modules	11
Module 1: Program Structure and the main() Function	11
Example	12
A Closer Look	13
Inside Information	15
Trying the Program	15
Program Notes	16
Chapter Summary	17

An Introduction to Using C

Introduction

Welcome to the C language tutorial. The tutorial is designed to introduce you to the C programming language. The first half of the tutorial helps you build a good foundation in the basics of C. The second half introduces you to more advanced features and programming techniques. This chapter is an introduction to the tutorial.

The following topics are presented:

- the purpose and organization of the tutorial
- tutorial format and approach
- using the tutorial with your computer
- a first look at a C program.

Tutorial Purpose

This tutorial is designed to teach you the basics of the C language as well as introduce you to some of the more advanced features of C. All you need to get started is an interest in C and access to a computer and C compiler. (If you are working on an IBM® PC compatible personal computer (with 512K of memory), you can begin with the C compiler provided with this tutorial.)

As you work through the tutorial, remember that hands-on experience is the best way to learn programming skills. After you read and look over the examples, try each of them. The more you try and experiment, the more you will learn about C.

There are some good reasons to learn to program using the C language. C is increasing in popularity among all levels and types of computer users. C has been used for a variety of applications. Some of the classic uses of C have been (and continue to be) to develop the software for operating systems, language compilers, and data base management. C is also used for numerous other applications such as document preparation systems, engineering and architectural design, games and graphics, and interactive training.

Why is C so popular? Initially, C was popular because of the popularity of the UNIX® operating system (C was developed in conjunction with UNIX). However, C can be used on a wide range of machines. Some of the reasons for C's continued success today include the following:

- C encourages structured, modular programming.
- C is efficient on most conventional computer architecture.
- C code is relatively easy to transfer (port) between computers.
- By design, C is a flexible language and a powerful development tool.

IBM is a registered trademark of International Business Machines Corporation.
UNIX is a registered trademark of AT&T.

Chapter 1

As a result, using C, you can create small and efficient applications that are not limited to a single computer hardware system.

Tutorial Organization and Conventions

Organization

This section explains how the tutorial presents the C language and the role the examples play. You will work with examples and programs that revolve around specific tasks that fit into an overall C application. By the time you complete the tutorial, you will have written the software for a variety of tasks within a larger system. In the world of C, this modular approach to building software is how things usually work.

To help you get started programming in C as quickly as possible, the tutorial is divided into basic and advanced chapters. Chapters 1 through 7 cover the basics of the C language. These chapters are designed to help you begin writing C programs that use fundamental aspects of most C features. Topics covered in these chapters include:

- introduction: an overview of C and the tutorial
- data: number representation and variables in C
- operators: expressions in C
- program flow: statements that provide program control
- input and output: simple ways to read and write data
- functions: how to write units of C program code
- arrays: how to handle groups of data or variables
- pointers: how to use addresses to manipulate data.

Chapters 8 through 11 expand on the material presented earlier and provide a more complete background in C and C programming techniques. The programs you will write in Chapters 8, 9, and 10 will complete the set of software for the system you develop throughout the tutorial. Topics covered in Chapters 8 through 11 include:

- more on operators and data types
- more on expressions and the C preprocessor
- working with data: files, structures, and storage
- introduction to data structures
- helpful hints and common mistakes.

As you can see, the tutorial takes you beyond the basics of C and introduces you to some of the more advanced concepts in C programming. The tutorial is structured to make this a friendly and interesting adventure. Some familiarity with computers is assumed (most likely a microcomputer), but you do not need any formal language background.

The tutorial is composed of learning modules. Each module focuses on a particular aspect of the C language. In each module you develop the C language skills to complete individual tasks.

In some modules, you will also see a section called **Inside Information**. This section contains extra information about language features presented in the module. You can read this section if you are interested in looking at the features in more detail, but you do not have to. To understand the contents of a module, you do not need to know these details, and in most cases, they will be presented in a later chapter.

If you are just beginning to learn the C language, you should start with Chapter 2 and work through the tutorial. If you have some experience with C you may want to skim Chapters 2 through 7 for a quick review but concentrate on the later chapters.

Key and Type Conventions

Whenever specific things need to be emphasized in the text, the following conventions are used:

<enter> means to press the RETURN or ENTER key, which sends a line to be processed.

CTRL-D sends a control character sequence by holding down the key labeled CONTROL and also pressing the key for the letter shown, in this case, D. The control key may be marked differently on your keyboard. If it is not marked CTRL or CONTROL, it may be CNTL or some other set of characters.

bold signals an important word or concept.

`monospace` indicates C language terms. Statements in the C language (and in other computer languages) are sometimes called *code*. The tutorial shows all C code in this typeface.

Using the Tutorial with Your Computer

This section provides an overview of the general procedures you need to know in order to begin to write and run C programs. This is only an overview because the exact steps you need to take depend on the computer you are using and the specific software you use to write and run C programs. To prepare C programs, the process goes something like this:

- Write your program using an editor.
- Submit your program to a **compiler** for syntax checks and translation to machine code.

Chapter 1

- Produce an executable file.
- Run your program by entering the name of the executable file.

The entire process is illustrated in **Figure 1.1**.

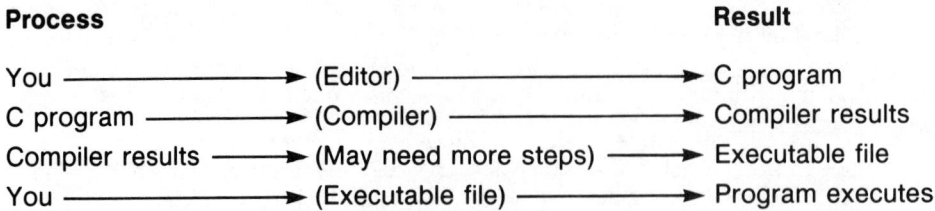

Figure 1.1 The Tutorial and Your Computer

The next sections provide more details on this process. (See also Part II, Chapter 12.)

Using an Editor

A **text editor** is a program used for recording and changing data. With an editor, you can create and build C programs. The editor may already be available to you as part of your computer system. For example, if you are using UNIX, you can usually work with either Ed or Vi. An IBM PC or compatible would probably include an editor such as "Edlin". If you are using a PC, the editor can also be a separate program that you need to get and run. Many popular editors, such as Wordstar® or WordPerfect,™ are available for PCs. In addition, many compilers (including the one provided with this book) supply their own editor.

When using an editor, the first thing you do is call up the editor on your system so that you can begin to type in your C program. This is usually done by typing the name of the editor or an abbreviation such as WP for WordPerfect. Next, you select the edit option that lets you create a new file. (A **file** is a collection of stored data, in this case, lines of text. Some systems use the term **data set** instead of file.)

When choosing filenames, keep the following in mind:

- Check your computer system's user guide for file naming rules.
- Choose a name that shows what the program does and that it is a C program.

Wordstar is a registered trademark of MicroPro International Corporation.
WordPerfect is a trademark of WordPerfect Corporation.

An Introduction to Using C

For example, if you are using MS-DOS® or PC DOS, two valid names are `list.c` and `balance.c`. The first part of the name indicates what the program does, and the second part reminds you that it is a C program source file. A **source file** means that the file contains your original C language code. The source file `list.c` might contain the C statements to print a grocery list, and `balance.c` might contain the code to balance your checkbook.

After you finish writing your program, save it, according to your editor's conventions, with the name you chose. You are now ready for the next step.

Compiling Your Program

The process of taking the source code that you wrote and translating it into a form the computer can read and understand is called **compiling** your program. A **compiler** is the program that checks your language statements for correct syntax and puts them into the proper form for the computer.

For example, the compiler takes the source file `list.c` and checks the C statements to be sure that you have written them correctly. If there are errors the compiler can detect, error messages are given and the translation process is not completed. If the statements are correct, the compiler produces a machine code version of your file (machine code being the computer's language) called an **object code** file (or **object module**). Note that the compiler is checking for syntax errors, not logic errors. Also, just because your program compiles without errors does not guarantee that it will behave as you expect. More on developing and testing your program can be found in Chapter 12.

Producing an Executable File

Some compilers, such as the one used with the UNIX operating system or the one supplied with the tutorial, let you execute your program as soon as it compiles. Others may require additional steps before a file is produced that you can execute. For example, there may be a **link** step that is necessary to turn the compiler translation (the object code file) into an executable file.

Sometimes, linking combines several separately compiled object modules into one module. The link step also ensures that any references between these files are correct or resolved. The linking process is transparent to users. In most cases the link step is performed because there are standard C routines or libraries that need to be included with your program. (You will learn more about the libraries in Chapter 5.) Linking is also needed if there is more than one source file involved in an application. For example, `credit.c`, `debit.c`, and `balance.c` might all be source files used in an accounting system program.

The linker is not usually specific to C or to your compiler. Usually, the linker program is operating-system specific. After the link step, your program is finally in a form that can be run.

MS-DOS is a registered trademark of Microsoft Corporation.

Chapter 1

These steps can be summarized as shown in **Figure 1.2**. (Note that the diagram shows MS-DOS style filenames ending in `.c` and `.exe`. Your computer system may have different name requirements for files.)

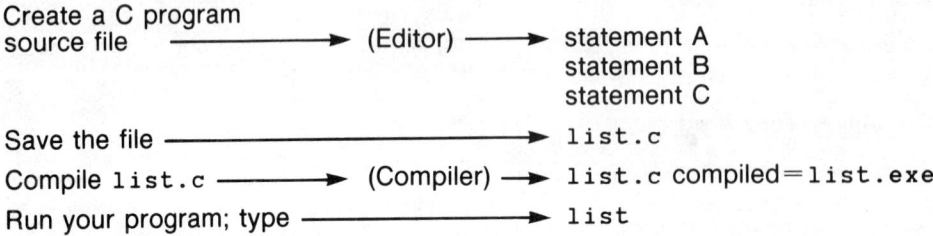

Figure 1.2   Compile and Execute

If your compiler requires a link step, the process will look something like **Figure 1.3**. (This figure shows MS-DOS style filenames ending in `.c`, `.obj`, and `.exe`.)

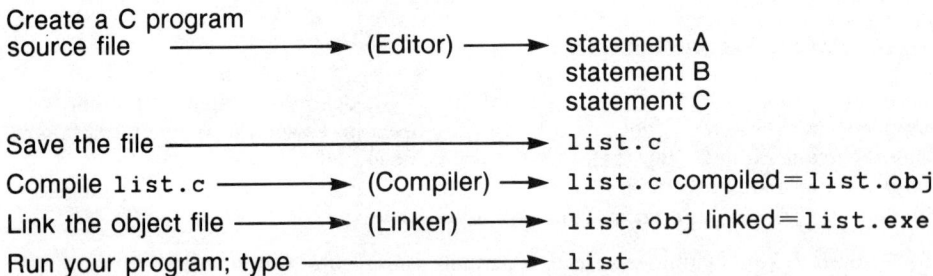

Figure 1.3   Compile, Link, and Execute

Consult the manual for your editor and compiler to find out the exact steps you need to take to create and run your C program. If you are using the compiler supplied with this text, Chapters 12 and 13 will help get you started.

An Introduction to Using C

A Note on Computers

There are a few more things you need to know about running the examples on your computer system before starting.

Computers differ in the way they handle some aspects of C. For example, the amount of space needed to store a number may vary among systems. This type of information (sometimes called **machine dependencies**) is most often listed in the user guide for the C compiler. If you are using the compiler that accompanies this tutorial, see Chapter 15.

If you are using this tutorial with a compiler that conforms to the Draft American National Standards Institute (ANSI) C, the examples in the text should run. In some cases, to illustrate characteristics of C in the most simple way, an example may not follow the Draft ANSI Standard exactly. A section entitled **Program Notes** includes additional information about the examples, especially where differences from ANSI exist. In addition, if there is a significant difference between the way a language feature is handled on a large (mainframe) computer and on a personal computer, the difference is mentioned. Some of the reasons for these differences are introduced in the next chapter on data representation in C.

Introduction to the Learning Modules

For the majority of the tutorial, you will be working on programs that can be incorporated into a larger system. (Many language features that you will learn are used in the system described in Chapter 10.) We hope you have fun with it, and as you become more proficient in C, you can add on and develop your own applications. Your first task is to print a list of some of the things a computerized home management system can do for you.

How you accomplish this task is covered in **Module 1** below, which is about the structure of C programs and the `main()` function.

Module 1: Program Structure and the main() Function

In this section, a very simple C program is reviewed. Concepts presented are

- the structure of C programs
- using a C function to print text
- using comments.

Keywords you need to note are

`main()`	comment statement
`printf()`	escape sequence
function	**header files**

Chapter 1

A C program is composed of one or more **functions**. A C function can be thought of as a self-contained set of code that performs a specific task. Functions are the basic building blocks of C programs. C programs begin with a function called `main()`. In C, `main()` must always be present: it signals the beginning of the main body of programming statements. Most C programs contain many other functions in addition to `main()`. Some of these functions are written by you. However, many are already written for you and are contained in C libraries that you can use in your program. (See Chapter 5 for more information about C libraries.)

Example

Read through the following C statements:

```
/* Your home management system */

main()
{
printf("Things to compute:\n");
printf("\tBest buy in food");
printf("\n\tCar maintenance schedule");
printf("\n\tInterest and payments");
printf("\n\nThat's all for now!");
}
```

You can probably tell that this program is going to print some lines of text. The program does this by including print statements as the **body** of the `main()` function. This program can do everything needed in the `main()` function.

The structure of the `main()` function is

    main()   (function name)
    {
      C statements;   (function body)
    }

Note in the example that a comment statement, set off by /* */, heads the `main()` function and that C statements printing lines of text compose the `main()` function body. Also note the semicolon (;) at the end of each statement; all C statements end in semicolons.

Points to remember are as follows:

- A C program consists of one or more functions.
- Each function has a name and a body of C statements.
- Each C program must include the function `main()`.
- A C statement ends in a semicolon.

An Introduction to Using C

A Closer Look

The example produces the following output:

```
Things to compute:
        Best buy in food
        Car maintenance schedule
        Interest and payments

That's all for now!
```

By examining each program statement in detail, you can see how this output was produced.

```
/* Your home management system */
```

The first line of code is a C **comment statement.** A comment is intended to help you understand your program, and it is ignored by the compiler. Comments always begin with /* and end with */ (with no spaces between the / and the *). Comments can be on the same line as a C statement or on a separate line. Commented text can continue for several lines before the comment is ended.* Although many C compilers allow you to nest comments, (that is, putting one comment inside another) you need to check your compiler documentation to be sure. In general, it is safer not to nest them.

Note that a blank line appears next. Blank lines can appear anywhere in a C program. Blank lines are not important to the compiler, but they often help make sections of code easier for you to find or read.

```
main()
```

As discussed earlier, `main()` is always present in a C program. Later, you will learn about statements that you can add before `main()`. Just remember that `main()` is followed by the executable part of the `main()` function.

```
{
```

The left curly brace marks the start of the `main()` function body.

```
printf("Things to compute:\n");
```

This is a simple C statement. This statement calls the C `printf()` function. `printf()` is a standard C function that produces **formatted** output. (Usually, this output goes to the screen by default. In Chapter 10, you will find out how to direct it elsewhere.)

In the example, a form of `printf()` is used to write the text "Things to compute:". Everything between the double quotes is written except for a special control character, \n, which is called an **escape sequence.** Escape sequences are included with the text

---

* Programmers often adopt different styles in formatting comments in code. This tutorial uses several styles so you will notice differences in the format of comments in sample programs.

13

Chapter 1

and give the computer information about how to format the output. Escape sequences used here are

\n   start a new line, which in C is commonly called newline character.

\t   tab (tabs are usually positions 8, 16, 24, and so on).*

The structure of the `printf()` used in the example is

`printf`   the function name

`(`   start of function value list (functions are covered in more detail in later chapters)

`"`   beginning of text to be written

`text`   text composed of characters (including blanks) and optional escape sequences

`"`   end of text

`)`   end of function value list

`;`   end of statement.

The next four `printf()` statements illustrate similar ways to print text. Note that the last `printf()` uses two newlines together (\n\n) to double-space the text.

   }

The closing brace marks the end of the `main()` function.

C imposes no limit on the maximum length of lines, although your particular editor or compiler might. In fact, C statements are completely free-form. For example, if you do continue a line, no special line continuation character is needed. Also, although the example has some lines indented, you can begin C statements in any column. In general though, it is a good idea to have only one C statement per line and keep statement length under 80 characters. Doing this makes the program easier for you to read and follow. Consider the following version of two lines from the program:

```
/* Your home management system */main(){
printf(
                "Things to compute:\n"
)     ;
}
```

The computer reads this perfectly well, but you may not want to.

One reminder: `main()` and `printf()` are both C functions. An important difference, however, is that you supply statements for `main()`, but the code for `printf()` is supplied in the C library. This means that `printf()` is a **standard** C

---

*When you use tabs in a program, you need to be aware that there is quite a bit of variation in the way different computer systems handle tabs. In other words, the output of a program that uses tabs may differ on two different systems.

14

function. (There are many of these functions in libraries provided with your compiler; you will find out more in Chapters 5 and 6.) In other words, the information you provide for `printf()` is what you want to print and, sometimes, how you want the output to look. You do not have to worry about the statements involved in telling the computer how to do it.

Inside Information

The compiler keeps information needed in order to use library functions (such as `printf()`) in files called **header files**. When you want to use a library function, you normally tell the compiler to include the header file for the function as part of your program. The way you do this is with an `#include` statement. Programs may have multiple `#include` statements. In the example program, you would typically put any `#include` statements first—before `main()`.

For the `printf()` function used by the example program, the header file is `stdio.h`. An `#include` statement for this header file, followed by `main()` looks like this:

```
#include <stdio.h>

main()
{
    Other program statements
}
```

As it happens, the sample program, which uses `printf()`, will run on many compilers (including the compiler supplied with this tutorial) even if you do not include `stdio.h`. Technically, however, including `stdio.h` for `printf()` is a must to follow the Draft ANSI C standard. Also, it is better programming practice to include header files for the functions your programs use. Actually, it can be very important: programs that use some functions will not run unless the appropriate header files are included. (You will learn more about header files and `#include` statements in Chapter 5.)

Trying the Program

The next thing you should do is use your editor to key in the example and compile it. Change the text and try different combinations of escape characters. You may get one or more error messages when you try to compile your program, if you have made a mistake in your code. If you have problems compiling the program, remember to check for correct statement format. Here is a hint on compiler errors: the mistake may be in a line sooner than the error message indicates so look beyond the indicated statement.

Chapter 1

If you are running the compiler supplied with this tutorial, you will find that programs in the tutorial are provided on a floppy diskette. You can copy the programs from the diskette if you do not want to type them in yourself. Chapter 13 explains how to access the diskette programs.

Program Notes

You may need to know about two additional statements that we did not put into the example program: the `return` statement and the `#include` statement. (See **Inside Information** earlier in this chapter.)

A `return` statement ends a function, such as `main( )`, and other functions that you write. It returns control to the point in the program where the function (in this case, `main`) was called. (Chapter 6 discusses this statement in more detail.) In the example program, you could put a `return` statement before the closing brace of `main( )`.

The sample program will run without a `return` statement on the compiler supplied with this tutorial. On some compilers, however, you may need to add the `return` statement for `main( )`.

Here is a `return` statement that could be added to the sample program:

```
return 0;
```

If you are unable to get the program to run on a different compiler, and you have checked all your errors and fixed them, you may need to add the `return` statement shown above.

The statement

```
#include <stdio.h>
```

gives the compiler information it needs when you use the `printf( )` function. (This statement is a special kind of program statement. You will learn more about it in Chapter 5. Notice that it does not have a semicolon at the end.) Many C compilers will run the sample program just fine without this statement, but if your compiler strictly follows the Draft ANSI standard, you may need to add this statement. (Check your compiler documentation to see if it follows ANSI rules.) Should you decide to add this statement, type it on the line after the comment, before `main( )`, like this:

```
/* Your home management system */
#include <stdio.h>
```

Chapter Summary

In this chapter you learned about the basic structure of a C program and used some basic C statements. The example shows that a C program consists of one or more functions. The example uses the `main()` function to demonstrate that a function has a name and body.

The next chapter explores different ways you can use C to represent and handle information. You will learn how the computer stores numbers and how you can tell the computer to store numbers by defining different kinds of variables.

New C Tools

Concepts

`main()` function

`printf()` function

; to end C statements

function name

function body

comment statement

escape sequences

Chapter 2
Data: Bits, Numbers, and Variables

Chapter 2

CONTENTS

Introduction 21
Module 2: Storage Concepts 21
    Bits and Numbers 21
    Inside Information 25
    Module 2 Summary 26
Module 3: Identifying Data Items in C 27
    Variables 27
    Basic Data Types 29
    Module 3 Summary 33
Module 4: The Declaration Statement 33
    Declaring Identifiers in C 33
    Assignment Statements 34
    Inside Information 39
    Module 4 Summary 40
Chapter Summary 40

Data: Bits, Numbers, and Variables

Introduction

In this chapter you will learn

- how the computer stores numbers and characters
- how to create and describe variables in C
- how to declare different types of variables.

When you write a program, you must consider the kinds of information the program will use. For example, your program may need to store numbers to use in a formula or letters to use as codes. In any case, the computer needs to know what kind of information to expect and where to find it. You give the computer this information by naming the data items you need and describing them in your program. This chapter helps you learn how to do this by providing some background on how the computer *sees* data items and how to write the C statements that describe these items.

Module 2: Storage Concepts

This module describes how the computer stores information in memory, which will help you understand how C handles data. Important concepts are

- units of storage
- coding schemes for information.

Keywords you need to note are

binary number system	**sign bit**
bit	**ASCII**
byte	**EBCDIC**
word	**one's and two's complement**

Bits and Numbers

The terms bit, byte, and word describe units of the computer's memory. Memory refers to that part of computer storage that retains information for later retrieval. Information is stored in computers in binary form; that is, as a series of 1s and 0s.

A **bit** (binary digit) is the smallest unit of memory and can be thought of as a switch that can be turned on (1) or off (0).

A **byte**, on most computers, is a set of eight bits. Eight bits provide 256 possible combinations of 0s and 1s. This means that the numbers from 0 to 255 can be represented by one byte. If one bit is used to represent the sign (+ or −) of a number, then the remaining seven bits can represent the signed numbers from −128 to +127. The next few paragraphs explain how the computer represents numbers using bits and bytes.

21

Chapter 2

A series of 0s and 1s can also represent characters as well as numbers. How this works will be explained later. For now, keep in mind that any letter can be encoded as a number, and the number can be represented with 1s and 0s.

In addition to the bit and byte, there is the **word**. A word is the typical unit of memory for a particular computer design. For most machines, a word equals 16 bits or two bytes. Larger machines use 32- and 64-bit words. The larger the word, the more information it can represent.

How the Computer Represents Numbers This section describes how the computer uses the binary number system (base 2) to store information. Some parts of this section are fairly detailed; for example, you will learn about counting in base 2 and how the computer handles negative and positive numbers. Of course, you can write perfectly good C programs without knowing this information or reading this section, so you may choose to skip it and move on to **Module 3**. Later, when you get to the discussion of data types, you may want more background information. You can then return to this section and read it. If you decide to read on, take your time until you feel comfortable with the material.

One of the key elements in storing information in a byte is the way each of the eight bits in the byte are referenced. The scheme used here numbers each bit position from zero to seven, beginning at the far right. The right-most bit is bit 0, and the left-most bit is bit 7. This system enables you to refer to the contents of a single bit; for example, bit 7 contains a 1, bit 3 contains a 0, and so on. **Figure 2.1** illustrates this.

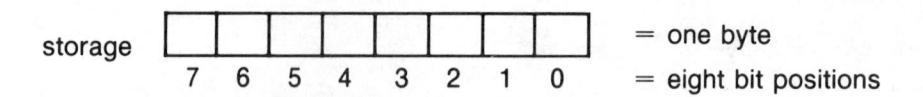

```
storage  [ ][ ][ ][ ][ ][ ][ ][ ]   = one byte
          7  6  5  4  3  2  1  0    = eight bit positions
```

Figure 2.1 Bit Positions in a Byte

To understand how the computer uses the bit positions to represent numbers and characters, you need to know about the **binary** (base 2) **number system**.

Consider an ordinary base 10 (decimal) number, for example, 19. Nineteen means, in decimal arithmetic, nine ones and one ten. Each position (the one's place, for example) can contain any digit from 0 through 9. To represent a ten, put a 1 in the ten's place, and a zero in the one's place. You can go up to 99 putting numbers in the ten's place and the one's place. To represent the next largest number (100), you need to carry a one over to the hundred's place; the one's and ten's places contain zeros.

Each position in the decimal number system, beginning at the far right, is a *power* of ten: the one's place is ten to the power of zero, the ten's place is ten to the power of one, the hundred's place is ten to the power of two or ten squared, and so on, adding

Data: Bits, Numbers, and Variables

places to the left. Using this idea of powers of ten, you can express some numbers in base 10 as follows:

$$19 = (1 \times 10^1) + (9 \times 10^0)$$

$$33 = (3 \times 10^1) + (3 \times 10^0)$$

$$100 = (1 \times 10^2) + (0 \times 10^1) + (0 \times 10^0)$$

The binary system is similar, except that it uses powers of two, instead of powers of ten. Also, the binary system has only two digits: 0 and 1, rather than 0 through 9, as in base 10.

Here is a sample of some powers of ten and powers of two together:

Powers of Ten	Powers of Two
$10^0 = 1$	$2^0 = 1$
$10^1 = 10$	$2^1 = 2$
$10^2 = 100$	$2^2 = 4$
$10^3 = 1000$	$2^3 = 8$
$10^4 = 10000$	$2^4 = 16$
$10^5 = 100000$	$2^5 = 32$
$10^6 = 1000000$	$2^6 = 64$

Here are the same base 10 numbers used earlier expressed in base 2:

Decimal	Binary
19	10011
33	100001
100	1100100

Using powers of two, you can express the numbers in base 2 as follows:

$$10011 = (1 \times 2^4) + (0 \times 2^3) + (0 \times 2^2) + (1 \times 2^1) + (1 \times 2^0)$$

$$100001 = (1 \times 2^5) + (0 \times 2^4) + (0 \times 2^3) + (0 \times 2^2) + (0 \times 2^1) + (1 \times 2^0)$$

$$1100100 = (1 \times 2^6) + (1 \times 2^5) + (0 \times 2^4) + (0 \times 2^3) + (1 \times 2^2) + (0 \times 2^1) + (0 \times 2^0)$$

Chapter 2

So, for the sample byte shown earlier, each bit position (7,6,5,4,3,2,1,0) represents 2 raised to the power of that position. Working from right to left, the positions and the numbers they represent are as follows:

bits								
2^{nth}	2^7	2^6	2^5	2^4	2^3	2^2	2^1	2^0
represents	128	64	32	16	8	4	2	1

With this notation, the number 3 is represented in binary as 11: one in the two's place and one in the one's place ($1 \times 2^1 + 1 \times 2^0 = 2 + 1 = 3$). In talking about the contents of a byte, the number 3 (11 in binary) uses two of the eight bit positions: the first two positions on the right. The other six unused positions can be filled in with zeros, so that a byte containing the number three can be represented as

0	0	0	0	0	0	1	1

Using a series of ones and zeros in the bit positions, one byte can represent 256 values; namely, the numbers from 0 to 255:

binary value	00000000	to	11111111
decimal value	0	to	255

There is a little more to this system of representing numbers that you need to know. So far, we have been talking about representing *unsigned* numbers, which are numbers without a + or − sign. You can use unsigned numbers in C, as you will see later, but you will also want to use signed numbers.

When you write signed numbers, you don't usually use the plus sign for positive numbers, but you do use the minus sign for negative numbers. However, the computer needs a way to represent both positive and negative. In order to represent a signed number, a byte has to give up one bit to be used to indicate whether the number is positive or negative. In the system we have been working with so far, the left-most bit (bit 7) is used. This bit is known as the **sign bit**. Because bit 7 is used for the sign, the maximum signed number that the byte can contain is now less than 255. The reason is that bit 7, which had been "2 to the 7th power," is now used for the sign.*

For an eight-bit byte, a value of 0 in bit 7 signals a signed positive number. The contents of the other bits mean the same as they would if the number were unsigned.

---

* The discussion of bits and bytes uses terms such as *sign bit* to refer to a bit in a particular position. In this case, the sign bit (bit 7) is on the far left and the zero bit (bit 0) is on the far right. Actually, the numbering of bit positions is machine dependent. On an IBM 370, for instance, the left-most bit (or high-order bit) would be bit 0, just the opposite of the example shown previously.

Data: Bits, Numbers, and Variables

A negative number has a 1 in bit 7. The contents of the other bits do not mean the same as they would if the number were unsigned. This is because, for negative numbers, there are usually additional steps to get to the exact binary representation. The exact method used to represent signed numbers depends on the kind of arithmetic your computer uses (probably two's complement arithmetic). (If you are interested in more details, refer to a section covering two's complement arithmetic in an introductory computer science text.)

Luckily, there is a general rule to determine decimal values for signed negative binary numbers. (This general rule is based on **two's complement** arithmetic, which is fairly common.) The rule is

> If the sign bit = 1, pretend that all eight bits are used, and calculate the number as though it were unsigned. Then, subtract 256 from that number.

The following are examples of binary signed numbers and their values:

> 0 1 1 1 1 1 1 1 = +127   (64+32+16+8+4+2+1)
>
> 1 0 0 0 0 0 0 0 = −128   (128 − 256)

How does all this relate to you and your computer? This way of representing information allows you (through the keyboard) and your program (after compilation) to communicate with your computer. For example, when you press a key on your terminal or computer, your system sends a numeric code for that character to the computer. There are two common schemes for encoding keyboard characters into a binary representation. One is the **ASCII** (American Standard Code for Information Interchange) and the other is known as **EBCDIC** (Extended Binary Coded Decimal Information Code). EBCDIC is used almost exclusively by IBM mainframe computers (although many IBM PCs use ASCII). Using C in an ASCII environment is much more common, so we will assume that you are working with ASCII code. In ASCII, different combinations of numbers are used to represent the keyboard characters. For example, in ASCII, a = 97, k = 107, a blank space = 32, and so on. (See the ASCII table in Appendix 2.)

Inside Information

The general rule given above for two's complement arithmetic illustrates how to get the decimal value for a binary, signed negative integer. Here are the steps to follow in changing a signed positive number to a signed negative number.

Suppose you want to represent the number −5 in eight bits using two's complement arithmetic.

- First, change the number to a positive binary number:

> 5 = 00000101

25

Chapter 2

- Next, in the binary representation, change every 0 to 1 and every 1 to 0.

    11111010

- Finally, add one. (In binary arithmetic, 1+1=0, with a 1 carried over to the next position; 1+0=1, with no carry.)

    11111011

Try it again using −4. You should get 11111100.

You may also have heard the term **one's complement** arithmetic. One's complement arithmetic also uses the sign bit to indicate positive and negative numbers (1 for minus and 0 for plus). To get negative numbers in one's complement arithmetic, you follow steps one and two above but not step three. (No final 1 is added.) In other words, you simply complement all the bits.

Intuitively, a one's complement way of handling numbers looks easier and probably is from a user's point of view. However, for many computers, two's complement is more efficient and is used instead.

Module 2 Summary

Module 2 gave you a brief look at how the computer stores data. Topics discussed include bits, bytes, and words, which are units of memory in a computer system. **Module 2** also reviewed the binary number system and how the computer stores information in bytes as a pattern of ones and zeros.

You learned the difference between signed and unsigned numbers. An unsigned number as large as 255 can be represented in a single 8-bit byte. The maximum size of a signed number is smaller than 255 because signed numbers use the left-most bit (bit 7) for the sign. Positive signed numbers have a zero in bit seven; and negative numbers have a 1. The reason is that the computer performs additional calculations to get the negative number. However, there is a general rule you can use to compute the decimal value of a negative signed binary number. **Module 2** prepared you for the next sections where you work with signed and unsigned numbers and other types of data in C.

New C Tools

Concepts

bits, bytes, words, and storage	ASCII and EBCDIC coding schemes
binary number system	one's and two's complement
signed and unsigned numbers	
sign bit	

Data: Bits, Numbers, and Variables

Module 3: Identifying Data Items in C

C provides many different ways to describe the data your program needs. In this section, you learn what to tell the computer about the data items your program uses.

Keywords you need to note are

object	**integer**
variable	**character**
identifier	**floating point**
data type	**double**

Variables

You just learned that bytes and words are storage areas of certain sizes in the computer's memory. You can give these areas in memory names so that your program can use them for saving and handling different kinds of data. The name lets the program refer to the actual value stored within the computer. For example, names could be `minutes` and `hours`. The values stored for each of these might be 0 and 5. If the value can change while your program is running, then the name is said to refer to a **variable**.

In C, areas of memory that are used to hold items like variable values are sometimes called *objects*. The more general term **object** is often used because it better reflects the variety of ways C allows you to define storage for data items. (Some of these ways are described in Chapter 7.) In fact, because you can identify storage in so many different ways, familiarize yourself with the C term **identifier**. A good way to think of an identifier is as the name of an object. But for now, consider the terms variable and identifier to mean the same thing.

A name can be as long as you like, but the number of characters recognized depends on your C compiler (the current standard is the first 31 characters, older versions may accept only 7 or 8).*

In C, names of variables (or identifiers) follow these rules:

- Begin the name with a letter or underscore (_).
- After the first character, use upper- and lowercase letters, numbers, and the underscore (_).
- Do not use spaces within a name.
- Do not use a C reserved name.

---

* You need to check your compiler documentation for the maximum number of characters that you can use in a name, and whether your compiler distinguishes between uppercase and lowercase characters (many do).

27

Chapter 2

The following are valid variable names:

```
VAR10
LAST_NAME
Count
```

These are not valid names:

```
!@ZOO
12DAYS
SAVE#
MON DAY
```

The name `!@ZOO` is invalid because ! and @ are not allowed. `12DAYS` is invalid because it begins with a number. The third name, `SAVE#`, is invalid because # is not allowed. Finally, `MON DAY` is not valid because of the blank space.

Remember that most C compilers distinguish between upper- and lowercase letters so that

`BIRTH` and `Birth`

are considered two different variables. If your compiler allows only eight characters in a name, the variables

`MONTHMAY1` and `MONTHMAY2`

will be considered the same variable `MONTHMAY`. (There are some special cases in which you may be limited to less than six characters. See Chapter 9 for more details.)

In your program, you will use variables for working with different kinds of data. In addition to having a specific name, a variable is also usually designed to hold a certain kind of data. Therefore, in addition to the name, a **data type** (described below) is associated with a variable. Think of a variable as a container. In your kitchen, for example, you might have one container named *recipe cards* and another named *iced tea*. The type of container is like a data type: a container for iced tea is designed for liquids (hopefully). While you might be able to put recipe cards in an empty iced tea container, the results may not be so good if you put iced tea in the recipe cards container.

On the level of the computer, a variable that counts something would hold integer values. An **integer** is a whole number, with no decimal point or commas, such as 2000 or 3. Another variable might contain a letter code like G for grocery or W for "wait until next month to pay." Or, you might be working with a physics problem that involves large numbers and exact precision. In order for the computer to distinguish between these different kinds of data, you give each C variable you name a specific data type. In C, data types tell the computer what kind of variable to represent and also how much storage is needed to represent it.

Data: Bits, Numbers, and Variables

Basic Data Types

C provides lots of freedom in terms of how you can describe data items. For example, C has several fundamental or basic data types. C also has data types that are derived from this basic set. (Beyond this, C allows you to create your own name for a data type.) For now, we are concerned with just the basic set. These are as follows:

`char`	for a character such as a letter of the alphabet, &, or $, and special character sequences. (`char` may remind you of a character data type in another language such as Cobol. Here, however, `char` refers to a data type for representing single characters. You will learn later how to handle sequences of characters, or *strings*.)

`int`
`short int`
`long int`
	for integer types used to represent whole numbers. `int`, `short int`, and `long int` can be prefixed by the word `unsigned`, which means that they cannot have negative values.

`float` `double`	for scientific notation or other numbers that require decimal points.

The Size of Data Types It is important to know how many units of storage your machine uses for each data type so you can define variables properly and efficiently for your computer system. The sizes of these types depends on the machine you are using for C. On most machines, a byte refers to eight bits. Recall from an earlier discussion, a 1-byte unsigned variable can represent any unsigned number from 0 to 255. For signed values, where a bit is used to indicate positive or negative, a 1-byte signed variable can represent −128 to +127. Because the way these types are represented in the computer is machine-dependent, a character on an IBM PC will be represented by 8 bits, but on another system, it might be 9 bits. Similarly, an integer, usually represented on an IBM PC by 16 bits, is 32 bits on an IBM 370 mainframe. Your computer most likely uses 8 bits per byte, so the following table will apply to you. If not (you will know how to tell shortly), consult your computer's reference guide.

Chapter 2

Table 2.1 Typical Ranges for C Variables on a PC (Machine Dependent)

Variable Type	Bits	Bytes	From	To
signed char	8	1	−128	+127
unsigned char	8	1	0	255
short	16	2	−32768	+32767
unsigned short	16	2	0	65535
int	16	2	−32768	+32767
unsigned int	16	2	0	65535
long	32	4	−2,147,483,648	+2,147,483,647
unsigned long	32	4	0	4,294,967,295
float	32	4	−1E+38	1E+38
double	64	8	−1E308	1E+308

Keep in mind, for the moment, that variables of type `char` can be integers as well as characters. (More details on this are given below under **Character**.)

When you are looking at the range of values for `int` types, remember that a two-byte storage area can hold a signed or unsigned integer. As a result,

- the value of the unsigned integer can range from 0 to 65535; that is, 65536 possible values.

- the value of the signed integer can range from −32768 to 32767; that is, 65536 possible values, including 0.

How do you choose which type to use and what are the advantages or disadvantages of each? To help you decide, the following sections examine each type in more detail.

Integer C has several different kinds of integer types. These types are used to hold whole numbers such as 89 or −9999. (Note that 9999.0 or 50,000 are not valid integer values because of the decimal and comma.) Integers can be specified as **signed** or **unsigned**. `int`, `short`, and `long` are called signed integers. These types have a negative to positive range. Their unsigned counterparts range from 0 to a larger positive number.

As mentioned earlier, the size of an integer is machine dependent. When considering type size, the only rules you can follow are

- `short` is smaller than `int`, or the same size.

- `int` is smaller than `long`, or the same size.

Data: Bits, Numbers, and Variables

This means that on one machine **int** and **short** may be the same size, while on another machine **int** and **long** will be the same size. Considering size is important if you write your program on one system and run it on another. An integer on one system may be able to handle larger values than an integer on the system you are moving your program to. This has obvious implications for program results. If you are not concerned with running your program on different systems, you can use **int** for most applications. (Programmers usually choose to use **int** as most efficient, in execution speed, for a given machine.) If you are working with very large integers, use **long**. If there is a difference between **short** and **int** on your system and you want to conserve space, use **short** for integer variables.

Character Character types (**char**) can hold a single character such as 1 or A. **char** can also be used to hold any sufficiently small integer value. Again, it depends on your computer, but usually character types are one byte long. In C, character types are used to represent the numeric value of a particular character. For the ASCII character set, this means that character types can be used to hold the value for a letter (A = 65), special characters ($ = 36), or even something unprintable, but useful, like the bell tone (beep = 07).

Earlier in this chapter, you learned that characters can be encoded as numbers, as they are in the ASCII set. For example, in ASCII, A is encoded as 65; B is encoded as 66, and so on. (There is a table of ASCII values in Appendix 2 at the end of the User's Guide.) Using a system that encodes letters (such as A) as numbers (such as 65) means that you need to tell the computer when you want the number (65) to be "65" and when you want it to be "A" (the letter associated with 65 in the letter encoding scheme). You do this by specifying the **char** type when you want the letter A and some other type (**int**, for example) when you want the number 65. However, since characters are encoded as numbers, in C, you can actually perform arithmetic on characters. You can add A and B, for example, which equals 131.

Adding letters is something that you may not want to do right away; however, you will want to add numbers. In this case, if you tell the computer that a number such as 4 is a **char** type, the computer stores it as the ASCII value associated with the character 4, which is 52. Similarly, the ASCII value for 2 is 50. So, if you add together 4 and 2 represented in the **char** type, you get 102. To get the correct value (4 + 2 = 6), you need to use another data type such as **int** that represents the numbers as they are, and not as their ASCII equivalents.

In comparing **int** and **char**, notice that the major difference between them is that **int** allows you to store larger values. For many computer systems, **char** types use only a single byte of storage, so that you can represent the numbers 0 through 255 using **char**.

You may be wondering how to store more than one character at a time. The answer can be found in **character strings**, which allow groups of characters. Unlike other languages, C does not have a special type for strings. One way to represent strings in C is to use the **char** type, but character strings are a world of their own in C. You

Chapter 2

can do so much with them that they get considerable attention later in Chapter 7, which covers arrays and strings.

Float and Double   If you are writing C programs that use decimal fractions or scientific notation, you will need to use the `float` and `double` types. (In scientific notation, a number is represented as a decimal fraction multiplied by a value of 10 raised to a power, for example, $10000 = .1 \times 10^5$.) These types require more storage space. Most computers use 32 bits to store a floating point number. The sign and exponent are stored in the left-most 8 bits with the nonexponent part stored in the remaining 24 bits. This means that floating point variables can hold real numbers with a precision of approximately 6 digits. Doubles (64 bits) are also used widely for floating point data, and they have a precision of about 16 decimal digits.

Although floating point types are needed for mathematical applications, remember that they take up more space and are slower to calculate. You should resist the urge to declare all your variables as `float` just because this type provides a greater range of values.

Finding Out About Size   As your program executes, all variables or objects are represented in the computer by a certain number of bytes. The size of the data object is the number of units of storage, normally bytes, used by that object. There is an operator in C called `sizeof` that finds the size of data objects. Here is a program that you can run to find out the size of the basic types on your machine.

```
/* This program lists the sizes of different data types */

main()
{
printf("Sizes of basic data types on this system are:\t\n");
printf("char size = %d bytes.\t\n",sizeof(char));
printf("int size = %d bytes.\t\n",sizeof(int));
printf("short size = %d bytes.\t\n",sizeof(short));

printf("long size = %d bytes.\t\n",sizeof(long));
printf("float size = %d bytes.\t\n",sizeof(float));
printf("double size = %d bytes.\t\n",sizeof(double));
printf("That's all!");
}
```

In this program the `sizeof` operator returns the length, in units of storage (usually bytes) of each data type.

There are some new things about the `printf` function here. A `%d` and `,` have been added. The `%d` means to look for a number or a variable containing a number, after the comma ending the quoted string. `%d` specifies the format to be used in printing out information. (It means "integer format—no decimal point.") The % and d must appear together with no space in between. You will learn much more about `%d` and other print formats in the next few sections.

Data: Bits, Numbers, and Variables

After you create and run this program, you will know the size your system uses for each of the basic C data types.

Module 3 Summary

In this section you learned that you need to identify variables in your C program to the computer by giving them a name and a data type.

New C Tools

Concepts	Code	
objects	`char`	`unsigned`
variables	`int`	`float`
identifiers	`short`	`double`
data types	`long`	`sizeof`

Module 4: The Declaration Statement

This section discusses how to write the C statements to declare your variables in terms of the basic C types. You also learn how to give each variable an initial value with simple assignment statements. Topics include the following:

- declaring identifiers in C
- using constants to initialize variables
- putting it all together in a sample program.

Keywords you need to note are

declaration statement   **character constant**
assignment statement
initialize
declare
define

Declaring Identifiers in C

In C, each variable you want to use in your program must be given a name and data type. You use a C **declaration statement** to do this. A simple declaration consists of only a variable name and data type. The name refers to a memory location and the data type specifies the kind of value the variable can be assigned and the storage needed to represent the variable. The way you can use a variable in your program is

Chapter 2

determined by its data type. If no data type is specified, a default type of `int` is assumed.

Examples of simple C declaration statements are as follows:

```
char acode;
short s;
float result;
long hugenum;
```

A C variable (or identifier) declaration has three parts. An example is the `acode` variable:

- data type: `char`
- name: `acode`
- semicolon: `;`

The declaration can also be in the form of a list of names separated by commas. The statement `int a,b,c;` defines three integer variables a, b, and c.

The qualifiers (`short`, `long`, `unsigned`) can stand alone as in the following:

```
short int a;      is equivalent to      short a;
unsigned int b;   is equivalent to      unsigned b;
```

When you **declare** a variable in C, you are stating that an object of a certain type is going to be used in a particular section of your program (program sections and scope of variables are discussed in Chapter 9). The term **defined** means to allocate storage for an object. For some types of variables, you only need to declare the variable: storage is allocated automatically. For other types of variables, you may need to provide definitions as well as declarations (more about these kinds of variables later). With the latter variables, a declaration only announces to the compiler that you are planning to use a variable with a particular name and type. Storage is allocated when you assign a value to the variable. You can read more about variable storage classes and how you use definitions of variables in Chapter 9.

Assignment Statements

There may be times when you want to give a variable an initial value or you may just want the variable to hold a certain value. To do this, you **initialize** the variable using a C statement called an **assignment statement**. Here is a sample assignment statement:

```
minutes = 5;
```

A C assignment statement means to take what is on the right side of the equal sign (=) and put its value into the variable on the left side. For example, `x=20;` means to take a copy of the value 20 and put it in the storage location called `x`. After this statement, `x` will have the value 20. Before this statement, the storage reserved for `x` contained whatever value happened to be there. This value might have been zero, but you can't be sure. If you expect variables to contain certain values before they are used in computations, be sure to assign starting values.

Data: Bits, Numbers, and Variables

Here is a short program that declares the variable **x**, assigns the value 10 to **x** and then prints **x**.

```
main()
{
int x;                    /* declaration */
x = 10;                   /* definition */
printf("\n x = %d\n", x);
}
```

You can also print several values at once with a `printf()` statement such as the one used below:

```
x=10;
y=5;
z=0;
printf("x= %d y=%d z=%d", x, y, z);
```

With this introduction to assignment, you are ready for some details on how you assign values to different data types.

Integer Constants In C, a number without a decimal place and without an exponent is assumed to be an integer. The following example initializes the integers **hours** and **lunches**:

```
int hours, lunches;

hours = 42;
lunches = -5;
```

An alternative way to initialize these is as follows:

```
int hours = 42;
int lunches = -5;
```

Remember that you cannot use commas or decimals. Long and short integers are initialized the same way. If you need to force an integer constant to `long`, you can put a capital L after its value. (A lowercase L looks too much like the number one.) For example, 200L would be stored as a long integer. (One example of a situation where you may want to force a constant to be stored as a `long` is if you plan to use it in a calculation in which you subtract another `long` from it.)

Character Constants A **character constant** is a single character or escape sequence between single quotes. This definition is important because it implies a restriction on what can be a character constant:

> A character constant may have only a single character as its
> value. The value must be enclosed in single quotes.

Chapter 2

Here is an example:

```
char grocery;
grocery = 'E';
```

or

```
char grocery = 'E';
```

Note that `grocery` cannot = 'eggs'.

One common use of character constants is to define special ASCII values. For example,

```
char skip;

skip = '\n';
```

defines the variable `skip` to be used as a newline ('\n'). Remember that '\n' is considered a single character—it is known as an escape character.

Float and Double Constants There are several valid ways to write floating point constants. The following is a common way to assign a starting value to the variable `leaf`:

```
float leaf;
leaf = 1.2222;
```

or

```
float leaf = 1.2222;
```

Other valid values for `leaf` are the following:

```
5e10    .99999    2000.    .6E-15
```

At some point in your programming career, you will probably encounter a message saying something like "floating point overflow". This means that a value has exceeded the limits for a `float` type variable. Usually your system handles this by replacing a value that is too large by the largest legal value and a value that is too small by 0. Check your system specifications to be sure what will happen. A possible solution (if your calculations are valid) is to declare the `float` variable in question as a `double` because on many computers, a `double` can be used to store larger values than a `float`. (See **Table 2.1** for the possible limits that `float` and `double` can have.)

Data: Bits, Numbers, and Variables

Example The following program contains several different types of variable declarations. Read it, then create and run the program as written. Next, try to run it with variables you create and assign.

```
/* Examples of Variable Declarations */

main()
{
char letter;     /* Declarations */
short s;
int i;
float duck;

letter = 'Z';    /* Initialization */
s = 22;
i = 9999;
duck = 2018.0;

printf("This program lists different kinds of variables\n");

printf("character is:   %d\n", letter);
printf("character is:   %c\n", letter);

printf("int = %d\n", i);
printf("short = %d\n", s);

i = -9999;
printf("int = %d\n", i);

printf("duck fixed: %.2f\n", duck);
printf("duck float: %f\n", duck);
printf("%f\n",5.2222);

printf("%f\n",3.0e10);
printf("scientific duck: %.4e\n", duck);

printf("ok!");

}
```

Your output should look like the following:

```
This program lists different kinds of variables
character is:   90
character is:   Z
int = 9999
short = 22
int = -9999
duck fixed: 2018.00
duck float: 2018.000000
5.222200
```

Chapter 2

```
3.0000000000.000000
scientific duck: 2.0180e+03
ok!
```

A Closer Look Here is a summary of what this program does: the first line is a comment explaining the program's purpose. The next two lines define the beginning of the `main()` function. These four lines are the declarations. Each is explained as follows:

`char letter;`	a character variable called letter
`short s;`	a short integer named s
`int i;`	an integer i
`float duck;`	a floating point variable called duck

The initializations are next. As a result, `letter` is assigned an uppercase Z; `s` contains the integer 22; `i` is assigned 9999; and `duck` gets the float constant 2018.0.

The next several print statements list the values of the variables in different ways with the `printf()` function. The first print statement prints a message about the program's purpose.

The next two print statements list different character values for the variable `letter`. Notice the symbols `%d` and `%c` in the `printf()` function. (You have seen `%d` before.) These symbols specify the format to use to print the information. `printf()` allows you to print information in different formats, but you need to tell it which format. Very simply, in this case, `%d` means print an integer. `%c` means print a character. Recall that variables of type `char` are stored as numbers so that you can, in fact, print them as numbers. The program prints the ASCII code associated with Z, namely, 90, and then prints the character Z.

The variables `i` and `s` are printed next. Notice that although they may be represented in storage as different sizes, the integer values are identical in form.

After `i` is given a new value (−9999), it is printed again. Notice that `%d` prints the sign for negative integers.

The next five statements illustrate different ways of assigning and printing floating point numbers. Notice the `%f` symbol indicates a floating point format to the `printf()` function. The statement

```
printf("duck fixed: %.2f\n", duck);
```

shows you how to print a floating point number. The number written is "2018.00". With `%f`, you can specify the amount of precision that you want for a value; that is, the number of places to the right of the decimal point. In this case, although the variable is an integer, two zeros are provided, because you asked for two places of precision. If you don't specify how many places you want to the right of the decimal point, you automatically get six places. You can see that there are 6 zeros in the next output line: no precision was specified. In the line after that, no precision is specified again, but only two places (filled with zeros) are added because 5.2222 already has four decimal places.

The next `printf()` statement prints 3.0e10, a value expressed in scientific notation in floating point form. (Notice the default of six decimal places.) This `printf()` also prints a value in scientific notation expressed by the format `%.4e`. This format requests four decimal places of precision.

The last statement prints a completion message, and the closing brace ends the `main()` function.

For fun, change some of the variable values so that they are greater than their defined limits and see what happens. By doing this, you can see how your system compensates for over- and underflow values. For example, assign `i` equal to 32768. (Most compilers give you a warning message when you make such an assignment to an `int` type.) If it comes out as a negative number, what is probably happening is that your computer converts the `int` type `i` to a `long`, but then puts it back in an `int` size space to write it out. In putting it back, the sign bit becomes one, and so the computer thinks the value is negative. If you get a positive value, your system probably uses a larger size for `int` type values.

You might want to see what happens when you use `signed`.

Inside Information

The example shows some of the common format specifiers you can use with `printf()` to print data of various kinds. You can print information in many other ways including the following:

- hexadecimal numbers (base 16)
- octal numbers (base 8)
- engineering notation with the precision (number of decimal places) that you specify—with or without a decimal point
- padded with zeros
- signed
- unsigned.

A discussion of all the format specifiers for `printf()` is a fairly detailed subject and is an advanced C programming topic. One reason is that the format specifier does more than simply format data. It also can convert variables from one type to another. The rules for these conversion operations depend on the original data type, the new type indicated by the format specifier, and other factors. Nevertheless, you should look at the discussion of the `printf()` function in Chapter 16 to get an idea of what `printf()` can do.

Chapter 2

Module 4 Summary

In **Module 4** you learned how to declare and initialize variables in C. Some rules and guidelines were provided to help you define constants of different types and assign variables starting values. More ways to code the `printf()` function were illustrated.

New C Tools

Concepts	Code
declaring and initializing variables	declaration statement assignment statement

Chapter Summary

In this chapter you learned how the computer stores numbers and letters. With this background, you can declare character and numeric data in your C program so that the computer can handle your program's variables correctly.

Declaring all variables is required in C. This requirement forces you to think about exactly what information your program needs to work with and what form it needs to be in. If you think about and declare variables at the beginning of each C function you need, you will write clearer and more efficient programs.

Your C skills now include the following:

- how numbers and letters are stored
- what basic C data types are
- how to declare variables using these types
- how to assign starting values for each type
- when to use each type.

The next chapter introduces basic C **operators**, both arithmetic and logical. You also graduate from writing simple print statements to writing assignment statements and simple expressions.

Chapter 3
Operators and C

Chapter 3

CONTENTS

Introduction	43
Module 5: Operators—a First Look	43
Arithmetic Operators	43
Relational Operators	46
Logical Operators	47
Inside Information	48
Module 5 Summary	49
Module 6: Introducing the C if Statement	49
Module 6 Summary	51
Module 7: Writing Expressions in C	51
Order of Evaluation in Expressions	52
Inside Information	54
More on Parentheses and Expressions	54
Example	55
A Closer Look	57
Inside Information	59
Program Notes	60
Module 7 Summary	60
Chapter Summary	60

Operators and C

Introduction

This chapter introduces you to some concepts and tools in C that will help you begin taking advantage of the computer's ability to perform tasks for you. Up to now, you have not written a program for anything that you could not have done as efficiently by hand. By learning about the mathematical and logical operators that C provides, you can begin to write C statements to perform calculations and make decisions faster and more precisely than you can by yourself. In this chapter you learn

- what the basic C operators are and how to use them
- how to handle conditional events by using the C **if** statement with operators
- how to write simple expressions in C.

Module 5: Operators—a First Look

C offers a rich variety of symbols to help you in programming tasks. You can use C operators to work with addresses of variables in storage, change values at the bit level, increment variable values in very efficient ways, and add, compare, or assign values. This section focuses on the C operators that you can use to do basic programming tasks like arithmetic, assignment, and comparison operations.

Keywords you need to note are

> **operator**
> **arithmetic operators**
> **binary operators**
> **unary operators**
> **modulus operator**
> **relational operators**
> **truth value**
> **logical operators**
> **conditional statement**

Arithmetic Operators

C provides a set of operators that allow you to code arithmetic expressions. (For now, think of an expression as a C statement involving operators and operands.) If you were working with two variables, **a** and **b** (the operands), you could use the following arithmetic operators:

    + addition   (sum of a and b)
    - subtraction   (difference between a and b)
    * multiplication   (product of a and b)

Chapter 3

    / division   (quotient of **a** divided by **b**)

    % remainder   (remainder of **a** divided by **b**)

Because the arithmetic operators must take at least two operands, they are said to be **binary operators**. C also has a set of **unary operators**. Some of them (-, for example) are the same symbols as binary operators, but they are used with only one operand.

+ Operator The + is a binary operator that indicates addition. For example, a = b + c; is a C statement that adds the values of the variables **b** and **c** and assigns the resulting value to the variable **a**. For now, think of + as addition involving two numbers of any arithmetic data type, for example, `int`, `float`, and `long`. Later, you will find out how to use addition with other types of operands (such as storage location indicators).

— Operator As a binary operator, the minus sign indicates subtraction, for example, a = b - c;. Again, for now, think of the operands as being of any arithmetic data type.

* Operator The * indicates binary multiplication, for example, a = b * c;. However, there is one other thing you need to remember about this operator that will save you from some programming difficulties later on:

> C has no exponentiation operator. Instead, C provides you with a library function. If you are familiar with another language where you write x** to raise a number to a power, remember to use a library function to do this in C. (See Chapter 16 for a description of the `pow` function.)

/ Operator The / binary operator indicates division. The operands can be of any arithmetic data type. In division, an integer divided by an integer gives an integer result. A floating-point number anywhere in a division expression yields a floating-point result (which you can use as such if your result field is defined as `float`). If you inadvertently divide something by zero, the result depends on how your C compiler handles division by zero. Check your compiler documentation to see what happens in this situation.

% (Modulus) Operator If you are dividing integers and there is a remainder, the result is truncated. In other words, the remainder is dropped. Suppose you want to know the remainder in integer division. You can use the % operator, which is called the **modulus operator**. For example, c = a % b; puts any remainder of the operation **a** / **b** into the variable **c**. There are some creative ways to use the modulus operator in C. For example, suppose you are developing a schedule and you want to note that a progress meeting should be held every six weeks. You could set an indicator to note this as follows:

```
meet = weeks % 6;
```

When the value of **meet** is 0 (indicating an even division by 6), your program should note that week.

Here is a short program that uses some arithmetic operators:

```
#include <stdio.h>

main()
{
int a, b, answer;
a = 12;
b = 4;

answer = a + b;   /* add the value of b to a; put */
                  /* the result in answer */

printf("The sum is %d\n", answer);

answer = a - b;   /* subtract the value of b from a; put */
                  /* the result in answer */

printf("The difference is %d\n", answer);

answer = a * b;   /* multiply the value of b and a; put */
                  /* the result in answer */

printf("The product is %d\n", answer);

answer = a / b;   /* divide the value of a and b; put */
                  /* the result in answer */

printf("The quotient is %d\n", answer);

a = 15;
answer = a % b;   /* perform modulus operation; put the result */
                  /* in answer */

printf("The result of a % b is %d\n", answer);
}
```

When working with numbers, you often need to know whether the result of one arithmetic operation is less than another or if a result is equal to some other number. To determine these kinds of relationships between numbers, C provides another set of operators.

Chapter 3

Relational Operators

In C, operators that compare numbers are called **relational operators**. These operators and what they mean are as follows:

<	less than
>	greater than
==	equal to
!=	not equal to
<=	less than or equal to
>=	greater than or equal to

For example, you could write a C statement to act on something if a is greater than or equal to b. The relational part of this would be coded **a >= b**. (Remember when you are coding operators that have two characters, like **>=**, there can be no space between them.)

If the relationship between the operands is true, the **truth value** for the expression is equal to 1. If it is not true, then the truth value is 0. We will examine this concept in more detail shortly. For now, note that you can test for the truth value in a relationship between numbers. For example, working with the variables a and b, possible truth values for each relational expression are given in **Table 3.1**.

Table 3.1 Relational Operators

Statement	Meaning	Variable Value	Truth Value
a < b	a is less than b	a = 1, b = 2	1 (true)
	a is not less than b	a = 2, b = 2	0 (false)
a > b	a is greater than b	a = 4, b = 2	1 (true)
	a is not greater than b	a = 2, b = 4	0 (false)
a <= b	a is less than or equal to b	a = 2, b = 3	1 (true)
	(otherwise)	a = 3, b = 2	0 (false)
a >= b	a is greater than or equal to b	a = 4, b = 3	1 (true)
	(otherwise)	a = 3, b = 4	0 (false)
a == b	a and b are equal	a = 2, b = 2	1 (true)
	a and b are not equal	a = 2, b = 4	0 (false)
a != b	a and b are not equal	a = 2, b = 4	1 (true)
	a and b are equal	a = 2, b = 2	0 (false)

Operators and C

The last two relational operators, == and != are frequently used. However, misuse of the first one, ==, often causes problems for C programmers. The == means *exactly equal to* and is used only in relational expressions. Recall that the = is used to assign a value to a variable. Try not to get the two confused. One way to remind yourself of the difference is that == stands for comparing two operands and = means to assign a value to one operand.

The next section covers some operators that you can use to tie relational expressions together.

Logical Operators

Logical operators provide a way for you to test for the logical value (true or false) of an expression that contains relational comparisons. There are three logical operators in C. They are

    && (AND)
    || (OR)
    ! (NOT)

Table 3.2 shows how each operator can be used and the truth values possible for each expression.

Table 3.2 Logical Operators, Use and Meaning

Statement	Possible Results	Truth Value
(a == 10) && (b == 10)	Both a and b are equal to 10	True (1)
	a is equal to 10, b is not	False (0)
	b is equal to 10, a is not	False (0)
(a == 10) || (b == 10)	Either a or b is equal to 10	True (1)
	Neither a nor b is equal to 10	False (0)
!(a < b)	a is greater than b	True (1)
	a is equal to b	True (1)
	a is less than b	False (0)

From this table, you can see that

- with the && operator, both conditions must be true for the entire expression to be true
- the || operator needs only one condition to be true for the entire expression to be evaluated as true.

Chapter 3

In C, logical expressions are always evaluated from left to right. As soon as any element is found that invalidates the expression as a whole, the evaluation stops. This is an advantage of the C language. It means that you can write logical expressions in which you are guaranteed that subsequent parts of the expression will not be considered at all if a previous part has already made the expression as a whole invalid.

As a programmer, you may want to use the `&&` (sometimes called *conditional AND*) to test whether two expressions are simultaneously true. If the first expression is false, the second is not evaluated. With the `||` operator (sometimes called *conditional OR*), if the first expression is true, the second is not evaluated.

Suppose, that you are working with the two variables `smoke` and `heat`:

```
int smoke;
int heat;
```

If `smoke`=1 and `heat`=0, then the following are some expressions with their truth values.

Expression	Truth Value
`smoke && heat`	False (only smoke is true)
`smoke || heat`	True
`!heat`	True
`!(smoke && heat)`	True ("not" false is true)
`(smoke < 5) || (heat > smoke)`	True
`(smoke < 5) && (heat > smoke)`	False

In the final example, the second expression `heat > smoke` is not evaluated unless, in the first expression, `smoke` is less than 5.

Inside Information

All the C operators presented in this section can be classified as unary or binary. (C also has a ternary operator, which is covered in Chapter 7.) Unary operators are used with just one operand. Usually the distinction between unary and binary operators is straightforward, but sometimes it depends on the context.

For example, for the arithmetic operators given above, the minus sign (-) can be used as either a unary or binary operator. As a unary operator it indicates the arithmetic negation of its operand: `-a` or `-(a + b)`, for instance. You can use the unary minus with any arithmetic data type. As a binary operator, - indicates subtraction of one number from another.

The `*` symbol in C is also used as a unary operator. You will probably use the `*` for this other operation more than you ever will for multiplication. The use of the `*` symbol as a unary operator is discussed in Chapter 8.

Module 5 Summary

In this section you have learned about the basic arithmetic, relational, and logical C operators. In the next section you will learn about a C statement that helps you put these operators to use.

New C Tools

Concepts	Code
operators	arithmetic operators +, -, *, /, %
operands	relational operators <, >, ==, !=, <=, >=
truth value	logical operators &&, ||, !

Module 6:   Introducing the C if Statement

Module 6 introduces the C `if` statement, which lets your program make choices based on different values for variables. Important concepts are

- conditional expression
- conditional statement
- alternate statement.

Keywords you need to note are

```
if                      header files
else                    #include
                        stdio.h
```

The `if` statement allows you to write the code to select alternative actions depending on different conditions or sets of conditions. Using this statement you can ask things like, "if the variable tested to end the program contains a 'Y' for yes, then print an appropriate message." Using the `if` statement, this can be written in C as follows:

```
if (end == 'Y')
   printf("Time to quit");
```

The syntax for a simple `if` statement is

   if (*expression***)**   (*expression* is what's evaluated)
      statement;   (*statement* is the action taken)

The **conditional expression** contains the expression to be tested and is evaluated as either true or false. If it is true, the statement, called the **conditional statement**, is executed. If the expression is evaluated as false, no action is taken.

Chapter 3

You can provide an alternative action if the conditional expression is not true by coding an **else** statement. The complete syntax then becomes

  if (*expression*)
    statement;
  else
    alternate statement;

Read and then try the following example:

```
/* Test for Blue */
#include <stdio.h>

main()
{
   int color;

   printf("Type a character and press ENTER:\n");

   color = getchar();
   if (color == 'B')
      printf("The sky is Blue\n");
   else
      printf("The fog is in\n");
}
```

The program first gets a character code, sees if it is equal to an uppercase B (66 in ASCII), then prints one message if it is B and another if it is not.

There are some new things in this example. One is the C function `getchar()`, which is in the C library. This function gets a character from the standard input device (in this case, your keyboard). The statement

```
color = getchar();
```

assigns the value of whatever letter you key in to the variable `color`. (Remember that characters are numeric values from the ASCII table.)

To be able to use this standard C function, you need to know about library **header files**. The compiler keeps information needed to use the library functions, such as `getchar`, in header files. You normally include the header file for the function you want to call as part of your program and can do this with an `#include` statement. (You will have more than one `#include` statement in a program when you use functions from different header files.) The header file for `getchar` is `stdio.h`. The statement

```
#include <stdio.h>
```

asks the compiler to include the C file that `getchar()` is in. `stdio.h` stands for *standard input output header file*. Many definitions of the most common C functions (such as `printf()`) are contained in this file. For this reason, you can usually code this statement as a matter of course in your C programs. Also, note the following

Operators and C

about the format of the `#include` statement:

- Do not terminate an `#include` statement with a semicolon.
- Surround the name of the header file with < >.
- Precede the word *include* with a # sign.

(Header or include files are covered in Chapter 5. Refer to that chapter for details.)

Notice how the == and the = operators are used in this example. Remember that == tests to see if two values are exactly equal. The = is used to assign a value to a variable.

Note that C does not make use of the word *then* as part of the `if` statement. Remembering this (and it is easy to inadvertently code it) can save you some time with syntax errors.

Module 6 Summary

In this section, you learned how to conditionally select an action using the C `if` statement. You are now ready to put all of this together and write some C statements that make use of more complex expressions.

New C Tools

Concepts	Code
conditional statements	`if` statement
	`else` statement
header files	`getchar()`
	`stdio.h`

Module 7: Writing Expressions in C

As noted earlier, an **expression** contains an operator and its operands. This section shows you how to write expressions using arithmetic, relational, and logical operators. Important concepts are

- order of evaluation
- precedence.

51

Chapter 3

Keywords you need to note are

expression	**associativity**
precedence order

You are already familiar with expressions as used in assignment statements such as **a = b + c;**. You can also create assignment expressions that use the same variable on both sides such as **b = b + c;**. This example reads: add the values of **b** and **c**, then put the result back in **b**.

C does not limit you, however, to writing line by line expressions. Expressions can be used anywhere a value is allowed. This means you can program statements such as **printf("%d", 100 + 200);**. The result of a statement like this is that the *value* of the expression (100 + 200) is written (300).

In C, each expression produces a result that can be nested inside a larger expression. This means that an expression really can be a combination of operators and operands ranging from one operand to complex sets of operators and operands. For example, the following are all valid expressions:

Expression	Value
20 + 6	26
41 > 40	1
x = 8 / 2	4
y = 5 + 3	8
z = 2 + (x = 8 / 2) + (y = 5 + 3)	14
z1 = z2 = z3 = 14	14

The last two expressions hint at how flexible C lets you be when constructing expressions. The next to the last expression includes the sum of two subexpressions. The last expression assigns the value 14 to all three **z** variables.

In order to write expressions in C correctly, you need to know how C evaluates operators and operands.

Order of Evaluation in Expressions

In expressions that have more than two primary components, the order of evaluation is important. For example, is 5 − 4 * 2 equal to 2 or −3? To give order to expression evaluation, all operators are assigned a **precedence**. Precedence rules specify the order in which operations are to be carried out. For example, multiplication is normally done before addition if both are present in a formula. This is because, traditionally, multiplication has a higher precedence than addition. Operations with the higher precedence are always performed first. (How parentheses can affect this is

Operators and C

covered below.) Some operators have the same precedence. To show the ranking of operators by their precedence value, **Table 3.3** ranks the operators from highest to lowest precedence and lists those with the same precedence on one line.

Table 3.3 Order of Evaluation for Operators—Highest to Lowest

Arithmetic Operators
* / %
+ -
Relational Operators
< > <= >=
== !=
Logical Operators
&&
||

As shown, the precedence among arithmetic, logical, and relational operators is

arithmetic
relational
logical.

When you have operators of equal precedence together in an expression (and no parentheses), the operation performed first depends on whether the operators are evaluated right-to-left or left-to-right. (This characteristic—right-to-left or left-to-right evaluation—is called **associativity**.) Here is the associativity for each of the groups of operators listed above:

```
* / %         left-to-right
+ -           left-to-right
< > <= >=     left-to-right
== !=         left-to-right
```

For example, obeying rules of precedence and associativity, you can be sure that $5-4*2$ is -3; that is, it is evaluated as $5-(4*2)$. Also, $5-4*5/2$ is -5.

In most cases (the exceptions are given shortly), you can use parentheses ( ) to change the order of evaluation in an expression. This is because expressions within parentheses are assigned a higher precedence. All expressions within parentheses are evaluated first. The result of that evaluation is then used with values outside of the parentheses. For example,

$$20 + 10 / 5 = 22 \quad \text{while} \quad (20 + 10) / 5 = 6$$

Chapter 3

You can also use parentheses in writing and testing the result of relational expressions involving complex operands. For example,

$(x + y) / z > (z + y) / x$

If the result of $(x + y) / z$ is greater than the result of $(z + y) / x$, then the truth value for the entire expression is 1.

Inside Information

If you read the previous **Inside Information**, you learned that there is also a set of unary operators in C. One of them is -. Another one (that you saw earlier in this chapter) is !. The ! is a negation operator. It changes an operand that is true (not zero) to false (zero) or changes an operand that is false to true. For example, you could use the ! operator with the following statement from the previous program example:

```
if (!(color == blue))
    printf("The fog is in \n");
```

Going back to the subject of precedence, if you include the ! and unary minus operators, the precedence order of all the operators covered so far is:

!
− (unary)
arithmetic
relational
logical

More on Parentheses and Expressions

For the operators introduced so far, you can use parentheses to force the order of evaluation in an expression in all cases except one. Parentheses do not affect grouping if there is more than one occurrence of the commutative and associative binary operator (for now just * and +). This means that the compiler is free (subject to some restrictions covered in later chapters, and depending on how closely your compiler conforms to the current Draft ANSI Standard) to interpret x * (a * b) * y as (x * a) * (b * y). For example, suppose you have the following:

```
result = x + y + z;
```

and you know that **x** is always a large negative number but that **y** and **z** are both always very large positive numbers. To prevent a possible overflow, you want to be sure that **x** and **y** are added together before the value of **z** is included. In C, you cannot force this by coding **(x + y) + z**. In order to force a particular grouping, you must break down the expression, and explicitly assign the value of **x + y** to another variable and then use that variable in the original expression. For example,

```
temp = x + y;
result = temp + z;
```

Evaluation of parenthesized subexpressions can be a programming problem because of another C convention:

> Except for logical operators, which are evaluated left to right, C does not specify the order of the evaluation of the operands of an operator, unless there is precedence.

This can be a problem in situations such as the following:

```
z = 10;
x = (y = z + 10) + (z = 100);
```

which could evaluate to either

```
x = (10 + 10) + 100    = 120    (y = z + 10) is evaluated first
```

or

```
x = (100 + 10) + 100    = 210    (z = 100) is evaluated first
```

(This example is not very good programming style anyway.)

The result may differ from compiler to compiler, so use temporary variables when in doubt. The example above could be rewritten as two statements to ensure a certain order of evaluation.

In general, to keep things clear, you should

- use spaces around arithmetic, relational, and logical operators
- use parentheses carefully
- make liberal use of comments to annotate more complex operations.

Note that although you should be careful with parentheses, they are good to use because they make the order of evaluation more obvious to anyone who may read the program.

Example

This chapter concludes by bringing everything together in an example. First, read through the following code:

```
/* Calculator Program - add, subtract, multiply, and divide */
/* integer numbers.  Print operands, operator, and results. */
/* The first statement includes the standard C input-output */
/* function header file.  The second statement includes a   */
/* header file needed by atoi, used in the getnum function. */

#include <stdio.h>
#include <stdlib.h>
```

Chapter 3

```
/* The main function begins next. */
main()
{

    /* Declare two integer variables to hold the values for the  */
    /* operands involved in the calculation.  Declare an integer */
    /* variable for the operator */

    int num1, num2, oper;

    /* Begin processing by printing a welcome message.  Next, ask */
    /* the user to enter the numbers he/she wants to use */

    printf( "Welcome to the Handy-Home Calculator\n" );
    printf( "...please use with integers only...\n\n");

    printf( "Enter the first number : " );  /* Enter operands */

    /* The following assignment statement takes the value         */
    /* returned by getnum and assigns it to num1. The number entered */
    /* by the user from the keyboard is the number "retrieved"    */
    /* by getnum(). */

    num1 = getnum();

    /* Go through the same process to assign the value of the second */
    /* number entered by the user. */

    printf( "\nEnter the second number : " );
    num2 = getnum();


    /* Ask the user to enter the operator for the operation to be  */
    /* performed.  The library function getchar() is used to retrieve */
    /* the operator and assign it to the variable oper.  Remember that */
    /* the ASCII numeric value for the operator characters (+ - / etc.) */
    /* is the value assigned. */

    printf( "\nEnter the operation to be executed + - * or x,/ ");
    oper = getchar();

    printf( "\n" ); /* skip to new line */




    /* The following statements do the actual calculations.  First, the */
    /* operation requested is determined by testing the value of oper.  */
    /* This is done by using an if-else structure.  Once the operator   */
    /* is determined, the calculation is performed in the context of a  */
    /* printf statement.  This saves programming steps.  Remember that  */
```

56

```
/* the %d indicates to printf that a decimal number is going to be */
/* substituted and printed.  The numbers involved follow the      */
/* format. */

if ( oper == '+' )
   printf( "%d + %d = %d\n", num1, num2, num1 + num2 );
else if ( oper == '-' )
   printf( "%d - %d = %d\n", num1, num2, num1 - num2 );
else if ( ( oper == '*' ) || ( oper == 'x' ) )
   printf( "%d * %d = %d\n", num1, num2, num1 * num2 );
else if ( oper == '/' )
   if ( num2 == 0 )
      printf( "I can't divide by zero.\n" );
   else
      printf( "%d / %d = %d\n", num1, num2, num1 / num2 );
else
   printf( "I don't understand what %c means.\n", oper );

} /* End the main function. */

/* getnum is a function written here that is used by main() to    */
/* get a number from the keyboard.  getnum() is discussed in more */
/* detail soon. */

getnum()
{
char buff [ 80 ];

gets( buff );
return( atoi( buff ) );
}
```

A Closer Look

The example asks you for two numbers and an arithmetic operator, calculates the result, and then writes the input with the result. The following paragraphs discuss the program in four sections to illustrate some new C features.

The program begins by including the standard library via `#include <stdio.h>`. `stdio.h` is needed for the `getchar()` function. `stdlib.h` is included for `atoi`, which is used by `getnum()`.

Next, the `main()` function is declared. Three integers are then declared. An opening comment is printed, and the real work of the program begins.

The statements that follow ask you to enter two numbers:

```
printf( "Enter the first number :  " );
num1 = getnum();
printf( "\nEnter the second number : " );
num2 = getnum();
```

Chapter 3

After each print statement, a new function, `getnum( )`, is called as part of an assignment statement. The `getnum( )` function retrieves the number you entered in response to each request and assigns the first number to `num1` and the second to `num2`. The `getnum( )` function is covered in more detail shortly.

After the operands have been entered and their values assigned to `num1` and `num2`, a request is made for the operation to be executed:

```
printf( "\nEnter the operation to be executed + - * or x,/  " );
oper = getchar();
```

Here, `getchar` gets the operator and assigns it to the variable `oper`. (Recall that `getchar( )` is a standard C function that retrieves a character from the standard input device, usually the keyboard.)

The next `printf( )` statement prints a blank line for spacing.

At this point, all the items necessary to perform the calculation are present. The next step is to decide which arithmetic operation was requested. Once the operation is determined, the calculation can be completed and the result written. The following statements accomplish both these tasks.

```
if ( oper == '+' )
    printf( "%d + %d = %d\n", num1, num2, num1 + num2 );
else if ( oper == '-' )
    printf( "%d - %d = %d\n", num1, num2, num1 - num2 );
else if ( ( oper == '*' ) || ( oper == 'x' ) )
    printf( "%d * %d = %d\n", num1, num2, num1 * num2 );
else if ( oper == '/' )
    if ( num2 == 0 )
        printf( "I can't divide by zero.\n" );
    else
        printf( "%d / %d = %d\n", num1, num2, num1 / num2 );
else
    printf( "I don't understand what %c means.\n", oper );
```

There are several things to note in these statements. Remember the use of single quotes to indicate a character constant. Each `if` statement tests the value of the variable `oper` in this way to determine the operator type. The `if` statements are combined with the use of `else` to provide a structure that progressively tests each possible value for `oper`. The form for this version of the `if` statement is as follows:

if (*expression1*)
    statement1;
else if (*expression2*)
    statement2;
else if (*expression3*)
    statement3;
else
    statement4;

The final `else` provides a default option in case none of the preceding tests is true.

Once the operator is determined, the calculation is performed as part of the `printf()` statement and the result is written. Note the use of the || logical operator to select the multiplication operation if either a * or x is entered. Notice also that the program provides for two error conditions. In the first case, if division is requested, the divisor, `num2`, is tested to be sure its value is not 0. If the result of the test is true, a message is written and the `else` clause containing the actual division is not executed. The last `else` statement in this series catches any values that were not recognized as valid operators and prints an appropriate message: "I don't understand what [the character] means." (Notice that `%c` is used to repeat the value of `oper` as a character.)

The final lines of code are for the `getnum` function. (`getnum` is a function that was created in this program; it is not in a library.) For now, know that the purpose of this function is to get a number (in the form of a string of characters) from the standard input device (keyboard) and convert it to a number. (`atoi` does the conversion.) Some of the components of this function are covered in more detail in a later chapter. It is introduced here so that you can use it along with `getchar()` in programming tasks.

Once the program runs successfully, try adding your own statements to make use of the modulus operator and some of the relational operators. For example, you could decide to select only numbers within a certain range for use as operands.

When you run this example, notice that you can only perform one operation each time the program executes. In the next chapter, you learn how to modify this program to make it much more dynamic and useful.

Inside Information

With `if`, you can use more than one conditional statement following the conditional expression that you are testing. Here is an expanded view of `if`:

```
if (expression) {
    statement;
    statement;
    statement;
        .
        .
        .
    statement;
}
```

Notice the use of left and right braces to set off a block of statements. You can use a block of statements in the same way (instead of a single conditional statement) with `else` and `else if`.

Chapter 3

Program Notes

One function used in this program is `gets`. `gets` is an I/O function that you will learn more about in Chapter 5. In the meantime, if you decide to work on some programs of your own, be careful if you use `gets`. Until you learn more about how this function behaves, you may get unexpected results.

Module 7 Summary

In this section, you learned how to write expressions in C. You also saw how to use the `if` statement with some C operators to build a simple calculator program.

New C Tools

Concepts	Code
"else if" form of the `if` statement	`getnum( )`
	`else if`
basics about C expressions (precedence and parentheses)	

Chapter Summary

In this chapter, you have learned about the arithmetic, relational, and logical operators: how they are defined in C and how to begin using them. You learned how to put these operators to use in expressions by coding the C statements for `if` and `else` clauses.

In the next chapter, you will learn more about how expressions can be used in C statements and how statements can be grouped in order to form sets of code that become the building blocks of C functions. You will also learn about some C statements that give your program the ability to loop through tasks and control program task flow.

Chapter 4
Program Flow - Control and Repetition

Chapter 4

CONTENTS

Introduction	63
Module 8: More Control - the C switch Statement	63
Program Notes	68
Module 8 Summary	68
Module 9: Looping with Control	68
An Introduction to Loops	69
C Statements for Program Repetition	73
The for Loop	73
Using break and continue	75
The while Loop	77
The do-while Loop	81
Which Loop?	84
Example	84
A Closer Look	85
Program Notes	86
Module 9 Summary	87
Chapter Summary	87

Introduction

This chapter introduces a special control structure that C provides for selecting actions based on mutually exclusive alternatives. This new structure is called a `switch`. As you learn about it, you will see how to group C statements to form executable blocks of code. Next, you will learn the keywords and C statements to use when you want your program to repeat (or *loop* through) sections of code. You will learn about various loops in C. These and related topics are covered in **Module 8** and **Module 9**.

Module 8: More Control - the C switch Statement

In the previous chapter, you learned how to make program choices using the `if` statement. Recall that the simple `if` allows you to choose whether or not to execute a statement based on the evaluation of a condition. The `if-else` construct makes it possible to choose between two alternatives. The `else if` structure is used to choose between multiple alternatives. In this section, you learn about another C conditional statement that provides a more efficient structure than `else if` for handling multiple choices. The key concept presented in this section is how to handle mutually exclusive alternatives using the C `switch` statement.

Keywords you need to note are

```
switch
case
break
default
```
simple statement
compound statement
block

You have learned that one of the advantages of using a computer is the computer's ability to select alternative actions quickly. When you need to select alternative actions based on a set of mutually exclusive possibilities, C provides you with a special control structure called the `switch` statement. By using a `switch`, your program can branch to perform an action if an expression evaluation matches any one of a set of constant values. The `switch` statement is an efficient way to make choices if you are working with a discrete set of integer values. For example, switches are often used to choose actions based on menu selections or to provide appropriate responses in computer games.

Chapter 4

The format of the C **switch** statement is as follows:

> **switch** (*integer expression*) {
>
>> **case** *integer constant1*:
>>> *statement_1*;
>>> .
>>> .
>>> .
>>> *statement_n*;
>> **break;**
>>
>> **case** *integer constant2*:
>>> *statement_1*;
>>> .
>>> .
>>> .
>>> *statement_n*;
>> **break;**
>>
>> **default:**
>>> *statement_1*;
>>> .
>>> .
>>> .
>>> *statement_n*;
> }

In a **switch**, the integer expression is evaluated first. If a case exists whose integer value matches the expression's value, then the program performs the action statement(s) associated with that case. If all the cases have been tested, and none match, the default action (if present) is executed. If there are no matches and no default case is coded, then no action is taken at all.

The following items are new:

- use of the keywords **switch**, **case**, **default**, and **break** to form the **switch** statement
- use of braces { } to delineate a set of C statements that form a **switch** statement.

The keyword **switch** indicates the start of a multiway branch structure in C. This part of the switch statement is coded as follows:

```
switch (integer expression)
```

For a menu selection based on a character entered from the keyboard, for example, this could be coded as follows:

```
switch (response)
```

Program Flow - Control and Repetition

Values for *response* could be '1', '2', '3', '4' or 'A', 'B', 'C', 'D'. Remember that in the ASCII character set, letters are represented by integer values. In other words, the integer expression following the keyword `switch` can be any valid expression in C that evaluates to an integer value.*

Each alternative in a switch is identified by a `case` label. The `case` statement indicates the action to be taken. Each `case` label must be unique. The action taken can be composed of one or more C statements. The format of the `case` statement is

> **case** *integer constant1*:
>   *statement_1*;
>   .
>   .
>   .
>   *statement_n*;
>   **break;**

Responses to a game menu could be coded as follows:

```
case 'A' : printf("Pursuit species equals: ANXIETIES\n");
                    break;
case 'B' : printf("Pursuit species equals: BEARS\n");
                    break;
case 'C' : printf("Pursuit species equals: CRAWLERS, NIGHT\n");
                    break;
case 'D' : printf("Pursuit species equals: DARKNESS\n");
                    break;
```

Note that a different constant value follows each `case` keyword. The action taken for a case can be specified by a single statement (as above), a function, or a series of statements. Remember that the colon and semicolon are required punctuation. (Use of the keyword `break` is optional. This is explained below.)

Coding `default` provides a way for you to flag or handle cases that you are not interested in or values that you might not be aware of. Otherwise, if no matching value is found, the value simply *falls through* the switch with no action taken at all. The default case is written simply as

```
default :
```

For the game example above, the default case might be coded as

```
default : printf("You're safe...for the moment!\n");
```

The keyword `break` is used often in C. `break` tells the program to jump out of whatever it is doing and begin again elsewhere. Used with `switch`, `break` causes program control to be transferred to the statement following the closing brace of the `switch` statement.

---

* Expressions involving `float` variables will not work. Also, `long int` may not work.

65

Chapter 4

As mentioned, **break** is optional. If you do not use **break**, execution will fall through to the next case. Therefore, even if the case constant for that case does not match the integer expression of the **switch**, it is still tested. If you want to get completely out of the **switch** after you encounter a matching case, you must use **break**. Note that if you choose not to use **break**, your **switch** statement may not work correctly (in fact, leaving it out when needed is a common source of program bugs).

Notice that the body of the **switch** statement is contained between a set of braces { }. Braces are used in C to group similar statements together into what C considers to be *one* executable statement.

Simple statements are considered to be the building blocks of C programs. Simple statements contain expressions, keywords, or any set of C elements that express a complete action to the computer. The simplest statement in C contains a single expression. You are already familiar with several simple C statements in the form of print, declaration, and assignment statements. (Strictly speaking, the most basic statement in C is a single semicolon, which does nothing. You will learn more about it and how it can be used in a later chapter.)

In many C constructs, such as **switch**, you can group similar simple statements together by enclosing them in braces. This structure forms a **compound statement** or **block**. You can use a compound statement in C instead of a simple statement. The format of a block in C is

```
{
    any number of C statements,
    each ending in a semicolon
}
```

The braces can be written on either end of a stream of statements (in other words, you can put the { on the same line as the first statement and the } on the same line as the last), but the form used above is easier to read. Notice that it is not necessary for the right (or closing) brace to be followed by a semicolon.

Within the **switch**, there may be times when you want two or more cases to be associated with the same action. For example, if you didn't need to distinguish between upper- and lowercase, you could code the following **switch**:

```
switch (letter) {
    case 'N' :
    case 'n' : netpay = gross - deductions;
        break;
    default  : netpay = gross;
}
```

In this example, you want to perform the same action for both upper- and lowercase values. Therefore, the **switch** is coded so that both 'N' and 'n' are associated with the same action statement. ('N' and 'n' have different ASCII values.)

Program Flow - Control and Repetition

Switches usually provide a clearer and more efficient way of handling multiple choices than `else if` statements. Here is the example from **Module 7** in the previous chapter coded as a `switch`.

```c
#include <stdio.h>      /* for printf and gets */
#include <stdlib.h>     /* for atoi */

main()
{
 int num1, num2, oper;

 printf("Welcome to the Handy-Home Calculator\n\n");

 printf("Enter the first number : ");
 num1 = getnum();
 printf("Enter the second number : ");
 num2 = getnum();

 printf( "\nEnter the operation to be executed + - * or x,/ :);
 oper = getchar();

 printf("\n");

 switch (oper)  {
     case '+'  :   printf("%d+%d = %d\n", num1, num2, num1+num2);
                   break;
     case '-'  :   printf("%d-%d = %d\n", num1, num2, num1-num2);
                   break;
     case '*'  :
     case 'x'  :   printf("%d*%d = %d\n", num1, num2, num1*num2);
                   break;
     case '/'  :   if (num2 == 0) printf("I can't divide by 0.\n");
                   else printf("%d/%d = %d\n", num1, num2, num1/num2);
                   break;
     default   :   printf("I don't understand what %c means.\n", oper);
                   }
     }

getnum()
{
char buff[128];
gets( buff );
return ( atoi( buff ) );
}
```

In this example, the `switch` is controlled by the value of the variable `oper`. Each case takes the place of one `else if` statement. Note that for multiplication, the cases are coded so that the value `*` falls through, allowing one action statement to be coded for both multiplication operators. For division, the check for division by zero is handled within the case as an `if` statement. The default case handles the action for any operator values that do not match one of the earlier cases.

67

Chapter 4

Program Notes

Depending on your compiler, you may need to add the following statement

```
return 0;
```

before the closing brace of `main`. Here is how it should look:

```
default  : printf("I don't understand what %c means.\n", oper);
  }
return 0;
}
```

Keep in mind the fact that you may need to add `return 0;` as you try the other examples in this chapter.

Module 8 Summary

In **Module 8**, you learned how to code a C `switch` to handle multiway branches. You also learned how to use braces to delineate blocks of C statements.

New C Tools

Concepts	Code
program switches	`switch`
simple statement	`case`
compound statement	`break`
block	`default`

Module 9: Looping with Control

In **Module 8**, you learned more about the power of computing in terms of decision making. **Module 9** introduces a companion tool: the power of repeating statements until a goal is achieved. Important concepts include

- what loops are and why you might want to use them
- how to create and use different kinds of loops in C.

Program Flow - Control and Repetition

Keywords you need to note are

loop control variable	**decrement operator**
initializing	`for`
incrementing	**entry condition loop**
loop body	`continue`
traverse	`while`
iteration	`do-while`
prefix	**exit condition loop**
postfix	`goto`
increment operator	

First, the concept of looping in general will be outlined. Then, you will learn about the C operators and statements involved in developing and using loops.

An Introduction to Loops

Suppose you want a quick way to retrieve and then sum ten numbers. You can do this in several ways. Suppose you always want to total only ten numbers at a time. The following logic would work:

Get a number from the keyboard and add it to the total.
Get a number from the keyboard and add it to the total.
Get a number from the keyboard and add it to the total.
.
.
.

(You get the idea. Seven more of the same follow.)

Of course, it would be better to tell the *computer* to do the C statements involved ten times instead of coding each of them ten times yourself. To do this, you must tell the computer to do the following:

1. Keep a counter, starting at 0, for the number of times you want to loop through the statements.

2. Tell the computer you want to do the statements ten times, beginning the count at 1, and requesting one number at a time.

3. Test to see if you have done the statements ten times, and get out of the loop if you have.

4. Code the C statements to get a number and add it to the total.

5. Add 1 to the counter, return to test the value, and do the statements again.

This approach of writing the program logic in English (or *pseudocode*) is a good idea.

Figure 4.1 illustrates this same process with a *flowchart*, which is a pictorial representation of the sequence of steps in the program.

Chapter 4

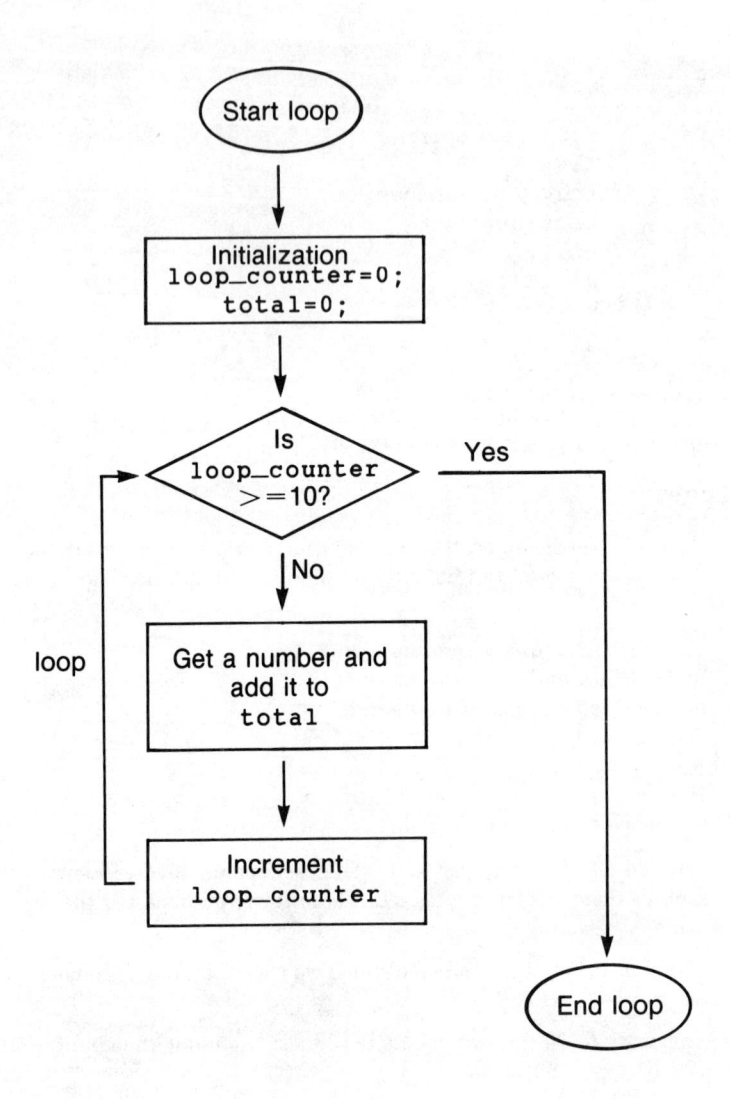

Figure 4.1 Program Loops

Program Flow - Control and Repetition

These steps can be summarized as follows:

1. Start a loop counter (initialize control variable)
2. Start the loop
3. Test the loop counter (conditional expression)
   (exit if >= 10)
4. Execute the statements (loop body)
5. Add 1 to the counter (reinitialize the control variable)
   (return to test step)

There are some conventional terms that go along with these steps. The loop counter is called the **loop control variable**. Starting the loop counter and progressively making it larger is called **initializing** and **incrementing** the loop control. As the computer goes through the statements you are repeating, known as the **loop body**, it is said to **traverse** the loop. Each complete pass through the loop is called one **iteration** of the loop.

To create a loop, you need C statements to do the following:

- Tell the computer to repeat a set of statements.
- Enter the loop if the test expression is true.
- Progressively update the test expression.

The key player in the above is the loop control variable. If its value changes incorrectly, your program results will be incorrect. If its value never changes, the computer will go on executing the loop forever, completely unaware of time, cost, or your increasing state of panic.

There are some special operators and shortcuts that you can use to make it easier to handle loop control variables. For example, in most programming languages, you would write something like the following to change the value of the loop control variable:

loop = loop + 1   or   i = i + 1
loop = loop - 1   or   i = i - 1

C has a special, compact way of saying the same thing:

```
loop++     ++loop     --loop     loop--
```

Chapter 4

These new symbols ++ and -- are called **increment** and **decrement** operators in C. An increment or decrement operator increases or decreases the value of its operand by 1. They can be used in the following two ways:

- If used before the operand, the operator is called a **prefix** operator, for example,

    ++points;

- If used after the operand, it is a **postfix** operator; for example,

    points++;

By themselves, both forms are equivalent; for example,

++points

simply adds one to whatever value is in points. That is, ++points and points++ both mean points = points + 1. However, used within the context of a larger expression or loop statement, incrementing before or after can make a difference. For example:

points++ (postfix form)	points is changed *after* its value is evaluated.
score = 10 * points++;	1. points is multiplied by 10.
	2. The result of step 1 is assigned to score.
	3. points is incremented by 1.
++points (prefix form)	points is changed *before* its value is used.
score = 10 * ++points;	1. points is incremented by 1.
	2. points is multiplied by 10.
	3. points' value is assigned to score.

In the example above, if points is 3, then after the first case score equals 30, while after the second case score equals 40. As you can imagine, you need to be careful with the prefix and postfix operators; errors can cause program bugs that are difficult to find. Also, as you become more familiar with how C programs are coded, you will probably note that poor programming style can be another result if these operators are not used correctly.

While you are pondering this, here are some more shortcuts that you can use:

```
a += b    is the same as saying    a = a + b
a -= b    is the same as saying    a = a - b
    (you can do the same with *, /, and %)
```

C provides lots of ways for you to create and use loops. The next section tells you more about what kinds of loops you can create, how to create them, and when to use them.

C Statements for Program Repetition

C provides three types of loop control structures: the `for` loop, the `while` loop, and the `do-while` loop. Each is introduced and diagrammed below.

The for Loop

You use the `for` loop whenever you want to do something a certain number of times, based on a progressively changing value or range of values. The `for` loop is illustrated in **Figure 4.2**.

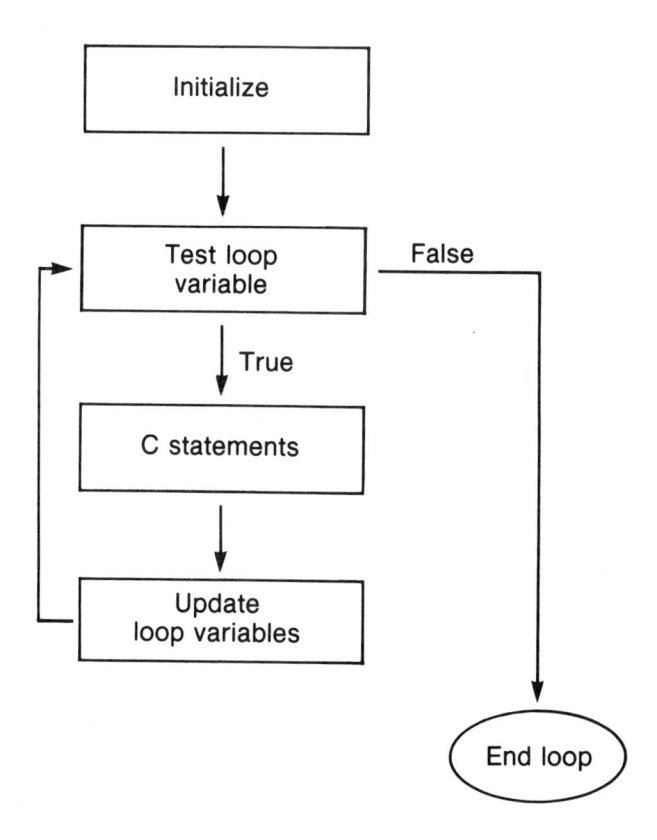

Figure 4.2 The `for` Loop

Chapter 4

The format of the `for` loop is as follows:

for (*expression1*; *expression2*; *expression3*)
   {
     statement(s)
   }

where

expression1   initializes the loop variable.
expression2   tests whether the loop should continue or stop.
expression3   updates the loop control variable.

The `for` loop is called an **entry condition loop**. This is because the test expression is evaluated *before* the loop body is executed. Following the `for` clause you can have a simple or compound statement:

```
for (expression1; expression2; expression3)
   {
     simple or compound statement
   }
```

Note: for a single statement, you don't need braces.

The loop continues until the leading test is found to be false. However, because the test is executed first, it is possible that the loop may never be traversed at all.

Returning to the earlier "number sum" example, a `for` loop to accomplish this looks like the following:

```
/*  Sum ten numbers   */

main()
{
int i, amount, total;
total = 0;

printf("Enter and Sum 10 Integers\n");

for (i = 0; i < 10; ++i)
   {
   printf("Please enter a number: \n");
   amount = getnum();
   total = total + amount;
   printf("Amount = %d, Total = %d\n", amount, total);
   }
}
     .
     .
     .

/*  Remember to include code for getnum here ... */
```

Program Flow - Control and Repetition

First, expression1 (`i = 0`) is executed. Then, expression2 (`i < 10`) is evaluated as either TRUE (`i` is still less than 10) or FALSE (`i` is equal to 10). If the result is TRUE, then the loop body (four statements including calls to `getnum()` and `printf()`) is executed *and* expression3 (`++i`) is done. Control then returns to expression2 completing one iteration of the loop.

If the result of expression2 is FALSE, meaning that `i` is no longer less than 10, then nothing else is done. The loop is considered finished, and control passes to the statement following the loop.

There are some things to remember as you work with `for` loops. You can, for example, leave out one or more of the expressions, but you must leave the semicolons as placeholders. A `for` loop with no expressions creates an infinite loop because in C, *no test* evaluates to TRUE. (If your "break" key is handy, you can try pressing it to get out of the loop):

```
for ( ; ; )
   printf("HELP...!\n");
```

You can use any valid C expressions in the test expression as long as you remember to always include the ; and end the loop. For example, you are not limited to increments or decrements by 1 or even by numbers. You could use

```
for (digit = '1'; digit <= '9'; digit++)
```

or, to increment by more than one,

```
for (amount = 25; amount <= 50; amount = amount + 2)
```

One more helpful hint about coding `for` loops. Remember that there is no semicolon after the `for` clause. The only time a semicolon might follow would be as a separate program statement. This could occur if you wanted the `for` clause to "stand alone" or not be followed by any statements that depend on the `for` clause. For example, this `for` loop

```
for (letter = 'a'; letter < 'z'; letter++)
   ;
```

executes 26 times, leaving `letter` with a value of 'z'+ 1.

The `for` loop can help illustrate how to use two loop control keywords to modify loop flow.

Using break and continue

Both `break` and `continue` are used to alter the flow of control in loop structures. You are already familiar with the keyword `break` in the context of program switches. You use `break` in a similar way here; it causes your program to jump completely out of the loop to whatever statement follows the loop body. `break` can be used with loops, for example, when you have a condition (such as an `if` statement) nested in a loop. If the condition is true, you can use `break` to leave the loop.

Chapter 4

continue, on the other hand, causes a jump to the next iteration of the loop. You do not leave the loop. You can also use it with conditions nested in a loop to stay in the loop if the condition is true.

The following examples show how this works. First, notice what happens when you use **break**:

```
#include <stdio.h>
main()
{

int i;

for(i = 10; i >= 0; i--)
   {
     printf("countdown! -%d\n", i);

     if (i == 5) {
        printf("Only 5 seconds left!\n");
        break;  /*------------------------->*/
        }       /*   end of if              |
                                            | control jumps here
                                            | */
   }            /*   end of loop            |
                                            |
       <-----------------------------------*/

printf("Mission ended...i = %d\n", i);

}  /*   end of main */
```

Here is what you get:

```
countdown! -10
countdown! -9
countdown! -8
countdown! -7
countdown! -6
countdown! -5
Only 5 seconds left!
Mission ended...i = 5
```

With **continue**, this happens:

```
#include <stdio.h>
main()
{

int i;

for(i = 10; i >= 0; i--)
   {
     printf("countdown! -%d\n", i);
```

Program Flow - Control and Repetition

```
     if (i == 5) {
        printf("Only 5 seconds left!\n");
        continue; /*------------------------->*/
     }          /* end of if           | control jumps
                                       | here
     <---------------------------------------*/
  }                    /* end of loop */

  printf("Mission ended...i = %d\n",i);

}                      /* end of main */
```

Here is the output:

```
countdown! -10
countdown! -9
countdown! -8
countdown! -7
countdown! -6
countdown! -5
Only 5 seconds left!
countdown! -4
countdown! -3
countdown! -2
countdown! -1
countdown! -0
Mission ended...i = -1
```

Using **break** causes the countdown (loop) to end after the message "Only 5 seconds left!" is printed. But, with **continue**, the message "Only 5 seconds left!" is printed, and then the countdown resumes.

Note: it is considered better programming to use **if** with an **else** when possible because it makes for clearer code. (Try rewriting the second example using **else** instead of **continue**.)

The while Loop

C also has a **while** loop and a **do-while** loop. The **while** loop is discussed first.

The **while** loop is an entry condition loop. The decision to go through the loop is made before the statements are executed. The **while** loop is illustrated in **Figure 4.3**.

Chapter 4

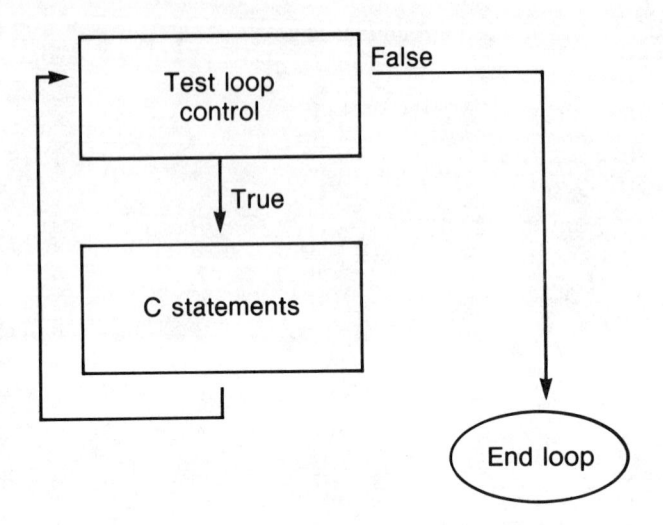

Figure 4.3 The `while` Loop

The format of the `while` loop is as follows:

   while (*conditional expression*)
     {
      statement(s)
     }

Following the conditional expression, a `while` loop may have a simple statement, or a compound statement (more than one statement between braces). This statement (or group of statements) is called the *object* of the `while`.

In a `while` loop, the conditional expression is always evaluated one time more than the loop body is executed. This structure is useful in situations where you want to perform a set of program tasks as long as a particular condition is true. A classic use of the `while` statement in C is to perform some action based on user responses, and continue it until the responses stop. For example, a program could continue to execute

Program Flow - Control and Repetition

based on codes entered from the keyboard, until a code indicating "the end" was encountered.

```
while ((letter = getchar()) != 'Q')
  {
    program statements
  }
```

The conditional expression is evaluated as either TRUE or FALSE. In this example, the keyboard character entered is tested to see if it is a Q. (Recall the discussion of TRUE and FALSE in Chapter 3 on testing a condition using relational operators.) Note that the conditional expression `while ((letter = getchar()) != 'Q'` is a shorthand way of coding these two statements:

```
int letter = 0;
    .
    .
    .
while ( letter != 'Q')
letter = getchar();
```

If the condition is evaluated as TRUE, the loop body is performed *and* the `while` is done again. If it is FALSE, the loop body (simple or compound statement) is skipped, the loop ends, and the program goes on to whatever statement follows the `while` loop.

Here is another example of a `while` loop. In this case, a control variable is incremented until the test expression is no longer true.

```
#include <stdio.h>

main()
{
 int fall, blocks;

 fall = 0;
 while (fall < 10) {
   blocks = 10 - fall;
   printf("Still standing %d blocks!\n", blocks);
   ++fall;
   }
 printf("Falling!!\n");
}
```

Chapter 4

Here is what you get:

```
Still standing 10 blocks!
Still standing 9 blocks!
Still standing 8 blocks!
Still standing 7 blocks!
Still standing 6 blocks!
Still standing 5 blocks!
Still standing 4 blocks!
Still standing 3 blocks!
Still standing 2 blocks!
Still standing 1 blocks!
Falling!!
```

Because you are starting to appreciate the value of C shortcuts, you could code the above statements in another way:

```c
#include <stdio.h>

main()
{
int fall, blocks;

fall = 0;
while (++fall < 10) {        /* increment AND test */
  blocks = 10 - fall;
  printf("Still standing %d blocks!\n", blocks);
  }
printf("Falling !!\n");
}
```

The results of this loop that increments and tests as part of the conditional expression are:

```
Still standing 9 blocks!
Still standing 8 blocks!
Still standing 7 blocks!
Still standing 6 blocks!
Still standing 5 blocks!
Still standing 4 blocks!
Still standing 3 blocks!
Still standing 2 blocks!
Still standing 1 blocks!
Falling!!
```

Notice that, in the last example, the first output value of **blocks** is 9, not 10, as in the previous example. This is because **fall**, initially 0, is incremented by 1 in **while (++fall < 10)** before it is subtracted from 10 in the statement **blocks = 10 - fall;**.

In most cases, using `for` or `while` is really a matter of personal preference. They are considered equivalent. For example, this `for` loop

```
for(expression1;expression2;expression3) {
 statement
 }
```

is equivalent to the following `while` loop:

```
expression1;
while (expression2)
   {
     statement;
     expression3;
   }
```

The do-while Loop

In contrast to a `while` loop, which is an entry condition loop, the `do-while` loop is an **exit condition loop.** The test expression is evaluated *after* the loop body is executed. The loop process then continues until the trailing test is found to be false. This means that the statements in the `do-while` loop body are always executed at least once. In this construct, the test expression is evaluated *after* each pass through the loop. The `do-while` loop is illustrated in **Figure 4.4.**

Chapter 4

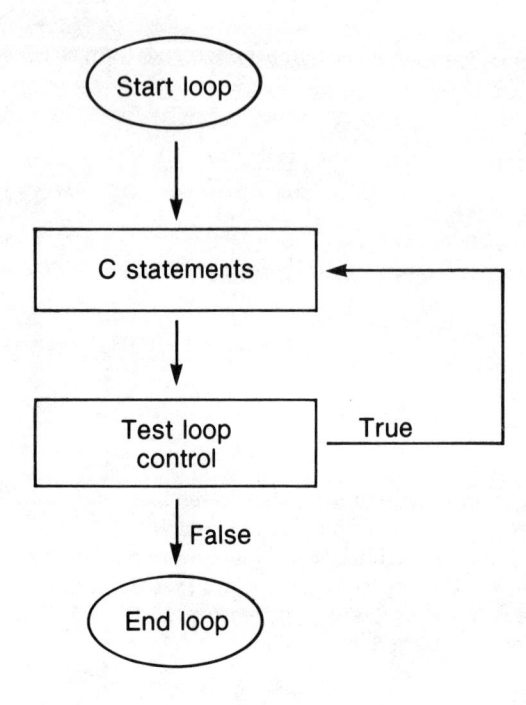

Figure 4.4 The do-while Loop

The format of the do-while loop is as follows:

do {
    simple or compound statement(s)
  } **while (***conditional expression***);**

The *statement* portion of the do-while loop is repeated until the *conditional expression* becomes false. This means that the statement portion is always done at least once.

The do-while loop is useful in situations where, no matter what the initial result of the test expression, you know you want to execute the loop body at least one time. For example, a `do-while` loop is useful in programming games, in order to give the player the chance to play at least once, for example:

```
main()
{
char play, winner;
(other declarations)

   do ─────────────────── outer loop ───────────────┐
   {                                                 │
       do ─────────────── inner loop ──────────┐    │
       {                                        │    │
           (game statements)                    │    │
                                                │    │
       } while(play != winner);  ◄──────────────┘    │
       printf("Want to give it another go ?\n");     │
                                                     │
   } while (getchar() != 'Q');  ◄────────────────────┘
   .
   . (other statements)
   .
}
```

Note in this example that one `do-while` is contained within another. This kind of code is called a *nested* loop. You can see that both loop bodies are always executed at least once. The inner loop controls the game itself while the outer loop determines whether or not play continues.

There is one more statement that you need to know with respect to program branching and repetition. You should be familiar with the concept because many languages, including C, use it. But, the main reason you need to be aware of it is to *avoid* using it.

goto When your program branches to *go to* some other part of your program, control is *unconditionally* transferred to the statement following the `goto` label. The use of `goto` is considered poor programming practice because its unrestricted use can cause the reader (and usually the program) to disappear into a labyrinth of code. In C, the format of the `goto` is as follows:

goto *label*;
label: *statements*;

The statement *label* may occur before or after the `goto`.

If you construct your logic carefully, using other C tools for repetition and choices, you should never have to resort to using `goto`. Of course, there is *one* exception. `goto` can be used for error handling, particularly in breaking out of the innermost

Chapter 4

loop of several nested loops. Here is an example of a hypothetical program using several `for` statements:

```
for (something)
  {
    for (something else)
    {
      various statements
            .
            .
            .
      completely lost
            .
            .
            .
      if(hopelessly lost)
         goto help;
    }
  }

help: printf("I quit!\n");
```

Which Loop?

Deciding which loop to use in your program can be confusing. The following guidelines may help:

- Determine if you need an entry or exit condition loop.
- If you need to control incrementing or decrementing the control variable, use a `for` loop.
- If there is little or no need for initialization or counting, use a `while` loop.
- Often, whether to use `for` or `while` is a matter of personal choice. Sometimes the specific use of the control variable is more visible with the `for`.
- A `while` loop should be used instead of a `do-while` except when you know you want to execute the loop body at least once.

Example

This chapter concludes with an example using the `while` loop. The program computes fuel economy.

```
/* Compute fuel economy from list of gas receipts */

#include <stdio.h>
#include <stdlib.h>
```

```c
main()
{
long int   start_odometer;      /* Odometer reading before first fillup */
long int   end_odometer;        /* Odometer reading after last fillup */
int   gallons;                  /* Gallons for each fillup */
int   total_gallons = 0;        /* Total gallons used */
int   count;                    /* Count of fillups */
double   mpg;                   /* Computed miles per gallon */

/* Get initial and final odometer readings.
   (An odometer measures how far you have traveled.) */
printf( "\nEnter starting odometer reading : " );
start_odometer = getnum();

printf( "Enter ending odometer reading : " );
end_odometer = getnum();

/* Get the list of gas purchases and total the number of
   gallons purchased */
printf( "\nEnter each gas purchase in gallons ( 0 to quit )\n" );

gallons = 1;   /* Initialize these variables so you can enter the */
count = 1;     /* loop at least once. */

while ( gallons != 0 ) {
   printf( "Gallons for fillup %d : ", count++ );
   gallons = getnum();
   total_gallons += gallons;
   }

/* Calculate the miles per gallon */
mpg = ( end_odometer - start_odometer ) / total_gallons;

printf( "\nYour gas mileage is %.1f miles/gallon\n",mpg );
}

/* A minimal input routine for reading numbers from the keyboard */
/* (No error checking or validity checking) */
int getnum()
{
char   buff[128];

gets( buff );
return ( atoi( buff ) );
}
```

A Closer Look

This program uses a `while` loop to sum the number of gallons of gas purchased over a period of time.

The first several statements define variables for use in computing fuel efficiency. The function `getnum()` is used to get responses from the keyboard for odometer readings. `getnum` is also central to the `while` loop. In the loop, shown below, the gallons are entered and totaled while a counter keeps track of the number of fillups.

```
while ( gallons != 0 ) {
  printf( "Gallons for fillup #%d : ", count++ );
  gallons = getnum();
  total_gallons += gallons;
  }
```

The loop continues until the keyboard response is '0', indicating no more receipt amounts to be entered.

The final statements compute and write the gas mileage as miles per gallon. Notice the use of the `printf()` format specifier `.1f`. This means that `mpg` is to be printed out with a precision of one decimal place.

Try the following alternative to construct the loop part by using `for` instead of `while`.

```
for (gallons=1, total_gallons=0; gallons!=0; total_gallons+=gallons)
    {
    printf( "Gallons for fillup %d : ", count++ );
    gallons = getnum();
    }
```

The structure of the `for` statement is a little more involved than you have seen so far, but once you understand it, it is really a simpler and clearer way to build the loop. Notice that by using the `for` statement, you can structure the entire loop in one clause.

Note also that the first expression in the `for` statement has two parts: `gallons=1, total_gallons=0`. The comma is a C operator often used in `for` loops. It causes left-to-right evaluation of the expressions `gallons=1` and `total_gallons=0`. (There will be more information on this operator in later chapters.)

Also, remember the `+=` just means `total_gallons = total_gallons + gallons`.

Program Notes

As mentioned previously, depending on your computer you may need to add the following statement right before the closing brace in `main()`:

```
return 0;
```

In the last example, this statement should go right before the last call to `printf()`:

```
printf("\nYour gas mileage is %.1f miles/gallon\n",mpg);
return 0;
}
```

Also, there is an alternative, and possibly better, way to code the loop in this program (although it is slightly more detailed). Right before the `while` loop, note that `gallons` is initialized to 1. This is done so that you can execute the loop at least once. But, if you are going through the loop at least one time, you really should think about using a `do-while` loop. Here is a way to recode the `while` loop as a `do-while` loop:

```
count = 1;
do {
   printf("Gallons for fillup #%d: ", count);
   count ++;
   gallons = getnum();
   total_gallons += gallons;
   } while (gallons != 0);
```

Module 9 Summary

In this section you learned how to use C to control statement repetition or looping. Several ways to write loops in C were presented with suggestions as to when to use each type of loop construction.

New C Tools

Concepts	Tools
creating and controlling loops	`for`
	`while`
	`do-while`
	`goto`
	`continue`
	`++`
	`--`

Chapter Summary

In this chapter, you learned about the `switch` statement, a control structure that handles multiple choices. You also learned how to group statements into blocks of code, and then how to repeat statements and blocks. Finally, you learned about `for`, `while`, and `do-while` loops. The next chapter covers basic input and output operations in C. You will put to use the tools presented in this chapter as well as some new ones. You will also build a menu that you can use in a later program and begin to fit together many of the things covered in the first several chapters.

Chapter 5
Introduction to Reading and Writing Data in C

Chapter 5

CONTENTS

Introduction	91
Module 10: Understanding Input and Output Operations	91
Using Standard C Files for Input and Output	93
Inside Information	94
Module 10 Summary	95
Module 11: How to Use the Basic C Input and Output Functions	95
Character Input and Ouput	96
getchar and putchar	97
getc and putc	98
fgetc and fputc	99
String Input and Output	100
gets and puts	100
fgets and fputs	101
Another Look at printf()	102
Module 11 Summary	105
Module 12: Using the C Preprocessor	105
#include	106
#define - Macros and Constants	107
Module 12 Summary	108
Creating a Simple Menu	109
Example	109
A Closer Look	111
Chapter Summary	113

Introduction to Reading and Writing Data in C

Introduction

This chapter introduces reading and writing data using C. You will learn some basics about input and output operations, including the standard set of files that C provides for handling data and a new set of C functions that you can use to read and write characters and strings of data. You will also learn how to supply additional information to your program with the C preprocessor feature. Then, to put what you have learned to work, you will write the first version of an interactive menu for a larger program. All these topics are covered in the following sections:

- understanding basic input/output operations in C
- how to use standard C input/output functions
- using the C preprocessor.

Module 10: Understanding Input and Output Operations

Most likely, the main reason you are learning C is to use the C language to write programs to perform tasks for you. This means that your program needs to produce some sort of output that is useful. In order to do this, your program will need a variety of input data to work with. This section introduces some general concepts about input and output operations, or more simply, I/O.

Keywords you need to note are

input	stream
read	text files
output	stdin
write	stdout
file	stderr
buffer	macros

Technically, the term **input** refers to the process of getting data into a processing system (your program) or a device (to save the data for later use). In this chapter, input is used more in the sense of **reading** data. That is, retrieving data from some form of storage or input medium (like your keyboard). **Output**, on the other hand, refers to the process of putting data out, which is **writing** or recording data in some form. This can mean saving data in storage or just sending it to your display screen.

This process is illustrated in **Figure 5.1**.

Chapter 5

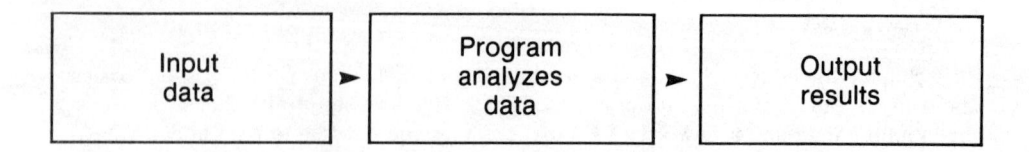

Figure 5.1 Input and Output of Data

In other words, I/O is used to communicate information to and from your program. In the simplest case, the process looks like **Figure 5.2**.

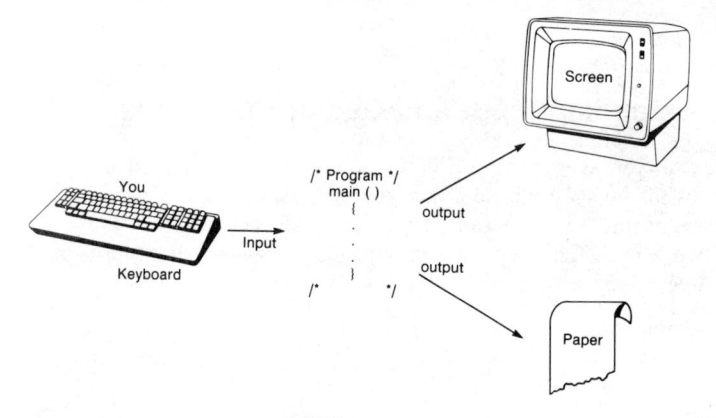

Figure 5.2 I/O Communication Process

Without input, you could not dynamically alter program flow of control. Without output, you could not see any meaningful results.

You can work with input and output data in two ways:

- a single item at a time (as when you enter a character via the keyboard)
- a set of related items.

Data items can be collected together and saved beyond the execution time of your program. Data stored in this way are usually referred to as a **file**.

Data can also be collected from a file (or from the keyboard) and saved in a temporary storage area. Such a temporary area is referred to as a **buffer**. Using a buffer to do I/O is called *buffered I/O*, and it is common in C. In buffered input, for example, portions of the data in a file or characters from the keyboard can be received, collected, and held in a buffer until your program needs them.

Buffering I/O is a very efficient way to process data. Suppose your program needs to read data from a file, for example. Without the use of a buffer, your program would have to go into the file every time it needed a piece of data. With a buffer, you could

Introduction to Reading and Writing Data in C

read a portion of the the file at once, and save it temporarily in the buffer. Then, you could let the program read from the buffer. It is faster to read and write data from a buffer than it is to return to the file each time you need to work with a data item.

In the opposite case, for example, data can be written quickly to a buffer from the program, and then the entire block of buffered data can be written back to a file. Having a buffer is really a simple engineering trick to speed up the overall performance of the system. In addition, buffering keyboard data lets you correct any keying errors before you send the entire buffer (via <enter>) to your program.

Working with buffered I/O in C has yet another advantage. C handles all the details of filling and emptying buffers for you. You only need to be concerned with getting the data to and from the buffered area. Here C helps you again by providing functions to handle the buffered data.

You may be wondering where buffers come from and what the data in a buffer looks like. The answer to the first question is C provides buffers for you to use exclusively for I/O. (You will learn more about these in a moment.) As for the second question, C handles this buffered data as a sequential **stream** of characters. You can think of this stream literally in that it is something that you can follow by starting at the beginning and continuing until the end with no breaks or jumps in between. Sometimes streams are called **text files** in C, but, because using buffered I/O is so common, thinking of the data in the buffer as a continuous stream of data may be more helpful. This idea is illustrated in **Figure 5.3**.

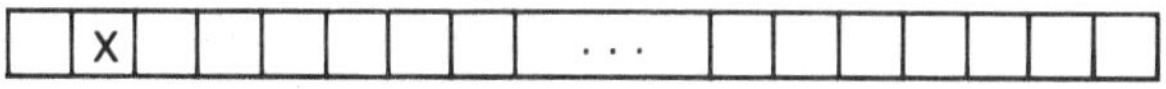

X = current position

direction of movement is left to right

Figure 5.3 Stream of Characters

C provides three standard streams for you. These are the exclusive I/O buffers mentioned in the last paragraph. These three standard streams are covered in this introduction to I/O, and other details on files and file handling are described in Chapter 10. By the way, C considers these streams to be files, and in fact they are called *standard files*. What they do, however, is let you buffer I/O.

Using Standard C Files for Input and Output

At the start of your program, C provides you with three special files for handling input and output operations. These files are as follows:

    `stdin`   standard input

    `stdout`   standard output

    `stderr`   output file available for writing error messages.

Although these are referred to as files (and technically they are files), note that they are *temporary* (created when your program starts up), unlike files containing data that you may have saved permanently. Thus, they fulfill the qualification of a buffer as a *temporary storage area*.

`stdin` normally refers to your keyboard (the standard source of input), and both `stdout` and `stderr` refer to your display screen (the standard target of output).

To use these three files, you use a set of C input and output functions. Using these files and their associated read/write functions is known as using *standard input* and *output* in C. To use them you must include the C library `stdio.h`. This file contains all the definitions, declarations, and other housekeeping tasks associated with input and output operations.

Before the `main` function is entered in your program, `stdin`, `stdout`, and `stderr` are prepared automatically for processing by your operating system and C compiler. When your program gets data from the keyboard, it normally comes in via `stdin`. When you write data using `printf()` (and other write functions you will soon learn about), the results usually appear via `stdout` or `stderr` on your terminal display screen.

In addition to handling the file management details for you, `stdio.h` also contains many functions and predefined lines of code called **macros** that you can use for reading and writing to the standard streams and other files. These standard I/O operations and functions are presented next. (The nonstandard ones use a different approach to I/O so they are covered later in Chapter 10.) Note that what is presented in the next section applies to most systems. You should, however, check your compiler documentation for the exact descriptions and implementations for these standard functions for your computer system.

Inside Information

Not all I/O in C has to be buffered. C provides functions that let you do I/O without the use of a buffer. This type of processing is called **raw** or **low-level I/O**. By contrast, **buffered I/O**, which lets you work with portions of a file in a buffer, is called **high-level I/O**. This chapter focuses on high-level I/O.

Here is a little more detail about the standard files (`stdin`, `stdout`, and `stderr`). As mentioned, the standard files are handled as streams in C. (Recall that a stream is a file that C has associated with a buffer to enable your program to read and write data efficiently.) For this reason, these files are sometimes referred to as **standard streams** in C. Standard streams imply text-only I/O operations. All the buffer handling is done for you automatically. Your program does not have to **open** or prepare the file for processing, nor does it have to **close** the file or tell the computer to conclude file processing.

Introduction to Reading and Writing Data in C

Module 10 Summary

In this module, you learned some basic concepts about data input and output operations. You also saw how C provides ways to help you with reading and writing data, including standard files and I/O procedures.

New C Tools

Concepts	Code
reading data	`stdin`
writing data	`stdout`
files	`stderr`
buffer	
streams	
standard input and output operations	

Module 11: How to Use the Basic C Input and Output Functions

In C there are no I/O statements. You use C library functions to handle all input and output operations. In this section you learn how to use C functions to read or write a character or a string of characters from `stdin` and `stdout`.

Keywords you need to note are

`getc`	`gets`
`putc`	`puts`
`getchar`	`fgets`
`putchar`	`fputs`
`fgetc`	`printf()`
`fputc`	

This section examines the basic I/O functions in two groups: those you use to read or write one character at a time and those you use to handle strings of characters. Then we will revisit `printf()` to take a closer look at formatted output.

Chapter 5

Character Input and Ouput

The standard C functions for handling character I/O are given in **Table 5.1**.

Table 5.1   Character I/O Functions

Input		Output	
getc	get the next character from the specified stream	putc	write a character to the specified stream
getchar	get the next character from stdin	putchar	write a character to stdout
fgetc	get the next character from a file	fputc	write a character to a file

All three sets of character functions let you handle input and output on a character by character basis. There are some differences between them, however, which are described next.

fgetc and fputc   All the information you give these functions is checked according to some specific rules. For example, as explained under the description of fputc in Chapter 16, this function writes a character. (Recall that characters are represented as ASCII values.) The character must have a data type of int. The compiler checks that it does have this type. Note that when you use fgetc and fputc to handle input and output, you are responsible for opening or closing the file and other file-specific details, unless the file you use is stdin, stdout, or stderr. In this section, you only need an introductory look at fgetc and fputc, so only the simplest form of these functions is presented.

getc, putc, getchar, and putchar   These functions are usually supplied with C compilers to make life easier than using fgetc and fputc. These two sets (getc, putc and getchar, putchar) are written in such a way as to take care of many of the file handling details associated with the full-blown functions fgetc and fputc. Although they are really macros instead of functions, for purposes of discussion, all of the I/O functions are referred to as functions. (Macros are discussed further in the next section.)

For now, be aware that there are differences between these sets of functions. The differences between fgetc, fputc and getc, putc, getchar, putchar will become important when you handle more complicated I/O.

Now you are ready to look at each of these on an individual basis.

Introduction to Reading and Writing Data in C

getchar and putchar

Using these two functions is the simplest way you can read or write a character in C using a standard file. When your program calls **getchar**, it waits for you to enter a character or string of characters from the console. **getchar** then gives you back just the first character (or the only character if just one was entered). Subsequent calls return the following characters (if any) in the line entered, one character per call. **putchar** operates in a similar manner in writing one character at a time to **stdout**. **Figure 5.4** is a flowchart of the way **getchar** works.

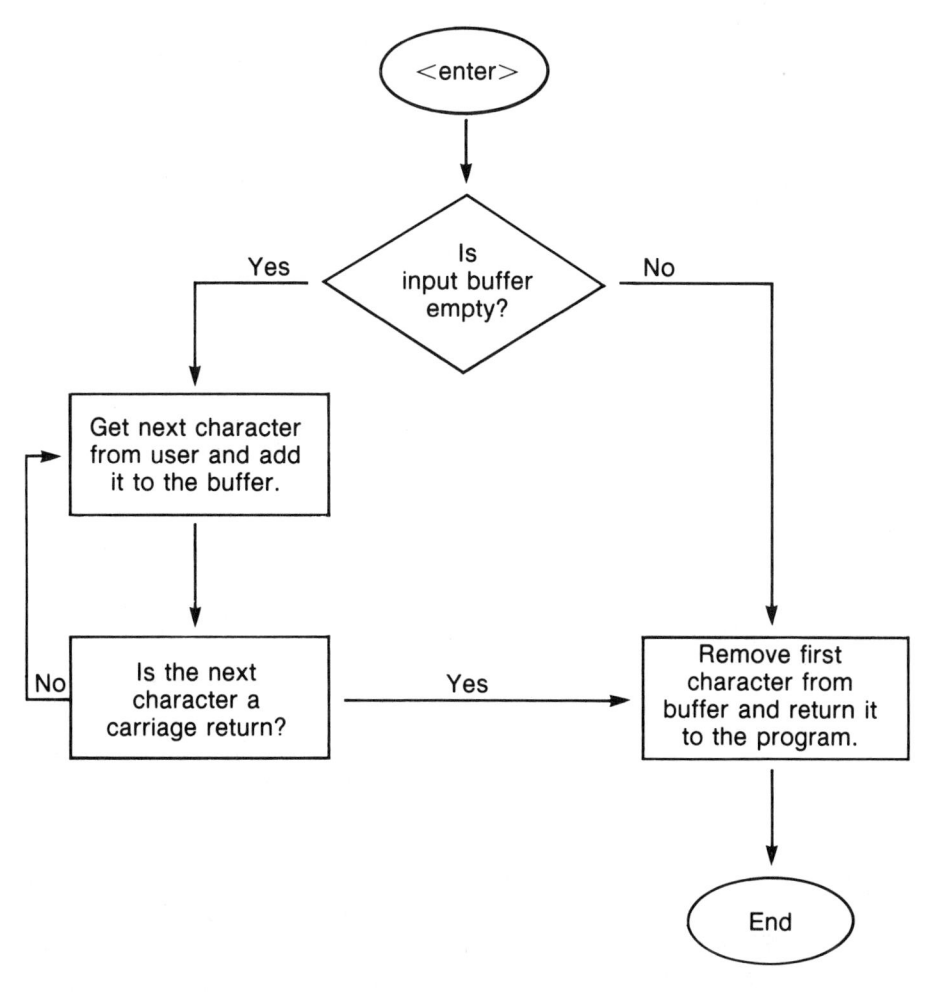

Figure 5.4 Diagram of getchar

Chapter 5

The following is an example of `getchar`:

```
#include <stdio.h>    /* Must be here because getchar() and putchar() */
                      /* are macros defined in stdio.h */
main()

{
 int c;

 c = getchar();
 putchar(c);
}
```

In this example, you type a character and the computer simply echos what you typed. Since I/O is buffered, you need to press <enter> after the characters in order to send the buffer to your program. Note that `getchar` needs no information (there is nothing entered between the parentheses). `getchar` just goes straight to `stdin` and returns the value of the first character. However, with `putchar`, you must give the name of the variable you want to write. Remember that because these are standard functions, you have to include the standard input/output library `stdio.h`.

getc and putc

`getc` and `putc` are equivalent to `getchar` and `putchar` except that they allow you to specify files other than `stdin` and `stdout`. Because, for now, you are only working with standard files, you won't notice much difference between these functions and `getc` and `putc` except that you have to specify the filenames. For example:

```
#include <stdio.h>
main()
{
 int c;

 c = getc(stdin);
 putc(c, stdout);
}
```

In this example, you have specified that you are reading a character from the standard input file. To echo the character read, you must give `putc` two pieces of information: the name of the variable and where you want to write it. In this case, you are writing to the standard output file.

Some C compilers give you a choice of functions like `getchar` and `getc`. One is for buffered I/O and the other for nonbuffered I/O. If you had to press the <enter> key before getting a response in either of these examples, then the function involved is set up for buffered I/O. If the letter you keyed as input was immediately echoed, then you are using a nonbuffered version. The buffered versions are useful when you need to read a line, hold it, and then process it character by character. The nonbuffered versions are useful in situations where you want the computer to take an immediate action based on a keyboard response, such as with a computer game. In any case, check your compiler documentation to see which kinds of `getchar` functions are available on your system.

fgetc and fputc

For our immediate purposes, these functions will not look much different from `getc` and `putc`. `fgetc` also returns the next character from a file or stream. Again, if the stream is the keyboard, the entire line (if more than one character) must be typed before any characters, including the first one, are available to your program. `fputc` appends or adds characters to the end of a file. You normally would use these functions to work with files other than `stdin`, `stdout`, and `stderr`. This means that the files involved must be opened or prepared for processing. (There are C functions for this that you will learn later.) Our work here is confined to the standard files, and they are already open and available for processing when your program begins execution.

Here is an example:

```
#include <stdio.h>
main()
{
int count, c;
count = 0;

while(count++ < 5)
  {
    c = fgetc(stdin);
    fputc(c, stdout);
  }
}
```

In this example, `fgetc` and `fputc` work just like `getc` and `putc` did. You supply the input file (again `stdin` for `fgetc`) and the variable and output file (`stdout` for `fputc`).

While we are on the subject of files, you may have wondered how the computer knows when it has reached the end of a file. In C, there is a special character assigned as an end-of-file (EOF) marker. The exact EOF character depends on your system, but knowing it is available means you can write things like the following:

```
#include <stdio.h>
main()
{
int c;
while ((c = getchar()) != EOF)
  putchar(c);
}
```

In this example, each time you press <enter>, the characters in the buffer are processed. Instead of just echoing one character and then stopping, using `getchar`

Chapter 5

(or another character function) with a `while` loop lets your program keep going until you stop it. What this statement says is

Call `getchar` to get a character from the keyboard.
When you get the character, put it in the variable called `c`.
Then, check the character to see if it is EOF. If not, keep going.

(By the way, this type of expression is often used in C, particularly with a `while` loop. This construct is commonly called an *embedded assignment statement*.) Notice that in your program, you do not have to define what EOF is; the compiler does it for you. (You need to know, of course. On most personal computer systems, CNTL-Z signals the end of keyboard input.)

String Input and Output

The next group of functions you will learn about are designed to allow your program to handle more than one character at a time. They are the standard set of string I/O functions and are listed in **Table 5.2**.

Table 5.2 String Input/Output Functions

Input		Output	
`gets`	get a string from `stdin`	`puts`	put a string to `stdout`
`fgets`	gets a string from a file	`fputs`	put a string to a file

You will work much more with these functions when you learn about handling strings with arrays and pointers in Chapter 7. They are still useful to know about in terms of standard I/O, so these functions are introduced here.

gets and puts

As with the other versions of `fgetc`, `gets` and `puts` are macro versions of `fgets` and `fputs`. `gets` keeps reading characters from `stdin` (for now, assumed to be the keyboard) until you <enter> the line. After the data are entered, the function detects the newline character and replaces it with a compiler generated character called a null character or '\0', which by C convention indicates the end of a string.

Here is an example of `gets`:

```
#include <stdio.h>
main()
{
char thoughts[80];   /* some space for your thoughts */

printf("What's on your mind?\n");
gets(thoughts);
printf("Pretty heavy thought! %s.\n", thoughts);
}
```

Note the unusual way `thoughts` is declared. The brackets after `thoughts` mean that it is an array. Specifically, it is a character array with room for 80 characters. (Counting the number of characters from 0 through 79, you get 80 characters.) Arrays are discussed in detail in Chapter 7. For now, however, think of an array as a space to store data temporarily (such arrays are also called buffers).

In this example, you can express a thought that is 79 characters long. Remember the '\0' ? The 80th character is reserved for it.

If you only want to echo the input string, use `puts` in place of `printf()` as follows:

```
puts(thoughts);
```

For now, remember that the difference between these functions and the next two are that `gets` and `puts` are macros and they work with `stdin` and `stdout`.

fgets and fputs

`fgets` reads data from a specified file until a newline is encountered, the input buffer is filled (including the '\0'), or an end-of-file (EOF) occurs. Input data are automatically appended with the character '\0'. If input comes from the keyboard and is terminated by a newline, then the '\0' character is added to the string after the newline character ('\n'). This means that if you stored the word *bye* from the keyboard, it would appear in the buffer as follows:

b	y	e	\n	\0

`fputs` copies a null-terminated string to whatever file is specified. In the case of standard output to the screen, `fputs` copies everything up to but not including the '\0'. This means that the '\n' (newline) is transferred, and any subsequent input will be read from the next line.

If a line is a character array, for example, `char line[40]`, then using standard files, `fgets` can be used as follows:

```
fgets(line, 40, stdin);
```

Likewise `fputs` is used as:

```
fputs(line, stdout);
```

For both functions, `line` is the name of the buffer for the string you are working with. For `fgets`, you must specify a maximum length for the string (in this case, 40). Because there is no standard convention, you choose the buffer size. Because you are using the standard C files, the last information in both cases is the standard file you want to work with.

Chapter 5

Here is an example that reads and displays text:

```
/* Read and Display Text Using Standard Files */

#include <stdio.h>

main()
{
char line[50];
int count;

count = 0;
printf("Enter any line < 50 characters\n");

while(count++ < 5)     /* read and echo five lines */
  {
    fgets(line,50,stdin);
    fputs(line,stdout);
  }
}
```

This example sets aside a storage area of 50 characters to hold a line of data. The `while` loop executes five times allowing five lines of data from `stdin` to be received and then displayed via `stdout`.

Caution: `fgets` is safer to use than `gets`. The reason is that with `fgets` you can specify the size of your buffer when you call `fgets`. In the previous example with `gets`, you had to remember how big the buffer was (79 characters) when you ran the program. With `gets`, you may try to write more characters into the buffer than the buffer can hold. (If you do this, you may get unexpected results. On a PC, for example, you could lock up your keyboard and have to restart your computer system.) Of course, one solution is to declare a buffer for `gets` larger than any string that could possibly be input. Another is to use `fgets`. With `fgets`, you have more protection against overreads.

Another Look at printf()

As you remember, `printf()` is used to produce formatted output. There is an expanded version of `printf()` that gives more flexibility in handling and defining output written to `stdout`. `printf()` converts, formats, and prints its arguments on standard output according to a format specified by a control string. Control characters and conversion specifications operate on each successive argument (item) that you are printing.

Recall the basic form of `printf()`:

printf(*format, arg1, arg2, . . . argn*);

The expanded `printf()` adds a full set of conversion codes and a set of modifiers that further specify the way your output is written. As pointed out earlier, the

Introduction to Reading and Writing Data in C

combination of a conversion code and modifiers in a `printf()` statement is sometimes called a *format specifier*.

The conversion codes include the following:

%d decimal
%o octal
%x hexadecimal
%u unsigned decimal
%c single character
%s string
%e float or double converted to exponential
%f float or double converted to decimal
%g use %e or %f, whichever is best

You have seen the %c, %d, %e, and %f codes earlier. %s was also used in previous examples in this chapter. Codes new to you are %o, %x, and %g. The %o and %x codes let you print the data as the computer sees it in octal (base 8) or hex (base 16). (Experiment and see for yourself.) The %g tells the compiler to select the best floating point format for your variable.

The modifiers that you can use with these codes are

digit string   A digit (or digits) indicates minimum width for an item to be printed. The decimal point is included in the width. A wider area is provided if the item does not fit. %5d allows five digits, for example. %5.1f allows one digit after the decimal point and three digits before it.

− (left justify)
    Data items are normally printed to the right of their field. The − indicates that the data should be printed starting at the left. For example if a value of "100" is printed using %5d, it will print as _ _ 1 0 0 (where _ indicates a blank space). If you use %-5d it will be 1 0 0 _ _.

. (decimal)   A decimal point indicates the precision or the number of digits to be printed to the right of the decimal. %5.2 prints with two decimal places as 326.00.

l   The converted data item is to be considered `long` instead of `int`.

Using all this, you can print some really interesting things, for example:

```
printf("ship is: %4.2f,slim is: %ld,punct is: %-5d,score is: %d%% \n", ship,slim,punct,score);
```

where

    `ship`   is printed as a two decimal float number
    `slim`   is specified as a long decimal
    `punct`   is left-justified
    `score`   is a number printed with the % sign by specifying %%.

Chapter 5

Here is an example, using several `printf()` statements. There are parentheses around some of the format specifiers to show you how the output can be justified using -.

```
#include <stdio.h>

main()
{
float ship = 1.34;
float boat = 69.5;
long int slim = 386913;
int punct = '?';
int score = 86;

printf("ship is: %4.2f\n",ship);

   /* field width of four, with two decimal places */

printf("ship is: (%5.2f)\nboat is: %4.2f\n",ship,boat);

   /* field width of five, with two decimal places */

   /* field width of four, with two decimal places */

printf("slim is: %ld\npunct is: %c\n",slim, punct);
printf("score is: %d%%\n",score);
printf("score is: (%4d)\n",score);

   /* field width of four */

printf("score is: (%-4d)\n,score is: (%-5d)\n",score, score);

   /* output is left justified. */

}
```

Here is what you get:

```
ship is: 1.34
ship is: ( 1.34)
boat is: 69.50
slim is: 386913
punct is: ?
score is: 86%
score is: (  86)
score is: (86  )
score is: (86   )
```

Note: there is an input function called `scanf()`, which complements `printf()` in that it lets you *read* formatted data. But because you will find out better ways to read formatted data in Chapter 10, for now keep in mind that `scanf()` is available.

Introduction to Reading and Writing Data in C

Module 11 Summary

In **Module 11,** you learned how to perform basic input and output operations using the standard C input and output files. The following chart summarizes this module:

Function Name	Operation
`getc, putc`	read/write a character
`getchar, putchar`	
`fgetc, fputc`	
`gets, puts`	read/write a string
`fgets, fputs`	
`printf`	produce formatted output

New C Tools

Concepts	Code
reading and writing data	`getc`
	`putc`
	`getchar`
	`putchar`
	`fgetc`
	`fputc`
	`gets`
	`puts`
	`fgets`
	`fputs`
	`printf`

Module 12: Using the C Preprocessor

When you think about processing your income tax return, you document all your deductions and income, complete your return as much as possible, and then take everything to your CPA. (If you don't, pretend you do.) The accountant looks at everything and then *preprocesses* your return by filling in amounts in appropriate places, pulling together additional information, and expanding things via formulas. After all the relevant data are present, the accountant processes your return and computes your income tax. All this makes life easier for you.

Chapter 5

You can think of the C preprocessor as performing the same kinds of things for your program that the accountant initially does for your tax return. The preprocessor substitutes all constants with their actual value, pulls in other needed information such as header files, and substitutes actual code for macros, for example, `getchar()`. In other words, the C preprocessor reads through your original C code and then writes new or *preprocessed* C code to use as input to the compiler. All of this saves you considerable time and effort. Following your directions, the preprocessor can also alter the way your program compiles code and conditionally include blocks of C code from other programs. In this section, you are introduced to the preprocessor by looking at two basic features: including other files in your program and substituting code for a name.

Keywords you need to note are

preprocessor

#include

#define

In this module, you will learn how the preprocessor

- includes all header files requested
- substitutes the actual value of constants
- substitutes all code defined by macros.

In some compilers, the preprocessor is a separate program that must be run on your source file as the first step in compilation. In other compilers, the preprocessor is part of the compiler, even though preprocessing of your source file is thought of as logically separate from the compilation step.

In C, commands for the preprocessor usually appear at the beginning of your program and are preceded by the `#` control character. This module introduces the following two preprocessor commands:

```
#include <filename>
#define  macro constant or code
```

Note: preprocessor statements do not end with a semicolon.

#include

You know that `stdio.h` defines and declares variables, constants, and functions relevant to the standard C files. The preprocessor makes these definitions available to your program. For example, in order to run a program that contains any I/O function, you know you need the definitions contained in `stdio.h`. Without a preprocessor, you would have to type in these definitions for each program. The `#include` statement provides you with an easy mechanism for including the contents of another file into your source program.

Introduction to Reading and Writing Data in C

There are many other header files that you can incorporate into your program via the preprocessor, for example, math and graphics headers. The header files save you from having to explicitly declare the data and functions associated with these applications in your source program. (You can also create your own header files. This is described in Chapter 10.)

A header file that you will find useful to include, especially when you are working with input and output, is `ctype.h`, and it includes some predefined code or macros that you can use to test the value of a character variable. These come in handy in I/O operations because you often need to know if someone has just entered a digit or an uppercase letter, or just random characters from the keyboard. Some of the most frequently used members in this file are shown in **Table 5.3**.

Table 5.3   ASCII Character Manipulation Macros in `ctype.h`

Macro	Description
`isalpha()`	test for alpha
`isupper()`	test for uppercase
`islower()`	test for lowercase
`isdigit()`	test for digits 0-9
`isspace()`	test for space
`ispunct()`	test for punctuation
`isalnum()`	test for alpha or digit
`isprint()`	test for printable character
`iscntrl()`	test for a control character

You use these macros by supplying the name of the character variable to be tested and then using the macro in an expression. For example, suppose you wanted to test if a keyboard response was numeric. You could use `isdigit` and code the test as follows:

```
char c;

if( isdigit(c) )
   printf("% is a digit\n",c);
```

As with many things in C, check your compiler documentation to see what character tests are available on your system.

#define - Macros and Constants

A **macro** is simply a name that is used as an abbreviation for a longer or more complicated expression. The `#define` preprocessor keyword is used to define these abbreviations.

Chapter 5

When the compiler finds a macro name in your program, it replaces the name with the code associated with it. The macro can be either defined by C, like `getchar`, or one you have defined earlier in your source program. In either case, when your program executes, the statement that is the replacement string is executed.

Macros can be used to

- associate a character string with an identifier so that each time the identifier is referenced the character string is substituted.

- define an identifier that the preprocessor expands into source code.

The simplest use of a macro is to define a constant. You can define constants for your program as follows:

#define *name body*

Defining items in your program like this allows you to define a frequently changing value (like "MAXLINES" or a date) in one place in your program without changing all occurrences of the code.

Some examples of constants that can be defined with #define are the following:

```
numeric     #define EOF   -1
            #define PI    3.14159

character   #define QUIT  'Q'
            #define NEWLINE '\n'

string      #define END   "job finished!"
            #define NAME  "John Doe"
```

The second use of a macro, substituting code, is illustrated as follows. Suppose you always want to print something a certain way. Rather than writing out `printf()` statements, you can define a macro and let the computer substitute the code for you each time it encounters the macro name. For example:

```
#define PNUM printf("num is %d.\n", num)
```

This #define statement instructs the compiler to substitute the `printf()` statement each time it encounters PNUM.

#define statements make your program more readable and flexible. (Note that you do not have to capitalize the name but capitalization like this is common practice.)

Module 12 Summary

This section introduced the C preprocessor. Now you have two preprocessor commands, #include and #define, to provide additional program information and flexibility.

Introduction to Reading and Writing Data in C

New C Tools

Concepts	Code
preprocessor	`#include`
	`#define`

Creating a Simple Menu

To help you put together what you have learned so far, this chapter concludes with an example. The following code shows how to use many of the I/O functions introduced in this chapter to create and display a menu, accept menu selections from the keyboard, and perform actions based on keyboard input. (In addition, you will see some new things where C functions are concerned, which hopefully will keep you curious enough to continue on to Chapter 6.)

Example

```
/* Menu Display and Selection Program */

#include <stdio.h>          /* needed for I/O functions */

#include <ctype.h>          /* needed for character tests */


/* You can declare functions too */
/* ...more details in Chapter 6 */

int get_one_char();    /* this one handles characters */
void calc();           /* these two don't handle anything yet */
void mileage();


#define FALSE   0          /* standard Boolean (logical) defines */
#define TRUE    !FALSE
#define PROMPT  "\nOption:"  /* macro for part of "Option:" request */


main()
{
int ch;                /* character to hold menu selection */
int done = FALSE;      /* Loop termination control */

while ( !done )
   {
```

Chapter 5

```c
      /* Display the menu */

      puts( "\n\nAvailable Functions\n" );
      puts( "   C)  Calculator" );
      puts( "   F)  Fuel Economy calculation" );
      puts( "   Q)  Quit" );

      fputs( "PROMPT", stdout );

      switch ( ( ch = get_one_char() ) )
        {
      case 'c':                /* Option C - Calculator */
      case 'C':
        calc();
        break;
      case 'f':                /* Option F - Fuel Economy */
      case 'F':
        mileage();
        break;
      case 'q':                /* Option Q - Quit Program */
      case 'Q':
        done = TRUE;
        break;
      default:                 /* Unrecognized option */
        printf( "\nUnsupported menu option <%c>\n", );
        break;
        }
      }

  return ( 0 );
}


/*--------------------------------------------------------------------*/
/*  get_one_char()                                                    */
/*     Reads a character from standard input, ignoring leading spaces */
/*     and removing trailer characters.                               */
/*--------------------------------------------------------------------*/

int get_one_char()
{
  int ch;      /* Storage for character read */
  int junk;    /* Temporary variable for discarding ext */


  /* Keep getting characters until you get something other than */
  /* a space or "return" */

  while ( isspace( ch = getchar() ) && ( ch != '\n' ) )
    ;
```

Introduction to Reading and Writing Data in C

```
    /* If the user just entered return, then return a space.*/
    /* This is useful for processing default answers. */

    if ( ch == '\n' )
       ch = ' ';


    /* Remove everything on line after the character */
    /* This is to empty the keyboard buffer */

    while ( ( junk = getchar() ) != '\n' )
       ;

    return ( ch );              /*  Return the character  */
}




/*-----------------------------------------------------------*/
/*  "Calc" and "mileage" are just function shells for now   */
/*  You can add the actual routines after Chapter 6         */
/*-----------------------------------------------------------*/

void
calc()
{
  puts( "\n\nHandy Home Calculator" );
}

void
mileage()
{
  puts( "\n\nMileage Checker" );
}
```

A Closer Look

This program begins with two `#include` statements. `stdio.h` is needed for calls to the I/O functions `getchar`, `puts`, and `printf`; `ctype.h` is needed for the call to `isspace`.

Following the `#include` statements are three function declarations. These are functions that will be written as part of the program; they are not included in the standard library, and their declarations are not in any header file, but they do use library functions, such as `printf`, whose declarations are in standard header files.

The `get_one_char` function is declared as type `int`. This means that after you call this function, it returns a value of type `int`. You can use a `return` statement to do this, as is done in this program. You may recall from earlier chapters that a `return` statement ends a function, and control returns to the point in the program where the

Chapter 5

function was called. As you will see, each of the three functions declared here is called by `main`, and each returns there. In the case of `get_one_char`, a value of data type `int` is returned. `void` means that the function does not return anything.

In order to produce an interactive menu, the `main( )` program function uses both a `while` loop and a `switch` statement. The `while` loop controls the menu display. Contained within the `while` loop is a `switch` statement that keys on the value returned by the function `get_one_char`. Depending on the value of the charact er returned, the program branches to execute one of three menu options. The display and selection process continues until the while loop condition is no longer true.

When you run this example, things should proceed as follows:

1. The menu is displayed, and it should look like this:

   Available Functions
   C) Calculator
   F) Fuel Economy Calculation
   Q) Quit

   Option:

2. After you type the option and then press <enter>, the menu choice you selected should be displayed. For example, if you typed c, the text string

   Handy Home Calculator

   should be displayed on your terminal screen.

3. After the selection is displayed, the menu is automatically displayed again, and the process continues until you select the Quit option.

In the `main( )` function, notice that `puts` is used to display the menu options and `fputs` is used to display the "Option:" line. In these two applications the functions are interchangeable. The only difference to note is that with `fputs`, you must specify the file you are using, `stdout`. The `puts` function assumes `stdout`, so you do not have to specify it.

Notice also, the expression that makes up the switch statement condition. You could assign the value returned by the `get_one_char` function to the variable `ch` in a separate statement and then key on "ch", like this:

```
ch = get_one_char();
switch ( ch )
```

But because C is so flexible, it makes sense to do it all in one statement if you can, as long as the intent is still clear.

The `get_one_char` function is needed to process the keyboard response in a more sophisticated way than one of the standard functions can alone. For example, the person entering a response might key a space and then the letter, or more than one letter. If only `getchar` were used and the user entered multiple letters, subsequent

Introduction to Reading and Writing Data in C

calls to `getchar` would return the next letter in the existing input buffer rather than the new response. For this and similar reasons, when processing input, especially from the keyboard, you need to think of all the things that can happen and provide for them so that your program will work properly. In `get_one_char` you can see that provisions are made to ignore blanks, deal with "no response" (user simply types <enter>), and the rest of the existing input buffer is cleared before returning the character value to the `main()` function.

You should modify and play with this program (and each I/O function) as much as you can to be sure that you understand what is going on. Practicing now with simple input and output operations will help you in understanding more about I/O later.

Chapter Summary

In this chapter you have learned about basic I/O operations in C. C functions for input and output and C preprocessor have been covered, and some other helpful things have been introduced along the way such as more detail on `printf()` and some useful character test macros. In the next chapter, you really begin to use the C features you have learned in order to understand and write C functions.

Chapter 6
Introduction to Functions in C

Chapter 6

CONTENTS

Introduction	**117**
Module 13: Function Basics in C	**117**
Module 13 Summary	120
Module 14: Function Structure	**120**
Defining a Function	121
Function Calls	124
Variable Use and Functions	128
Guidelines for Using Local and Global Variable Names	130
Helpful Hints for Function and Parameter Declarations	131
Module 14 Summary	133
A Function for Fun - The Shell Game	**133**
The Shell Game	133
Program Notes	144
Chapter Summary	**145**

Introduction to Functions in C

Introduction

Functions are the building blocks of C programs. Each program you write is composed of a set of tasks or routines that accomplish a specific goal. In C, your program can be structured in terms of these tasks, all coded as independent units, called functions. Each function is related in some way to the larger purpose of your program. You have already used some of the standard precoded C library functions such as `printf()`. In this chapter, you learn how to write and use your own C functions. After covering the basics, you will learn by doing more hands-on programming than you have done in earlier chapters. The following topics get you started:

- function basics in C
- the structure of C functions
- learning to use C functions.

Module 13: Function Basics in C

When you need to perform a particular task in several different places in your program, you can write the lines of code involved each time you need them as part of the `main()` function. To make your program more readable and efficient, you can write code for each program task once, name it, and then use that unit of code each time the task is needed. To help you begin thinking in terms of functions, this module explains how you can structure your C program in terms of program tasks.

Keywords you need to note are

function

call

structured programming

In C, a **function** is a self-contained set of code that performs a specific program task. Using functions is one of the advantages of C because it means you can build your program by fitting together task-specific modules of code to form a clear and efficient application. (The idea of a function may not be entirely new to you. If you know another language, you may have used something similar in your programs, such as a subroutine or procedure.)

When the `main()` function is encountered in your program, it begins to execute. However, you must retrieve or **call** all other functions in C by name in order to execute them. You can call library functions and functions you have written from `main()`. You can also call functions from other functions. As **Figure 6.1** shows, C programs are written in terms of functions. Writing programs like this, in terms of task-specific modules of code, is known as **structured programming**. C lends itself to this kind of programming very well.

Chapter 6

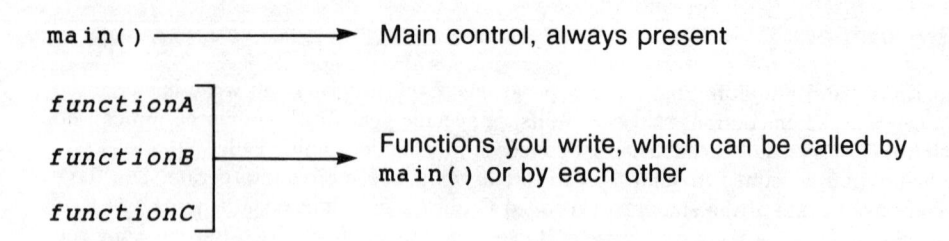

```
main()  ─────────────▶  Main control, always present
functionA ⎤
functionB  ────────▶  Functions you write, which can be called by
functionC ⎦            main() or by each other
```

Figure 6.1   Sample Program Structure: `main()` and Three Other Functions

Suppose you are writing a program to play the old familiar shell game. Your goal as a player is to guess which shell a pea is under. The basic functions you need to program this game include a function to display three shells (with a pea under one of them), a function to move the shells around (simulate animation on your screen), and a function to handle guesses and provide responses. You would write the following functions:

`main()`	to provide overall program control
`display`	to show the game screen
`animate`	to simulate mixing up the shells
`guess`	to handle user interaction.

You can structure your program around these tasks as shown in **Figure 6.2**.

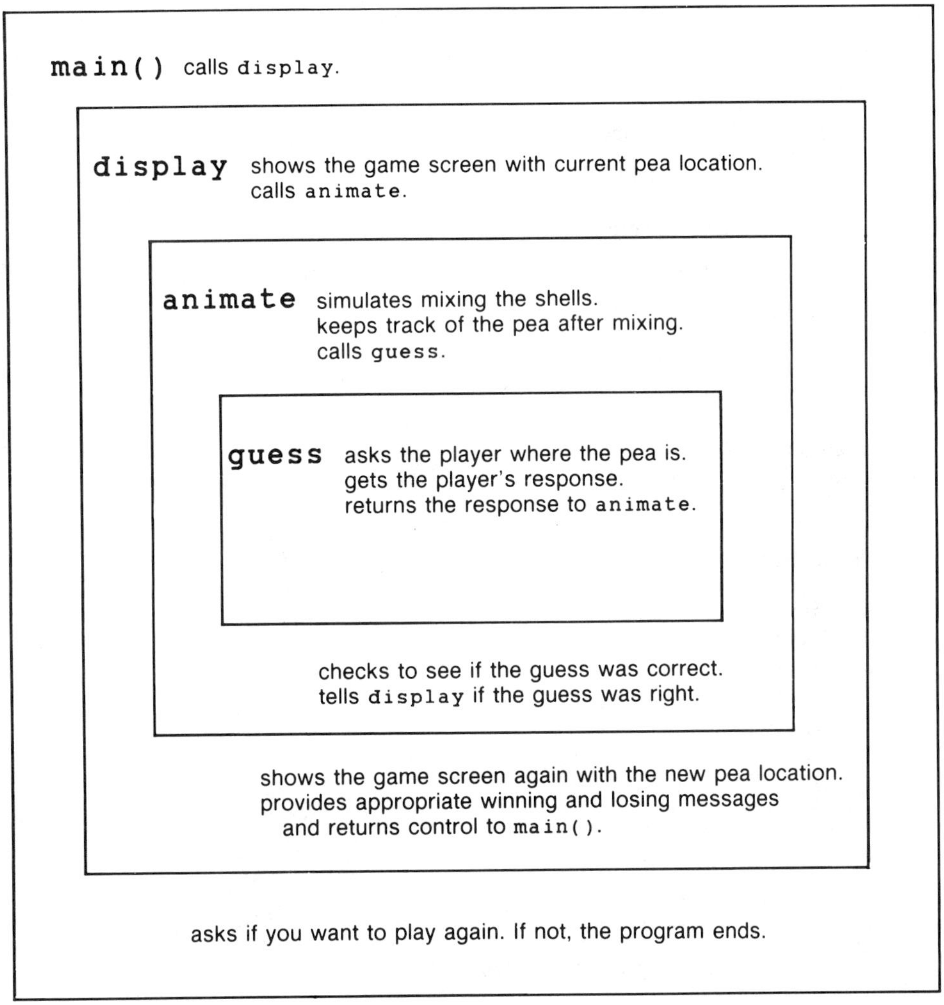

main() calls `display`.

> **display** shows the game screen with current pea location.
> calls `animate`.
>
>> **animate** simulates mixing the shells.
>> keeps track of the pea after mixing.
>> calls `guess`.
>>
>>> **guess** asks the player where the pea is.
>>> gets the player's response.
>>> returns the response to `animate`.
>>
>> checks to see if the guess was correct.
>> tells `display` if the guess was right.
>
> shows the game screen again with the new pea location.
> provides appropriate winning and losing messages
> and returns control to `main()`.

asks if you want to play again. If not, the program ends.

Figure 6.2 Shell Game Program Structure

Chapter 6

As you can see, there is quite a bit of communication going on between the functions involved, which raises the following questions:

- How do you say you want to execute a function?
- How do you give the function information it might need?
- How do you get the results?

And, within the function itself:

- How do you tell C where function code starts and stops?
- How do you get any information you need from the "outside"?
- How do you define variables you might need in the function?
- How do you send back a result to the calling function?

The answers to these and similar questions are provided by C function definitions, function declarations, and function calls. These are all covered in the next section on function structure.

Module 13 Summary

In this module, you have learned how a C program is composed of task-oriented units of code called functions. Writing C programs in terms of functions provides program structure and efficiency.

New C Tools

Concepts

function

structured programming

Module 14: Function Structure

In this module, the first thing you learn is how to write or define a function. Next, you will see how to tell the compiler you want to use functions you have already defined by declaring them. Finally, you will learn how to execute or call a function.

Introduction to Functions in C

Keywords you need to note are

function definition	**formal parameters**
function type	**function declaration**
function name	**call by value**
function parameters	**call by reference**
function body	**local variables**
`return`	**global variables**
function call	**function prototypes**
function arguments	
actual parameters	

Defining a Function

Like many other items in C, functions must be defined. You need to write a function definition in order to tell the compiler what types of data the function will work with and what type of information the function will return. To communicate these things to the compiler, you write a **function definition.** The function definition includes the type of value returned by the function (like `int` or `float`), the name followed by parameter (or argument) declarations (if needed), and a function body that includes one or more return statements. The basic structure of a C function looks like this:

function_type function_name   *(parameters)*   ⬅— type, name, parameters
parameter declarations;   ⬅— parameter declarations
{
    statement1;
    .
    .   ⬅— function body
    .
    statement_n;

    return *value-of-function_type*;   ⬅— function type value
}

C functions work with copies of variable values (with one exception that you will learn about in Chapter 7). A simple function to exchange the copies of values for two numbers follows. (You will learn how to use this function later in this section.)

```
/* exchange function */

int xchange(num1, num2)
int num1, num2;
```

Chapter 6

```
{
int hold;

hold = num1;
num1 = num2;
num2 = hold;

return num1;

}
```

Using this function as an example, the parts of a function definition include*

```
int xchange(num1,num2)      /* function type, name,
                               and parameters (if needed) */

int num1,num2;              /* parameter declarations (if needed) */

{                           /* function body  (enclosed in braces) */

int hold;

hold = num1;
num1 = num2;
num2 = hold;

return num1;

}
```

If you do not need to pass any information to a function, you do not need to code any parameters. In fact, the minimum requirements when defining a function are the function name and the function body, for example,

```
future_code() { }
```

If you called this from **main( )**, program control would branch to **future_code( )**, do absolutely nothing, and return. Coding functions like this as *placeholders* is useful when you are developing a program and know you need a function but have not yet developed the code. Of course, there will be more involved in the functions you write. The following sections look at each part of a function in closer detail.

Function Type, Name, and Parameters The concept of a **function type** in C is easier to understand if you remember that *functions are typed according to the kind of value they return*. The type of result may be character, integer, or double, for example (or,

---

* If you are familiar with the Draft ANSI Standard, you may note that ANSI would handle the declaration of **xchange** a little differently, showing the types of the arguments, as well as the function itself:

```
int xchange(int num1,int num2)
```

as you will see in subsequent chapters, it may be more complex than any of these). The associated function type would then be considered to be `char`, `int`, or `double` (or another valid C data type). A function in C returns *one* value or object. In this chapter, you will be working with functions that return one of the basic C data types covered so far. Then, in Chapter 7, you will learn how to return a value that indicates an area of storage containing several values.

As mentioned, a function does not have to return a result or value. You could write a function that simply printed message lines. If a function does not return a value and you want to declare it as such, you use the type `void`. The function type is always coded before the function name. Some programmers code the type and name on the same line as is done here. Others place the type on a separate line above the name. This choice, however, is largely a matter of taste.

In the next few paragraphs, you will learn about the `return` statement. (You may already be familiar with this statement from **Inside Information** in previous chapters.) While on the subject of function types, you need to know that if you do not declare a type for a function (as in the `future_code()` example above) you should code

```
return 0;
```

as the `return` statement for the function.

The **function name** can be any valid C name recognized by your compiler. The function name must be unique within your program. Following the name, variables communicating information between the function and the outside world are coded within parentheses. These variables are referred to as **function parameters**. The parentheses following the name are required whether or not any parameters are present. If you need several parameters, you separate them with commas.

Parameter Declarations You provide information about the kinds of parameters used by a function by coding a declaration statement for each parameter. Parameter declarations are coded immediately after the function definition statement.

The Function Body The C task statements associated with the function are called the function body. The function body is enclosed in braces. Any valid C statements, including complex blocks of statements and calls to other functions, can be used within the function body. (A function can also call itself. This is covered in a later chapter.)

Return Use a `return` statement if you need to send output from the function back to whatever called the function. If the function alters data in some way (such as sorting it) and produces no single result value, you do not need a `return` statement. When you do use a `return` statement, it does two things within a function:

- It causes the value of whatever expression is given as a function result to be communicated to the caller.

Chapter 6

- It also signals the end of function execution and gives control back to the calling function.

There can be more than one return statement, and `return` does not need to be coded as the last statement in the function. Because a function may or may not return a result, `return` has two forms:

> **return;**   no value returned
>
> **return** *expression*;   any valid C expression representing the function result

A good way to think of the relationship between functions, parameters, and `return` statements is to remember that parameters communicate values to a function and `return` communicates a value back to the calling function.

Function Calls

Functions are accessed or **called** by coding their name and parameters. (In the function call, parameters are more properly referred to as **function arguments**.) The call can be part of any valid C expression. This is important because it means that you have great flexibility in using function calls. For example, a function call can be used in an assignment statement such as the following:

```
error_code = get_error();
```

where the variable `error_code` is assigned the value returned by the `get_error` function.

If a function does not need parameters, you code the call by giving the function name followed by parentheses as follows:

```
error_message()
```

where `error_message` might be a function that prints a line and returns.

If you need to provide information to the function, then you assign the variable values needed to the parameters before the function call is made. In C, a distinction is made between parameters passed in the function call and the parameters coded as part of the function definition. Parameters used in the call statement are termed **actual parameters** because they are the variables you are working with in the calling function. When you call the function, the variables coded as parameters in the function definition are given copies of these actual variable values.

Parameters defined in the function are called **formal parameters**. Their only purpose is to hold temporary copies of the actual arguments passed from the calling function.

Introduction to Functions in C

When parameters are involved, the process and call look like **Figure 6.3**.

```
int error_number;
   .
   .
   .
error_number = 5;
error_message(error_number);
```
code in calling function
(actual parameter = error_number)

```
int error_message(error_type)
int error_type;
{
   if(error_type == 5)
   /* print message */
   .
   .
   .
}
```
code in called function
(formal parameter = error_type)

Figure 6.3 Calling a Function with Formal Parameters

This way of handling parameter values makes C a **call by value** language. Since the function only uses temporary copies of actual parameter values, any processing of the formal (function copy) variables does not affect their original (actual) value. Here is a simple example of what happens:

```
#include <stdio.h>

main()
{
int new;
int actual_val = 5;
new = change(actual_val); /* call change, passing copy of actual_val;
                             put what change returns into new */

printf("actual_val is: %d\n new is: %d", actual_val, new);
return 0;
}

int change(formal_val)
int formal_val;
{
formal_val = formal_val + 3;   /* compute formal_val + 3 and
                                  put the result back in formal_val */
return formal_val;             /* return contents of formal_val */

}
```

Chapter 6

This is the output for the program:

```
actual_val is: 5
new is: 8
```

Most other languages use **call by reference** in which the location of the actual parameter is passed to a function and the function then works with the actual variable, not a copy of the value. Both ways have advantages and disadvantages; this is discussed in more detail in Chapter 11. For now, just remember that C functions work with copies of actual argument values.

C does one other thing behind the scenes during a function call. When parameters are passed to the called function, C automatically *upgrades* the actual and formal parameter types. `float` parameters are converted to `double`, and `char` and `short` parameters are converted to `int`.* You still declare and handle the parameters according to their original types. C just provides this feature for efficiency and insurance.

Calling Functions Before Their Definitions In C, you cannot have the code of one function body contained within another function body, but you can code calls to other functions from within a function body. Functions called from one C function are defined elsewhere. They are either written by you and located in your code, or, if you are using library functions, they are in a header file which you `#include`. Thus, it is important to add declarations for any function called within another function. If this is not done, the compiler is unable to perform some of its error checking tasks. (In addition, the compiler assumes that any function not declared is type `int`.)

To avoid worrying about the order of function calls, you can code declarations for all the functions you have defined before the `main()` function. For example:

```
int display();
int animate();              ◄────── function declarations
int guess();
    .
    .
    .
main()
{
int new_loc, guess, pea;

display();
new_loc = animate(pea);     ◄────── function calls
answer  = guess(pea);
    .
    .
    .
}
```

---

* This type of conversion is typical behavior in the absence of a function prototype. You will learn about prototypes later in this chapter.

Introduction to Functions in C

```
int display()    ◄──────────────  function definitions
{

}
```

To help tie some of these concepts together, try the following example.

```c
/* Exchange two things */

#include <stdio.h>       /* Defines standard functions */

int xchange();           /* A function declaration */

int main()
{
int loc = 1;         /* Starting pea location is shell 1 */
int shell1 = 1;      /* Simple way to keep track of shells */
int shell2 = 2;

printf("Before exchange pea is under Shell %d\n", loc);

loc = xchange(shell1,shell2);   /* Function call assigning return
                                    value of new location */

printf("After exchange pea is under Shell %d\n", loc);
printf("Shell1=%d and shell2=%d\n", shell1,shell2);

}

/* exchange function */

xchange(num1, num2)          /* Exchange copies of values */
int num1, num2;

{
int hold;
printf("Before exchange num1=%d  num2=%d\n", num1,num2);  /* values are . . . */

hold = num1;
num1 = num2;
num2 = hold;

printf("After exchange num1=%d  num2=%d\n", num1,num2);  /* values are . . . */
return num1;

}
```

In this example, there are two user-defined functions, `main()` and `xchange`. Each function is declared and named. A declaration for `xchange` is given before `main()` begins. (If you do not declare a function, the default declaration is `int`.) Each function has a body of task statements enclosed by braces { }.

Chapter 6

In `main()`, `loc` is declared with the original pea position (1 = shell 1). `loc` is then assigned the new pea position using the result of the `xchange` function coded as the assignment statement

```
loc = xchange(shell1,shell2);
```

On the right side of this expression is the function call `xchange(shell1,shell2)`. The two call parameters, `shell1` and `shell2` were given actual values when they were declared.

The function `xchange` has two parameters, `num1` and `num2`, enclosed in parentheses. Following this, they are declared as integers so they can hold copies of the integer values passed from the call in `main()`. The left brace then signals the start of the function body.

When the `xchange` function is called, the value of the first parameter, `shell1` (1) is assigned to the variable `num1`. The value of the second parameter `shell2` (2) is given the variable `num2`.

Within the function body, the values of `num1` and `num2` are exchanged. The value of the variable `num1` containing the exchanged number is then sent back or **returned** via a `return` statement to the `main()` function. Note that only a copy of the values has been exchanged. (There are ways to exchange the actual values of variables and they are discussed in later chapters.)

Variable Use and Functions

Suppose you are writing the shell game program, and you want people to have the option to play a *basic* version and a more difficult or *advanced* version. You want to keep track of wins and losses for both versions. You also want to know combined or total wins and losses. You do this in C by defining variables for use just within each function and variables that can be used by both functions. In this case, you would define the counters needed as **local** and **global variables.**

You can specify local and global variables in your program by expanding the variable definition or by default, according to where the variable declaration occurs in your program. In this chapter, you will learn that where you define a variable can make a difference in where it can be used. Here is an outline of the game example:

```
/* Shell Game - Basic and Advanced Versions */
main()
{
   int play;    /* Control type of play */
         .
         .         /* Game control statements */
         .
}
```

Introduction to Functions in C

```
            int tot_wins;           /* Global variable used by
                                       both basic() and advanced() */
       basic();
          int basic_wins = 0;       /* Local variables used only */
          int winner = 0;           /* in basic() function */
                .
                .
                .
          if(winner) { basic_wins += 1;
                      tot_wins += 1; }
       }
       advanced();
       {
          int adv_wins = 0;         /* Local variables used only */
          int winner = 0;           /* in advanced() function */
                .
                .
                .
          if(winner) { adv_wins += 1;
                      tot_wins += 1; }
       }
```

Global Variables   When you declare a variable outside of all functions, including `main()`, that variable becomes global in scope and you can use it in all of your subsequent functions in the program. Global variables are created when your program begins and last for the life of your program. Global variables are also automatically initialized to zero unless you initialize them to something else. (It is better to explicitly initialize variables, of course.)

In the shell game above, you keep track of total wins with the global variable `tot_wins` defined after the `main()` function. (You could have defined `tot_wins` before `main()`. This is a matter of personal choice.) This declaration allows both functions, `basic()` and `advanced()`, to update the total number of wins.

Local Variables   When you declare variables within the body of a function (after the opening brace) you are declaring local variables.

Caution: local variables exist *only* while the function is active (executing). They are automatically created upon entry to the function and automatically destroyed on return from the function. For this reason, local variables are sometimes called *automatic variables* (more on this later). They are not, however, automatically initialized. You must initialize them in the function before they are referenced.

Chapter 6

In the shell game example above, `basic_wins` is declared as a local variable to keep track of wins for as long as the basic version of the game function is active. Similarly, `adv_wins` keeps track of the advanced version totals.

Remember, local variables are valid only for the life of the function. If you want to separate total wins into game totals for basic and advanced versions, you would have to define two more global variables, `tot_bas` and `tot_adv`, and update them from each function.

In summary, the purpose of local variables is to provide a way for a function to have a private set of variables for its own use. The purpose of global variables is to define variables that can be used by all functions in your program. The following general guidelines should help.

Guidelines for Using Local and Global Variable Names

- A local and global variable can have the same name. The local variable version will be used within the function containing its definition. Otherwise, the global name prevails.

- You can have two local variables with the same name occurring in two different functions because each is recognized only within its specific function. This is useful for variables with a similar purpose such as `counts` or `totals`.

- All local variables within a function must have different names.

- All function names are considered global names. Parameter names are considered local names (with one exception that you will learn about in later chapters).

The complete basic definition of a function is shown in **Figure 6.4**.

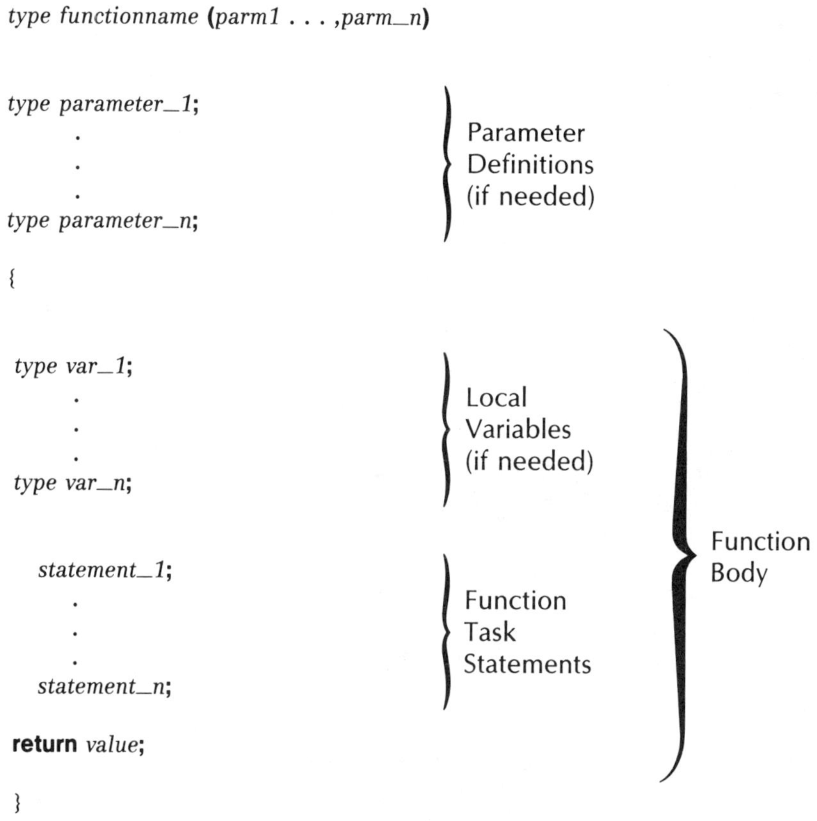

Introduction to Functions in C

type functionname **(***parm1* . . . ,*parm_n***)**

    type parameter_1;
        .
        .
        .   } Parameter Definitions (if needed)
    type parameter_n;

    {

        type var_1;
            .
            .   } Local Variables (if needed)
            .
        type var_n;

        statement_1;
            .
            .   } Function Task Statements
            .
        statement_n;

    return *value*;

    }

} Function Body

Figure 6.4   Basic Definition of a Function

Helpful Hints for Function and Parameter Declarations

Argument mismatches occur when a calling function passes a different type argument than was expected by the called function. This can cause problems in interpreting parameter values. For example, if a function is expecting a signed integer and receives an unsigned value, the bit patterns will be interpreted incorrectly. (Recall Chapter 2 and data representation.) Similarly, if a function is expecting a `short` but is passed a `long`, it may assign an incorrect value to its parameter because it may make use of the wrong two bytes of `long`.

In order to deal with possible argument mismatches, C provides a feature that lets you optionally define **function prototypes.** By prototyping functions, you can declare the function type *and* its argument types earlier in your program in a function declaration. By comparing the prototype to the call or definition of the function, the compiler can detect a mismatch between an argument and a parameter. It will then print a

Chapter 6

diagnostic message to inform you of this error. The following program outline shows you how prototypes could be coded for the functions **xchange** and **animate**.

```
int xchange(int, int);         /* prototype */
int animate(int);              /* prototype */

void main()
{
int shell1, shell2, loc;
    .
    .                          /* code for main function */
    .
    xchange(shell1, shell2);   /* calls to functions */
    animate(loc);              /* with arguments */
    .
    .
    .
}

int xchange(num1, num2)        /* function declarator */
int num1, num2;                /* with parameters */
{
    .                          /* code for xchange function */
    .
    .
}

int animate(x)                 /* function declarator and parameters */
int x;
{
    .                          /* code for animate function */
    .
    .
}
```

By coding prototypes you can be sure only integer values are used in the **xchange** and **animate** functions.

Function misdeclarations can also occur. If a function type has not been declared before a function is called, the function type defaults to **int**. Since functions are typed on the basis of their return value, an incorrect type may result in program errors.

The best way to address this potential problem is to declare all functions before they are used. Frequently such declarations are made in a header file that you use in your source program via **#include**. In fact, most system **#include** files (for example, **stdio.h**) contain function prototypes of standard functions.

Introduction to Functions in C

Module 14 Summary

In this module, you have learned the basics about writing C functions. This includes knowing how to code a function definition, how to include a function declaration, and how to use or call a function you have written. You also learned how to declare and use local and global variables. Finally, some potential function definition problems were covered and suggestions were made on how to avoid them. The next section puts all of this to work when you code your first major application.

New C Tools

Concepts	Code
function declaration	function structure (type, name, parameters, body)
function definition	call statement
call by value	`return`
local and global variables	

A Function for Fun - The Shell Game

After reading about the famous shell game throughout this chapter, you might enjoy programming and running it. This program makes use of many of the function features discussed so far. Later, you will see how to write some functions more efficiently, but for now, try this version. It will take a while to work through this example, but most C programs are composed of more than two or three functions. This application will give you some practice in working with more extensive C code. Besides, you know enough to make all kinds of changes to this version to make it a little more challenging. A short explanation follows the code, but you will also find helpful information in comments in the code.

The Shell Game

The shell game works like this:

You have three shells

   [ ] [ ] [ ]

with a pea (*) under one of them

   [ ] [*] [ ]

The program displays the original shell set-up, then simulates mixing the shells on your display screen. In reality, variables are used to hold the exchanged shell values as in the earlier example. The program then asks you to guess the location of the pea and provides encouraging messages if you are wrong.

Chapter 6

To do all this, the following functions are involved:

`main( )`	controls the game.
`show_pea`	displays the pea in one of the shells.
`animate`	exchanges the shells.
`trade`	simulates exchange on the display screen.
`issamepair`	keeps track of shell exchange.
`first` `second` `third`	used with the `trade` function to simulate shell movement.
`space`	used in `trade` to space where the shells are displayed.
`delay`	pauses during the game so the player can look at the screen.
`getnum`	handles the guesses.
`get_one_char`	controls whether or not the game continues (used in a `switch`).

The next thing you should do is key in the code for the game.* Play the game until you get a feel for what is happening. If you have problems, jump ahead to the section following the code. It gives you an overall summary of what parts of the program do. If you choose to key in the code, key carefully to help prevent compiler errors (if you are using the compiler provided with this tutorial, and you get errors, refer to Part II, the User's Guide). Each section of the source file is explained in a comment block preceding that section. You do not have to key all the comments, but adding some later is good programming practice. Good luck!

```
/* The first section of the source file is a series of #include
   statements. Each of these causes the inclusion of a header
   file containing macros and/or function prototypes to be used
   by your program. */


#include <stdio.h>    /* C library for Standard I/O functions   */
#include <stdlib.h>   /* C library for more standard functions  */
#include <time.h>     /* C library for useful time functions    */
#include <ctype.h>    /* C library for character check macros   */


/* Now comes a series of your own macro definitions you will use
   in the remainder of the program */

#define SHELL1  0     /* Constant values to use in shell */
#define SHELL2  10    /* manipulation */
#define SHELL3  20
```

---

* If you are using the compiler provided with this tutorial, the code for this program is on diskette 2.

Introduction to Functions in C

```c
/* Each function used in your program should have a prototype.
   For the standard library functions, these are found in the
   usual header files.  The prototypes that follow are for the
   functions you define in your own program. */

void show_pea( int );                /* Function Prototypes */
int animate( int );
void trade( int, int );
int issamepair( int, int, int, int );
int first( int, int, int );
int second( int, int, int );
int third( int, int, int );
void space( int );
void delay( int );
char get_one_char();                 /* Function declarations */
int getnum();


/* The main() function is defined next.  Usually this will be
   the first function definition in the file.  main() need not
   be defined first, but the source file has a better logical
   organization if it is.  */

int main()         /* Control game flow via do-while and switch */
{

   /* The first statements in any function are the definitions of
      local variables used in the program.  Keep in mind that any
      of these you don't initialize will have unpredictable values. */

     int   initial;
     int   final;
     time_t time_val = time( NULL );  /* Get system time value in secs. */
     int   finished;                  /* NULL just tells the function */
     int   guess;                     /* that's all you want to do */
     int   wins = 0;
     int   losses = 0;


   /* Print a "sign-on" message and do any necessary initialization. */

     puts( "\n\nWelcome to Honest Abe's Shell Game Emporium \n" );

     srand( (unsigned) time_val );   /* Get seed (start value) for
                                        random number generator using
                                        system time value */
```

Chapter 6

```c
/* This is the primary part of the main() program.  It is a loop
   which displays the shells, mixes them, prompts for a guess,
   responds to the guess, and gives you a chance to play again. */

      do {                     /* Start of main do-while */

         initial = irand( 3 );  /* Randomly choose starting pea location */

         puts( "OK, keep your eye on the shell with the pea.\n" );
         show_pea( initial );   /* Display initial pea location */
         delay( 5 );            /* Pause for 5 seconds */

         final = animate( initial );  /* Mix shells, start with initial
                                         position; return final location */

         fputs( "\n\nWhere do you think the pea is? ", stdout);

         guess = getnum();      /* Get player's guess about location */

         if ( guess == final )  /* Correct guess */
            {
            puts( "\nLucky guess." );
            wins++;
            }
         else
            {
            printf( "\nSorry, the pea was in shell number %d\n", final );
            show_pea( final );   /* Show where the pea really is */
            putchar( '\n' );
            losses++;
            }

         fputs( "\n\nWould you like to give it another shot?", stdout );

         switch( get_one_char() )  /* See if player wants to try again */
            {
            case 'Y':               /* Either a capital Y or a small y */
            case 'y':
               finished = 0;
               break;
            case 'N':               /* Either a capital N or a small n */
            case 'n':
               finished = 1;
               break;
            default:
               puts( "\nI'll take that as a yes..." );
               finished = 0;
               break;
            }
      } while ( !finished );  /* End do-while if player wants to quit */
```

Introduction to Functions in C

```
/* The final few lines are referred to as "termination code".
   They display your success rate and print a termination message.
   Notice that a "return" statement ends the main() function even
   though it appears that main() does not return anywhere.  Actually
   main() is called from a "start-up" routine supplied with your
   compiler, and the "return" allows the operating system to detect
   overall success or failure of the program.  (Usually 0 means
   success and 1 indicates failure--more on how to do this in a later
   chapter).  Although the "return" is not really necessary in this
   case, its omission may cause a "function value return mismatch"
   since main() should always be declared as returning an "int". */

   printf( "\n\nFinal standings You: %d    Honest Abe's:%d\n\n",wins, losses);
   if ( wins > losses )
       puts( "Say!, how would you like to work for Honest Abe's" );
   else
       puts( "Come back again..." );

return(0);

}

void show_pea( loc )    /* show_pea function - prints shells
                           revealing pea in shell */
int loc;                /* number of location--where 1 <= loc <= 3 */
{
  switch (loc)
     {
  case 1:
     putchar('\r');               /* Move to beginning of line*/
     space( SHELL1 );             /* Move to location of first shell */
     fputs("[*]", stdout);        /* Print a shell (with pea) */
     space( SHELL2 - ( SHELL1 + 3 ) );   /* Space to the location of
                                            the second shell--this is
                                            location SHELL2.  We
                                            already spaced to SHELL1
                                            and then 3 more spaces by
                                            printing "[* ]". */

     fputs("[ ]", stdout);        /* Print an empty shell */
     space( SHELL3 - ( SHELL2 + 3 ) );   /* Space to SHELL3 */
     fputs("[ ]\r", stdout);      /* Print the last shell,
                                     and return the cursor
                                     to the beginning of the
                                     line (via \r). */
     break;                       /* That's it for this case */
```

Chapter 6

```
      case 2:                     /* Cases 2 and 3 are identical to
                                     case 1, except for printing the
                                     pea in the correct shell. */
   putchar('\r');
   space( SHELL1 );
   fputs("[ ]", stdout);
   space( SHELL2 - ( SHELL1 + 3 ) );
   fputs("[*]", stdout);
   space( SHELL3 - ( SHELL2 + 3 ) );
   fputs("[ ]\r", stdout);
   break;
   case 3:
   putchar('\r');
   space( SHELL1 );
   fputs("[ ]", stdout);
   space( SHELL2 - ( SHELL1 + 3 ) );
   fputs("[ ]", stdout);
   space( SHELL3 - ( SHELL2 + 3 ) );
   fputs("[*]\r", stdout);
   break;
   }
}

animate( from )      /* animate function - makes 10 iterations of
                        shells. Takes starting position as "from";
                        returns the pea location after shell
                        "movement". */
int from;

{
  int  current = from;
  int  i;

  for ( i = 0; i < 10; i++ )     /* Move the shells 10 times */
     {
     switch ( irand( 3 ) )       /* Pick one of the 3 possible swaps.
                                    This routine just updates and
                                    returns the current pea location */

        {
       case 1:                   /* Trade locations 1 and 2. trade() */
          trade(1, 2);           /* does the screen animation */
          if ( current == 1 )    /* Update the pea's location. If it was */
             current = 2;        /* at location 1, it is now at location */
          else if ( current == 2 ) /* 2, and vice versa. If it was at */
             current = 1;        /* location 3, nothing changes. */
          break;
```

138

Introduction to Functions in C

```c
         case 2:                    /* Trade locations 2 and 3 */
            trade(2, 3);
            if ( current == 2 )
               current = 3;
            else if ( current == 3 )
               current = 2;
            break;
         case 3:                    /* Trade locations 1 and 3 */
            trade(1, 3);
            if ( current == 1 )
               current = 3;
            else if ( current == 3 )
               current = 1;
            break;
         }
      }

   return ( current );
}

void trade( loc1, loc2 )       /* trade function - provides visual
                                  display only */

int loc1, loc2;                /* visually trades shells at loc1 and */
{                              /* loc2 to update the display screen */
   int pos1 = SHELL1;
   int pos2 = SHELL2;
   int pos3 = SHELL3;
   int offset;
   int done = 0;
   int swap_type;

/* Find out which type of exchange is happening.  There are only
   three types:  swapping 1 and 2; swapping 2 and 3; or swapping
   1 and 3.  However, it is possible that the requested swap is 2 and
   1, or 3 and 2, or 3 and 1, so the issamepair function checks to see
   if the second pair of numbers is the same as the first, except
   possibly reversed. */

   if ( issamepair( 1, 2, loc1, loc2 ) )
      swap_type = 1;
   else if ( issamepair( 2, 3, loc1, loc2 ) )
      swap_type = 2;
   else if ( issamepair( 1, 3, loc1, loc2 ) )
      swap_type = 3;

   putchar('\r');
   space( SHELL1 );
   fputs("[ ]", stdout);
   space( SHELL2 - ( SHELL1 + 3 ) );
   fputs("[ ", stdout);
```

Chapter 6

```c
    space( SHELL3 - ( SHELL2 + 3 ) );
    fputs("[ ]\r", stdout);

    do
       {
       switch ( swap_type )
          {
          case 1:                      /* Exchange 1 and 2 */
             pos1++;                   /* Move shell 1's location right */
             pos2--;                   /* Move shell 2's location left */
             done = ( pos2 == SHELL1 ); /* Done if shell 2 is in the */
                                       /* first location */
             break;
          case 2:                      /* Exchange 2 and 3 */
             pos2++;                   /* Move shell 2 right */
             pos3--;                   /* Move shell 3 left */
             done = ( pos3 == SHELL2 ); /* Done when shell 3 is in */
                                       /* shell 2 location. */
             break;
          case 3:                      /* Exchange 1 and 3 */
             pos1++;                   /* Move shell 1 right */
             pos3--;                   /* Move shell 3 left */
             done = ( pos3 == SHELL1 ); /* Done when shell 3 is in */
                                       /* shell 1 location. */
             break;
          }
       putchar( '\r' );

       space( first(pos1, pos2, pos3) );  /* Space the first shell */
                                          /* position.*/
       fputs( "[ ]", stdout );            /* Draw a shell */
       offset = second( pos1, pos2, pos3 ) -
                ( first( pos1, pos2, pos3 ) + 3 );

       space( offset );                   /* Space to the location on */
                                          /* the second shell */
       fputs( "[ ]", stdout );   /* Draw the shell */
       offset = third( pos1, pos2, pos3 ) -
                ( second( pos1, pos2, pos3 ) + 3 );

       space( offset );                /* Space to the final location */
       fputs( "[ ]", stdout );  /* Draw the last shell */

       space( SHELL3 - third( pos1, pos2, pos3 ) );
                                       /* Draw spaces to the end of
                                          the line. This helps keep
                                          the animation smooth, by
                                          printing about the same
                                          number of characters all
                                          the time. */
```

Introduction to Functions in C

```
            putchar( '\r' );
            } while ( !done );
      }

issamepair( a, b, from, to )         /* checks if a and b are the
{                                       same pair, ie., possibly
                                        exchanged as "from - to".
                                        Expression reduces to
                                        single Boolean result. */

   return ( ( ( a == from ) && ( b == to ) ) |
            ( ( b == from ) && ( a == to ) ) );
}

first( a, b, c )    /* first function - determines which shell is
                       the leftmost shell during an exchange
                       operation. */
{
   int smallest = a;

   if ( b < smallest )
      smallest = b;
   if ( c < smallest )
      smallest = c;

   return ( smallest );
}

second( a, b, c )   /* second function - determines which shell is
                       in the middle during an exchange operation. */
{
   int smallest = a;
   int middle = b;
   int largest = c;
   int temp;

   if ( middle < smallest )
      {
      temp = middle;
      middle = smallest;
      smallest = temp;
      }
   if ( largest < middle )
      {
      temp = middle;
      middle = largest;
      largest = temp;
      }
   if ( middle < smallest )
      {
      temp = middle;
```

Chapter 6

```
      middle = smallest;
      smallest = temp;
      }

  return ( middle );
}

third( a, b, c )      /* third function - returns the rightmost location
                         of the three locations passed. */
{
  int largest = a;

  if ( b > largest )
     largest = b;
  if ( c > largest )
     largest = c;

  return ( largest );
}

void space( count )   /* space function - moves the cursor "count"
                         spaces.  Space to go forward, or backspace,
                         if negative. */
{
  int i;

  if ( count < 0 )
     for ( i = count; i < 0; i++ )
        putchar( '\b' );
  else
     for ( i = 0; i < count; i++ )
        putchar( ' ' );
}

irand( range )        /* irand function - randomly retrieves an
                         integer between 1 and "range" */
int range;
{
  int  rand_val;

  rand_val = rand() % range;   /* rand_val will be 0, 1, or 2 */

  return ( rand_val + 1);      /* rand_val needs to be 1, 2, or 3 */
}

void delay( secs )    /* delay function - pauses "secs" seconds */
```

```c
{
  time_t time_val = time( NULL );

  while ( time( NULL ) < time_val + secs )
      ;                  /* do nothing--pause */
}

getnum()     /* getnum function - reads a number from stdin (keyboard) */

{
  char buff[80];

  fgets( buff, 80, stdin );
  return ( atoi( buff ) );
}


char get_one_char()    /* get_one_char function - reads a character
                          from standard input, ignoring leading spaces
                          and removing trailer characters. */
{
  char ch;             /* Storage for charcter read */
  char junk;           /* Temporary variable for discarding extras */

  /* Get first non-whitespace character (except return) */

  while ( isspace( ch = getchar() ) && ( ch != '\n' ) )
      ;

  /* If the user just entered return, then return a space.
     This is useful for processing default answers. */

  if ( ch == '\n' )
     ch = ' ';

  /* Remove everything on line after character
     This is to empty the keyboard buffer */

  if ( ch != ' ' )
     while ( ( junk = getchar() ) != '\n' )
         ;

  return ( ch );           /* Return the character */
}
```

Chapter 6

Program Notes

As mentioned previously, the comments give detailed information about the program. Overall, the program works as follows:

1. The `main` function prints a welcome message.
2. Because chance is involved, you need to generate random numbers to use in mixing up the shells. The numbers are based on a C time function.
3. The `do-while` loop begins and performs the following steps:
   - call `irand` to get possible positions (1,2,3).
   - call `show_pea` to show current pea location.
   - `show_pea` calls `space` to show initial location.
   - call `delay` so player can see pea before swap.
   - call `animate` to switch the pea.
   - `animate` calls `trade` to move the pea.
   - `trade` calls `issamepair` to see which pair is being swapped. `trade` simulates animation by using a `do-while` loop and the `first`, `second`, and `third` functions to determine spacing and location offsets.
4. Call `getnum` for player's guess as to final pea location.
5. Use `if-else` to track a win or loss.
6. Switch on `get_one_char` to determine if play continues. If yes, return to `irand` call and loop. If not, end loop.

When looking over this example, notice how function communication takes place. To begin with, function prototypes are defined to ensure correct function and parameter types. The function parameters and return values are shown below.

Function	Parameters	Return Value
`main()`		`void`
`show_pea`	`loc` - pea location	`void`
`animate`	`from` - start location	`int`-current (new) location
`trade`	`loc1, loc2` - trade locations	`void`
`issamepair`	`a, b, from, to` - pairs to compare	`int` - Boolean (true/false)
`first`	`a, b, c` - locations	`int` - smallest of `a, b, c`
`second`	`a, b, c` - locations	`int` - middle of `a, b, c`
`third`	`a, b, c` - locations	`int` - largest of `a, b, c`
`space`	`count` - number of spaces	`void` e
`irand`	`range` - maximum return value	`int` - random value
`delay`	`secs` - seconds to wait	`void`
`getnum`		`int` - number
`get_one_char`		`char` - nonspace character

Take your time looking over the code. You might notice some different ways of declaring variables or assigning values.

In looking at the `issamepair` function, notice that **a** and **b** are not declared. This seems unusual, but in fact, these variables are of type **int**, as you will see from the prototype at the beginning of the program. Since these variables are also used as **ints** in `issamepair`, they do not need to be declared there (but it would be a good idea). A similar situation occurs with `first`, `second`, `third`, and `space`.

You may also have noticed that the program uses the `rand` function with a modulus operator to compute `rand_val`:

```
rand_val = rand() % range;
```

This method of computation is simple, but the results are, in fact, statistically weighted. An alternate, and slightly more sophisticated approach might be the following:

- Define a value MAXRAND to be the maximum value for `rand` to use:

    ```
    #define MAXRAND 32767.0
    ```

- Recode the above line as follows:

    ```
    rand_val = ((double) rand() / ((double) MAXRAND + 1.0 )) * (double) range;
    ```

Note that this line contains casts to type `double`. (Each `double` inside parentheses forces what follows it to type `double`. See Chapter 8 for more on casts.) Also, your compiler may have a predefined value (such as **RAND_MAX**) available so that you may not need to define MAXRAND (or some other constant) via `#define` as was done here. Check your compiler documentation.

Chapter Summary

Chapter 6 showed you how to write your own C functions. You are aware of the basics of function definitions, declarations, and calls. To top it all off, you have gone through a simulation of the shell game, which was your first major C program. In the next chapter, you enter into the domain of pointers and discover the real power of C.

Chapter 7
Introduction to Arrays and Pointers

Chapter 7

CONTENTS

Introduction **149**
Module 15: Working with Arrays in C **149**
    Declaring Arrays 149
    Inside Information 151
    Initializing Arrays 152
    Inside Information 153
    Using Subscripts 153
    More About Text Strings 155
    Inside Information 156
    Module 15 Summary 158
Module 16: An Introduction to Pointers **158**
    Getting to Know Pointers 159
    Declaring Pointers and Using Pointer Operators 160
    Using Pointers 163
    Inside Information 170
    Module 16 Summary 170
Converting Units of Measure **171**
    A Closer Look 176
    Program Notes 178
Chapter Summary **178**

Introduction

In this chapter, you will explore how to handle multiple data values by using arrays. You will also learn how to access areas of storage by using a special type of C variable called a pointer. Because a good understanding of arrays and pointers is essential to becoming a good C programmer, each topic is introduced with several short examples that emphasize the concepts involved. At the end of the chapter, you will use some major C features such as functions, arrays, and pointers in a program. After the following three sections, you are well on your way to becoming a C programmer:

- working with arrays in C
- getting started with pointers
- example.

Module 15: Working with Arrays in C

An **array** is a sequence of objects of the same type. You have been working with single data items or **scalars**. Arrays can hold multiple items of data. You can think of an array as an area of storage (or buffer) that can hold numbers or characters. For example, you can think of a collection of ten boxes to hold ten numbers.

This module answers many questions about arrays, including the following:

- How do you define an array?
- How do you get values into an array?
- How do you use values in an array?

Keywords you need to note are

> **array element**
> **array subscript**
> **initializing arrays**

Declaring Arrays

Like other storage objects in C, arrays must be declared before they can be used. In C, an array of ten integers is declared as follows:

```
int numbers[10];
```

In the declaration, `int` specifies the data type of the array. This means that the array `numbers` contains integer items. Each item in an array must be of the same data type. The name of the array, `numbers`, follows the data type. Following the name, enclosed in brackets, is the array size. In this example, the array can hold ten numbers. Explicitly stating the size between the brackets in the declaration is one way to tell the

Chapter 7

compiler how large to make the array. (More about what can go in the brackets in a moment.)

You can think of an array as an area of memory as shown in **Figure 7.1**.

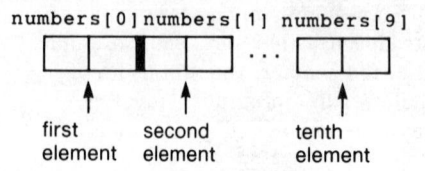

```
numbers[0] numbers[1]    numbers[9]
```
↑ first element ↑ second element ↑ tenth element

Figure 7.1   The Ten Elements in the Array `numbers`

Here it is assumed that an integer is two bytes. If an integer were four bytes long (remember size is machine-dependent), the array would look like **Figure 7.2**.

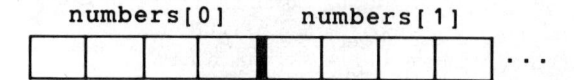

```
    numbers[0]        numbers[1]
```

Figure 7.2   Array `numbers` with 4-byte Elements

In the array declaration, you define the array by stating the kind of data the array will hold, the name you are going to use to refer to this set of data, and how many data items will be in the array. The format of an array declaration is as follows:

  type array_name **[***size***]**;

Reviewing the example above, you declared an array of `integer` type called `numbers`, and you allowed ten integer storage cells to hold the contents.

Each individual array object is called an **array element.** Each element is distinguished from other elements by its unique position in the array. The brackets [] signal to your compiler that this is an array. The number enclosed in the brackets is the number of elements you decide the array needs to contain the data items involved.

The array in the example above is said to have ten elements. You may have noticed that the elements are numbered from 0 to 9 instead of 1 to 10. Numbering elements beginning with 0 is a C convention. This means that in storage, the example array `numbers` looks like **Figure 7.3**.

Introduction to Arrays and Pointers

Element number	0	1	2	3	4	5	6	7	8	9
Contents	8	5	9	0	0	2	4	6	0	0

Figure 7.3 Contents of Array `numbers`

In an array of ten items then, the elements are numbered 0 to 9. An array of five items would be numbered from 0 to 4.

To reference an element of an array in C, you give the array name and the location of the item you want. To pull out the number in the first cell of the array `numbers`, you would refer to location 0. To get to the number in the last cell, you refer to location 9. For example,

```
i = numbers[9];   /* assign to i the last element */
                  /* of the array "numbers" */
```

When you enclose a specific cell or element number in brackets, that number is known as an **array subscript**. Using subscripts allows you to get to a particular element in the array. (Subscripts are discussed further in **Using Subscripts** below.)

Once you have located the cell you want, you will most likely want to do something with the contents of that cell. So, you will usually use an array reference as part of a larger expression, such as an assignment statement. For example:

```
int value;
int numbers[10];    /* array declaration */
    .
    .               /* code to initialize array */
    .
value = numbers[0];  /* assignment */
value = numbers[9];
```

In the first assignment statement, `value` will equal 8, which is the value of the number contained in the first array cell (subscript 0). After the second assignment statement, `value` will equal 0, which is the number in the last array cell (subscript 9).

Inside Information

In this chapter, the discussion of arrays is limited to arrays that are composed of a row of cells. These arrays have only one dimension, *length*. Sometimes these arrays are known as **vectors**. You can also have arrays with rows and columns. These are called two-dimensional arrays. You will use multidimensional arrays in later chapters.

Chapter 7

Initializing Arrays

You can use arrays for various purposes, such as holding data items temporarily or storing data to be used throughout the program. If you want to store the items in an array, you need to be able to **initialize** the array by putting data in the array elements.

How and whether you can initialize an array depends on how storage for the array is defined or where it is defined. How storage is defined is discussed in Chapter 10. For now, where the array is defined in your program is important. Global arrays, which are declared outside `main()` or any other function, can be initialized. Some compilers also permit the initialization of local arrays, but others do not (check your compiler documentation). Global arrays are automatically initialized to zero. Local arrays contain whatever is sitting in storage where they are, which is usually garbage. But if you need specific values, you can initialize global numeric arrays as follows:

```
int months[12] = {1,2,3,4,5,6,7,8,9,10,11,12};
main()
{
    /* month elements can now be used in main() and other functions */
}
```

The first line is the initialization part of the array definition, which consists of a list of numbers separated by commas and coded between a set of braces. From the definition above, the compiler will assume that the array has twelve elements (numbered 0 through 11) containing the numbers 1 through 12, respectively.

Arrays that are declared as holding character data can be initialized in two ways. The first method is to initialize the array as an *array of characters*, for example,

```
char name[]= { 'h','a','w','k','\0'}; /* long way */
```

The second method is to initialize the array as a *string constant*. An example of this shorter method is as follows:

```
char name[] = "hawk";    /* short way */
```

Note that the array length defaults to the number of elements you define. In other words, the compiler can determine the size of an array from the initialization. Note also that by using the first method (array of characters), you define an array of characters, one by one. With the second method (string constant), the array of characters becomes a string that can be manipulated in its entirety. In the string constant form, a null character, '\0', is automatically added.

If you want to initialize a text string the short way and the string contains double quotes, you can precede the double quotes with a backslash so the compiler knows that these quotes do not mean the end of the string. For example:

```
char string[] = "he said \"yes \""
```

Unless your program makes a change to a globally-defined array, the elements remain as they were assigned. Local arrays within functions are treated as any other local variable. They are declared, initialized, and remain available only for the life of the function.

Introduction to Arrays and Pointers

Inside Information

Most C compilers define, in a standard header file, a constant called null. Null, or '\0', is a character constant that stands for actual numeric zero. (The ASCII character set code for 0 is 48.) This special null character has many uses in C. Here it is used to provide a way to mark the end of a string.

Using Subscripts

In defining an array, a number enclosed in the brackets refers to the number of items in the array. In using the array, the value in brackets (the subscript) indicates the position of a particular element in the array. For example, suppose you were building a program that deals with freight trains in some way (perhaps keeping track of the inventory of each boxcar). You may have an array named `train`. The array elements would be the engine and boxcars. `train` could be defined as:

```
int train [10];
```

The array `train` has 10 integer elements (or cells), where the engine and the boxcars represent elements 0 through 9 (10 altogether). The value of an element (`train [6]`, for example) equals the amount of freight in a boxcar. (`train [0]`, of course, is the engine, which probably carries no freight.)

To initialize the array and figure out which number is in cell 5, try this:

```
#include <stdio.h>

int train[10] = {10, 20, 30, 40, 50, 60, 70, 80, 90, 100};

int main()
{
int boxcar = 0;

printf("Enter boxcars 0-9,  99 to quit\n");

while ((boxcar = getnum()) != 99)
{
 printf("Boxcar %d contains %d\n",boxcar,train[boxcar]);
}

return 0;
}

getnum()
{
char buff[80];
gets( buff );
return(atoi(buff));
}
```

Chapter 7

Your output should look like this:

```
Enter boxcars 0-9, 99 to quit

5                         (you enter a 5)

Boxcar 5 contains 60      (response)
```

Note that boxcar 0 contains 10, that is, the initial or starting element of the array contains the value "10".

Code that checks the value returned by `getnum( )` to be sure it is 0 - 9 or 99 was purposely not provided. Try this example entering a number that is not within that range and see what happens. You will find that C does not care if your request was reasonable and returns whatever happens to be in storage. This will be explained shortly.

You can use increment and decrement operators with integer variables to work your way progressively through an array. The following example uses code to copy one string to another.

```
#include <stdio.h>

char string1[100];     /* declare two character arrays */
char string2[100];

int main()
{

int index = 0;         /* start at the beginning of arrays */

printf("Enter a line and it will be copied: \n");

gets(string1);
printf("\nString 1 contains: %s\n", string1);

 while (string1[index] != '\0')
   {
    string2[index] = string1[index];   /* copy a single element */
    ++index;                /* move index to next element */
   }

string2[index] = '\0';
printf("String 2 now contains: %s\n", string2);
printf("%d elements copied plus '\0'\n", index);

return 0;
}
```

Introduction to Arrays and Pointers

Here is another example that takes a lowercase string and prints an uppercase version.

```c
/* Print a string from lower to upper character: array version */

#include <stdio.h>              /* try also using getchar() */
#include <ctype.h>

char lower[] = "contents";

int main()
{
 int i;
 puts(lower);

 for (i = 0; lower[i] != '\0'; i++)
     lower [i] = toupper (lower [i]);

 puts(lower);

 return 0;
}
```

Before executing the loop, the array `lower` contains the following:

'c' 'o' 'n' 't' 'e' 'n' 't' 's' '\0'

After the loop, `lower` contains this:

'C' 'O' 'N' 'T' 'E' 'N' 'T' 'S' '\0'

As was mentioned earlier, arrays can be any valid C type. Recall that the memory size of a variable is determined by its type. An `int` type on most machines is two bytes, and `char` is one byte. Values in an array are stored contiguously in memory. Fortunately, C keeps up with size for you; in other words, C knows to move two bytes to find the next `int` element.

C does not, however, keep track of subscripts in terms of the maximum number of array elements specified. You are responsible for being sure that you don't request an item greater than the last element number in your array. For example, as you saw in the boxcar program, if you entered a 10, nothing stopped C from going past the end of the array and into the next space in storage.

More About Text Strings

Strings are special cases of character arrays. A string is a constant like "hello world" or a character buffer filled with a string. Each array element contains one character of the string. The last element contains the null character '\0' to mark the end of the string.

Chapter 7

In memory as a text string, the word "express" looks like this:

| e | x | p | r | e | s | s | \0 |

Suppose you have defined strings like those given above, and now you want to perform some basic operations on them. For example, you may read a string from the keyboard into an array using the `gets` function discussed in Chapter 5. Once you read in the string, you may want to know exactly how long it is to determine, for example, if the string used all the space you allowed for it. You might also want to copy the string elsewhere. To handle these and other common string manipulations, your C library provides a number of handy string functions, which are usually contained in a header file called `string.h` (or something similar; check to be sure).

Some of the more common and useful string functions are

> `strlen`   find out the string length
> `strcpy`   copy string characters
> `strcat`   concatenate two strings
> `strcmp`   compare two strings

The `strlen` function returns the number of non-null characters. For example,

```
char train[] = "express";
strlen(train);
```

would return a 7. (Remember that `train` is a character array and the total size is 8, counting the ending null character.)

Inside Information

If you coded `sizeof(train)`, the value returned is 8 because the terminating null is counted. Anytime you initialize a character array with a string constant, the `sizeof()` operator returns a value one unit larger than indicated by `strlen`.

The `strcpy` function copies one array of characters into another. It is your job to be sure the receiving array is large enough. For example:

```
char train[40] ;
strcpy(train, "midnight");
```

Here, the string "midnight" is copied into the character array `train`.

`strcat` concatenates one character array to the end of another. For example,

```
strcat(train, "rider");
```

Introduction to Arrays and Pointers

tacks the text string "rider" onto the end of the text string contained in the array `train`. The result looks like this:

| m | i | d | n | i | g | h | t | | r | i | d | e | r | ... |

The function `strcmp` returns a value giving the results of comparing two strings based on the sorting sequence of their characters (remember the ASCII character set). The strings are compared on a character by character basis. The result is negative if one string would sort lower than the other, zero if there is no difference, and positive if one string would sort higher than the other. For example:

```
result = strcmp("aa", "zz");     /* "aa" < "zz", result negative */
result = strcmp("zz", "aa");     /* "zz" > "aa", result positive */
result = strcmp("abc", "abc");   /* equal, result is zero */
```

You can print the results of string functions by using the `%s` format in `printf()`. For example,

```
printf("String is: %s\n", string);
```

Notice that you use the array name as the name of the string to be printed.

These functions are illustrated in the following program:

```
#include <stdio.h>
#include <string.h>             /* needed for string functions */

char string[40];                /* array to hold 39 char. + NULL */
char string1[] = "midnight";    /* string array */
char string2[] = " train";      /* string array */

int main()
{
    int result = 0;             /* to hold function return values */

    result = strcmp(string1, string2);
    printf("Compare result is: %d \n", result);     /* compare */

    strcpy(string, string1);                         /* copy */
    printf("String is: %s \n", string);

    strcat(string, string2);                         /* concatenate */
    printf("String is: %s \n", string);

    result = strlen(string);                         /* length */
    printf("Total string length is: %d \n", result);

    return(0);

}
```

157

Chapter 7

The results look like this:

```
Compare result is: 77
String is: midnight
String is: midnight train
Total string length is 14
```

If you were going to use `strcmp` to decide how to sort the two strings "midnight" and "train," a negative value (returned by `strcmp`) means that the first string would precede the second (alphabetically). A positive number means that the second string would precede the first, alphabetically. The result of the `strcpy` example is that `string1` "midnight" is copied into the `string` array. `strcat` concatenates the string "train" onto the string "midnight," giving a total string length in `string` of 14.

Module 15 Summary

In this section you learned how variables having multiple values can be stored as arrays. You also learned how to define and use simple integer and character arrays.

New C Tools

Concepts	Code
array	subscripting
subscript	text string functions
character arrays and strings	

Module 16: An Introduction to Pointers

This module introduces the pointer, one of the key elements of the C language. Pointers and pointer operations work with the storage addresses of data items. Pointers provide you with another way to reference and work with variables and arrays. In Chapter 10, you will see that by using pointers, you can also work with more complex objects, performing many programming operations more simply than would otherwise be possible.

Keywords you need to note are

- **pointer**
- **variable address**
- **indirection operator**
- **address operator**
- **memory address**
- **pointer arithmetic**

Introduction to Arrays and Pointers

Getting to Know Pointers

When you visit your neighborhood post office, you usually see a section containing individual post office boxes. Each box has a unique number identifying it. You could think of a row of boxes as an array, and choose one relative to its distance from the first box in the row. For example, when the postmaster assigns you your box, he could say, "You have the third box from the left on the fifth row." A better way would be to identify a post office box by a number or *address* that points you directly to the box you want. For example, "You have box number 53." This way you can access any box just by knowing the address. Unlike arrays, you do not need to know the position of the box relative to other boxes.

You can think of computer memory as a set of post office boxes. In **Module 15,** you learned how to handle rows of boxes using arrays. You can even pick out one box by using array subscripts. But, C makes it even easier for you to handle locations in storage. You can *point* to a specific location using another type of C variable called a **pointer.**

Suppose you are looking at the first row of post office boxes, 1-10. (It's a small town.) You have declared this row as an array as follows.

    char boxes[10];

You now know that in storage this looks like

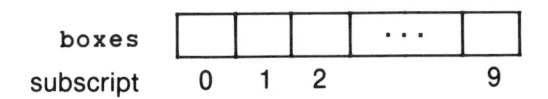

```
boxes     [   ][   ][   ] . . . [   ]
subscript   0    1    2          9
```

This row exists somewhere in computer memory. You know that the computer contains millions of addressable bytes. Assume that this row is in bytes 10001 to 10010, which means the address of the first byte is 10001.

```
address   10001  10002  10003         10010
boxes     [    ][     ][     ] . . . [     ]
subscript    0      1      2             9
```

You can declare a variable called **box_ptr** (to mean "box pointer"), and assign the address of the initial box to it. This variable then becomes a pointer to that box, allowing you to access the contents or value at that location by pointing to the initial box via its address. To do this, you need to know how to declare a pointer and how to use some new operators.

Chapter 7

Declaring Pointers and Using Pointer Operators

The first new operator is the *****. You have seen the ***** symbol used previously for multiplication. In the context of pointer operations, however, the ***** acts as a unary operator instead of the binary version used in multiplication. The ***** is called the **indirection operator,** and it will be used first in declaring pointer variables.

C pointers are declared to point to a specific data type. The form of a pointer declaration is

   type ******ptr_name*;

where *type* is a valid C data type, and ***** denotes a pointer variable follows. (Short names that use the letter **p** or the term **ptr** are helpful identifiers.) The following are all valid pointer declarations:

```
int *p1;        /* the object pointed to by p1 is an int */
char *name;     /* the object pointed to by name is a char */
long *calc_ptr; /* the object pointed to by calc_ptr is a long */
short *unit;    /* the object pointed to by unit is a short */
```

The pointer declaration tells you two things: that the variable is, in fact, a pointer and the object pointed to is of the specified type. So the declaration,

   `char *name;`

means that **name** is a pointer to type **char**. In other words, **name** points to character data. The declaration

   `int *box_ptr;`

means that **box_ptr** is a pointer to type **int**, which means that **box_ptr** points to integer data.

The C **address operator** **&** produces the address of a variable. To use this address, you declare a pointer variable. The pointer gets the address with an assignment statement. Here is how it looks:

   `box_ptr = &boxes[0];`

Since **boxes** is an array, and **boxes[0]** is its initial element, the **&** operator produces the address of **boxes[0]**. Unless otherwise specified, the address of an array is the address of the first element. This address is then assigned to **box_ptr**.

You want to get the address of the box (using **&**) so you can use the contents of the box. To get the contents, you need to use the indirection operator *****. Once you know the address of a box, to retrieve the value, you use the ***** with the pointer variable to produce the value stored at a particular address. The C statement to assign the *value* stored at an address to a variable is as follows:

   `box_value = *box_ptr;`

This statement means, "assign the value of the object pointed to by **box_ptr** to **box_value**." Here you can see why the ***** is called an *indirection* operator because it means "the object pointed to by . . . ." In other words, the pointer name is not the

160

Introduction to Arrays and Pointers

name of the object. Rather, the name indirectly leads you to the object by giving you the object's address.

To summarize, the indirection operator * has two uses: to declare a pointer and in an indirection operation.

Look at the whole process once more. Suppose your compiler has assigned a storage location to the first element of the array `boxes` at location 10001. The statement

```
box_ptr = &boxes[0];
```

assigns the storage location value 10001 to `box_ptr`. To use the value stored at that address, the statement

```
box_value = *box_ptr;
```

retrieves the *value* stored at location 10001, say 10, and assigns that value to the variable `box_value`.

Notice that the following two statements mean the same thing in our example.

```
box_value = *box_ptr;
```

```
box_value = boxes[0];
```

This is because for any variable, for example, `prize`, the expressions

```
prize
```

and

```
*&prize
```

refer to the same object in storage. This may seem confusing at first, but it is easy to understand if you remember that

```
&prize
```

means "the address of the variable `prize`" while * means "the object pointed to by . . . ." (Remember that you can think of an address as *pointing to* an area of memory.) Then,

```
*&prize
```

means the object pointed to by the address of `prize` or just the object at the address of `prize`. Of course, what object is at `prize`'s address? Just `prize` itself! So, you have discovered that

```
prize == *&prize;
```

is always true.

Chapter 7

The process works the same with other variables. The address of a non-array variable (or scalar) is the address of that item in storage. Here is one more example using two integer variables **x** and **y**.

```
x = 10;         /* assign starting value of 10 to x */
x_ptr = &x;     /* assign the address of x to pointer x_ptr */
x = x + 10;     /* add 10 to x, x now contains the value 20 */
y = *x_ptr;     /* assign the VALUE stored at x's address to the variable y */
```

This is what happens in memory.

1.   x = 10; y=0;   x : | 10 |
2.   x_ptr = &x;   (10012)   .
                                        .

                                    y : | 0 |
                                    (10016)

                                    x_ptr : |10012|

3.   x = x + 10;   x : | 20 |
                            (10012) .

                                    y : | 0 |
                                    (10016)

                                  x_ptr : |10012|

4.   y = *x_ptr;   x : | 20 |
                            (10012) .

                                  y : | 20 |
                                  (10016)

                                x_ptr : |10012|

To begin with, **x**, at address 10012 in memory, contains the value 10. The pointer variable **x_ptr** is assigned the address of the variable **x**, which is 10012. At this point the variable **y** contains 0. In statement 4, 10 is added to **x** making the value now contained in **x**, 20. **y** and **x_ptr** are unchanged. In the last statement, **y** is given the value stored at the address of **x**, which is 20.

In this introduction, you have learned that you can locate and work with variable values by using storage addresses and pointers. In the next section, you will learn how to define pointers to different types of variables and how to use pointers with arrays and other types of variables.

Introduction to Arrays and Pointers

Using Pointers

Before continuing, now that you know what a pointer is you may be wondering why it is such a desirable C tool.

Pointers are used in many C applications. A primary reason to use pointers is that, once you get used to them, your C code can become much cleaner and efficient. For example, using pointers is a more succinct way of writing code to deal with C storage objects such as arrays. Your code is more efficient because instructions using pointers are closer to the way the computer handles things (via instructions involving addresses at the machine level).

There will be many times that you will want to work with an object's address in C. Recall that in C there are many types of storage objects, and only about two-thirds of them have been covered. With more complex objects, pointers become a convenient way to refer to the object in an expression. Pointers are also needed to create some of the more complex C objects.

Finally, in working with functions, pointers enable you to simulate *call by reference*. (Remember C is a *call by value* language as explained in Chapter 6.) By passing functions pointers to variables, you can change the actual value of the variable instead of just working with a copy.

In summary then, there are three basic reasons to use pointers in C:

- to write tighter, faster code.
- to construct and use complex objects in storage (such as structures and the linked lists introduced in Chapter 10).
- to achieve the effect of call by reference.

Even though arrays and subscripts may be more familiar, you will find it easier to refer to objects in storage (including arrays) when you use pointers. Actually, behind the scenes, your compiler converts and conducts array operations in terms of pointers anyway because pointers move around in storage faster. In your C programs, pointers mean faster and more efficient code.

Looping Through Arrays Using Pointers You can use pointer increment and decrement operators to move a pointer through an array. For example, suppose you have declared the following array and pointer:

```
char letters[4];
char *ptr;
```

Chapter 7

you can put something into the array like this,

```
ptr = &letters[0];   /* equivalent to: ptr = letters */
                     /* -more on array names and pointers soon */

*ptr = 'b';          /* assign the letter 'b' to object pointed to by ptr */

ptr = ptr + 1;       /* add 1, ptr points to next */
                     /* element in letters[] */

*ptr = 'o';
ptr = ptr + 1;       /* repeat process */
*ptr = 'x';
ptr = ptr + 1;
*ptr = '\0';         /* signal end of array with null */
```

The array **letters** now looks as follows:

| b | o | x | \0 |

You could shorten this example by using the following code:

```
ptr = letters;
*ptr++ = 'b';
*ptr++ = 'o';
*ptr++ = 'x';
*ptr   = '\0';
```

Here ***ptr++ = 'b';** means store the character **b** at the address pointed to by **ptr** and then increment **ptr** by one. This statement is equivalent to any of the following:

```
*ptr = 'b';
ptr++;
```

or

```
*ptr = 'b';
ptr += 1;
```

or

```
*ptr = 'b';
ptr = ptr + 1;
```

Introduction to Arrays and Pointers

The way in which memory would change as this code executes is shown below:

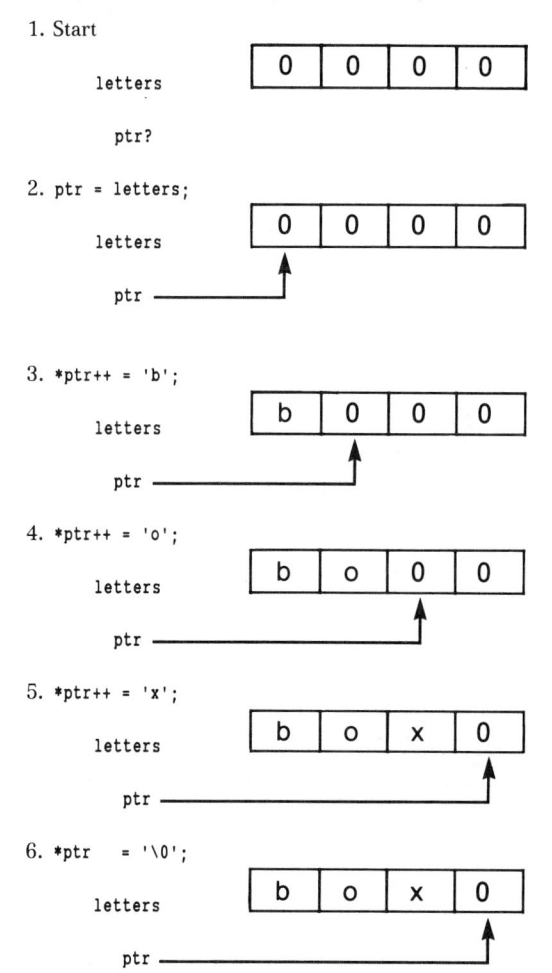

1. Start

    letters | 0 | 0 | 0 | 0 |

    ptr?

2. ptr = letters;

    letters | 0 | 0 | 0 | 0 |
    ptr ─────────↑

3. *ptr++ = 'b';

    letters | b | 0 | 0 | 0 |
    ptr ─────────────↑

4. *ptr++ = 'o';

    letters | b | o | 0 | 0 |
    ptr ─────────────────↑

5. *ptr++ = 'x';

    letters | b | o | x | 0 |
    ptr ─────────────────────↑

6. *ptr = '\0';

    letters | b | o | x | 0 |
    ptr ─────────────────────↑

Chapter 7

Assuming that the array `letters` contains the string "box", you could retrieve each individual letter by doing this:

```
char letters[4];
char *ptr;
char letter;
    .
    .
    .
ptr = letters;      or      ptr = &letters[0];

letter = *ptr;  /* letter = value of initial element, 'b' */
++ptr;
letter = *ptr;  /* letter now has the next value, 'o' */
    .
    .
    .
/* Process continues */
```

As shown above, pointer values have been incremented. (You can also decrement them.) Note, however, that the value of a pointer is not an integer, but a **memory address**. When you move from one memory address to another, your C compiler automatically keeps track of whether it needs to move two bytes (to the next integer) or one byte (to the next character). This means that **pointer arithmetic** involves locations automatically computed in the appropriate number of storage units. You only need to be concerned with where you move the pointer and not the details involved in how it gets there.

In review, you change the location of a pointer by using the C increment and decrement operators introduced earlier: ++ and --. To assign a value to `box_value`, and then move to the next value of `boxes`, for example, you would code

```
box_value = *box_ptr++;
```

You could also write

```
box_value = *++box_ptr;
```

The latter, however, would have a different effect. It would first increment the pointer, and then assign what is pointed to as the value of `box_value`. As in loop processing, whether you increment before or after depends on whether you want to move the pointer before or after the expression it is used in is evaluated.

Arrays and Pointers   In many contexts, an array name is treated as a pointer to the first element in the array. In other words, the value of an unsubscripted array name is considered to be the address of the initial element of the array. The following statements are the same:

```
box_ptr = &boxcars[0];
box_ptr = boxcars;       /* boxcars with no subscript
                            means the first element */
```

Remember that, even after this assignment, `sizeof(box_ptr)` and `sizeof(boxcars)` will have different values. `sizeof(box_ptr)` will be the size of a pointer, which is machine-dependent, while `sizeof(boxcars)` will be the size (in bytes) of the entire `boxcars` array.

To assign the address of the first element in an array to a pointer, you can code

```
box_ptr = boxcars;
```

To assign the address of any element of the array, you can code

```
box_ptr = &boxcar[2];
```

which gives the address of the second element.

You can also use the subscript operator and the indirection operator on both arrays and pointers. The following are the same:

```
boxcar[2]      (and)     *(boxcar + 2)

box_ptr[2]     (and)     *(box_ptr + 2)
```

In the last case, if you use a subscript on a pointer, it means to refer to the value located at that address plus the subscript (recall the earlier discussion of pointer arithmetic).

Pointers, Arrays, and Functions In Chapter 6, it was mentioned that there is a way to return more than one value from a function. You can do so by using a pointer to an array. You pass the address of an array to the function when the function is called. In C, you cannot pass an array as a function argument, but you can pass its address or (equivalently) a pointer to the array. (Recall that the value of an unsubscripted array name is the address of the first element of that array.)

In C, passing the address of the first element of an array is one of the most important uses of a pointer. Here is an example:

```
/* Pass arrays to function converting lower to uppercase (pointer version) */

#include <stdio.h>
#include <ctype.h>

char lower[] = "contents";
char upper[20];

int main()
{
puts(lower);          /* passes address of array to puts() */
convert(lower, upper); /* passes addresses of arrays to convert() */
puts(upper);          /* passes address of array to puts() */

return 0;
}
```

Chapter 7

```
convert(lower, upper)
char *lower, *upper;
{
int i;
for (i = 0; *(lower + i) != '\0'; i++)
    upper[i] = toupper (lower[i]);
}
```

The following is another example of pointers and functions using the **xchange** function introduced in Chapter 6. Note that because you are pointing to the location of the variable in storage, this version actually exchanges the caller's values. Using pointers with functions in this way simulates call by reference in C. (Refer to Chapter 6 for a review of call by reference versus call by value.)

```
/*  xchange function using pointers */

#include <stdio.h>

int main()
{
int loc = 1;
int shell1 = 1;
int shell2 = 2;

int *s1, *s2;       /* declare two pointers to integers */

printf("Pea is under shell %d\n", loc);
printf("shell1=%d, shell2=%d\n", shell1, shell2);

s1 = &shell1; /* set s1 to point to the int variable shell1 */
s2 = &shell2; /* set s2 to point to the int variable shell2 */

loc = xchange(s1, s2); /* call xchange function    */
                       /* pass pointer variables s1 and s2 */

printf("Pea now under shell %d\n", loc);
printf("shell1=%d, shell2=%d\n", shell1, shell2);

return 0;
}

xchange(p1, p2) /* exchange function parameters */
           /* declared as pointers     */
int *p1, *p2;  /* to integers    */
{
  int temp;     /* variable to hold exchanged value */

  temp = *p1;  /* assign VALUE in variable pointed */
               /* to by p1 to temp  */
```

Introduction to Arrays and Pointers

```
    *p1 = *p2;    /* assign value in variable pointed */
                  /* to by p2 to variable */
                  /* pointed to by p1 */

    *p2 = temp;   /* assign value in temp to variable */
                  /* pointed to by p2 */

    return *p1;   /* return value in variable pointed to by p1 */

}
```

Differences Between Arrays and Pointers Consider these two declarations:

```
char measure[] = "apounce to zzzzz";
char *units    = "apounce to zzzzz";
```

Earlier it was noted that an array name frequently means the same thing as a pointer variable containing the address of the initial array element. There is a difference between the two, however. The array name denotes an array in memory, and its value cannot be modified because that would imply changing the location of the array. A pointer variable, on the other hand, denotes an address (which *may* be a place in memory where an array starts).

You can see the difference by using the `sizeof` operator:

```
sizeof(units)    == 2
sizeof(measure)  == 17
```

The pointer `units` equals 2 because on most systems, the size of a pointer variable is two bytes. The array `measure` equals 17 because that is the total string length (including the terminating null character).

Another important difference is that you cannot code

```
measure = units;   /* WRONG */
```

because you need a variable name on the left side of the assignment. An array name is not considered a variable in C. What can appear on the left side of the assignment is described in a later chapter. For now, keep in mind that this assignment is incorrect because the name of an array is not a variable, but the names of its elements are.

Arrays of Pointers You can also declare an array that contains nothing but pointers. For example:

```
char *units[5];
```

means that `units` is an array of five pointers to characters. Arrays of pointers are often used to handle tables. The declaration above could be defined further as

```
char *units[] = {"oz", "lbs", "sec", "min", NULL};
```

Chapter 7

The NULL entry is used here to end the table. NULL is equivalent to 0. A NULL pointer does not point to anything. (When NULL is used to refer to a pointer, it is written in uppercase.) In storage this table might look like **Figure 7.4**.

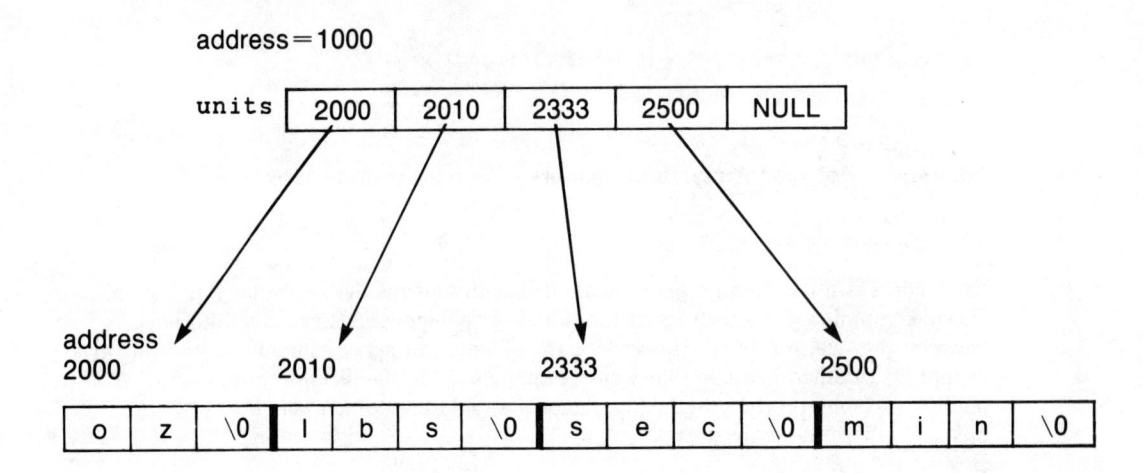

```
                address=1000

        units  | 2000 | 2010 | 2333 | 2500 | NULL |

address
2000              2010              2333              2500

| o | z | \0 | l | b | s | \0 | s | e | c | \0 | m | i | n | \0 |
```

Figure 7.4 An Array of Pointers

In this example, the initial element of the array `units` points to another array in storage beginning at address 2000. This array contains the text string "oz".

Inside Information

Pointers can also point to other pointers. This is called **double indirection**. For example:

    int **ptr; /* pointer to pointer to int */

You will see examples of this in Chapter 10 when you work with lists and other data structures.

Module 16 Summary

In this module, you learned how to use storage addresses and pointers to access variables. You learned how to declare pointers and how to use pointers with arrays and functions.

Introduction to Arrays and Pointers

New C Tools

Concepts	Code
pointers and storage addresses	indirection operator
	address operator
arrays of pointers	
memory address	
pointer arithmetic	

Converting Units of Measure

To conclude this chapter, you will work with a program that converts units of measure. For example, you can convert pounds to ounces or decades to days. When you run the program, you are prompted for a unit to convert *from* and a unit to convert *to*. The program accesses three tables to check for unit compatibility and conversion factors. The program then performs the requested conversion and displays the results.

Read over the following code and then run the program. See if you can get a sense of what is happening on your own. A detailed discussion follows the example, so do not get discouraged if you encounter some things that are unclear the first time through.

```
/* Units Conversion Program */

#include <stdio.h>
#include <ctype.h>
#include <math.h>

/* Use the preprocessor to define Boolean values. */

#define FALSE    0
#define TRUE     !FALSE


#include "table.c"

/* This include statement pulls in the three tables used in the
   conversion routine.  These tables are:
        unit_name: array of pointers to common unit names
                such as "acre" or "yr"
        conversion_factor:  an array of standard unit values
                corresponding to each unit name.  The unit values
                equal whatever the usual unit of measurement is
                for that unit name.  For example, the unit value
                for "minutes" would be "sec" (seconds).
        standard_unit: an array of pointers to text strings naming
                the standard unit appropriate for each unit_name. */
```

171

Chapter 7

```c
/* Find number of entries in the conversion_factor array
   by dividing the total number of bytes in the array by
   the number of bytes used for each element. */

int    num_units = sizeof( conversion_factor ) / sizeof( double );

/* Function prototypes */

char *get_word( char * );
int  find_unit( char * );
char *fget_word( char *, FILE * );

int main()
{
   int   mult_factor;     /* factor to convert from unit to standard */
   int   div_factor;      /* factor to convert standard to
                              wanted unit */
   char  from_unit[32];   /* name of unit to convert from */
   char  to_unit[32];     /* name of unit to convert to */
   int   done = FALSE;    /* Main loop termination flag */

 puts( "\n\nWelcome to the Handy-Home unit conversion master.\n" );
 puts( "I will try and convert almost any unit you can think of \n");
 puts( "to any other unit you would like. \n");
 puts( "After this brief introduction, you will be asked to enter" );
 puts( "the conversion you wish to perform.  You will be prompted" );
 puts( "for a from unit and a to unit.  If I can't find either unit");
 puts( "I will print a message saying so, and start over." );
 puts( "\nUnit names must be singular, and one word. \n");
 puts( "Enter EOF to end.\n");

   /* M A I N   L O O P */

   while ( !done )

   /* The while loop continues to prompt the user for a unit
      to convert from and to, until the user decides to stop
      by specifying End of File. */

      {
```

```
/* Prompt for from_unit and get value to be converted. */
   If EOF exit the program */

printf( "Convert from :  " );
if ( get_word( from_unit ) == NULL )
    {
    /* If the user entered NULL character
       then exit the program */
    done = TRUE;
    break;
    }

/* Look up the requested unit, and get the index of the unit
   in the tables. */

mult_factor = find_unit( from_unit ); /* get index of unit to */
if ( mult_factor == 0 )               /* be converted  from */
    {
    printf( "Can't find unit <%s>\n", from_unit );
    continue;
    }


/* Prompt for to_unit and get the value to be converted to. */

printf( "Convert to :  " );
if ( get_word( to_unit ) == NULL )
    {
    /* If the user entered NULL character
       then exit the program. */
    done = TRUE;
    break;
    }


/* Get index of unit to be converted to. */

div_factor = find_unit( to_unit );
if ( div_factor == 0 )
    {
    printf( "Can't find unit <%s>\n", to_unit );
    continue;
    }
```

Chapter 7

```
        /* Make sure that both units specified can be converted to
           the same standard unit by comparing text with strcmp(). */

        if ( strcmp( standard_unit[mult_factor], standard_unit [div_factor]))
           {
           printf( "Units are not compatible.\n" );
           }

        /*  If the units are compatible, then proceed with the
            conversion.  The conversion process works as follows.
            Tell the user what the conversion factor is.  The
            conversion factor is derived by first converting a user's
            from_unit to a standard unit.  This number is just
            obtained by reading the appropriate conversion factor
            for that number from the table.  This number is then
            divided by the conversion factor for the to_unit.  This
            converts the standard unit back into the user's to_unit. */

        else
           {
           printf( "Multiply a %s by %g to obtain %s.\n",
                    unit_name[mult_factor],
                    conversion_factor[mult_factor] /
                    conversion_factor[div_factor],
                    unit_name[div_factor] );
           }
        }

   return 0;
   }


/* get_word - return a word from the stdin file.
   This routine simply calls fget_word with stdin as the file
   parameter. */

char *get_word( buffer )
char *buffer;      /* pointer to buffer for word */
   {
   return( fget_word( buffer, stdin ) );
   }
```

Introduction to Arrays and Pointers

```c
/* find_unit - use a simple loop to search the input table for the
       named unit, returning the index of the entry if found and 0
       if not in table. */

find_unit( unit )
char *unit;         /* Pointer to unit name to search for */
{
  int  i;   /* Index of the table entry --the "number" of the array
               element that is found. */

  for ( i = 0; i < num_units; i++ )
     {
     if ( !strcmp( unit, unit_name[i] ) )  /* unit_name is a global */
        {                                  /* variable from the */
        return( i );                       /* header file table.c */
        }
     }

  return( 0 );
}


/*  fget_word - read a word from the specified file.
       Returns NULL on EOF condition. */

char *fget_word( buff, file )
char *buff;         /* pointer to storage for word */

/* file is a pointer to data type FILE,
   in this case, stdin - more on FILE
   in Chapter 10. */

FILE *file;     /* pointer to file to get input from */
{
  char *ptr = buff;
  int   ch;

  /* While reading spaces, ignore them. */

  while ( isspace( ch = fgetc( file ) ) )
      ;

  /* Check to see if we are at end-of-file. */

  if ( ch == EOF )
     {
     *ptr = '\0';
     return( NULL );
     }
```

175

Chapter 7

```
    /* Save the character just read. */

    *ptr++ = ch;

    /* While reading non-space characters, add them to the buffer. */

    while ( !isspace( ch = fgetc( file ) ) && ( ch != EOF ) )
       {
       *ptr++ = ch;
       }

    /* Terminate the string with an end-of-string marker. */

    *ptr = '\0';
    return( buff );
    }
```

A Closer Look

This example shows you how you can combine pointers, arrays, and functions to code a units conversion program efficiently. The program uses three tables to compare the *from* and *to* unit names, ensure that they are compatible, and then convert using a conversion factor. (You will learn later that arrays can be used to work with tables.) The three tables are included at the beginning of the program in a source file called **table.c**. These tables look like this:

```
char *unit_name[] = {      /* Array of pointers to character */
       "acre",             /* Each string is the name of a   */
       "angstrom",         /* unit of measure. */
          .
          .
          .
       "yr" };


double conversion_factor[] = {     /* Array of doubles */
       4046.86,             /* Common conversion factor */
       1e-10,               /* between like units. */
          .
          .
          .
       3.15569e+07 };


char *standard_unit[] = { /* Array of pointers to character */
       "m2",               /* Each string is the name of a  */
       "m",                /* standard unit                 */
          .
          .
          .
       "sec" };
```

176

Introduction to Arrays and Pointers

The following functions are involved:

```
main()          /* control the conversion process loop */
get_word()      /* calls fget_word using stdin */
find_unit()     /* search for name in unit_name table, if */
                /* name is found return the index where name */
                /* is located */
fget_word()     /* read a word (unit name) from specified file */
```

The program works like this:

1. Prompt user for unit to convert from (from_unit).
   Call find_unit().
      find_unit() searches the unit_name table and returns
      the location (i = index) of the from_unit name.
      assign this index to mult_factor .

2. Prompt user for the unit to convert to (to_unit).
   Call find_unit().
      find_unit() searches the unit_name table and returns
      the location (i = index) of the to_unit name.
      assign this index to div_factor.

3. Make sure both from and to units are compatible (that is,
   you cannot convert feet to ounces).
   Use strcmp() to do this.

4. If the units are compatible, proceed with the conversion.

For example, if you convert days to decades, you get the following results:

```
Convert from : day
Convert to : decade
Multiply a day by 2.73791e-04 to obtain a decade.

Convert from : decade
Convert to : day
Multiply a decade by 3652.42 to obtain a day.
```

This conversion is accomplished as follows. **Day** is located at element 35 in the **unit_name** array. **Decade** is located at element 36. So **find_unit** assigns 35 to **mult_factor** and 36 to **div_factor**. The standard unit is **sec** for both **from** and **to** units. You find this by looking up entries 35 and 36 in the **standard_unit** table. Both entries use "sec" (seconds) for their standard units. In the **conversion_factor** table, the conversion factor for the **day** is 86400. The conversion factor for **decade** is 3.15569e+08. Dividing **day** by **decade** gives the appropriate amount for converting days to decades, or 2.73791-04.

Look at the arrays in **table.c** and play with the program until you are sure you understand the code involved.

Chapter 7

Program Notes

Note the quotation marks around `"table.c"`. In the `include` statement, the reason for quotation marks is that this file is not a standard `include` file. Typically <> are used to set off standard header files. A compiler looks in a different place for standard header files than for files set `off by " "`. (If you are using the compiler provided with this tutorial, see Part II, the User's Guide.)

Chapter Summary

In this chapter, you learned about arrays as well as pointers (one of the most powerful features of C). You learned how to use pointers with arrays and functions. In the example, you put everything together to produce a compact and efficient units conversion program. Now you have covered most of the C basics in terms of defining and using data and C functions. You are ready to go on to more advanced parts of the tutorial where you will learn even more about the world of C.

Chapter 8
Expanding the Basics: More on Operators and Types

Chapter 8

CONTENTS

Introduction	181
Module 17: More Operators - Working with Bits	181
Bitwise Logical Operators	182
Inside Information	183
Setting Bits	183
Bitwise Shift Operators	186
Module 17 Summary	187
Module 18: More About Expressions	187
Assignment and lvalues	187
The Conditional Operator (?:)	189
The Comma Operator (,)	189
Module 18 Summary	190
Module 19: An Introduction to Advanced Data Types	191
The New Data Types: Enumerations, Structures, and Unions	192
Creating Your Own Names for Data Types - typedef	200
Converting Data Types	201
Module 19 Summary	203
The Calculator Program Revisited	203
A Closer Look	212
Chapter Summary	214

Expanding the Basics: More on Operators and Types

Introduction

In this chapter and those that follow, you are introduced to some of the more advanced features of C. You learn how to use these features in some interesting programming applications. In these chapters, you continue building the C foundation you established in Chapters 1 through 7. After working through the concepts and examples that follow, you will know how to perform many common programming tasks using C. You will also have a good idea of where you can go with more advanced applications.

Chapters 8 and 9 add to the basics by introducing topics such as bit manipulation and structures. In Chapter 10, you apply what you have learned as you build and use a data base to add to the C tools you developed in previous chapters. Chapter 11, the last chapter in the Tutorial, is similar to a help session. Some common programming mistakes are listed and discussed and information on making your programs more efficient and compatible with other C compilers is provided.

Do not worry about these areas being called advanced topics. You are building on what you already know, and you will find that these areas introduce a whole new world of very interesting C applications. So, take your time, and enjoy these remaining chapters.

As mentioned above, this chapter adds to the basics covered in earlier chapters. You will learn about the remaining C operators and data types. You will also learn more about expressions, assignment statements, and data type conversions. The following topics are covered:

- C operators for working with bits
- more about expressions
- introduction to advanced data types.

Module 17: More Operators - Working with Bits

In Chapter 2, you learned how the computer stores information in terms of bits, bytes, and words. You discovered that the position of a bit and whether it was *on* (1) or *off* (0) made it possible to represent numeric and character data. In this module, you learn about C operators that let you work with the individual bits in a byte.

You may be wondering why you would ever want to work at the bit level. In the course of everyday applications programming, you probably will not need to. But, if you are interested in learning how to write code to interact with I/O devices, working with computer sound and graphics, or conserving memory, you will want to know how to use C to work at the bit level. Because these applications (especially graphics) are compiler and operating system dependent, you will be introduced to some basic bit operations and applications. Then, you can take it from there by referring to the documentation for your particular system.

Chapter 8

Keywords you need to note are

bitwise logical operators	OR
flag	exclusive OR
hexadecimal	bitwise shift operators
bitwise negation operator	left shift operators
mask	right shift operator
AND	

Bitwise Logical Operators

C provides several operators that enable you to manipulate the bits in a byte. Recall that, for purposes of discussion, the bits in a byte can be represented like this:

bits								
bit position	7	6	5	4	3	2	1	0
2^{nth}	2^7	2^6	2^5	2^4	2^3	2^2	2^1	2^0
decimal value	128	64	32	16	8	4	2	1

Also, as discussed in Chapter 2, numbers are represented in the computer by the values associated with each bit position. For example, the following numbers are represented in memory, as shown:

Decimal number	Bit settings
0	0 0 0 0 0 0 0 0
3	0 0 0 0 0 1 1 0
255	1 1 1 1 1 1 1 1

Suppose you are writing a function, and you want to keep track of certain kinds of errors that might occur during the function's processing. When the function has completed, you want to print appropriate error messages, depending on which errors or combinations of errors occurred. You could do this by defining the variables `err1-err_n` to store *n* error numbers. You could, however, be more efficient in your use of memory and use each bit in a byte as a **flag** to represent a particular kind of mistake.

For example, bit position 1 could be turned on (set or toggled from 0 to 1) if division by zero was attempted (division by zero is undefined in algebra). Your function could then check this bit to see if any error had occurred and pass information about this error, and any others you had defined, to an error processing function. To help you do this, C provides logical bit operators that allow you to set and test bit positions. These operators and associated concepts are covered next.

182

Expanding the Basics: More on Operators and Types

Inside Information

In C programming, bit patterns are often represented using hexadecimal notation. Hexadecimal is an alternative notation for representing binary numbers. The word **hexadecimal** means *based on sixteen* or *base sixteen* (hexa (6) and deci (10)). The hexadecimal number system groups bits into units of four. Hexadecimal values include the ten decimal digits (0–9) and the letters A through F; A, B, C, D, E, and F represent the numbers 10 through 15, respectively. Hexadecimal constants are written in C with a "0x" prefix. Each number following the prefix represents the value contained in one set of four bits. For example, the number 1 looks like this:

```
0x01 = 1    where 0x is the prefix and
            0 = 0000   1 = 0001
```

The number 47 would be written as follows in hexadecimal:

```
0x2F = 47   where 0x is the prefix and
            2 = 0010   F = 1111
```

Reading the value for all eight bits gives you the value 47:

```
0 0 1 0  1 1 1 1
   32  +  15  = 47
```

It is a C programming convention to use hexadecimal notation when working with bit operations. In the following sections hexadecimal notations are given along with decimal values so you will become more familiar with the hexadecimal numbering system.

Setting Bits

Bitwise operations work on any integer type data, including `char`. In practice, however, `unsigned int` is often used because the absence of a sign bit gives you one more bit to work with. For our error flag example, a variable could initially be defined as

```
unsigned error_flag = 0;
```

Assume an unsigned integer is two bytes (sixteen bits) in size. As a set of bits, this integer contains all zeros in memory and looks like this:

```
00000000 00000000
```

For purposes of illustration, the following examples work with just one byte of data, which will be the right-most (or lowest) byte.

Chapter 8

Suppose also, you want to define four errors, turning on bits 0, 1, 2, and 3, respectively, depending on which error occurs, as follows:

error 1	0 0 0 0 0 0 0 1	(error_flag = 1 or 0x01)
error 2	0 0 0 0 0 0 1 0	(error_flag = 2 or 0x02)
error 3	0 0 0 0 0 1 0 0	(error_flag = 4 or 0x04)
error 4	0 0 0 0 1 0 0 0	(error_flag = 8 or 0x08)

bit number   7 6 5 4 3 2 1 0

From this example, you can begin to see the possibilities for processing errors that `error_flag` provides. You can test for individual errors, but you can also control further processing based on the severity of error. For example, you could decide to abort processing entirely if the value of `error_flag` rose higher than a certain number, such as 10. To reach a value of 10, both error 4 (bit 3) and error 2 (bit 1) must occur (0 0 0 0 1 0 1 0 = 8 + 2 = 10).

C provides one unary and three binary operators to help you manipulate and test the bits in a byte. These operators are covered next. All these operators are called *bitwise operators* because they operate on each bit in a byte, independently of any other bits.

Bitwise Negation Operator (~)   This unary operator, sometimes known as *one's complement*, changes each 1 to a 0 and each 0 to a 1.* Another way of putting this is to say that the ~ operator *flips bits*. For example, if `error_flag` equals 9, then (on most machines) the negation would be as follows:

```
unsigned negation = 0;       /* 0 0 0 0 0 0 0 0 */
unsigned error_flag = 9;     /* 0 0 0 0 1 0 0 1 */

negation = ~ error_flag;     /* 1 1 1 1 0 1 1 0 */
```

You could also use hexadecimal values as follows:

```
unsigned negation = 0x00;
unsigned error_flag = 0x09;

negation = ~ error_flag;
```

The next three bitwise operators are binary operators. They are all used to test and modify bits (0 or 1). In an expression involving one of these operators, the bit settings of the operand on the left of the operator are tested bit by bit using each bit value in the operand on the right. Because the operand on the right contains a specific bit pattern that *overlays* the field to be tested, this operand on the right is sometimes called a **mask**.

---

* Refer to a computer science text for more information on one's complement.

Expanding the Basics: More on Operators and Types

The AND Operator (&)   The & operator compares one operand to the other bit by bit. For each bit position, the bit in the result variable is set to 1 only if *both* corresponding bits in the operands are 1, for example,

```
unsigned a = 0x00, b = 0x0C, c = 0x06;

/* a = 0 0 0 0 0 0 0 0  = 0  */
/* b = 0 0 0 0 1 1 0 0  = 12 */
/* c = 0 0 0 0 0 1 1 0  = 6  */

a = b & c;     /* a = 0 0 0 0 0 1 0 0  = 4 (0x04) */
```

Here, **b** is the operand tested and **c** is the mask. When the integer values 6 and 12 are compared using the & operator, the resulting bit pattern is represented by the value 4 in variable **a**. This is because only bit position 2 (remember to count from the right starting with 0) is turned on (1) in both **b** and **c**.

The OR Operator (|)   This operator can be used to turn on specific bits. For each bit position in a bit-by-bit comparison, the resulting bit is 1 if *either* of the corresponding bits in the operands are 1, for example,

```
unsigned a = 0x00, b = 0x0C, c = 0x06;

/* a = 0 0 0 0 0 0 0 0  = 0  */
/* b = 0 0 0 0 1 1 0 0  = 12 */
/* c = 0 0 0 0 0 1 1 0  = 6  */

a = b | c;     /* a = 0 0 0 0 1 1 1 0  = 14 (0x0E) */
```

In this example, the | operation on **b** using the mask in **c**, results in **a** having the value 14.

The Exclusive OR Operator (^)   This operator enables you to toggle a bit in the result if *either but not both* of the bits in the operands are 1, for example,

```
unsigned a = 0x00, b = 0x0C, c = 0x06;

/* a = 0 0 0 0 0 0 0 0  = 0  */
/* b = 0 0 0 0 1 1 0 0  = 12 */
/* c = 0 0 0 0 0 1 1 0  = 6  */

a = b ^ c;     /* a = 0 0 0 0 1 0 1 0  = 10 (0x0A) */
```

Here, the exclusive OR operation is applied to **b** using the mask in **c**. This results in **a** having the value 10.

Routines using these concepts and operators are illustrated in the example at the end of this chapter.

Chapter 8

Bitwise Shift Operators

C also provides two operators that you can use to shift the bits in an integer to the left or to the right. You can use these operators to move through the bits in a field or as a way to multiply and divide using powers of 2.

The Left Shift Operator (<<) This binary operator shifts the bits in the left operand by the number of places you specify in the right operand. As the bits are shifted left, the vacant ones on the right are set to zeros. Bits shifted to the left *disappear* as they fall off the left end, for example (shown in decimal for clarity),

```
unsigned error_flag = 0;      /* error_flag = 0 0 0 0 0 0 0 0 */

error_flag = ( 2 << 2 );      /*       2   =  0 0 0 0 0 0 1 0 */
                              /* (2 << 2) =  0 0 0 0 1 0 0 0 */

                              /* error_flag now equals 8      */
```

As you can see, shifting left is equivalent to multiplying the variable value by a power of two. In this example, `error_flag` is assigned a value of 2, shifted two places to the left. Two to the second power (two places were shifted) equals four. Multiplying 2 by 4 equals 8, which is the resultant value after shifting `error_flag`.

The Right Shift Operator (>>) This binary operator shifts the bits in the left operand by the number of places you specify in the right operand. As the bits are shifted right, the vacant ones on the left are set to zeros. Bits shifted to the right disappear as they fall off the right end, for example,

```
unsigned error_flag = 0;      /* error_flag = 0 0 0 0 0 0 0 0 */

error_flag = ( 8 >> 2 );      /*       8   =  0 0 0 0 1 0 0 0 */
                              /* (8 >> 2) =  0 0 0 0 0 0 1 0 */

                              /* error_flag now equals 2      */
```

As you might guess, shifting right is equivalent to dividing the variable value by a power of two. In this example, `error_flag` is assigned a value of 8, shifted two places to the right. Eight shifted two places equals 8/4, or 2. Two is the resultant value of the right shift operation.

You will see another example using these operators in the *bitwise calculator* example at the end of this chapter.

Hints on Use of Bitwise Operators Here are some helpful hints on using these kinds of operators in C. First, try not to confuse the logical operators && and || with the bitwise logical operators & and |. Remember, they give very different results, for example,

```
0xF0 || 0x00 == 1           /* Result is 1(TRUE) 16 or 0 */

0xF0  | 0x00 == 0xF0        /* 16 | 0 equals 16 */
```

Expanding the Basics: More on Operators and Types

When using the shift operators, remember that shifting is safest when done with unsigned integers or unsigned long integers. And, when using the shift operators, do not shift an integer to the point that all its bits disappear. Also, be careful of using right shift operators with a negative number. The resulting value varies depending on your computer.

Module 17 Summary

In **Module 17,** you learned that you can work at the bit level in C. You also were introduced to the C bitwise operators.

New C Tools

Concepts	Code
bit operations	bitwise negation operator ~
mask	bitwise logical operators &, |, ^
	bitwise shift operators <<, >>

To become familiar with the remaining operators in C, move from the bit level to expressions. The next section tells you more about exactly what can appear on the left side of an expression and introduces two more operators to use in expressions.

Module 18: More About Expressions

In this module, you will look at assignment statements in more detail, in that you will learn what kinds of objects and expressions can appear on the left side of the assignment operator. Also, two more operators that you can use in forming expressions are introduced.

Keywords you need to note are

lvalue
ternary operator
conditional operator
comma operator

Assignment and lvalues

Module 19 introduces more complex C objects than you have worked with so far. In order to use these objects (and pointers or arrays) correctly in expressions, you need to learn more about what can and cannot go on the left side of an assignment operator. The C term **lvalue** is used in discussing what kind of values can appear on the left side of the assignment operator.

187

Chapter 8

As shown in the examples in Chapters 1 through 7, the assignment operator is basic to programming in C. When you first learned about the assignment operator and assignment statements, you learned that the operand on the left side of the assignment operator (=) is a variable name and the operand on the right side is a value. Also, the purpose of the assignment statement is to assign the value on the right to the variable on the left.

In Chapters 6 and 7, you learned about two other C objects in addition to variables: arrays and pointers. You also used these objects in assignment statements and expressions. With assignments involving variables, it is usually apparent what can and cannot go on the left side of an assignment. For example, you would not think of saying `999 = abc` because 999 is a number. You cannot assign a value to a number or a constant because the value of a constant cannot be changed (that is what makes it a constant).

In this chapter, however, you learn about some of the more complex data types in C. With these kinds of objects, distinctions concerning when and where values can be changed may not be quite as clear.

One way you can think about lvalues is that an lvalue is an expression that refers to a C object in a way that allows that object to be altered. To alter the value of an object you need to be sure that your program can *get to* that value in storage. An lvalue is simply a way of thinking about values that can be used in expressions (such as a value on the left side of an assignment) that allow you to refer to the location of a C object in storage. To refer to a location in storage, an lvalue must be the result of an expression that references storage, such as an identifier or the result of a pointer operation.

Here is another way of putting it: in order to change the value of a C object you must be able to reference that object in storage, and to do that, you must use an lvalue to access that variable or object.

The following can generally be used as lvalues:

- the name of a variable declared as any arithmetic type
- the name of a variable declared as a pointer
- references to individual array elements (but *not* the array name)
- an indirection expression (`*ptr_name`).

Some common expressions that are *not* lvalues are

- array names
- address-of expressions (for example, `&var`)
- function names.

The `&`, `++`, and `--` operators require that their operands be lvalues. The left side of an assignment statement also always requires an lvalue.

Expanding the Basics: More on Operators and Types

Before you learn about the remaining C data types, there are two operators that can help you write complex expressions more clearly and efficiently.

The Conditional Operator (?:)

You have already learned about unary and binary operators. C also has a **ternary operator**, which is an operator requiring three operands. This operator is called the **conditional operator** because it is used to form a shorthand version of the conditional `if-else` statement. A conditional expression using this operator looks like this:

```
smallest = ( x < y ) ? x : y;
```

which means

```
if (x < y)
    smallest = x;
else
    smallest = y;
```

You can see that there are really three operands involved, each of which can be an expression:

expression1 **?** *expression2* : *expression3*;

In this kind of conditional expression, *expression1* is evaluated first as TRUE or FALSE. If *expression1* is TRUE then *expression2* is evaluated and its value becomes the value for the expression result. If *expression1* is FALSE, then the value for *expression3* is given as the result.

In a conditional expression, *expression1* must have a scalar (single item of data) type. Both *expression2* and *expression3* may have an arithmetic type, or the same structure, union, or pointer type. If necessary, the types of *expression2* and *expression3* are promoted to the same level before *expression1* is evaluated.

The conditional operator is useful when you want to make a choice between two alternatives. Using the `?:` form instead of an `if-else` construct produces more succinct source code.

The Comma Operator (,)

You have seen the comma , as a separator for punctuation in declarations and function arguments. The comma, however, has another use in C as an operator. Recall from the discussion in Chapter 3 that C uses rules of precedence in evaluating expressions. A compiler is free to evaluate subexpressions (items inside parentheses) in a statement in any order. The comma operator provides you with a mechanism to force expressions to be evaluated in a particular order. You will probably make the most frequent use of this facility in `for` loops and progressive assignments of values to variables. Here is how both work.

Chapter 8

The comma operator enables you to use more than one expression as part of the `for` loop initialization or update, for example,

```
/* track time */

main()
{
int secs, mins;

for(secs = 1, mins = 0; secs <= 120; secs++, mins = secs/60)
{
   printf("secs = %d\n", secs);
}
printf("mins = %d\n", mins);
}
```

In this example, the comma first serves as punctuation in the declaration of `secs` and `mins`. But then, in the `for` statement, the comma operator ensures that `secs` is initialized before `mins` and, more importantly, that `secs` is incremented before `mins` is calculated.

You can also use the comma operator to help form expressions. In the next example, the statements that swap values in the shell game can be written as one statement by using the comma operator. In this example, the comma operator ensures that the expression is evaluated left to right. This is how it looks:

```
hold = a, a = b, b = hold;      /* swap values */
```

However, a disadvantage is that complicated comma expressions often make your code harder to read. Because this statement is equivalent to the following three statements, the following coding is usually preferred:

```
hold = a;
a = b;
b = hold;
```

You should use the comma operator only when it is needed, which is usually to force evaluation in a complex expression to take place in a certain order.

Module 18 Summary

Module 18 introduced the concept of lvalues. Using this concept, you learned some basics about what can and cannot appear on the left side of expressions involving the data types covered so far. You also learned how to use two more C operators: the conditional and comma operators. Now you are ready to discover more about C types.

Expanding the Basics: More on Operators and Types

New C Tools

Concepts	Code
lvalues	conditional operator
	comma operator

Module 19: An Introduction to Advanced Data Types

This module reviews the basic data types and introduces three new types, including one that you will use extensively in later chapters. You will also learn how to create your own names for data types and how to handle conversions between data types.

Keywords you need to note are

enumerated types	**dot operator**
enumerator list	**structure pointer operator**
enumerator tag	**unions**
structure	`typedef`
structure members	**type conversions**
structure tag	**casts**

Recall from Chapter 2 that an *object* in C refers to a region of storage. Also, objects are *typed* according to the kinds of values they can represent and the operations that are valid for those values. In previous chapters, you learned about the following basic types of C objects:

- character
- integer
- floating point
- void.

You also learned about the following three types that are based on or derived from these basic types:

- function
- array
- pointer.

This section introduces you to one additional basic type and two new derived types. **Figure 8.1** helps complete the picture. (The new types are shown in capital letters.)

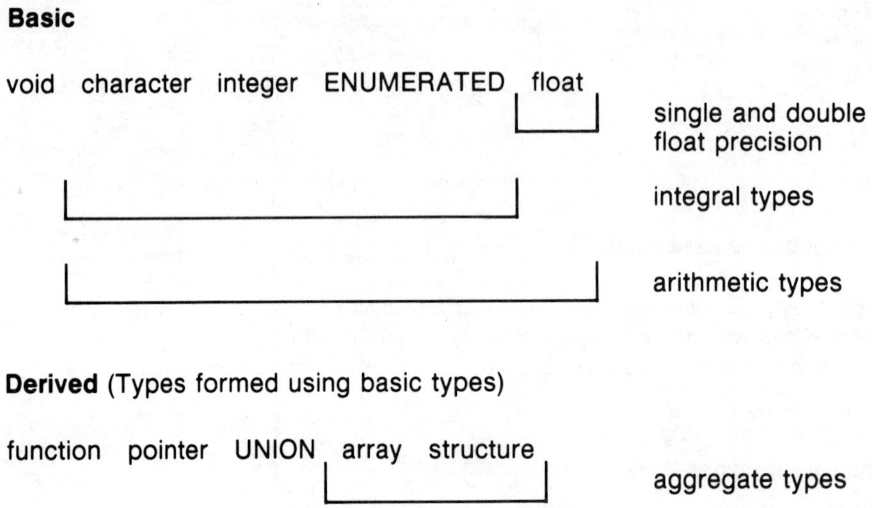

Chapter 8

Basic

void   character   integer   ENUMERATED   float
                                          └─────┘ single and double
                                                  float precision
       └──────────────────────────────────┘ integral types

       └──┘ arithmetic types

Derived (Types formed using basic types)

function   pointer   UNION   array   structure
                             └──────────────┘ aggregate types

Figure 8.1   C Types

Character, integer, enumeration, and float types can be grouped together as arithmetic types because you can perform basic arithmetic operations on each of them. Character, integer, and enumeration types are often called integral types because they work with integers.

Arithmetic types can also be grouped with pointer types as scalar types because they are single items. Arrays and structures are called aggregate types because each array and structure may be composed of a number of items (array elements or structure members).

The New Data Types: Enumerations, Structures, and Unions

The following sections introduce the basics about each of these new types. In Chapter 10, you will get lots of practice working with these new types.

Expanding the Basics: More on Operators and Types

Enumerated Types   Using the `enum` keyword in C allows you to assign meaningful names to a range of integer values. (Because enumerated types work with integers they are considered one of the basic C data types.) For example, if your program worked with the days of the week, it might be clearer if you could use the identifiers `Sunday`, `Monday`, . . ., `Saturday` instead of the integers 1 to 7. Using an enumeration can often take the place of using a large number of `#define` statements to give meaningful names to numeric values.

An `enum` object takes its value from an **enumerator list**, a collection of identifiers that are treated as `int` constants. You can explicitly assign values to list members. If no explicit value is assigned to the first list member, its value is zero. If no value is assigned to any other member, its value is one greater than that of the previous member.

Here is an example of an enumerator list with an **enumerator tag** associating a name with the list.

```
/* Define an enumerator list with the enumerator tag = unit */

enum unit { cafe, clinics, maternity = 4, pediatrics, labs };

        /* Values associated with units are:

           cafe = 0
           clinics = 1
           maternity = 4
           pediatrics = 5
           labs = 6
        */

/* Define a variable "floor" to be of type unit */

enum unit floor;
```

In summary, the declaration of an `enum` variable has the following two parts:

- an enumeration list associating integer values with a collection of meaningful identifiers
- a declaration that associates a variable name with the enumeration list.

Structures   C structures make it possible for you to group *fields* or variables of different basic types (and other derived types) together into a discrete unit or *record*. For example, you might want to organize your exercise data, with variables concerning aerobic activity, weight training, and so on, in terms of daily activity. Each variable could be represented by a field in a daily activity record. In C, the term **structure** is used to refer to the daily activity record. Different types of objects form the fields and are called **structure members**.

Chapter 8

A C structure, then, refers to a complex object that can be made up of any other types of C objects except functions. The concept of a C structure is analogous to the concept of a *record* in other languages. This section discusses the basics about structures: how they are declared and why you would want to use them. In Chapter 10, you will work with structures in more detail.

Use structures when you want to group several different kinds of data together into a logical unit, for example, your exercise record. This differs from arrays and enumerations where you group *homogenous* objects (objects all of the same type). Take a simple example; suppose you wanted to represent your date of birth using a structure. You could code the following:

```
struct {
   int year;
   int month;
   int day;
} birth;
```

The compiler interprets this as a pattern or template for your date of birth. This pattern or *template* is only telling the compiler how to represent your birth date in storage, it does not set aside any storage space at this point. A minimum structure declaration, then, looks like this:

struct {
  declaration list (minimum of one member);
} *identifier*;

A more workable definition is to provide a name or **tag** and variable definitions, as follows:

struct *tag* {
  declaration_1;
  .
  .
  .
  declaration_n;
} *variable_1, . . . , variable_n*;

In this format, **struct** is a keyword, and *tag* can be any valid C identifier. The list of declarations for structure members follows the tag, and it is enclosed in braces. Following the member declarations are definitions for variables of that structure type. In other words, if you define a tag for the structure, you do not have to redefine the entire structure each time you want to define a variable of that structure type.

Expanding the Basics: More on Operators and Types

In this case, the first reference is interpreted as shown in **Figure 8.3**.

```
       field pointed to in structure
                          ┌──────┐
       date_ptr -> year
       └────────┘
       pointer to structure
```

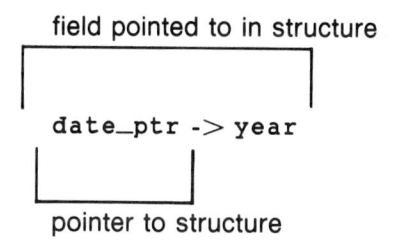

Figure 8.3 Using the Structure Pointer Operator

In terms of results, the two methods of reference are equivalent. In general, however, you should use the form **x.y** when **x** is a structure and **y** is a field in it. Use the form **x -> y** when **x** is a pointer to a structure and **y** is a field in the structure being pointed to.

In the example at the end of the chapter, you will see how a simple structure is defined and used. For now, move on to the final C type discussed in this module.

Unions   A common definition of *union* might refer to joining two or more things into one, or a collection of elements belonging to two or more sets that occupy the same logical space. In C, the data type **union** refers to an area of storage defined so that it can hold two or more different types of objects in the same memory space. In a sense, unions allow you to *redefine* a storage space depending on the type of data you need to work with. Unions are useful when you want your program to interpret the data in one storage location more than one way.

Unions are similar to structures in that you define a storage template and then declare variables of that template type. The difference is that you can define several templates that occupy the same space in storage. A programmer uses a union to represent a

Chapter 8

variable that in some contexts should be thought of as one type while in other contexts it should be thought of as another. Only one union component or template is active at a time, however. The syntax for defining a `union` is as follows:

union *optional_tag* {
  declaration of type_1;
  declaration of type_2;
  .
  .
  .
  declaration of type_n;
};

where **union** is a keyword and the declarations are for each component type that can occupy that storage space.

Suppose you want a variable called `time` that in some cases will be measured in years and in others, it will be measured in seconds. You could use the union

```
union time {
        short years;
        long  seconds;
      };
```

because a length of time measured in seconds may be very large while a similar length measured in years is much smaller.

A union is a space-saving device because, unlike structures, the fields in a union overlap. The `time` union takes up only as much space as a `long` (the largest field). Compare the above union to the following structure:

```
struct stime {
        short years;
        long  seconds;
      };
```

The structure takes up an amount of space equal to the size of a `short` *plus* the size of a `long`. In other words, the total space is the sum of the sizes of the structure's fields.

When you use a structure, all fields in the structure may be used simultaneously. This means the value stored in one does not affect the value stored in another. This is not true of a union because its fields overlap. The `time` union and `stime` structure are illustrated in **Figure 8.4**.

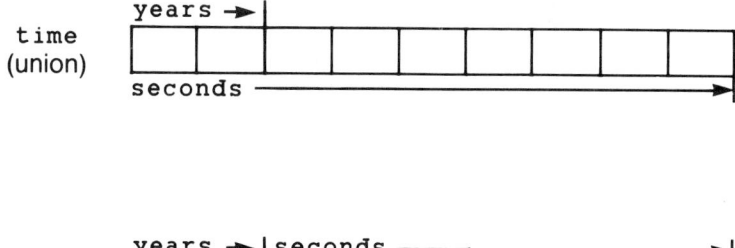

Expanding the Basics: More on Operators and Types

```
          years →
time     ┌──┬──┬──┬──┬──┬──┬──┬──┐
(union)  │  │  │  │  │  │  │  │  │
         └──┴──┴──┴──┴──┴──┴──┴──┘
         seconds ─────────────────→


           years → seconds ───────────────→
stime      ┌──┬──┬──┬──┬──┬──┬──┬──┬──┬──┐
(structure)│  │  │  │  │  │  │  │  │  │  │
           └──┴──┴──┴──┴──┴──┴──┴──┴──┴──┘
```

Each box represents one byte.

Figure 8.4 Space Requirements of a Union Versus a Structure

Therefore, in the following section of code, the function `time_function` is called:

```
struct stime s;
    .
    .
    .
s.years   = 1;
s.seconds = 123456789;

if (s.years == 1)
   time_function();
```

If a union is used, however, `time_function` is not called because the assignment to `t.seconds` results in the value of `t.years` being overwritten.

```
union time t;
    .
    .
    .
t.years   = 1;
t.seconds = 123456789;

if (t.years == 1)
   time_function();
```

199

Chapter 8

Structures can be components of unions. Using the structure `birth` discussed earlier, you could have the following:

```
union birth_dates {
    struct birth;
    char    date[12];
};
```

This would allow you to use a date in either structure or array form.

You can combine structures and unions with arrays and pointers to create just about any record type or data structure you can think of. In Chapter 10 you will work with some of these constructs in the form of lists and hierarchical trees of data. The purpose here has been to introduce you to the data types you will be working with.

There are two additional topics relevant to C data types that need to be discussed before continuing. One is the feature that C provides to let you create your own name for a type. The other concerns what happens when you convert, intentionally or not, from one C type to another.

Creating Your Own Names for Data Types - typedef

The `typedef` feature in C allows you to create your own name for a particular data type. You can do this for any C data type. In fact, this feature becomes very important in creating certain kinds of advanced data structures. For now, think of this feature as a way to create more descriptive labels for types of data.

For example, suppose you want to make it clearer in your program when an object is used to point to strings. In other words, you would like to define a data type, call it *string*, and use it in declaring pointers to strings.

You create descriptive names for data types like this:

   typedef *type alias*;

where **typedef** is a keyword, *type* is any valid C data type, and *alias* is the new label you want to give this data type.

For example, instead of coding

```
char *name;     /* pointers to char */
char *address;
```

you can code

```
typedef char *string;
```

which declares `string` as a *pointer to character*. You can then use `string` in your program anywhere you want to define a pointer to type `char`, for example,

```
string name, address;    /* same as char *name, *address */
```

You will see some more uses for the `typedef` feature in the example at the end of this chapter. For now, remember that `typedef` allows you to give more meaningful symbolic names to data types or functions and that it does not *create* new data types.

Expanding the Basics: More on Operators and Types

Converting Data Types

There are three categories of **type conversions** in C:

- arithmetic
- implicit
- explicit.

Arithmetic conversions are performed by the compiler in order to facilitate arithmetic or logical operations. Implicit conversions occur when the compiler finds it necessary to modify the type of an object in order to perform a program operation. Explicit conversions are those that you initiate on purpose through your program code.

Some general circumstances under which each kind of conversion can occur are as follows:

Arithmetic One operand may be converted by the compiler to a different type to perform an arithmetic or logical operation. For example, if **x** and **y** are long integers and **i** is an integer, then in an expression such as

```
x = y + i;
```

i is converted to a long integer before the addition is done.

Implicit Functions may have actual arguments converted to a different type prior to the function call. Function return values may be converted to a different type prior to return from the function. A variable or other storage object may be converted to a different type during assignment of an lvalue if the lvalue differs from the original type. If **c** is a character variable, for example, then in the function call

```
func(c);
```

c is converted to an `int` before the call is made.

Explicit A special expression in C can be used to cause the conversion of one value to another type value. For example, in the statement

```
p = (char *) time;
```

the variable `time` is explicitly converted to a character pointer.

In general, for operations involving two different types, an attempt is made to convert or promote to the higher ranking type. Remember, however, that each type in C contains a specific range of values (see Chapter 2). Therefore, in some operations where you might try to assign values across types, the results might be unpredictable. For example, on many microcomputers, `int` variables can only represent integer values from -32768 to 32767. If you try to assign a floating point number outside this range, your results will be incorrect.

Type conversion is another area in C where machine dependencies must be taken into consideration. Check the documentation provided with your compiler to be sure

Chapter 8

exactly what happens on your system, particularly with implicit conversions and conversions involving signed types.

There are, however, some general rules that you can reference for arithmetic and implicit type conversions. These are listed in **Table 8.1**. When your program performs arithmetic operations or passes parameters to a function, values are often converted or promoted in type automatically. These basic conversions are listed first.

Table 8.1 General Rules for Arithmetic and Implicit Type Conversions

Original Type	Type Converted To
Arithmetic Conversions	
`char`	`int`
`short`	`int`
`float`	`double`
either operand is `double`	operands and result converted to `double`
either operand is `long`	operands and result converted to `long`
either operand `unsigned`	operands and result converted to `unsigned`
array name	pointer, when name is passed to a function
Implicit Conversions	
`char`	`int`, `short`, `long`
`int`	`char`, `short`, `long`, `float`, `double`, `unsigned`
`short int`	(Signs will be extended if there is a promotion to
`long int`	a wider type; conversion to a narrower type may cause truncation.)
`float`	`double`
`double`	`float` (Result is rounded and may be truncated. Conversion to any other type from float or double is machine-dependent and results are unpredictable if the value being converted from is too large for the type being converted to.)

Explicit Conversions   In C, you can force a conversion of one type to another with a **cast**. In a cast, an expression is written that forces or *coerces* variables into one of the conversions mentioned above. The syntax for a cast expression is

(*type*) *expression*

For example, suppose you wanted to be sure that the argument to a function is always of type `double`. You could write a cast expression within the function call to ensure that any other type would be converted to `double`. (Note: the compiler would at least *attempt* a valid conversion.) You could code this as follows:

```
calculate ((double) number);
```

Expanding the Basics: More on Operators and Types

The `(double) number` portion of the function call is a cast expression forcing `number` to be of type `double`. Cast expressions can become very complex in C. Casts are used in the example at the end of this chapter.

Module 19 Summary

In this module, you learned the basics about some new C data types. You also learned how you can define new names for data types. Finally, some guidelines were given for conversion between data types.

New C Tools

Concepts	Code
enumeration type	`enum`
structure type	`struct`
union type	`union`
type conversions	`typedef`
casts	structure member operators (. and ->)

The Calculator Program Revisited

In this example, you return to the calculator you built in Chapter 3. This time, however, the program code is written more efficiently, making use of `typedef`, enumerations, arrays, structures, and pointers. The example also shows how to use the bitwise operators in program code.

The program provides you with a menu containing certain calculation options. After you select an option, you are asked to enter two numbers. The operation selected is then performed using the two numbers requested. A message is printed detailing the operation, operands, and results. This is how the program output should look:

```
Enter the operation to be executed:
    +) Add
    -) Subtract
    x) Multiply
    /) Divide
    &) And
    |) Or
    ^) Exclusive Or
    ~) Negate
    <) Shift Left
    >) Shift Right
    q) Quit
```

Chapter 8

```
Option: __

Enter first number  [0000000000000000] : __
Enter second number [0000000000000000] : __

0000000000000000 + 0000000000000000 = 0000000000000000
```

As you can see, the main difference between this calculator and the one you programmed earlier is that the calculations are performed using binary numbers. There are also some differences in the way the code is structured. These differences are highlighted after you have read and executed the program. The basic program flow is illustrated in **Figure 8.5** using the Add option.

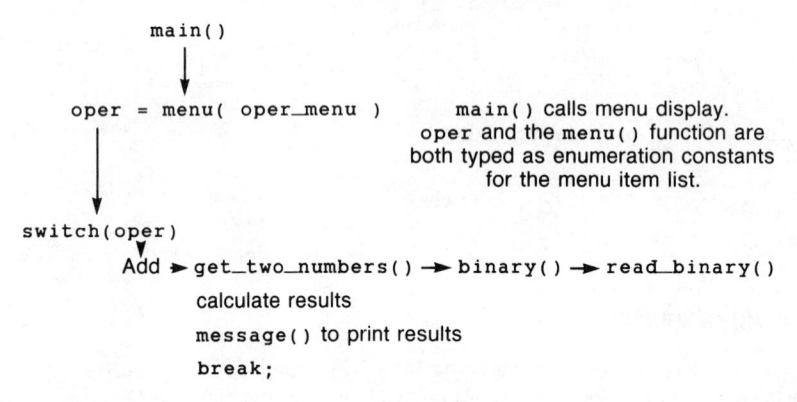

```
              main( )
                 |
                 v
    oper = menu( oper_menu )          main( ) calls menu display.
        |                             oper and the menu( ) function are
        |                             both typed as enumeration constants
        |                             for the menu item list.
        v
switch(oper)
        v
       Add ─► get_two_numbers( ) ─► binary( ) ─► read_binary( )
             calculate results
             message( ) to print results
             break;
```

Figure 8.5 Program Flow Using the Add Option

Read over the program and run it. Try to follow and understand the structure, type definitions, and arrays involved before looking at the notes following the program text.

```
/*  Binary Calculator  */

#include <stdio.h>
#include <ctype.h>

/*
 *  standard Boolean defines
 */
#define FALSE   0
#define TRUE    !FALSE

/*
 * Menu_return type contains symbolic representations of all possible
 * values returned by the menu function.
 */
enum menu_enum { Add, Subtract, Multiply, Divide, And, Or, Xor,
                 Negate, Shift_left, Shift_right, Quit };
typedef enum menu_enum  menu_return;
```

Expanding the Basics: More on Operators and Types

```c
/*
* Define a structure that can contain all the information needed for the
* menu function: A string of option characters that will invoke a
* description, and the return value associated with that option.
*/

struct menu_struct {
   char *options;                  /* string of options that are equivalent */
   char *description;              /* description of option */
   menu_return  return_code;       /* return value for option */
   };
typedef struct menu_struct    menu_entry;

/*
* Function prototype for all included functions
*/
char get_one_char();
void error(menu_return);
menu_return menu(menu_entry[]);
void get_one_number(int *);
void get_two_numbers(int *, int *);
char *binary(int);
int read_binary();
void message(char *,int,int,int);
void message1(char *, int, int);

/*
* Definition of main menu information
*/
menu_entry oper_menu[] = {
   { "+aA",    "Add",           Add },
   { "-sS",    "Subtract",      Subtract },
   { "xX*mM",  "Multiply",      Multiply },
   { "/dD",    "Divide",        Divide },
   { "&",      "And",           And },
   { "|Oo",    "Or",            Or },
   { "^eE",    "Exclusive Or",  Xor },
   { "~nN",    "Negate",        Negate },
   { "<lL",    "Shift Left",    Shift_left },
   { ">rR",    "Shift Right",   Shift_right },
   { "qQ",     "Quit",          Quit },
   { NULL,     NULL,            Quit }
   };

int result = 0;              /* Result of last operation is
                                used as default number for input */
```

Chapter 8

```c
main()
{
  int num1, num2;           /* numbers to be worked on */
  int done = FALSE;         /* flag to terminate program */
  menu_return oper;         /* current operation */

  printf("Welcome to the Handy-Home Calculator\n\n");

  /*
   * While the user wants to continue
   */
  while ( !done )
     {
     printf("\nEnter the operation to be executed:\n");
     oper = menu( oper_menu );

     printf("\n");

     /*
      * Process the selected option
      */
     switch (oper)
        {
        case Add:
           get_two_numbers( &num1, &num2 );
           result = num1 + num2;
           message( "+", num1, num2, result );
           break;

        case Subtract:
           get_two_numbers( &num1, &num2 );
           result = num1 - num2;
           message( "-", num1, num2, result );
           break;

        case Multiply:
           get_two_numbers( &num1, &num2 );
           result = num1 * num2;
           message( "*", num1, num2, result );
           break;

        case Divide:
           get_two_numbers( &num1, &num2 );
           if (num2 == 0)
              printf("I can't divide by 0.\n");
           else
              {
              result = num1 / num2;
              message( "/", num1, num2, result );
              }
           break;
```

Expanding the Basics: More on Operators and Types

```
            case And:
                get_two_numbers( &num1, &num2 );
                result = num1 & num2;
                message( "&", num1, num2, result );
                break;

            case Or:
                get_two_numbers( &num1, &num2 );
                result = num1 | num2;
                message( "|", num1, num2, result );
                break;

            case Xor:
                get_two_numbers( &num1, &num2 );
                result = num1 ^ num2;
                message( "^ ", num1, num2, result );
                break;

            case Negate:
                get_one_number( &num1 );
                result = ~ num1;
                message1( "~", num1, result );
                break;

            case Shift_left:
                get_two_numbers( &num1, &num2 );
                result = num1 << num2;
                message( "<<", num1, num2, result );
                break;

            case Shift_right:
                get_two_numbers( &num1, &num2 );
                result = num1 >> num2;
                message( ">>", num1, num2, result );
                break;

            case Quit:
                done = TRUE;
                break;

            default:
                printf("I don't understand what that means.\n");
            }
        }

    return 0;
}
```

Chapter 8

```
/*
 * get_one_number()
 * Read a string representing a binary number and return its
 * value, the return value is returned in the parameter,
 * therefore the parameter must be a pointer to the number to
 * be changed.
 */

void get_one_number( ret_val )
int *ret_val;
{
  printf( "Enter a number [%s] : ", binary( result ) );
  *ret_val = read_binary();
}

/*
 * get_two_numbers()
 * Just like get_one_number, except that it returns two numbers
 */
void get_two_numbers( ret_val1, ret_val2 )
int *ret_val1, *ret_val2;
{
  printf( "Enter first number [%s] : ", binary( result ));
  *ret_val1 = read_binary();
  printf( "Enter second number [%s] : ", binary( result ));
  *ret_val2 = read_binary();
}

/*
 * read_binary()
 * Read a binary number from the standard input.
 */
read_binary()
{
  char buff[80];              /* Temp. storage for input string */
  char *b_ptr = buff;         /* Pointer for scanning string */
  int  temp = 0;              /* Temp. value for converting value */

  /*
   * Read a string, if the string is empty then use the result of the
   * previous expression.
   */

  fgets( buff, sizeof(buff), stdin);
  if ( buff[0] == '\n' )
     {
     return result;
     }
```

Expanding the Basics: More on Operators and Types

```
  /* ignore leading spaces */
  for ( ; isspace( *b_ptr ); b_ptr++ )
     ;

  /* while the strings contains 0's and 1's keep building the temp value
   */
  while ( ( *b_ptr == '1' ) || ( *b_ptr == '0' ) )
     {
     temp = ( temp << 1 ) + ( *b_ptr == '1' );
     b_ptr++;
     }

  return temp;
}

/*
  binary()
* Convert an integer to a string of 0's and 1's, that is the binary
* representation of that number.
*NOTE 1
* This routine returns a pointer to an internal static, and subsequent
* calls to the routine will overwrite the previous value, so care must
* be taken to ensure that the string is copied somewhere else if it
* is needed for longer than until the next call to binary.
*NOTE 2
* Check the standard header file "limits.h" for a definition of
* CHAR_BITS on your machine.  Substituting this definition
* for numeric constants in buffer array references is one way to
* make the program more general (instead of assuming 16 bits per
* int). For example:

        static char buffer[(CHAR_BITS *sizeof(int)) + 1]
                instead of
        static char buffer[17];
*/

char *binary( val )
int val;
{                                    /* Static storage is discussed */
                                     /* in the next chapter. */
  static char buffer[17];            /* Static buffer for returning */
  int i;                             /* Element being processed */

  /*
   * For each of the 16 bits in an integer value set the corresponding
   * element of the buffer string.
   */
  for ( i = 0; i < 16; i++ )
     {
     buffer[15 - i] = ( val & ( 1 << i ) ) ? '1' : '0' ;
     }
```

Chapter 8

```c
    /* terminate the string with a 0 */
    buffer[16] = '\0';
    return buffer;
}

/*
 * message1()
 * Print out the result string of a unary operation, given the operands, result,
 * and a string representation of the operator.
 */
void message1( oper_string, val1, val2, )
char *oper_string;
int val1, val2;
{
    char buff1[17];      /* Temp storage for storing binary string */

    strcpy( buff1, binary(val1) );

    printf( "%s %s = %s\n", oper_string, buff1, binary(val2));
}

/*
 * menu()
 * Routine to actually search through the menu list, print the menu, and
 * get a valid response.
 */
menu_return
menu( selections )
menu_entry selections[];
{
    char ch;                    /* character user typed */
    int  valid = FALSE;         /* Do we have a valid option yet? */
    menu_return return_val;     /* Value to return */
    int i;                      /* Loop counter */

    /* Print the menu. */
    for ( i = 0; selections[i].options != NULL; i++ )
       {
       printf( "   %c)  %s\n", *selections[i].options,
                               selections[i].description );
       }

    /*
     * Loop until we get a valid option selection.
     */
    while ( !valid )
       {
       fputs( "\nOption: ", stdout );

       ch = get_one_char();
```

210

```
    /*
     * If the user types '?' list the menu again.  (If you modify the
     * menu and one of the things you add is a '?', then you should
     * change the character used here.)
     */
        if ( ch == '?' )
           {
           puts( "\n\nOptions\n" );
           for ( i = 0; selections[i].options != NULL; i++ )
              {
              printf( "    %c)  %s\n", *selections[i].options,
                                 selections[i].description );
              }
           }
        else
           {
           valid = FALSE;

           /*
            * Search the menu for a match.
            */
           for ( i = 0; selections[i].options != NULL; i++ )
              {
              /*
               * If the user's character is in the options string, it's a match
               */
              if ( strchr( selections[i].options, ch ) )
                 {
                 return_val = selections[i].return_code;
                 valid = TRUE;
                 }
              }

           /*
            * They entered a bad option, tell them so.
            */
           if ( !valid )
              {
              printf( "<%c> is an invalid option\n", ch );
              }
           }
      }

   return ( return_val );
}

/*
 * get_one_char()
 *    Reads a character from standard input, ignoring leading spaces
 *    and removing trailer characters.
 */
```

211

Chapter 8

```
char get_one_char()
{
  char buff[80];              /* Buffer containing input line */
  char *ptr;                  /* Pointer for scanning array */

  /*
   * Read a line from input into buffer.
   */
  if (fgets( buff, sizeof( buff ), stdin ) == NULL )
     { fprintf( stderr, "Read Error." \n");
         exit( 1 );
     }

  /* Get first non-white space character (except return). */
  for( ptr = buff; isspace( *ptr ); ptr++ )
      ;

  /*
   * If the user just typed return (or blanks followed by return)
   * return a space, so that it can be used to check for the default
   * case.
   */
  if ( *ptr == '\0' )
     *ptr = ' ';

  return ( *ptr );            /* Return the character. */
}

/*
 * Print an error message if the main program does not understand an
 * option from menu. This should only get called if there is a program
 * error.
 */
void
error( value )
menu_return value;
{
  fprintf( stderr, "Invalid return from menu()\nReturn code
= %d\n",value );
}
```

A Closer Look

Here are some notes on the three new components involved in the program and how they work. This is the code for the menu entries:

```
enum menu_enum {Add, Subtract, Multiply, Divide, And, Or, Xor,
                Negate, Shift_left, Shift_right, Quit};

typedef enum menu_enum  menu_return;
```

Expanding the Basics: More on Operators and Types

This code creates an enumeration, `menu_enum`, to be used in defining menu options. The `typedef` creates a type called `menu_return` of type `enum menu_enum`. The variable `oper`, used as a switch in `main( )`, is of this "menu list type". Therefore, because enumeration constants are identifiers for integers, you can switch on the integer values of `oper` and yet also use the more meaningful enumeration constant names "Add", "Subtract", and so forth as objects of the case statements in the switch. The end result of all this is clearer code.

The next new item is the menu structure. This code sets things up:

```
struct menu_struct {
        char *options;        /* pointer to option string */
                              /* "+aA" and so on */

        char *description;    /* pointer to operator descriptor */
                              /* "Add", "Subtract" and so on */

        menu_return return_code;  /* option return value */
        }

typedef struct menu_struct menu_entry;
```

Here, a `typedef` is used to define the identifier `menu_entry` to be a structure of type `menu_struct`. Once `menu_entry` has been defined as a type, you can use it to provide a more descriptive type name for other variables, for example,

```
menu_entry oper_menu[] = {
   { "+aA",    "Add",     Add },
               .
               .
               .
   { NULL,     NULL,      Quit }
   }
```

By using `menu_entry` as the type, the variable `oper_menu` is defined as an array of arrays of type `struct menu_struct`. In other words, each element of `oper_menu` is an array that contains three elements that will be used by each component of a variable of `menu_struct` type.

In the same way, `selections` in the function `menu` is of `menu_struct` type:

```
menu_return
menu( selections )
menu_entry selections[];
```

Note that you are passing a pointer to the first element of an array of type `menu_entry` via the array name. Notice also that the function `menu` returns a value of type `menu_return`, which is an enumeration type containing the symbolic representations of all possible values that can be returned by the menu function (Add, ..., Quit).

The `binary` function uses `<<` and `&` operators introduced in this chapter. This function takes an integer value and converts it to a string of 0s and 1s representing

213

Chapter 8

how the number would appear in binary form. This is done by progressively moving through the integer value (right to left) using the << operator. Each bit is tested using the & operator, and the corresponding element in the array is set according to the result of the AND operation. The result is a string of 0s and 1s representing the binary value.

Chapter Summary

This chapter covers several new concepts ranging from bitwise operations to structures. Of greatest importance is your understanding of the interplay between structures, types, and functions because in following chapters, you will quickly build on the basic concepts presented here. The next chapter adds a major dimension to all we have talked about so far: the concept of scope and storage classes. You also learn more about how you can use C preprocessor commands.

With this chapter, you have completed your introduction to all the C operators. You learned about bitwise, conditional, and comma operators. You also covered cast expressions and structures. To help summarize what you have learned, this chapter concludes with a table providing a quick reference guide to all the C operators.

Table 8.2   C Operators

Operator by Precedence	Operation	Associativity
( )	function call	left to right
[ ]	array element	left to right
->	structure/union member pointer	left to right
.	structure/union member reference	left to right
-	unary minus	right to left
++	prefix/postfix increment	right to left
--	prefix/postfix decrement	right to left
!	logical negation	right to left
~	bitwise negation	right to left
*	pointer	right to left
&	address of	right to left
sizeof	size of an object	right to left
(*type*)	cast (type conversion)	right to left

(continued)

214

Table 8.2 (*continued*)

Operator by Precedence	Operation	Associativity
*	multiplication	left to right
/	division	left to right
%	modulus	left to right
+	addition	left to right
-	subtraction	left to right
<<	bitwise left shift	left to right
>>	bitwise right shift	left to right
<	less than	left to right
<=	less than or equal to	left to right
>	greater than	left to right
>=	greater than or equal to	left to right
==	equal to	left to right
!=	not equal to	left to right
&	bitwise AND	left to right
^	bitwise exclusive OR	left to right
|	bitwise OR	left to right
&&	logical AND	left to right
||	logical OR	left to right
?:	conditional evaluation	right to left
=	assignment	right to left
*=	assignment	right to left
/=	assignment	right to left
%=	assignment	right to left
+=	assignment	right to left
-=	assignment	right to left
&=	assignment	right to left
^=	assignment	right to left
!=	assignment	right to left
<<=	assignment	right to left
>>=	assignment	right to left
,	comma operator	left to right

Chapter 9
More on Expressions and the C Preprocessor

Chapter 9

CONTENTS

Introduction	219
Module 20: Storage Classes and Scope	219
Introduction	219
Storage Classes	221
Scope	226
Module 20 Summary	227
Module 21: More on the C Preprocessor	228
Introduction	228
#define	229
Inside Information - #define	230
Defining Macros	230
#undef	233
#include	234
Conditional Compilation	235
Directives for Portability and Advanced Applications	237
Module 21 Summary	238
Language for Fun - An Example Using the Preprocessor	239
A Closer Look	248
Chapter Summary	248

More on Expressions and the C Preprocessor

Introduction

The concepts introduced in this chapter will help you in writing expressions using C objects in single and multifile applications. This chapter presents two new topics: storage classes and scope. You also learn more about using the C preprocessor. These topics help you write more efficient programs, as well as provide some basics to build on if you ever work with multifile applications in C. These features are covered as follows:

- understanding storage classes and scope
- using the C preprocessor.

Module 20: Storage Classes and Scope

In previous chapters, you learned that where you declare or define a variable in your program determines whether the program recognizes the variable as available only to a function or available for use by the entire program. In this module, you learn about storage classes and scope and how they affect identifier use.

Keywords you need to note are

scope
storage class
automatic
external
static
register

Introduction

All the programs you write in this tutorial involve a single source file. This is done to keep things relatively simple, both in terms of program text and compiler steps. However, there may be times when you will want to separate an application into several task-specific source files (modules). These modules might be compiled separately but linked and executed as one program. (Refer to Chapter 2 for a review of the compile and link steps.)

For example, in a multifile application, you could write a main module called `ctools.c` and use it to control the processing of some of the other programs you have written. In other words, you would include the fuel economy program, calculator, shell game, menu, and assorted utility functions as separately compiled files in `ctools.c`. The `main` function in `ctools.c` would use functions and variables in these other files to form a complete application.

Any program can be organized by having a separate file for each function. Usually, however, a file contains functions that are logically related or functions that are of the

Chapter 9

same type. You could, for example, put all the I/O functions in one file, the arithmetic functions in another, and so on.

Larger applications are sometimes implemented as a set of communicating functions that run relatively independent of each other except for occasional exchanges of information. In this type of cooperative processing, many of the functions involved share the same data structures and variables. In large and complex applications like this, many C functions can be called during the course of program execution.

Whether you have a single or multifile application, coordinating and defining variable use between functions is central to C programming. Making C objects available for use in different areas of your program requires understanding the concepts of *scope* and *storage class*. The extent to which a variable is known to your program is called the **scope** of that variable. You can control the scope of a variable by specifying how visible that variable is to other parts of your program. To do this, you specify a **storage class** for that variable.

You were briefly introduced to these concepts in the discussion of local and global variables in Chapter 6. Recall that the location of a variable definition determines the extent to which the variable is recognized within the program. In C, some declarations within a file occur outside of any function. These are called **external declarations**. Externally-declared identifiers are visible (available) from the point of declaration to the end of the file. Declarations within functions are visible from the point of declaration to the end of the enclosing block (usually this is the end of the function).

There are four storage classes in C (the C keyword is in parentheses):

- automatic (`auto`)
- external (`extern`)
- static (`static`)
- register (`register`)

The storage class affects a variable's storage duration and availability. The storage classes are shown below with variable availabilty and duration.

Table 9.1 Availability and Duration of C Storage Classes

Storage Class	Available to Functions in Other Source Files?	Storage Duration
`extern`	yes	entire program
`static`	no	entire program
`auto`	no	block or function
`register`	no	block or function

More on Expressions and the C Preprocessor

Remember that many C declarations not only describe an object but also request that storage be allocated for it. These declarations are termed *definitions*. Only definitions should have initializers. Both the storage class and whether or not a definition can be made are determined by the placement of the declaration in your program and the use of a storage class keyword. **Table 9.2** shows storage class keywords and whether or not definitions can occur for external and internal identifiers.

Table 9.2 Storage Class Keywords and the Use of Definitions

	Storage Class Keyword Used	Storage Class	Definition Allowed?
External Declarations*	none used	external	yes
	`extern`	external	no
	`static`	static	yes
Internal Declarations**	none present	automatic	yes
	`extern`	external	no
	`static`	static	yes
	`auto`	automatic	yes
	`register`	automatic	yes

* made outside of all functions.
** made inside a function.

Note that a variable with an `extern` storage class can never be initialized.

The next section discusses each C storage class in detail. After the storage classes are described, the discussion of scope is continued.

Storage Classes

Recall that the basic syntax for declaring an identifier is

  data_type identifier(s);

If you want to specify a storage class, just add the storage class to the beginning of the declaration:

  storage_class data_type identifier(s);

You can provide the storage class in the original definition for a variable, as well as any subsequent declarations of the variable made to facilitate its use. The following sections cover each storage class in detail.

Automatic Automatic identifiers are local identifiers that are automatically created upon entry to a block and *removed* when the block is exited. (Recall that a *block* consists of one or more C statements set off by braces.) Note that this means if you declare a variable as `auto` within a block or sub-block of code, the variable exists, or is recognized, only within that portion of code.

Chapter 9

By default, variables declared within a function are considered to be automatic. (Note that the formal parameters of a function are not really automatic variables although they behave in much the same way.) An **auto** variable comes into existence when the function containing it is called. When control returns to the caller, the variable *disappears*. You must declare **auto** variables at the beginning of a block or function. If you try to assign an automatic storage class to an identifier outside of a function, the compiler will not accept the declaration.

The syntax for an **auto** declaration is

  auto *data_type identifier*;

External   Specifying the **extern** storage class allows you to use a global or external variable that is defined in another source file or is defined later in the same file. Remember, external variables are permanent identifiers that are used to communicate between functions, including independently compiled functions residing in completely different files. External definitions or declarations are made outside of all functions (including **main**).

The **extern** storage class allows a function to use an external variable even if its definition appears later in the program or in another file that is part of the program. If you define a variable outside of all functions and it is only used within the file containing the functions, the **extern** keyword can be omitted. In this case, the *location* of the variable definition makes the storage class external and the variable global in scope.*

Remember, there can be only one definition of an external variable among files, although there may be several external declarations used to access it across functions. **Figure 9.1** illustrates this.

---

* Some systems have restrictions on the number of characters in the name of an **extern** variable. Check your system's documentation.

More on Expressions and the C Preprocessor

Correct: one definition of i

file1.c	file2.c	file3.c
`int i;`	`extern int i;`	`extern int i;`
(external) definition	declaration	declaration

Incorrect: multiple definitions of i

file1.c	file2.c	file3.c
`int i;`	`extern int i;`	`int i;`
(external) definition	declaration	(external) definition

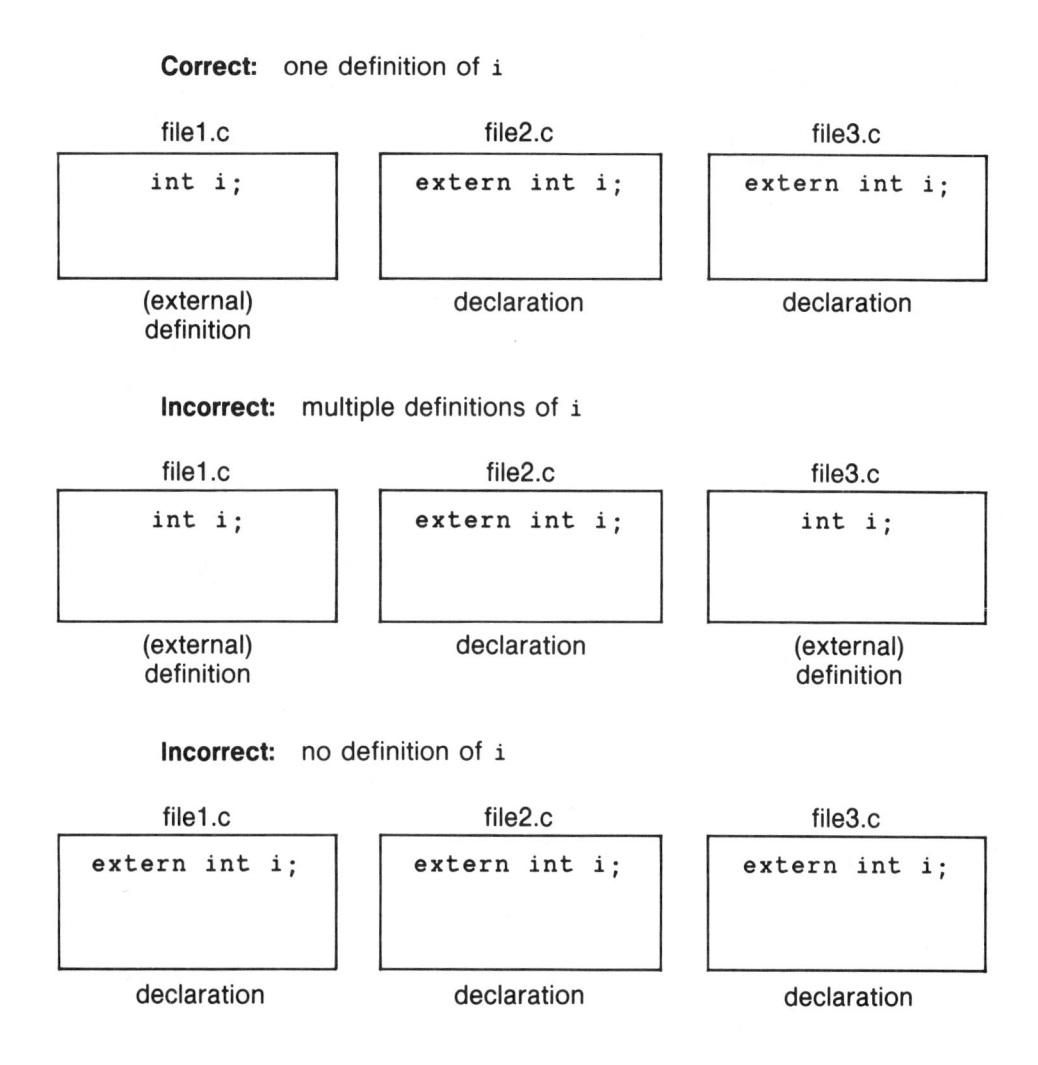

Incorrect: no definition of i

file1.c	file2.c	file3.c
`extern int i;`	`extern int i;`	`extern int i;`
declaration	declaration	declaration

Figure 9.1   Definition of an External Variable

Chapter 9

Initialization of an external variable is done when it is defined. For most compilers, a variable declared outside of any function must be defined only once between all the functions that use it. When `extern` is specified, the compiler assumes that a definition for this variable exists somewhere external to this particular file.

The syntax for an external declaration is

    extern *data_type identifier*;

When declaring an external array, the array size must be given in the original definition. The size can then be optionally included in any `extern` declarations made to reference the array.

In summary, code an `extern` declaration for a variable in the following cases:

- when an external variable is referred to before it is defined
- when an external variable is defined in a source file different from the current one.

Table 9.3 will help you decide when to explicitly code the keyword `extern`.

Table 9.3   When to Use the Keyword `extern`

Variable Use	Code as `extern`?	Where Defined	Declared Later?	Where to use `extern`
In one file and in some functions	no	Outside of all functions where used	no	—
In one file and in all functions	no	Before any function	no	—
In two or more files and in some functions	yes	In one file before functions where used	yes	In other files, where used
In two or more files and in all functions	yes	In one file, before all functions	yes	In other files, where used

Static   Variables declared as `static` are local identifiers that retain their values among block executions. Such identifiers are allocated at the beginning of program execution and exist for the life of your program. You can think of a `static` variable as a local variable whose value remains unchanged. Or, you can think of a static

More on Expressions and the C Preprocessor

variable as a global variable whose visibility is limited to the block (or file) in which it is defined.

Using the `static` storage class enables you to tell the computer to remember the values of variables declared within a function. Otherwise, these variables would be `auto`, and their values would disappear between function calls. At the same time, `static` allows you to *hide* the variable from other functions. Try the example below to see the difference `static` makes.

```
int main()
{
 int i;

 for (i = 1; i <= 3; i++)    /* Loop through print and function. */
  {
    printf("Function call: %d \n", i);
    sample();
  }
 return 0;
}

int sample()     /* Print auto and static values. */
{
 auto int auto_v = 1;
 static int static_v = 1;

 printf("Auto value = %d  Static value = %d\n", auto_v, static_v);

 auto_v += 1;
 static_v += 1;
 return 0;
}
```

The program output looks like this:

```
Function call: 1
Auto value = 1  Static value = 1
Function call: 2
Auto value = 1  Static value = 2
Function call: 3
Auto value = 1  Static value = 3
```

Note that the automatic variable `auto_v` is reinitialized each time the function is entered. The `static` variable `static_v`, however, retains its value after each successive function call.

You can also define external `static` variables that are visible to the entire file. If you declare a `static` variable outside of a function, it can be used by any functions in the source file that follow its definition. Such external statics are useful if you want two or more functions in the same file to share the same variable. In addition, it is sometimes very useful to declare a function as `static` so that its name will not be known outside of the source file containing it.

Chapter 9

Register Variables declared as `register` are similar to auto identifiers except that they are stored in machine registers for faster access. Registers are areas in memory that can be accessed and used more rapidly than other memory locations. If you know that a variable is going to be used frequently, specify this storage class to help minimize program run time.

However, there are some drawbacks, primarily the limited number of registers available. If the compiler cannot assign the variable to a register, its storage class will default to `auto`. In addition, you are not allowed to take the address of a `register` variable, so you cannot use the `&` operator on it.

The syntax of a `register` declaration is

  register *data_type identifier;*

Helpful Notes Here is a list of some important points to remember about storage class:

- If the storage class of an identifier is not specified explicitly, the identifier's storage class is determined by where its definition is located in the program.
- If the identifier is defined inside a function, its storage class defaults to `auto` (local).
- If an identifier is defined outside of a function, its storage class defaults to `extern` (global).
- You can leave out `auto` in variable declarations.
- In single file applications, you can leave out the keyword `extern`.
- In more complex single file applications, it is good programming practice to code `extern` whenever it applies, rather than relying on it being the class assigned by default.
- In multifile applications, you must specify `extern` when variables or objects are used across files in order to ensure that they are recognized by all functions involved.

Scope

At the beginning of this module, the **scope** of a variable was defined as the extent to which that variable is known to your program. This section helps you summarize the concept of scope as related to storage class.

As described in the previous section, there are two ways to view the scope of a variable: internally and externally. The *internal* scope of a variable is the extent to which the variable is known within a single source file. The *external* scope is the extent to which a variable is known among files.

More on Expressions and the C Preprocessor

Also, a scope can be implicit or explicit. An *implicit* scope is one that is dependent on where the variable is defined. An *explicit* scope is one that is specified by coding a storage class in the variable declaration or definition.

The following list summarizes the scope of a variable whose storage class is defined implicitly:

- An identifier defined within a block of code is recognized only within that block.
- The scope of an identifier defined outside all functions ranges from its declaration or definition to the end of the source file.
- The scope of a formal function parameter is the function itself.
- The scope of enumeration constants, structure and union component names, and type definitions is the same as a variable defined in the same program area.

It you specify a storage class explicity, the following rules apply to the scope of identifiers:

- The scope of automatic identifiers is limited to the block in which they are defined.
- An identifier declared as external is recognized by all the files forming an application.
- The scope of a static variable declared within a block is the block itself (differing from other local variables in that the value remains across function calls).
- Variables declared with the register storage class have the same scope as automatic variables.
- The scope of a static variable declared outside a function is limited to the source file containing the declaration or definition.

Module 20 Summary

In this module, you learned about storage classes and scope. This background will help you to ensure the integrity of identifiers in single and multifile applications. In the next module, you will learn more about the C preprocessor. Some new preprocessor commands will be introduced, and you will learn some ways to use the preprocessor to write clearer and more efficient C code.

New C Tools

Concepts	Code
scope	`auto`
storage class	`extern`
	`static`
	`register`

Chapter 9

Module 21: More on the C Preprocessor

Module 12 in Chapter 5 introduced the C preprocessor. As explained in that module, the preprocessor reads your source code before the compiler does and modifies your source code according to preprocessor commands or directives (the two terms are interchangeable). You learned how to include header files in your program with `#include`, and how to form simple constants and macros with `#define`. In this module, the rest of the preprocessor commands are introduced, and you will see more ways to take advantage of the preprocessing step in your programs.

Keywords you need to note are

manifest constant	`#endif`
parameterized macro	`#else`
`#define`	`#ifdef`
macro expansion	`#ifndef`
`#undef`	`#elif`
`#include`	`defined`
conditional compilation	`#line`
`#if`	`#pragma`

Introduction

Recall that a preprocessor command or directive begins with a `#` and can be one of several different instructions to the preprocessor. You are already familiar with `#define` and `#include`. This section looks at these commands (or directives) in more detail before introducing other preprocessor commands. The remaining commands are generally used in larger programming applications, particularly those where code must be as portable as possible. These other directives are also used in writing compilers and translators as well as programs that write other programs (code generators).

You may, however, find uses for many of the commands in everyday programming applications. Preprocessor commands make your program more flexible, and, when used properly, easier to understand. For example, the preprocessor can

- help make program modification easier by defining constants.

- enable you to form macros that simplify program code.

- provide a way for you to include additional files (declarations, data, blocks of code) to make modular program development easier.

- enable selective compilation of portions of code, helping you create different versions of your program.

More on Expressions and the C Preprocessor

Before you get started on this section, you need to know that preprocessor directives are compile-time options and not run-time options. This means that the preprocessor commands are executed before your program runs. How preprocessor commands are handled at compile time differs among C compilers. Many compilers allow you to *turn on* preprocessing options contained in your program from the command line when you invoke the compiler. Others only work with the preprocessor commands as they are encountered in your program.

Because compilers differ in preprocessor implementation, the focus here is on how you use preprocessor commands in your program only. Refer to the compiler documentation for your system for more information on the preprocessing step. In particular, find out if it is possible to enter preprocessor information from the command line when you invoke your compiler.

Each preprocessor command is discussed next. Some examples are given that show you how to use a command. However, many of these directives are for advanced systems applications beyond the scope of this book. But, the basics presented here should help you if you become interested in working with different kinds of hardware or other advanced applications.

In Chapter 5, `#define` was used to substitute a text string for an identifier. This module expands upon using constants and macros created by `#define`. Then you learn how to *undefine* a `#define` identifier using `#undef`, followed by another application for `#include`.

#define

The `#define` directive is used to

- define a preprocessor identifier (constant or macro name).
- define a macro for simple text string substitution.
- define a macro that the preprocessor expands into C code.

Defining an Identifier In order to use many of the preprocessor commands, you use `#define` to create special identifiers that are only recognized by the preprocessor. You use `#define` identifiers as constants or macro names in preprocessor commands that specify how you want the preprocessor to act on your source code. These identifiers or objects of the `#define` directive are often called **manifest constants**.

You create an identifier recognizable to the preprocessor by specifying the `#define` directive followed by at least one space and then a unique name. Note: do not use a semicolon after preprocessor directives.

Here are some examples of defining preprocessor identifiers.

```
#define DEBUG
#define SMALL_BUF
#define COMPATIBLE
```

Chapter 9

`#define` identifiers are most often used to tell the preprocessor that you want a particular preprocessing option to be in effect. In a later section you will learn how you can use identifiers to define preprocessing options in the section on conditional compilation. For now, just remember that preprocessor commands must work with identifiers that are known only in the preprocessing step, and the way you create such identifiers is with the `#define` command. Remember, `#define` identifiers are only available for use by the preprocessor. The identifiers you use in the `#define` statements are no longer available to your program after the preprocessing step.

Inside Information - #define

If you are using a compiler that allows you to enter directives from the command line, the syntax may look something like this:

```
cc program.c -DDEBUG
```

where `cc` means compile, `program.c` is your source file, and `-D` signals that a preprocessor identifier follows. The identifier, `DEBUG`, is an option to activate compile time activities that generate information needed later by a program debugger. (See Chapter 18 for more on the debugger included with this package.) As with other identifiers, `DEBUG` would be defined in your program with a `#define` command.

Defining Macros

In Chapter 5, you learned that you can define two kinds of macros in C. One type lets you do simple text string substitution. The other lets you define and expand C code and involves the use of parameters.

Simple Macros   In a simple macro, the preprocessor replaces all occurrences of an identifier with the text string coded after the identifier name. This means you can define something once. Then, if the value changes, you only need to change the value of the macro. For example, if you were processing text and wanted to be able to change the size of a buffer depending on the amount of text you were expecting, you could code:

```
#define BUFFER    40
    .
    .
    .
char text [ BUFFER ];    /* text = 40 element array */
```

To change the size of all occurrences of `text` you only need to change the value specified for `BUFFER`.

Here are some more examples of simple text replacement macros:

```
#define OUNCE   28.350          /* grams */
#define AND     &&              /* logical */
#define HELLO   "Hello World!"  /* output string */
```

230

You can also use simple text substitution macros if you want to make your code more readable. A common example is to define the following:

```
#define BEGIN  {
#define END    }
```

In this example, every occurrence of a { in your program would be replaced with the word BEGIN and every occurrence of a } would be replaced with the word END. This is a convenient way to delineate long or complicated blocks of code.

Defining Macros with Parameters You can do more with macros than simple text replacement. You can associate code containing symbolic variables with a macro identifier. When you use the macro in your program, you code the actual values in the macro call. The preprocessor replaces the formal parameters with the actual values. These kinds of macros are called **parameterized macros**.

The syntax for defining a parameterized macro is

#**define** identifier(parm_1, . . ., parm_n) text containing parm_1, . . ., parm_n

The #**define** command is followed by a name identifying the macro. Immediately after the name, with no spaces in between, is a list of parameters that are used in the C code defined to replace the macro where it occurs in your program.

Here is how it works. The macro definition is coded using formal parameters. The macro call in your program uses actual parameters. The first thing the preprocessor does when it encounters a parameterized macro in your program is replace the formal parameters in the #**define** with the actual parameters from the program. Then, the preprocessor substitutes the C code defined for the macro where the macro occurs in your program. The entire process is called **macro expansion**.

Suppose you want to print error messages. You could define a macro to print a message to the standard error file. Here is how it would look:

```
    /* Macro definition */
#define error_msg(text)  fprintf(stderr, text);
    .
    .
    .
    /* Macro call */
error_msg( "error: attempted zero-divide" );
```

The message `error: attempted zero-divide` or any other message text you supply will be printed when you call `error_msg`. The preprocessor recognizes a macro definition when it encounters the #**define** with an identifier immediately followed by a parenthesized parameter list. In the example there is only one parameter, `text`, enclosed in parentheses following the macro identifier `error_msg`. The preprocessor substitutes the actual error message for the formal parameter `text` in the macro definition. Then, the expanded macro text is substituted in the program.

Chapter 9

The following is what is compiled after the preprocessing step:

```
fprintf(stderr, "error: attempted zero-divide");
```

In this case, coding a macro saved you only a little coding time, the program is made clearer by specifying a call to print an error message.

Reviewing this process, you create a parameterized macro by coding a parameter list immediately after the macro identifier. The parameters are separated by commas and enclosed in parentheses. Note: there must be no space between the macro identifier and the first parentheses. If there is a space, the compiler assumes anything that follows is just text to be substituted instead of a macro definition.

As you might have guessed, macros can be much more complex. For example, you can define blocks of code to be substituted as long as you *continue* multiple line macros with a backslash. Here are three examples to help give you some ideas for using parameterized macros in your programs.

```
#include <stdio.h>

/* Define two macros to compute the maximum and minimum
 * of any two numbers.  Define a third macro that will exchange
 * the values of any two numbers.
 */

#define max(x,y)         ((x) > (y) ? (x) : (y))
#define min(x,y)         ((x) < (y) ? (x) : (y))

#define xchange(type,x,y)  { \
                            type _temp = (x);     \
                            (x) = (y);            \
                            (y) = _temp;          \
                           }
#define error_msg(text)    fprintf(stderr, text);

main()
{
 int a = 4, b = 5;

 printf( "a=%d, b=%d\n", a, b);  /* print original values */
 xchange ( int, a, b );          /* exchange two values */
 printf( "a=%d, b=%d\n", a, b ); /* print exchanged values */

 error_msg( "test error message \n");  /* use error print */

 printf( "%d %d\n", max(1,2),  max(2,1) );  /* use max macro */
 printf( "%d %d\n", min(1,2),  min(2,1) );  /* use min macro */

 return 0;
}
```

232

More on Expressions and the C Preprocessor

Look at each macro involved. The `max` and `min` macros are defined as taking two parameters `x` and `y`. The macro text for `max` that will be substituted in your program is the conditional expression `((x)>(y)?(x):(y))`, which compares `x` with `y` and returns a Boolean value depending on whether the result of the comparison is true or false. The call for `max` is made as part of a `printf()` statement. In the preprocessing step, the actual values 1 and 2 are substituted for the formal parameters `x` and `y`. The preprocessor then replaces the macro in the line of code with the expanded text for the conditional expression. The same process occurs for the `min` macro.

Similar processing steps occur for the `xchange` macro. The code to be substituted is enclosed in braces to delineate a block. A temporary variable `_temp` is defined to be whatever type is passed, in this case `int`. The variable name `_temp` is coded beginning with an underscore as a matter of style. (For program clarity, you may want to adopt the convention of beginning variable names with an underscore if the variable is part of a macro definition.) After preprocessing, the expanded version of `xchange` appears in your program wherever the `xchange` macro is encountered. In the example, the expanded code will look like this:

```
{
  int _temp = a;
  a = b;
  b = _temp;
}
```

You may be wondering why you should bother coding a function for something when you can use macros. A general rule is that you should use a macro if the code is relatively brief and you do not need a value returned from the call. However, even though function calls involve more work from the compiler's point of view, macro code can use more storage than a function. More importantly, programs using lots of macros can become very difficult to debug.

One last note: when defining macros, be careful about including extraneous operators or semicolons. For example, if you end a macro with a semicolon and then use the macro in a context where a semicolon already appears in the regular C code, the results can be unpredictable.

#undef

The `#undef` directive is used to *undefine* something that has been defined earlier with a `#define` directive. This command makes the compiler stop recognizing an earlier definition of the identifier involved.

For example,

```
#define TEST
    .
    .
    .
#undef TEST
```

causes the identifier `TEST` to cease to be recognized by the preprocessor.

Chapter 9

Remember that preprocessor commands can appear anywhere in your program. This makes the `#undef` command especially useful if you want to process something one way in part of your program and another way later. This directive is also useful if you want to change or suspend the way something is defined in a header file. Instead of changing the header file you can just use `#undef` on whatever `#define` you want to change.

For example, suppose an I/O buffer is defined in a header file, and you want to change the size. The following code would accomplish this:

```
#define IO_BUF  500        /* code in header file */
    .
    .                      /* code in your program */
    .
#undef IO_BUF              /* terminate that definition */
#define IO_BUF 1000        /* define as you want it */
```

The `#define` that you code remains in effect for the rest of your program unless you nullify it with a subsequent `#undef`.

#include

You know from Chapter 5 that files can be made available for use in your program by using this command. This means that you can keep constants, data, various type declarations, function declarations, and definitions in files separate from your main program.

For example, recall the discussion on structures in Chapter 8. Suppose you had a long and detailed structure, such as your monthly financial statement. You would probably use this same structure in a number of programs, such as checkbook balancing, investments, tax records, and so forth. Instead of coding the structure for each program, you could code the structure once and include it as a header file in your program, as follows:

```
#include <mydata.h>   /* personal finance record structure */
```

This include file would contain the structure tag definition, which might look something like this:

```
/* My finance data */

struct master {         /* contains summary of your finances */
    char type_code[5];  /* type of data - bank, auto */
    char begin_date[6]; /* start of transaction period */
    char end_date[6];   /* end transaction period */
    int payment_sum;    /* total all payments */
    int receipt_sum;    /* total all receipts */
         .
         .
         .

    } ;
```

More on Expressions and the C Preprocessor

If you need to modify a member of this structure, you only make the change in one place. You can use `#include` for structure definitions, constants, and any other definitions too long or cumbersome to repeat in several programs.

Conditional Compilation

There are preprocessor commands that allow you to specify that only those sections of your program satisfying a certain set of conditions are compiled. In other words, these directives enable you to create different versions of your program by including certain sections and excluding others. This is called **conditional compilation**.

Conditional compilation is used at the end of this chapter in a simple language translation program. In the program, you include some files if the language selected is Spanish, but you use another set of code for some sections of your program if the language selected is French.

You use the following preprocessor commands to conditionally compile your program:

```
#if
#endif
#else
#ifdef
#ifndef
#elif
```

#if, #endif, #else   The `#if` directive is conceptually closer to the regular C `if` statement than other forms of preprocessor conditional commands. Using `#if` allows you to execute code based on whether or not a condition is evaluated as true or false. The format for `#if` looks like this:

#if *identifier*
   C statements
#endif

Note that the `#if` construct ends with an `#endif`.

You can pair `#if` commands with `#else` directives just like regular C `if` and `else` clauses, as follows:

#if *identifier*
   C statements executed if #if is TRUE
#else
   C statements executed if #if is FALSE
#endif

The condition evaluated for the `#if` command is a constant expression represented by an identifier that has been defined by `#define`. The statements following `#if` or `#else` can be any lines of C code, including other preprocessor directives.

Chapter 9

In both cases, the constant expression is evaluated as true or false depending on whether its value is non-zero or zero. In the simple #if, if the condition is true, the C statements are executed. If not true, they are not executed. When #else is used, the statements following the #else clause are executed if the #if condition is evaluated as false.

For example, suppose you want to vary the size of arrays in your program depending on the amount of data you were working with. You would code a #define for the buffer size relevant to a particular program execution. The preprocessor would note the presence of this #define. Using a simple #if, your code could look something like this:

```
#if SMALL
#define BUFFER 100
#endif
#if MEDIUM
#define BUFFER 250
#endif
#if LARGE
#define BUFFER 500
#endif
```

You could then define SMALL in a separate header file that you would include with #include (or you could define SMALL from the command line, if possible with your compiler).

If you only want to choose between two sizes or default to a size if an option is not in effect, you can use #else and code something like this:

```
#if LARGE
#define BUFFER 500
#else
#define BUFFER 250
#endif
```

If LARGE was not defined (that is, FALSE), a size of 250 is defined.

#ifdef, #ifndef, #elif   These directives are really additional forms of the #if preprocessor command.

The #ifdef directive tests to see if an identifier has been defined previously with #define and not undefined by #undef. The result (TRUE if the identifier exists and FALSE if the identifier is not defined) can be used in conditional inclusion of program statements.

The #ifndef directive, on the other hand, tests to see if an identifier has not been defined. The result of the conditional test is TRUE if the identifier does not exist and FALSE if the identifier is currently defined. #ifndef is also used to conditionally include program statements. For example, in the program at the end of this chapter,

More on Expressions and the C Preprocessor

these commands are used as follows:

```
#ifdef FRENCH      /* if FRENCH has been defined    */
    .              /* execute the code that follows */
    .
    .
#endif             /* end the #ifdef                */
```

In this case, the portion of code relevant to the French application is executed only if a **#define** exists for **FRENCH**. You could accomplish the same thing by saying:

```
#ifndef SPANISH    /* if SPANISH has NOT been defined */
    .              /* execute the code that follows   */
    .
    .
#endif             /* end the #ifndef                 */
```

Here, the code following the **SPANISH** is executed if **SPANISH** is not defined. You could use this construct if you want to execute the same code for all languages (French, German, and so on) except Spanish.

The **#elif** directive is a recent addition to the C language. It follows the C **else if** construct, and it is used to simplify nested **#if** statements. Here is how it looks:

#if *identifier_1*
   statements executed if identifier_1 TRUE
#elif *identifier_2*
   statements executed if identifier_2 TRUE
#elif *identifier_3*
   statements executed if identifier_3 TRUE
   .
   .
   .
#endif

Directives for Portability and Advanced Applications

The following directives are used most often to ensure portable code.

defined   This preprocessor command is also a recent addition to the C language and does not appear in many C compilers. **defined** is actually considered a preprocessor *operator* instead of a true directive (note the absence of #). This is because you apply the keyword **defined** to an operand; in this case, a preprocessor identifier created with **#define**. **defined** removes the need for using **#ifdef** and **#ifndef**. For

Chapter 9

example, instead of using a series of **#ifdef** directives like this

```
#ifdef A
#ifdef B
     .
     .
     .
#endif
#endif
```

you could use **defined** as follows:

```
#if defined (A) && defined (B)
     .
     .
     .
#endif
```

Check your compiler documentation for the use of **defined** on your system.

#line   The compiler keeps track of the lines in your code with line numbers. You notice these numbers if you have syntax errors because they are associated with the line in error. This directive forces the compiler to reset the line count. This can be done for the current program or for another file.

#line is used mainly in writing and debugging program generators or preprocessors. You may be involved with this type of application later. Under most circumstances, however, you will not need this directive.

#pragma   This is another command you will probably never use unless you become involved in writing compilers or C code that will be used on several different hardware implementations.

In a general sense, a *pragma* is a programming statement that gives information to the compiler about a particular implementation. For example, you would use **#pragma** if you want your code to run on two different kinds of microcomputers, and you want to tell the compiler about the different attributes involved for each.

This directive is also used in creating very efficient or *optimized* code for a particular machine or compiler. But again, in most of your applications, use of **#pragma** will not be necessary.

Module 21 Summary

In this section you learned more about what the C preprocessor can do to make your programs more flexible and efficient. Although you may not use all of the commands, knowing their general attributes is good background if you venture into more complex C applications.

More on Expressions and the C Preprocessor

New C Tools

Concepts	Code
preprocessor	`#define`
macro	`#undef`
conditional compilation	`#include`
	`#if`
	`#endif`
	`#else`
	`#elif`
	`#ifdef`
	`#ifndef`
	`defined`
	`#line`
	`#pragma`

Language for Fun - An Example Using the Preprocessor

In this example you work with a program that provides a template for practicing language translations. The program is structured for two topics. Under each topic you have a choice of two languages to use for translation practice. Although Spanish and French are used as examples, you can easily substitute any language text.

The main purpose of this example is to show you how to use the preprocessor to conditionally include blocks of code. In the example, you include either Topic 1 or Topic 2 in Spanish or French versions, depending on what you define as active to the preprocessor.

The example runs based on a series of pairs of phrases and translations. You are prompted for the correct translation for a phrase followed by a list of possible choices. The choices are formed from all the translations available. After entering a choice, the program tells you if you chose correctly. The number of questions for translation depends upon the number of phrase/translation pairs you have defined in the program.

Chapter 9

When you run the example, your output will look like the following (definitions are active for Topic 1, Spanish, and for three phrases).

```
Topic #1

What is the translation of: Spanish Phrase 1

1) Translation 2
2) Translation 3
3) Translation 1
Translation # ? _2_      ( <--- you enter your choice)
Correct.

What is the translation of: Spanish Phrase 2

1) Translation 3
2) Translation 1
3) Translation 2
Translation # ? _1_
Sorry, the correct answer is Translation 2.

What is the translation of: Spanish Phrase 3

1) Translation 3
2) Translation 2
3) Translation 1
Translation # ? _3_
Correct.

You got 2 right out of 3.
```

The basic program flow is as follows. The `main` function calls a function named `ask_question`. `ask_question` controls the processing calling: `scramble` to mix up the translations to the phrases, `print_options` to display the choices, and `getnum` to get your response. `ask_question` returns your score to `main( )` where it is printed. Read over the code and try the program. Following the code is a summary of the program components: the preprocessing step, each function, and the data objects involved.

```
/* Program to translate basic Spanish and French phrases. */

/* Translations are done in two topic areas.              */


/* Include standard I/O and utility ("isdigit") header files */
#include <stdio.h>
#include <ctype.h>

/* Define maximum number of questions that can be handled */
#define MAX_QUESTIONS    30
```

More on Expressions and the C Preprocessor

```c
/*  Define standard Boolean values  */
#define FALSE 0
#define TRUE  !FALSE

/*  Declare the structure for the translation data.
 *  Members are character pointers to the phrase
 *  to be translated and the translation.
 */
struct pair {
  char *phrase;
  char *translation;
  };

/*  prototypes for functions defined in this program  */

void scramble( struct pair[], char *[], int );
int ask_questions( struct pair[], int );
void print_options( char *[], int );
int getnum( char *, int );

/*  Begin preprocessor directives for conditional compilation.  */

/*  Define an identifier to determine the active language.
 *  Only one language can be "active" at a time.  The presence
 *  of "SPANISH" and absence of "FRENCH" means that Spanish
 *  is the language used in this occurrence of the program.
 *  The same is true for the topic area selected. In this case,
 *  TOPIC1 is active since it is defined.
 */

/*  N O T E: Only ONE language and topic can be active    */

                   /* ---------------------------------- */
#define SPANISH    /* S E L E C T    L A N G U A G E     */
#define TOPIC1     /* A N D    T O P I C                 */
                   /* ---------------------------------- */


/* _____*/


#ifdef TOPIC1       /* Begin code relevant to Topic 1.  */

char *topic = "Topic #1";  /* Pointer to text describing topic 1 */


/* --------------------------------------------------------- */
#ifdef SPANISH      /* If Spanish is defined (active) use this code. */
```

241

Chapter 9

```
    /* Define an array of phrase/translation pairs.
     * Array is two-dimensional, each element is an
     * array consisting of two elements of type "struct pair".
     */

    struct pair questions[] = {
      { "Spanish Phrase 1", "Translation 1" },
      { "Spanish Phrase 2", "Translation 2" },
      { "Spanish Phrase 3", "Translation 3" },
    };


    /* Let the computer calculate the number of questions.
     * Divide the total number of bytes used (sizeof) for the
     * phrase/translation pairs by the width in bytes of one
     * phrase/translation object.
     */

    int num_questions = sizeof( questions ) / sizeof( struct pair );

    #endif   /*  END Spanish  */



    /* -------------------------------------------------------- */
    #ifdef FRENCH      /* If French is defined (active) use this code */

    struct pair questions[] = {

      { "French Phrase 1", "Translation 1" }
      { "French Phrase 2", "Translation 2" }
      { "French Phrase 3", "Translation 3" }
    };

    int num_questions = sizeof( questions ) / sizeof( struct pair );

    #endif   /*  END French  */

    #endif   /*  END Topic 1  */




    /* _____ */

    #ifdef TOPIC2        /* Begin code relevant to Topic 2 */

    char *topic = "Topic #2";  /* Pointer to text describing topic 2 */



    /* -------------------------------------------------------- */
    #ifdef SPANISH     /* If Spanish is defined (active) use this code. */
```

```
   struct pair questions[] = {
     { "Spanish Phrase 1", "Translation 1" },
     { "Spanish Phrase 2", "Translation 2" },
     { "Spanish Phrase 3", "Translation 3" },
     };

   int num_questions = sizeof( questions ) / sizeof( struct pair );

   #endif   /* END Spanish */


   /* -------------------------------------------------------- */
   #ifdef FRENCH      /* If French is defined (active) use this code. */

   struct pair questions[] = {
     { "French Phrase 1", "Translation 1" }
     { "French Phrase 2", "Translation 2" }
     { "French Phrase 3", "Translation 3" }
     };

   int num_questions = sizeof( questions ) / sizeof( struct pair );

   #endif   /* END French */

   /* -------------------------------------------------------- */

   #endif   /* END Topic 2 */


   /* End of preprocessor statements.  The main() function begins.
    * main() calls the function ask_questions which drives the
    * translation process.
    */

   main()
   {
     int score;
     printf( "\n\n%s\n\n", topic );
     score = ask_questions( questions, num_questions );
     printf( "\nYou got %d right out of %d\n", score, num_questions");
     return 0;
   }
```

243

Chapter 9

```
/*  This function receives a pointer to the first element of the
 *  array containing the phrase/translation pairs and a count
 *  indicating the total number of questions.
 *  An integer value called "score", containing the number of correct
 *  guesses, is returned to main().  ask_questions asks what the
 *  appropriate translation is for each phrase; calling the function
 *  scramble to mix up the translations.  The question and answer
 *  process continues until all phrases have been used.
 */

ask_questions( array, count )
struct pair array[];
int count;
{
  char *mixed[MAX_QUESTIONS];
  int i;                          /* three variables, local in scope */
  int score = 0;
  int guess;
  int valid_guess = 0;

  scramble( array, mixed, count );    /* mix up the translations */

  for ( i = 0; i < count; i++ )
    {
    printf( "What is the translation of: %s\n\n", array [i].phrase);
    print_options( mixed, count);
    valid_guess = 0;

    while (! valid_guess ) {
     guess = getnum("Translation #?", 0);
     valid_guess = (guess > 0) && (guess <= count);
    }

    /* If response equals the translation member for that */
    /* element of the array of phrase/translation structures */
    /* print "Correct", otherwise provide correct answer. */

    if (array[i].translation == mixed[ guess - 1 ] )
        {
         printf( "Correct.\n" );
         score++;
        }
    else
        {
         printf( "Sorry, the correct answer is %s. \n",
                 array[i].translation );
        }
    }
  return (score);
}
```

More on Expressions and the C Preprocessor

```c
/* Mix the translations to phrases.  Keep track of the
 * translation locations in an array of pointers to character
 * named "mixed".
 */

void scramble( array, mixed, count )
struct pair array[];
char *mixed[];
{
  int i;
  int place;

  /* First fill "mixed" with NULL's, up to "count" elements */
  /* "count" is the total number of phrase/translation pairs */

  for ( i = 0; i < count; i++ )
     {
       mixed[i] = NULL;
     }


  /* Randomly mix the translations, replacing each NULL
   * with a pointer to a translation member.
   */

  for ( i = 0; i < count; i++ )
     {
       for (;;)
          {
            place = rand() % count;
            if ( mixed[place] == NULL )
              {
                mixed[place] = array[i].translation;
                break;
              }
          }
     }
}
```

Chapter 9

```c
/*  Print the possible translations as multiple choices for a phrase.
*/
void print_options( options, count )
char *options[];
{
    int i;

    for ( i = 0; i < count; i++ )
        {
        printf( "%2d)   %s\n", i+1, options[i] );
        }
}


/*  A more sophisticated version of getnum(). Provides greater */
/*  error checking.  */

getnum( prompt, default_value )
char *prompt;
int default_value;
{
    char buffer[80];
    int i;
    int valid = FALSE;
    int digits = 0;

    while ( !valid )
        {
        fputs( prompt, stdout );

        valid = TRUE;
        digits = 0;

        /* Try to read a line, if fail, abort the program. */

        /* Use sizeof to avoid hardcoding a buffer size */
        if ( fgets( buffer, sizeof( buffer ), stdin ) == NULL )
            {
            fprintf( stderr, "Unexpected error reading number.\n" );
            exit ( 1 );
            }

        /* If got a full line, remove the trailing <RETURN>
         * (Use "i" as a temporary variable so you don't have
         * to recalculate the string length)
         */

        if ( buffer[ (i = strlen( buffer ) - 1) ] == '\n')
        buffer[i]= '\0';
```

246

More on Expressions and the C Preprocessor

```c
    /* Skip leading spaces */

    for ( i = 0; isspace( buffer[i] ) && ( buffer[i] != '\0'); i++)
       ;

    /* If a blank line or string of spaces, return the default */

    if ( buffer[i] == '\0' )
       return ( default_value );

    /* Check string for validity, ignore leading sign
     * since that's valid for a number.
     */

    if ( buffer[i] == '-')
       i++;

    /* Skip over string of digits */

    for ( ; isdigit( buffer[i] ) && ( buffer[i] !='\0'); i++)
       digits++;

    /* Skip over trailing spaces. */

    for ( ; isspace( buffer[i] ) && ( buffer[i] !='\0'); i++)
       ;


    /* If everything has been handled that "could" be
     * a number and not yet at end-of-string, then
     * rest of input is invalid, tell user, and
     * try again.
     */

    if ( ( buffer[i] != '\0' ) || ( digits == 0 ))
       {
        printf( "Invalid number <%s>\n", buffer );
        valid = FALSE;
        }
    }

/* buffer contains a valid string representation of number,
 * so convert it and return it
 */

return( atoi( buffer ) );
}
```

Chapter 9

A Closer Look

The most important new concepts in this program are the preprocessor statements that determine which topic and language are used, and the structure template for the phrase/translation pairs.

In the first part of the program, `#define` is used to define constants for the maximum number of questions (`MAX_QUESTIONS 30`) and standard Boolean values. The new use of `#define` is

```
#define SPANISH
#define TOPIC1
```

These identifiers indicate to the preprocessor that the code for Topic 1 and Spanish is to be used instead of Topic 2 or French. This conditional compilation is accomplished with the use of `#ifdef` in later statements.

Data for translation processing is in the form of a structure template called `struct pair` whose members are a pointer to the phrase to be translated and a pointer to the translation for that phrase.

```
struct pair {
   char *phrase;
   char *translation;
   }
```

These phrase/translation pairs are defined in a two-dimensional array called `questions`, which is of type `struct pair`. The array phrase/translation elements are initialized in the array definition.

```
struct pair questions[] = {
         { "Spanish Phrase 1", "Translation 1" },
         { "Spanish Phrase 2", "Translation 2" },
         { "Spanish Phrase 3", "Translation 3" },
      };
```

The functions `ask_questions( )` and `scramble( )` both receive a pointer (via the array name) to the first element of the phrase/translation array `questions`.

Take the time to diagram and work through each function. Be sure that you understand what parameters are being used and what return values, if any, are present.

Chapter Summary

In this chapter, you learned more about the C preprocessor. You also learned about scope and storage class and how these concepts apply to objects you have defined. In the next chapter, you continue to build on the concepts. You learn more about I/O operations, especially in terms of handling more complex data structures. The basics for some advanced data structures are introduced and you get an opportunity to apply what you have learned in building and using a simple data base.

Chapter 10
Working with Data: Files, Structures, and Storage

Chapter 10

CONTENTS

Introduction	251
Module 22: More on I/O - Working with Files in C	251
Some Background on C I/O Operations	252
Standard File I/O Functions	253
Additional I/O Options: Random and Low-Level I/O	257
Module 22 Summary	258
Module 23: An Introduction to Data Structures	259
What is a Data Structure?	259
A Simple Data Base of Names and Addresses	260
Concepts and Tools for Developing the Data Base	264
Implementing the Data Base Operations	274
Module 23 Summary	303
Chapter Summary	303

Working with Data: Files, Structures, and Storage

Introduction

In this chapter, you will learn more about working with data in C. You will see how to work with collections of data in file form and as a data base. The chapter begins with a brief section covering the remaining I/O functions, focusing on the file I/O functions that you will use later. For the remainder of the chapter, you will develop and work with a data base of names, addresses, and telephone numbers.

The data base programming example that you construct in this chapter is considerably more complex than the ones in previous chapters. It is designed both to help you build a useful tool to add to your C programs, and to illustrate some features of the C language and functions in the C library that you have not seen in an actual application. Remember, you will need to work through the example over a period of time. Try not to become discouraged if some concepts and code are not clear after more than one read through the chapter.

The data base program is built in sections. Each section is discussed in detail: new concepts and code are identified each step of the way. If you have access to a PC running MS-DOS or PC DOS, you will also find it helpful to print a complete listing of the program. The program is `CH10EX1.C` on the examples diskette included with the Student Compiler. Also, print a listing of the header file `db.h`. (You can then refer back to variable definitions and so forth while you are studying the text.) Then, run the example, and study each section of code. If you have access to a debugger (one is included with the Student Compiler), you will find it very helpful to step through the program as it is executed. Again, take your time with the concepts and code presented here. Understanding this application provides a good introduction for studying C at a more advanced level.

The chapter is organized into two sections:

- working with files in C
- introduction to data structures.

Module 22: More on I/O - Working with Files in C

In Chapter 5, you learned how to read and write data using the standard files that C provides: `stdin`, `stdout`, and `stderr`. In this module, you learn some new I/O functions and how to work with files other than the standard files: files you create or other files existing outside the C environment.

The basics about each file I/O function are covered, but consult your compiler's reference guide for more details about how each function is implemented on your system.

You will also learn how to perform basic error checking for some of these functions in the data base example discussed in the following module. But, again, refer to your reference guide for more complete details on handling I/O errors on your system.

Chapter 10

Keywords you need to note are

standard I/O	`fopen`
low-level I/O	`fclose`
text file	`fread`
binary file	`fwrite`
random access	`fseek`
file pointer	`ftell`
`FILE`	

Some Background on C I/O Operations

As mentioned earlier in this tutorial, C was developed in close conjunction with UNIX operating systems. Therefore, the C input and output model was originally structured around UNIX concepts. The basic features of the traditional UNIX I/O model include the following:

- A **file** is a sequence of bytes. A file contains no information other than these bytes.
- A file is divided into **lines** by the newline ('\n') character.
- The bytes in a file are numbered sequentially starting at 0.
- It is possible to position a file efficiently to any particular byte.
- There are no arbitrary restrictions on the length of lines or the size of a file. (Some newer versions of UNIX operating systems do have an option to set a file size limit.)
- Files may be opened for reading, writing, or both.

UNIX operating systems also define two I/O interfaces: standard I/O and low-level I/O. **Low-level I/O** is sometimes referred to as *unbuffered* I/O because you work with the data directly instead of having it read into a buffer. **Standard I/O** refers to operations involving buffered I/O where many of the file handling details are done for you by the compiler. Standard I/O is focused on here.

Today, C programs are run under many different operating systems. For example, if you are using the C compiler provided with this book, you are probably using a PC DOS operating system, which handles files differently from UNIX operating systems. To ensure that C is compatible across most systems, language standards are being developed by the Draft ANSI Standard. The Draft ANSI Standard defines a somewhat different I/O model from UNIX operating systems to take into consideration variations in operating systems.

One of the main differences is that ANSI distinguishes between **text** and **binary** files. Let's look at PC DOS as an example to see why this distinction is necessary.

Working with Data: Files, Structures, and Storage

PC DOS separates lines of text using a two-character sequence: carriage return (CR) followed by a line feed (LF). UNIX operating systems, however, recognize only the newline character as separating the lines in a file. So, to allow a line-oriented C program to execute under PC DOS, the C library must translate a CR/LF to a newline character on input and vice versa on output. To handle this situation, the ANSI I/O definition specifies that when a file is accessed as a **binary stream**, the C implementation must read or write the characters without modification. When a file is accessed as a **text stream**, C is obliged to present the file to the program as a series of lines separated by newline characters.

The Student Compiler is based on the ANSI I/O model, which can be summarized as follows:

- There are two ways to process a file: as a text stream or as a binary stream. In binary mode, what you work with in your program is the exact sequence of characters that appear in the file. In text mode, what appears in the file may be translated in the buffer. In other words, CR/LF pairs are translated to the newline character.

- A file accessed as a text stream appears to the program as a sequence of lines separated by occurrences of the newline character ('\n').

- When a file is accessed as a binary stream, its characters are numbered sequentially starting at 0. It is possible to position a binary stream to any particular character. (Text streams are addressable, but not necessarily by a character number.)

- Files may be opened for reading, writing, or both.

Now you are ready to look at the C functions for file I/O operations.

Standard File I/O Functions

These functions work with standard files and can be used with either the standard C files or files you create or access.

fopen `fopen` initially takes an external filename, such as the MS-DOS or PC DOS filename `myfile.c` or `names.txt`, and performs some tasks associated with preparing a file for processing. `fopen` then returns a pointer, called a **file pointer**, to the internal structure that the compiler uses to hold information about the file. You use this pointer when you work with the file in various I/O operations (read, write, and so on).

The structure that the compiler fills with information about your file is represented in `stdio.h` by a structure definition called `FILE`. You use the type name `FILE` to declare a file pointer to this structure. The format is as follows:

  FILE *fp*;

where fp is a pointer to a structure of type `FILE`.

Chapter 10

The format for the **fopen** call in your program looks like this:

fopen(*name*, *mode*)

where *name* is the name of a file and *mode* indicates how you want to use the file, such as read, write, append, or a permissible combination such as read/write. (Append means to add data to the end of an existing file.) Both the name of the file and the access mode are character strings or pointers to character strings.

The most common modes are shown in **Table 10.1**. (Refer to the discussion of **fopen** in the reference guide for your compiler for more options.)

Table 10.1   File Modes in C

Mode	Access	Create File
"r"	read only	no
"w"	write only	yes
"a"	append only	yes
"r+"	read, write	no
"w+"	read, write	yes
"a+"	read, append	yes

Appending b to any mode causes a file to be opened in binary mode; otherwise, the mode is text mode. For example, **rb+** reads and writes an existing file in binary mode.

In the data base example, the function that creates the data base file uses **fopen**. Here is how it looks:

```
dbread(name)       /* data base read routine */

char *name;        /* pointer to name string */
{
   FILE *fp;
         .
         .
         .
   if ((fp = fopen(name, "rb+")) == NULL)
     {
        fprintf(stderr, "Can't open file: %s \n", name);
        return(0);
     }
```

Working with Data: Files, Structures, and Storage

This code opens the named file for reading and writing as a binary file. **fopen** returns a NULL pointer value (remember NULL is defined for you in `stdio.h`) if the open operation fails (for example, if you try to read a file that doesn't exist).

In review, the function call to **fopen**

```
fp = fopen(name, "rb+");
```

means, "call the **fopen** function, passing as parameters the name string pointed to by **name** and the access mode string `"rb+"` to open an existing file in read/write mode for binary data."

After calling **fopen**, the file then can be read by any of the standard I/O read functions such as **fread**. Or, as you will see shortly, the file can also be positioned for reading by **fseek()** or another random access I/O function.

fclose This function completes the processing of a standard I/O file. Any operations in progress, such as writing data to the file, are completed before breaking the bond between the file pointer and the name established via **fopen**.

If the close operation is successful, **fclose** returns a zero. If **fclose** is not successful (the file does not exist or has already been closed), **fclose** returns a -1.

The format for **fclose** is

fclose(*filepointer*)

where *filepointer* is a pointer to the file you are working with.

fread This function reads data from the standard file pointed to by **fp**. The **fread** function groups data to be read into blocks. You specify the size of the block and the maximum number of blocks of data that will be read. **fread** is designed to work primarily with binary data.

The format for **fread** is

fread(*buffer, size, count, file*)

where *buffer* is the area you have specified to hold a block of data, *size* is the size of each block in bytes, *count* is the maximum number of blocks you want to handle at one time, and *file* is a **FILE** pointer for the file that you have opened for input.

fread returns the number of complete blocks that were read. If the end of the file is reached in the middle of a block, the partial block will be stored in the buffer, but not included in the count. If an error occurs, **fread** returns a zero, which means no blocks of data could be read. Actually, if the return value is less than **count**, then your program can check two other C functions, **feof** and **ferror**, to determine what happened.

Chapter 10

Frequently, a block size of 1 is used by programmers in order to get an exact count of bytes read from the file. For example, in the data base program, **fread** is coded like this:

```
FILE *fp;
struct dbentry db;
int rsize;
    .
    .
    .
rsize = fread((char *)&db, 1, DBSIZE, fp)

/* size of 1 block == 1 char, reading DBSIZE blocks */
```

Now look at each part of this statement.

    rsize = . . .

rsize is an integer variable that will contain the number of blocks actually read. This is the value returned by the **fread** function.

    fread(. . .)

This call to **fread** takes four parameters coded as follows:

    (char *)&db

This parameter tells **fread** the location of the buffer to be used. In this case, **db** is a structure of type **dbentry** (data base entry containing name, address, and phone number data). The address of this structure is cast to a character pointer. This is necessary because **fread** requires the first parameter to be a character pointer to the first block of data, so you must cast the address of the structure to type `char *`.

The 1 tells **fread** that you want to read blocks of data that are one byte in size.

DBSIZE is defined earlier in the program as

    #define DBSIZE sizeof(struct dbentry)

to be the size of a structure of type **dbentry**. The size of this structure is the number **fread** should return if successful. Looking at this again, the number returned by **sizeof** is the size of the structure **dbentry**. You want **fread** to read as much data as will fit in the structure, or, in other words, as many one-byte pieces of data as the structure holds. If successful, **fread** should return the size of one structure (the number of bytes read).

fp is the pointer to the input file you opened earlier.

fwrite   The **fwrite** function is the inverse of the **fread** function. **fwrite** writes blocks of data to a file opened for output. As with **fread**, you specify the size of the block and the maximum number of blocks of data that will be written.

Working with Data: Files, Structures, and Storage

The format for **fwrite** is

fwrite(*buffer*, *size*, *count*, *file*)

where *buffer* is the area you have specified to hold a block of data, *size* is the size of each block in bytes, *count* is the maximum number of blocks you want to handle at one time, and *file* is a `FILE` pointer to a file that you have opened for output.

`fwrite` returns the number of complete blocks that were written. If an error is encountered, `fwrite` returns a value less than `count`.

If you want to write a data base entry to an output file, the same construct can be used as was used for `fread`:

```
FILE *fp;
struct dbentry db;
int wsize;
    .
    .
    .
wsize = fwrite((char *)&db, 1, DBSIZE, fp);
```

Additional I/O Options: Random and Low-Level I/O

You probably will not use either of these types of I/O processing as often as the other functions discussed so far. But, the basics are described here so that when you do need these functions, you will be familiar enough with them to understand more extensive descriptions in your compiler reference guide.

Random Access   The kind of file processing described so far has involved starting at the beginning of a file and reading the data sequentially until the end. But, what if you want to skip over some data at the beginning of a file and then start reading (or writing)? C provides functions to do this type of random processing. Two of the main random access I/O functions are discussed next.

fseek   This function allows you to move to any particular byte in a file that has been opened by `fopen`. The format for `fseek` is

fseek(*fp*, *offset*, *origin*)

where *fp* is a pointer to a file, *origin* is where you want to begin looking, and *offset* is how far you want to go from the starting point. The offset must be coded as a `long` and can be positive or negative in value. You have three choices for *origin*:   start at the beginning of the file (0), start at the current position (1), or start at the end (2), for example:

```
fseek(fp, 0L, 0);   /* seeks to the beginning of the file */
```

Chapter 10

ftell   By using `ftell`, you can find out what your current position is in a file you are processing. The format of `ftell` is

ftell(*fp*)

where *fp* points to a currently opened file. You could use `ftell` as follows:

```
long pos;
     .
     .
     .
pos = ftell(fp);
```

In this case, `pos` would contain the number of bytes the current position is offset from the beginning of the file.

Low-level I/O   Because this is an introductory text, we'll just mention that this type of I/O is available. To learn more about using low-level or nonstandard I/O functions in C, consult an advanced text (some suggestions are given in the References section in Part III). You can also check your compiler documentation for the function descriptions for `open`, `close`, `read`, and `write` as implemented by your compiler.

Module 22 Summary

In this module, you learned more about processing files in C, and some background was provided on the evolution of the C I/O model. The focus of this module was on standard I/O operations, with examples given for the most commonly used functions.

New C Tools

Concepts	Code
standard I/O	`FILE`
low-level I/O	`fopen`
text file	`fclose`
binary file	`fread`
	`fwrite`
	`fseek`
	`ftell`

Working with Data: Files, Structures, and Storage

Module 23: An Introduction to Data Structures

In this module, you will work through building and using a data base of personal information (name, address, and telephone number). Each phase of the program is presented and discussed along with the concepts being illustrated.

Keywords you need to note are

data structure	**binary tree**
data base	**recursion**
dynamic memory allocation	`malloc`
data base operations	`free`
linked list	`exit`
node	

What is a Data Structure?

For your programming purposes, it is easiest to think of a **data structure** as an area of memory (data) that is organized (structured) in a way that helps you represent certain information used by your program. Typical examples of data structures are linked lists, binary trees, stacks, and queues (stacks and queues are special forms of lists). Data structures help you manipulate or store information that is related in a complex way. You will work with a linked list and tree in the example. Linked lists and trees are defined later in this module.

Every language has certain simple *built in* data structures. In C, the simple data structures are arrays, structures, and unions. By making clever use of these simple data structures (particularly C structures and unions), you can create complex data structures such as lists and trees. Rather than continuing to think abstractly about complex data structures, a program is designed here that makes use of them. Then you can see how to create and use these kinds of objects.

In the following sections, you will construct a simple data base program for creating and manipulating a data base of names, addresses, and telephone numbers. This will allow you to see applications of C file I/O and complex data structures. This program is implemented in such a way so as to introduce you to these features of the C language and library. The major point of the example is to familiarize you with the processes involved, and it is not to produce the most efficient data base implementation possible. (An *implementation* refers to the specific way something is designed or made to satisfy the needs of a particular application.) In any case, the program does succeed in implementing a name, address, and phone number data base that you can use, and you are encouraged to modify and improve the program after you become familiar with it.

You can think of a **data base** as a collection of interrelated data values. A data base exists in the form of a complex data structure. The data for the data base is stored in a

Chapter 10

simple structure form in a data base file. **Figure 10.1** illustrates the relationship between the data, data file, and data base.

personal data in the form
of a C structure

```
┌─────────┐
│ name    │
│ address │    represented by  | D |  (for data)  below
│ phone   │
└─────────┘
```

    data base file   used to build   D A T A   B A S E

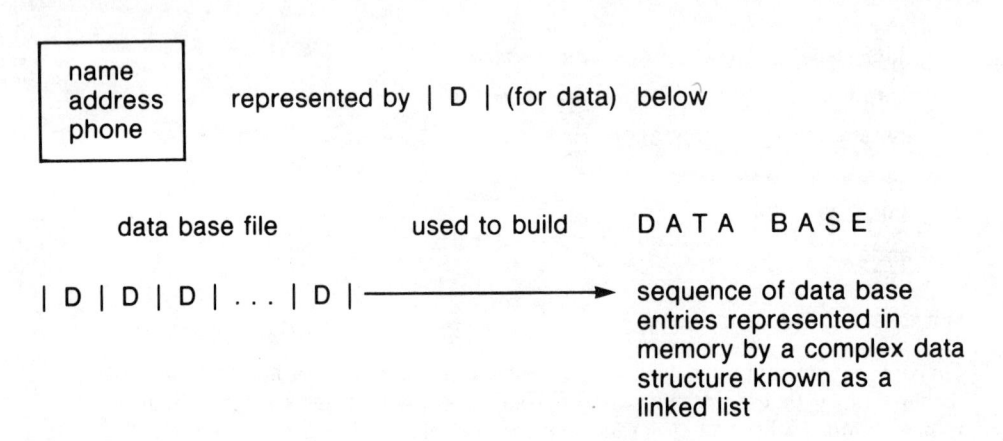

| D | D | D | ... | D | ───────▶ sequence of data base entries represented in memory by a complex data structure known as a linked list

Figure 10.1   Relationship Between Data, Data File, and Data Base

A Simple Data Base of Names and Addresses

A handy tool to have on your computer is a data base of the names, addresses, and telephone numbers of people you communicate with. These could be business associates, long time friends, people to whom you send Christmas cards, and so on. For each such person, you will want to store the following information:

    name   (first, middle, last)
    address   (number, street, city, state, zip code)
    telephone (area code, exchange, number)

There are several ways you might choose to represent information of this type in C, but the easiest and most natural way is to use C structures.

To begin, you can think of a person's name as consisting of three character strings corresponding respectively to the first, middle, and last names. A character string is simply an array of characters, so each part of a person's name can be thought of as such an array. How long should these arrays be? Well, that depends upon how long you expect the longest name in your file to be because each such array must be capable of holding that name. If you know someone named "John Jacob-Anthony-Peter

Working with Data: Files, Structures, and Storage

Smith" then you know that your name arrays must be able to hold at least 20 characters ("Jacob-Anthony-Peter" plus the '\0' null character terminating the string). To be safe, you should probably allow even more room.

You need not make an immediate decision about exactly how long your name arrays should be. Instead, you should use a macro whose value you may later define via a **#define** directive at the top of your file when you settle on the length. You could represent the name of a person with this C structure:

```
struct {
        char first[MAXNAME];
        char middle[MAXNAME];
        char last[MAXNAME];
} name;
```

where **MAXNAME** is defined with a **#define** statement at a later point in your program.

A similar approach can be applied to the address, except that some information in the address is better stored in a form other than that of a string. Consider the address to be represented by the structure:

```
struct {
    char city[MAXCITY];
    int state_index;
    char street[MAXSTREET];
    short number;
    long zip;
} address;
```

Here both the city and street are represented as character strings (whose maximum length will be **MAXCITY** and **MAXSTREET**, respectively). The state is represented by a number that is an index into a table of state names (more on this later). The street number is represented as a short integer, and the zip code is represented as a long integer (in case the Post Office decides we need very long zip codes).

Likewise, you can represent the telephone number as a structure consisting of three fields:

```
struct {
        short area;   /* area code */
        short exch;   /* exchange  */
        short num;    /* number    */
} number;
```

All of this information can now be consolidated into a single representation of a *person* in terms of name, address, and telephone number. Such a representation can be

Chapter 10

called a `dbentry` (data base entry) because these will be the pieces (or entries) making up the data base. Each such entry will look like the following:

```
struct dbentry { /* Entry in data base */
    struct fullname { /* Representation of person's name */
        char first[MAXNAME];
        char middle[MAXNAME];
        char last[MAXNAME];
    } name;
    struct { /* Representation of address */
        char city[MAXCITY];
        int state_index;    /* index of state name in state_names */
        char street[MAXSTREET];
        short number;
        long zip;
    } address;
    struct { /* representation of phone number */
        short area;
        short exch;
        short num;
    } number;
};

#define DBESIZE  sizeof(struct dbentry)
```

Notice that what is defined here is a structure tag `dbentry`, and that structures of this type (`struct dbentry`) consist of three substructures called `name`, `address`, and `number`. `DBESIZE` is defined to make memory allocation, read, and write operations easier to code. (Memory allocation is discussed further in the next section.)

Figure 10.2 illustrates each entry in your data base.

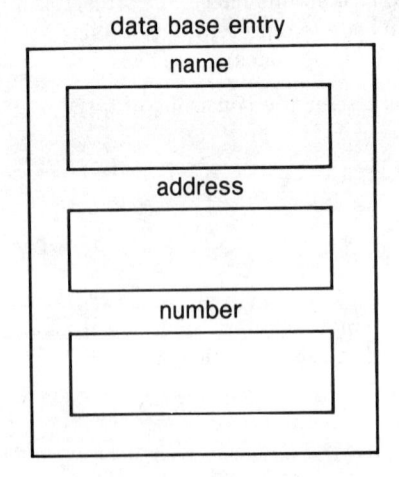

Figure 10.2   A Data Base Entry

Working with Data: Files, Structures, and Storage

Your data base will consist of a sequence or list of these entries.

You might wonder why a tag has been defined for the `dbentry` and `fullname` types of structures and not for the other internal structures. Tags could have been defined for these as well, and certainly no harm would come from doing so. But, as you will see, you will not need tags for such internal structures. You will, however, need a tag for the `dbentry`s and `fullname`s. This is because you will need to dynamically allocate memory for these entries, and so you will need to refer to the type of object (the tag) for which you are allocating this memory.

Dynamic Memory Allocation Memory is usually allocated for variables (and other C objects) by the compiler as your program is compiled. For example, when you define an array, the compiler knows how much space to allocate for the elements involved by looking at the array type and size. The compiler allocates memory, then, for all variables defined in your program. What if you do not need all the space allocated for an array all the time? Or, what if you need space for a variable or object some times but not others? In instances like these, C allows you to use a special part of memory set aside for dynamic allocation of objects. **Dynamic allocation** means that the storage for a variable is defined while the program is executing.

For example, in the data base program, you define a structure for a data base entry. If you define the following:

```
struct tag {
    .
    .
    .
} ;
```

no space is actually allocated because this is just a storage template. If you define a variable like this

```
struct tag {
    .
    .
    .
} name ;
```

storage is allocated for *one* copy of this structure. But, when you work with many copies of this structure at once, as in a linked list, one copy is obviously not sufficient. You need to be able to get enough space for this kind of structure every time it is needed. Instead of defining many instances, you only need to allocate memory each time a structure is needed, only for as long as it is needed. You can then free the memory involved when the storage is no longer needed.

The C functions involved in memory allocation are discussed shortly. Basically, though, if you allocate memory for the entry, you automatically allocate memory for its parts. Therefore, you do not need to refer to them by type. This will become clearer as you go along.

Chapter 10

You can think of the name, address, and number information as being written on three index cards, and you can think of the entry as being a paper clip holding these cards together.

Operations on the Data Base Now that you know how to represent the information in your data base, you need to think of what you want to do with, or to, this information. There are at least three **data base operations** you might want to apply to an entry:

- addition — create a new entry to add a person's information to the data base.
- deletion — delete an existing entry from the data base.
- search — search the data base for a given entry.

Also, you do not want the data base to disappear between program runs. Rather, you want the data base to serve as a permanent reference for name and address information. To ensure this permanence, you should store your data base in a file (on your disk if you are using a PC), and, of course, your data base program should be able to create, read, and update this file.

There are several ways to achieve these goals. The one chosen here is largely for purposes of illustration and may not be particularly efficient, but it provides you with a workable data base program. The following section shows you how to design this program step by step, learning about complex data structures along the way.

Concepts and Tools for Developing the Data Base

Before beginning, you should execute the data base program to get an idea of the processes involved. When you execute the data base example, the following menu is displayed:

```
          ADDRESS DATA BASE MENU

1)   Create a new data base file
2)   Load an existing data base
3)   Add a data base entry
4)   Search for a data base entry
5)   Delete a data base entry
6)   Save the data base
7)   List the current data base to a file
8)   Abandon current data base
9)   Quit
```

The first time you work with the example, choose option 1 to create a new data base file. After the file has been created, choose option 3 to add entries to the data base.

Working with Data: Files, Structures, and Storage

You will be prompted for name, address, and phone number information. After you have made entries (the data base is no longer empty), you can search for an entry, delete an entry, list the data base to a file (in printable format), save, or abandon the data base. (Note: once you have selected option 6 to save the data base, the data base will be read and stored once again as a data base file. In other words, it no longer exists in memory. To work with it again, choose option 9 to quit. Then, execute the program again, this time selecting option 2 to reload the data base.)

Each option is outlined next, so you will know what to expect as you run the program.

Selection: 1
Name of file to load: (any valid name)
Created file: (echoed as per your request)
Press ENTER to continue:

Selection: 2
Name of file to load: (name of an existing file)
File (your file) now loaded
Press ENTER to continue:

Selection: 3
Last name: (you fill in each request for data)
First name:
Middle name:
City:
State:
House number:
Street:
Zip code:
Area code (3 digits):
Exchange (3 digits):
Number (4 digits):

Selection: 4
Name to search for:
Last name: (you fill each part of the name entry)
First name:
Middle name:

Found entry: (entry is listed, if found, else "name not found")
name . . .
address . . .
phone . . .

Chapter 10

Selection: 5
Name to delete:
Last name: (you fill each part of the name entry)
First name:
Middle name:

Entry deleted
Press ENTER to continue

Selection: 6
Data base saved to (your file name)

Selection: 7
Name of output file: (you select a name)
Data base listed to file
Press ENTER to continue

Selection: 8
Data base is abandoned

Selection: 9
Program terminates

To build the data base, you will need a variety of macros, global variables, functions, a menu, and a basic understanding of the data base file and data structures involved.

Some Handy Macros As you learned in Chapter 9, macro definitions and #include statements can be placed in your own header file. You can call this header file db.h (for data base header file). These macro definitions will be of use later in the program. You will also need to use #include for some standard header files that you will need in the program. The part of db.h you need first is listed below.

```
#include <stdlib.h>
#include <stdio.h>
#include <ctype.h>

#define MAXNAME   40   /* maximum length of a name */
#define MAXCITY   40   /* maximum length of a city name */
#define MAXSTREET 20   /* maximum length of street name */

/*
 * The macro repl_nl() takes one argument x that is a buffer, and
 * another argument y that is an index into that buffer.  If a
 * newline character is found at y-1, it is replaced with a string
 * terminator.
 */

#define repl_nl(x,y)  {if (x[y-1] == NL) x[y-1] = EOL;}
#define NL      '\n' /* newline character */
#define EOL     '\0' /* End of Line (string terminator */
```

Working with Data: Files, Structures, and Storage

The files `stdio.h` and `stdlib.h` are included so that symbols such as `NULL`, `stdin`, `stderr`, and `FILE` are defined. The file `ctype.h` is included because it defines the macro `toupper`, which is used later in the program.

Macros for the maximum length of names are chosen in anticipation of how long such names are likely to be. If you later discover that you miscalculated, you need only change these macro definitions because definitions of various arrays will be made by using the macros rather than the numbers themselves.

The `NL` and `EOL` symbols are defined to make typing the program a little simpler. The macro `repl_nl` means "replace the newline character with an end-of-line character." `repl_nl` is used when `fgets` is called later in the program.

Data Structures for the Data Base You can think of the data base as a sequence of `dbentry`s stored in a file on disk. This example program needs to be able to create such a file and a list of `dbentry`s, and then read this list from the file into internal memory, and write this list from internal memory out to the file. When the list is in internal memory, the program may be required to modify it by making additions or deletions. Therefore, it must be in a form that makes additions and deletions fairly easy. In addition, the program must be able to search the list to find a given entry, and this searching should be made efficient.

Given these requirements, the internal representation of the data base is implemented as a complex data structure called a **linked list**. A linked list consists of an ordered sequence of data elements called **nodes**. When the program opens a data base file and reads its entries into memory, a linked list is created. (As you will see, a major advantage of linked lists is that they are dynamic and can grow or shrink as needed.)

Figure 10.3 illustrates a simple linked list.

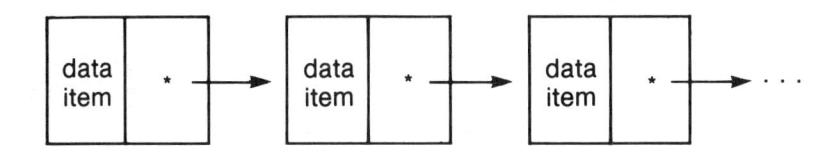

Figure 10.3 A Simple Linked List

Each list node consists of a structure containing a data item and a pointer to the next data item. In the example, the nodes are a little more complicated than this because each node has two pointers: one to a data base item and one to the next entry.

Chapter 10

For the purpose of searching, it is preferable to have the entries ordered (or *sorted*) in a way that makes searching a bit more efficient than simply looking at each entry in a list until you find the one you want. To search for an entry, the data base will be transformed from a linked list into a **binary tree**, which is sorted in a particular way that is described later. Like a linked list, a tree is also a collection of data stored as nodes, but the tree is structured differently (as you might have guessed from the name). **Figure 10.4** illustrates a simple binary tree structure.

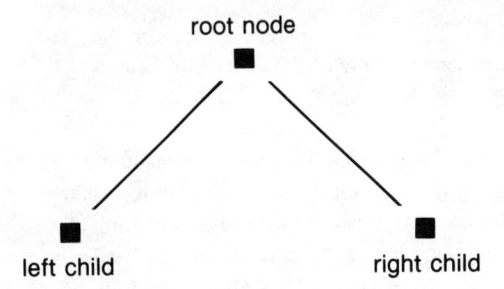

Figure 10.4 The Components of a Simple Binary Tree

Figure 10.5 illustrates a more extensive tree.

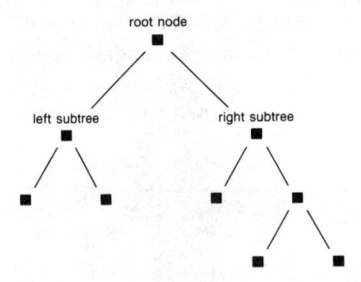

Figure 10.5 A More Extensive Binary Tree

This approach to searching the data base requires you to transform the internal data base from list to tree and from tree to list, but in this example, such transformations have been made as infrequently as possible. The primary advantage to this approach is as a teaching tool: it allows you to see how both a linked list and a binary tree may be implemented in C. (After you understand the program, you may wish to modify it by eliminating the linked list entirely and having the program work only with the tree.)

In order to construct these complex data structures you need to define a data structure that can represent a node in the linked list and one that can represent a node in the binary tree. By using a union, you can define one type of node that will do for both

Working with Data: Files, Structures, and Storage

applications. In this example, such a data structure is called a `list_node` and defined as follows:

```
struct list_node {
  struct dbentry *dbe;
  union {
        struct list_node *next;  /* next node in linked list */
        struct {
                struct list_node *left;   /* left child */
                struct list_node *right;  /* right child */
            } c;  /* children nodes of this node in a binary tree */
      } u;  /* union for use in either linked list or binary tree */
};

typedef struct list_node LIST_NODE;
```

Remember that you are defining pointers to the same type of structure within the structure definition (not actual occurrences of the structure inside itself). The structure tag is available to the compiler as it encounters each subsequent reference. The compiler then knows that each area of type `struct list_node *` will be filled with an address.

The new type of `LIST_NODE` is defined in order to simplify declarations of `list_node` structures. Rather than declaring

```
struct list_node ln;
```

you can declare

```
LIST_NODE ln;
```

Each `LIST_NODE` will point to a `dbentry`. If you are constructing a linked list, the field `u.next` of the `LIST_NODE` will point to the next `LIST_NODE` in the list (and the fields `u.c.left` and `u.c.right` will not be used). But, if you are constructing a binary tree, the field `u.c.left` will point to the left child of the current `LIST_NODE` while `u.c.right` will point to the right child (and the field `u.next` will not be used).

Chapter 10

The linked list will look like **Figure 10.6**, while a binary tree will look like **Figure 10.7**.

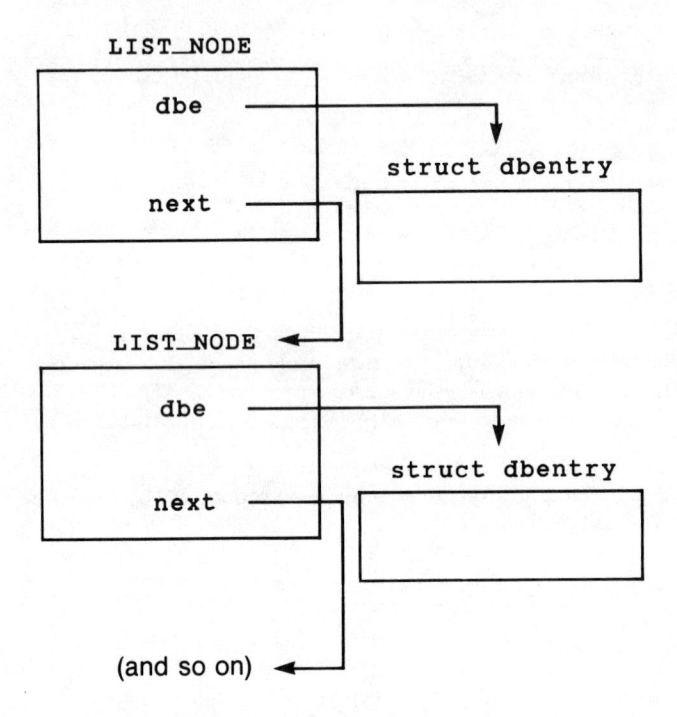

Figure 10.6 Construction of the Linked List

Working with Data: Files, Structures, and Storage

```
              LIST_NODE
            ┌──────────┐
            │   dbe    │
            │ u.c.left │──────▶ struct dbentry
            │ u.c.right│       ┌──────────┐
            └──────────┘       │          │
           ↙            ↘      └──────────┘
  LIST_NODE              LIST_NODE

  (and so on)            (and so on)
```

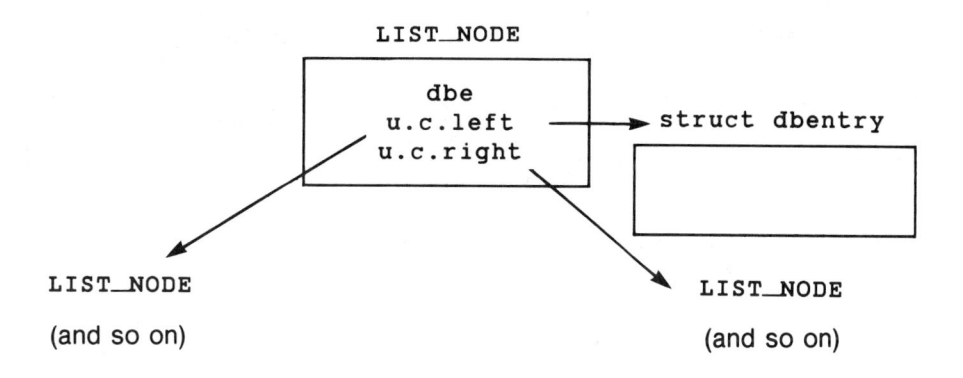

Figure 10.7 Construction of the Binary Tree

The following are global variables that you need to define in order to keep track of the list and tree.

```
LIST_NODE *dbfirst,  /* head of linked list of nodes */
         *dblast;    /* pointer to last node in list */

LIST_NODE *name_tree; /* pointer to top of tree sorted by name */
```

The variable **dbfirst** points to the beginning of the linked list of dbentries and **dblast** points to the last **dbentry** in the list. The variable **name_tree** points to a binary tree that has been sorted by name.

In order to keep track of the status of the linked list, tree, and other features you define a variable **flags** and several bit patterns that indicate the various states of the program and data base (remember the discussions on working with bits in Chapter 8).

```
short flags;  /* bit flags indicating state of data base */

#define NAME_SORTED 0x0001 /* data base is currently sorted */
#define LIST_OK     0x0002 /* linked list is up to date */
```

If you want to, you can include these defines in **db.h**.

Chapter 10

In addition to these dynamic data structures (dynamic in that the linked list and the tree will change at different points of the program), you will need a static array to hold the names of all the states. If you look at the definition of the `dbentry` structure, you will see that a state is represented as an integer index into a table of state names. This saves space over the alternative of representing each state by its name as a separate character array. Searching for a state name by using a table consisting of pointers to state names is more efficient.

The table of state names is simply an array of character pointers initialized to the names of the states:

```
char *state_names[] = {
"Alabama","Alaska","Arizona","Arkansas",
"California","Colorado","Connecticut",
"Delaware","D.C.","Florida","Georgia","Hawaii",
"Idaho","Illinois","Indiana","Iowa",
"Kansas","Kentucky","Louisiana",
"Maine","Maryland","Massachusetts","Michigan","Minnesota",
"Mississippi","Missouri","Montana",
"Nebraska","Nevada","New Hampshire","New Jersey","New Mexico",
"New York","North Carolina","North Dakota",
"Ohio","Oklahoma","Oregon",
"Pennsylvania","Rhode Island","South Carolina","South Dakota",
"Tennessee","Texas","Utah","Vermont","Virginia",
"Washington","West Virginia","Wisconsin","Wyoming",
"UNKNOWN STATE"
};
```

The last slot in this table is used to hold a standard name for any input the user may type that does not match a known state name.

To facilitate the coding of certain statements (those that search this table), you can define a macro for the number of elements in this array:

```
#define NUM_STATES   (sizeof(state_names)/sizeof(char *))
```

Here, `sizeof(state_names)` is the size in bytes of the `state_names[]` array and `sizeof(char *)` is the size of one of the elements in that array. Remember that the array consists of pointers to the actual state names, not character strings, so `sizeof(state_names)/sizeof(char *)` is the number of elements in the array.

The Data Base File At any given time the program will be working with, at most, one data base file. It may read from this file or write to this file. The file must be opened (or created) prior to such operations, and no other file may be opened or created while the current file is still open.

To keep track of these things, you define the following:

```
FILE *dbfp;   /* file pointer to currently opened file */
char dbfname[MAXNAME+1];   /* current data base file name */
```

```
#define FILE_LOADED 0x0004   /* a file is currently loaded */
```

Again, the `#define` statement can be placed in `db.h`.

Working with Data: Files, Structures, and Storage

Function Declarations Many of the functions you will be defining will return pointers rather than integers, or will be of type `void`. These must be declared prior to their use in order to avoid errors in the program or warnings from the compiler. The functions you need to declare are

```
FILE *dbcreate();
LIST_NODE *make_list();
struct dbentry *dballoc();
LIST_NODE *lnalloc();
char *alcmem();
LIST_NODE *name_search();
void add_entry();
void del_dbe();
void free_list();
void free_tree();
void get_name();
void get_addr();
char get_one_char();
void get_phone();
void disp_entry();
LIST_NODE *find_last();
void pause();
void disp_menu();
```

Their definitions will occur later in the program.

The main() Function and Menu Now you can are ready to sketch the design of the `main()` function and the menu for the program. These are defined as

```
void
disp_menu()
/* Display the menu */
{
 printf("\n\n\t\t\tADDRESS DATA BASE MENU\n\n");
 printf("\t\t(1) Create a new data base file\n");
 printf("\t\t(2) Load an existing data base file\n");
 printf("\t\t(3) Add a data base entry\n");
 printf("\t\t(4) Search for a data base entry\n");
 printf("\t\t(5) Delete a data base entry\n");
 printf("\t\t(6) Save the data base\n");
 printf("\t\t(7) List current data base to a file\n");
 printf("\t\t(8) Abandon current data base\n");
 printf("\t\t(9) Quit\n\n");
 printf("\t\tSelection: ");
}
```

Chapter 10

```c
main()
{
  int code;
  struct dbentry dbent;
  LIST_NODE *ln;
  LIST_NODE *parent;

  while (1)
  {
      disp_menu();  /* display the menu and ask for choice */
      switch(get_one_char()) { /* switch on selection */
          default:
                  puts("\n\t\t*** UNRECOGNIZED  CHOICE ***\n");
                  break;
          case '1': /* Create */
                  break;
          case '2': /* Load */
                  break;
          case '3': /* Add entry */
                  break;
          case '4': /* Search */
                  break;
          case '5': /* Delete */
                  break;
          case '6': /* Save */
                  break;
          case '7': /* List */
                  break;
          case '8': /* Abandon */
                  break;
          case '9': /* Quit */
                  exit(0);
      } /* end of switch */
  } /* end of while */
  return(0);
}
```

The `disp_menu()` function simply displays the program menu. The `main()` function consists of a loop that first displays the menu and prompts for a selection, gets a character indicating the selection, and switches on this character to execute the desired action. We have defined several automatic variables at the beginning of `main()`, and these will be used later in our development. Now we need only fill in each of the cases with code that will accomplish the desired goal.

Implementing the Data Base Operations

The following sections describe the code necessary to perform operations on the data base such as adding an entry, deleting an entry, and so forth. **Figure 10.8** summarizes what you will be doing.

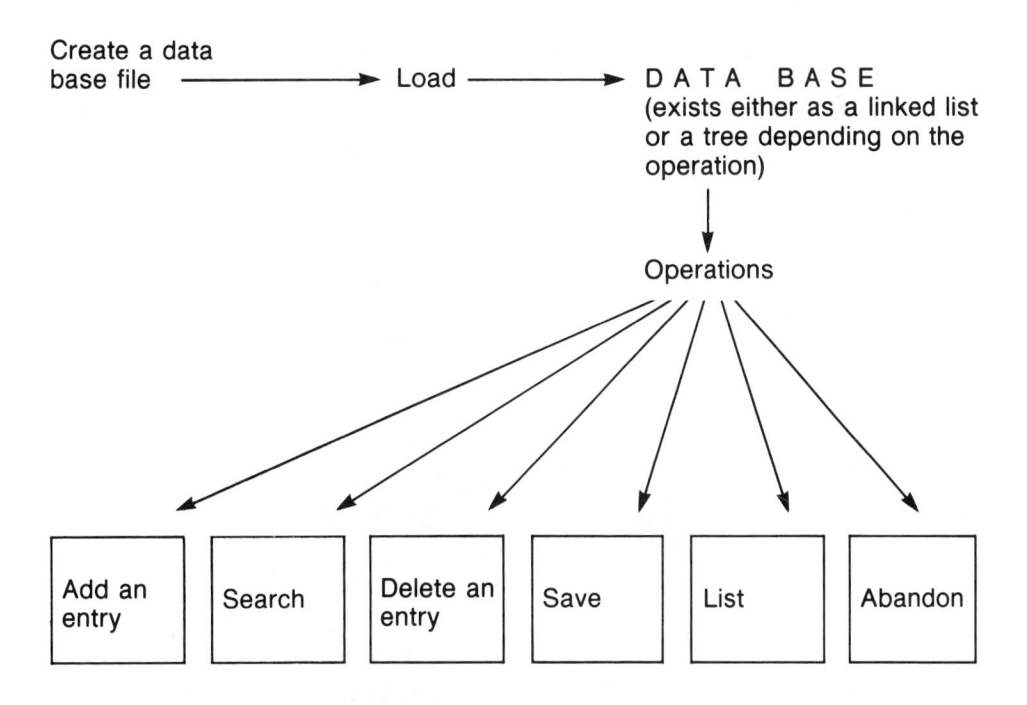

Working with Data: Files, Structures, and Storage

Create a data base file ⟶ Load ⟶ DATA BASE (exists either as a linked list or a tree depending on the operation) ⟶ Operations ⟶ Add an entry | Search | Delete an entry | Save | List | Abandon

Figure 10.8 The Data Base Operations

Creating a Data Base File In order to create a data base file you will need to write a function called **dbcreate** that takes as a parameter the name of the file to create and the creation mode. In certain circumstances it may not be possible to create the desired file. This may be because you do not have the permissions on your system that are necessary to create such a file, or because the file already exists. (**dbcreate** will be written in such a way that it refuses to create a file that already exists in order to protect the user from destroying an existing data base.) Because of this, **dbcreate** indicates why it has failed via an additional parameter that it can "fill in" with its reason for failure.

In the case that **dbcreate** succeeds, it returns a **FILE** pointer for the created file. In the case that it fails, it will return **NULL** as this pointer.

Chapter 10

Here is **dbcreate( )**:

```
FILE * dbcreate(name,mode,code)
char *name;
char *mode;
int *code;
{
  FILE *fp;

  if ((fp = fopen(name,"r")) != NULL)  /* file already exists */
    {
    *code = 1;  /* assign code of 1 to integer pointed to by 'code' */
    fclose(fp); /* close the file */
    return(NULL);
    }

  if ((fp = fopen(name,mode)) == NULL)
    {
    fprintf(stderr,"Can't create file: %s in mode %s\n",name,mode);
    return(NULL);
    }

  return(fp);
}
```

In order to test whether the file already exists, an attempt is made to open it for reading. If this is successful, you know that the file is already there and the integer pointed to by **code** is assigned the value 1 indicating this. The file is then closed because you should never leave a file open if you do not intend to use it. The return code in this case is **NULL**.

If the file does not already exist, it is created by opening it in mode **wb+** (see the code below for **case '1'**). This makes the file a binary file (because you will be writing binary data to it) that you may either read or write. This mode also causes the file to be created if it does not exist (not all modes do this, for example, **r** does not cause a file to be created).

If this open operation is successful, the **FILE** pointer to the opened file is returned, otherwise a **NULL** pointer is returned.

Working with Data: Files, Structures, and Storage

You can now fill in the `case '1'` clause of the `main()` function as follows:

```
case '1': /* Create */
        if (flags & FILE_LOADED)
            {
             printf("File %s is currently loaded\n",dbfname);
             break;
            }
        else
            {
            printf("Name of file to load: ");
            /* get new file name */
            fgets(dbfname,MAXNAME,stdin);
            repl_nl(dbfname,strlen(dbfname));
            if ((dbfp = dbcreate(dbfname,"wb+",&code)) == NULL)
               {
               if (code == 1)
                   printf("File %s already exists\n",dbfname);
               break;
               }
            flags |= (FILE_LOADED | LIST_OK);
            printf("Created file: %s\n",dbfname);
            }
        break;
```

In processing this case, a check is first made to see whether a file is already loaded. You will know this by checking the `FILE_LOADED` bit setting in the `flags` variable. If the bit is *on* (1), you don't open another file.

If no file is currently loaded, a prompt is made for the name of the file. The name is obtained from the command line via `fgets`, and the newline that `fgets` leaves in the buffer is replaced with a string terminator. (This last operation would not be necessary if you used `gets` rather than `fgets`, but `fgets` allows you to limit the amount read from the input while `gets` does not. It is possible with `gets` to accidently overwrite the end of the buffer and cause a bug that is difficult to find. The use of `fgets` is less prone to error.)

The next step is to call `dbcreate` to create the file. If this is successful, you can set the `FILE_LOADED` and `LIST_OK` flags and announce that the file has been created. The code

```
flags |= (FILE_LOADED | LIST_OK);
```

is equivalent to

```
flags = flags | (FILE_LOADED | LIST_OK);
```

and means "`flags` equals the result of the bitwise OR operation of `FILE_LOADED` with `LIST_OK` ORd with the contents of `flags`."

The `FILE_LOADED` flag indicates that a file has been loaded, while the `LIST_OK` flag indicates that the linked list (pointed to by `dbfirst`) is up to date; that is, the linked

Chapter 10

list does not require recreation from the sorted tree. (In this case, it is NULL because neither the list nor the tree exists.)

The **pause()** function is called to ensure that any messages displayed will not be forced off the screen by the menu before the user can read them:

```
void
pause()
{
  char buffer[80];

  printf("Press ENTER to continue: ");
  gets(buffer);  /* get input and ignore it */
}
```

Loading a Data Base   In order to load the data base, write a function called **dbread** that opens a file for reading and then reads the **dbentry** structures in that file into a linked list like the one described above. **dbread** looks like this:

```
dbread(name)
char *name;
{
  FILE *fp;
  struct dbentry db;
  struct dbentry *dpe;  /* pointer to a dbentry */
  LIST_NODE *ln;  /* pointer to a list node */
  int rsize;  /* size read */

  if (dbfp != NULL)
    {
    printf("A file is currently open: %s\n",dbfname);
    return(0);
    }
  if ((fp = fopen(name,"rb+")) == NULL)
     {
     fprintf(stderr,"Can't open file: %s\n",name);
     return(0);
     }
  dbfp = fp;
  while ((rsize = fread(&db,1,DBESIZE,fp)) == DBESIZE) {
    /* While another full dbentry has been read */
    /*
     * If either the dbentry or the list node cannot be
     * allocated, return 0.
     */
    if ((dpe = dballoc()) == NULL)
      return(0);
```

Working with Data: Files, Structures, and Storage

```
      memcpy(dpe,&db,DBESIZE);  /* copy buffer to allocated memory */

      if ((ln = lnalloc()) == NULL)
         return(0);
      ln->dbe = dpe;   /* hook it to the list node */

      if (add_dbe(ln->dbe) == 0)  /* add it to the data base */
                                  /* entry list */
         return(0);    /* return 0 if not possible to add to list */
   }
   if (rsize != 0)  /* partial entry read */
   {
      fprintf(stderr,"Error reading data base file\n");
      pause();
      return(0);
   }
   flags |= (FILE_LOADED | LIST_OK);  /* set file loaded flag */
   return(1);   /* Everything okay */
}
```

First, check to be sure that the data base file pointer **dbfp** currently has the value **NULL** before reassigning a value to it. (Remember, **dbfp** is external to this function.) In the context of the entire program, this check is not really necessary because you will check the **FILE_LOADED** flag prior to calling **dbread**. It is, however, a good precaution against error.

Next, open the named file for reading (and writing) as a binary file, returning **NULL** if this is not possible. The **rb+** mode is used because it allows the program to write to the file as well as read it. This is because you may want to update the data base and save the updated version, which will require writing it out to the file in its new form.

In order to read the **dbentry** structures from the file, a **while** loop is entered that does the following:

1. reads enough bytes from the file to fill a **dbentry** buffer (**db**) that you have defined
2. allocates new space to save this entry by calling **dballoc**
3. allocates a **LIST_NODE** by calling **lnalloc**, which is made to point to the new **dbentry**
4. adds this new **LIST_NODE** to the linked list pointed to by **dbfirst** and **dblast**.

The **while** loop terminates when the amount read from the file is not the size of a **dbentry**. If this amount is 0 bytes, then the end of the file has been reached and everything has gone as expected. If this amount is not 0 (and not the size of a **dbentry**), then something is wrong because the file is supposed to contain just a sequence of **dbentry** structures. In this situation an error message is displayed.

Chapter 10

A number of new functions are called by `dbread`. Before examining them, fill in the `case` statement in `main( )` where `dbread` is called:

```
case '2': /* Load */
        if (flags & FILE_LOADED)
           {
           printf("File %s is currently loaded\n",dbfname);
           break;
           }
        printf("Name of file to load: ");
        fgets(dbfname,MAXNAME,stdin); /* get new file name */
        repl_nl(dbfname,strlen(dbfname));
        if (dbread(dbfname))
           printf("File %s now loaded\n",dbfname);
        pause();
        break;
```

Notice that again the `FILE_LOADED` flag is checked before loading a new file. The user is prompted for the name of the file to load, and the file is then loaded.

Now you can go on to look at the functions called by `dbread`.

Memory Allocation and Deallocation Functions Making linked lists and trees requires memory to be dynamically allocated for structures such as `dbentry` and `LIST_NODE` objects. Remember, in order to fill in the structure template with data, the data must have a place to occupy in memory. So, you need to allocate enough memory to hold the data while you work with it.

Because this will be done fairly frequently, it is convenient to have functions tailored to your application requirements rather than simply calling the C memory allocation function `malloc` in a number of different contexts. The C function `malloc` allocates a block of dynamic memory of the size requested (`malloc(size)`). `malloc` returns the address of the first character of the new block of memory. It is good programming practice to always check the return from `malloc` to detect an *out of memory* condition, and it is better to do so at one point in the program rather than everywhere a memory allocation function is called. In accordance with these guidelines, the following memory allocation functions are defined:

```
char * alcmem(nbytes)
int nbytes;  /* number of bytes to allocate */
{
   char *p;

   if ((p = malloc(nbytes)) == NULL)
       fprintf(stderr,"Out of memory\n");
   else
       memset(p,0,nbytes);  /* zero it out */
   return(p);
}

struct dbentry * dballoc()
```

Working with Data: Files, Structures, and Storage

```
{
   return((struct dbentry *) alcmem(sizeof(struct dbentry)));
}

LIST_NODE * lnalloc()
{
   return((LIST_NODE *) alcmem(sizeof(LIST_NODE)));
}
```

The `alcmem` function provides two services:

1. it checks for an error return from `malloc` and displays an error message if this occurs
2. it zeros out the memory allocated so that you do not have to code a number of assignment statements to initialize pointers in our allocated structures to `NULL`. This makes the program smaller and more efficient.

The `dballoc()` function allocates a chunk of memory large enough to hold a `dbentry` structure, and the `lnalloc()` function does the same for a `LIST_NODE`. Because both functions call `alcmem`, each has a built-in error check and results in the memory being initialized to zeros.

When you want to write one data base out to a file and then read in another one, the memory used for the old linked list and binary tree must be released so it can be reused for the new ones. In C, to deallocate memory means to *free* memory. The C function `free` is used to free a block of memory previously allocated by the `malloc` function. `free` takes as a parameter a pointer to the block of memory to be deallocated. The memory deallocation functions needed for linked lists and binary trees are as follows:

```
/* free a linked list of LIST_NODEs */

void free_list(list,entries)
LIST_NODE *list;
int entries;
{
LIST_NODE *next; /* next node to be freed */

if (list == NULL)
 return; /* can't free a list that isn't there! */

for (next = list->u.next; list != NULL; list = next,
     next = next->u.next)
 {
  if (entries) /* free dbentry as well */
     free((char *)list->dbe);
  free((char *)list); /* free current top node in the list */
 }
dbfirst = dblast = NULL; /* pointers no longer valid */
}
```

Chapter 10

```
/* free a binary tree of LIST_NODEs */

void free_tree(tree,entries)
LIST_NODE *tree;
int entries;
{
if (tree == NULL)  /* no tree to free */
   return;

/* If the current node has no children, free it */
if (tree->u.c.left != NULL)  /* there is a left sub-tree */
   free_tree(tree->u.c.left);  /* free the left sub-tree */

if (tree->u.c.right != NULL) /* there is a right sub-tree */
    free_tree(tree->u.c.right);  /* free the right sub-tree */

/* There are no more child nodes of tree, so free it */
if (entries)  /* free dbentry as well */
   free((char *)tree->dbe);
free((char *)tree);
}
```

Notice that each of these functions is of type `void` because they return no values. Good programming practice dictates that the return value from `free` should always be checked. This is a modification you should make, and when you do so, you will probably want to change these functions from type `void` to type `int` to return an error code.

The `free_list` function starts at the `LIST_NODE` pointed to by `list` (normally `dbfirst`) and frees each node, stopping when `list` has the value `NULL`. If the `entries` parameter is nonzero, the data base entry (`dbentry`) for the node is freed as well. If the `entries` parameter is zero, it is not freed.

The `free_tree` function performs virtually the same service for a binary tree, but its implementation is a bit more complicated because of the nature of such trees. This function is **recursive,** meaning it calls itself. Recursion is needed because in order to free a given node in the tree, all of the nodes below that node must be freed first.

To accomplish this, `free_tree` frees all the nodes in the left subtree of the given node, and then frees all the nodes in the right subtree of the given node. Finally, it frees the given node itself. It is essential that the first action of `free_tree` is to determine whether it is being asked to free a `NULL` tree and, if so, to return immediately. Requests to free memory at address 0 (this is the value of `NULL`) most often result in very unfortunate consequences. On many operating systems, such an action causes an *access violation* or *memory fault*. On less robust operating systems, the result will be the death of the operating system itself, in which case you must reboot the system and begin again.

Adding an Entry to the List   The `dbread` function calls `add_dbe` to add a `dbentry` structure to the linked list. `add_dbe` is very simple; it links the new entry to the end

Working with Data: Files, Structures, and Storage

of the existing list, if there is one. If there is no existing list, **add_dbe** makes both **dbfirst** and **dblast** point to the new entry, creating a list with a single member. The **add_dbe** function looks like this:

```
add_dbe(dbptr)
struct dbentry *dbptr;   /* new entry to add to list */
{
  LIST_NODE *ln;

  if ((ln = lnalloc()) == NULL)
     return(0);  /* return 0 if not enough memory */

  ln->dbe = dbptr;  /* hook the entry to this list node */
  /* Append this node to the list */
  ln->u.next = NULL;  /* no next node -- this is now the last */
  if (dbfirst == NULL)  /* this is first node in list */
    {
      dbfirst = ln;  /* head of list */
      dblast = ln;   /* also the tail */
    }
  else
    {
      /* The old last node is now followed by this one */
      dblast->u.next = ln;
      /* and this one becomes the last node */
      dblast = ln;
    }
  flags &= ~NAME_SORTED;  /* no longer sorted */
  return(1);  /* return success */
}
```

First, a **LIST_NODE** is created, and its **dbe** field is made to point to the **dbentry** you want to add to the list. If there is an existing list (**dbfirst** is non-NULL), then the new **LIST_NODE** is assigned as the **next** field of **dblast**, and **dblast** points to the new node. Otherwise, both **dbfirst** and **dblast** point to the new node.

Because an entry has been added to the list, the **NAME_SORTED** flag is reset to indicate that the current binary tree (if there is one) no longer reflects the current linked list.

The function **add_dbe**, called by **dbread**, is also useful when you want to select option 3 to add an entry to the data base. The code for this case is

```
case '3':  /* Add entry */
     if ((flags & FILE_LOADED) == 0)
        {
          puts("No data base file currently open\n");
          pause();
          break;
        }
     else
         add_entry();
       break;
```

Chapter 10

It is first essential to check that a data base file has been loaded before an entry is added to its list (even if this list is for a newly created file and is NULL), because a data base operation can take place only if a data base file is open. If the file is open, **add_entry( )** is called to prompt for and add the entry:

```
void add_entry()
{
  struct dbentry *dbe;

  if ((dbe = dballoc()) == NULL)
     return;
  get_name(dbe);  /* get the name */
  get_addr(dbe);  /* get the address */
  get_phone(dbe); /* get the phone number */

  add_dbe(dbe);   /* add the entry to the list */
}
```

add_entry( ) creates a **dbentry** structure and then calls the functions **get_name**, **get_addr**, and **get_phone** to fill in the various parts of this structure. These *get* functions all act in a similar manner:

```
void get_name(dbe)       /* get a name */
struct dbentry *dbe;
{
  char buffer[MAXNAME+1]; /* input buffer */
  int l;  /* for length of string in buffer */

  printf("Last name: ");
  fgets(buffer,MAXNAME,stdin); /* get line from standard input */
  buffer[MAXNAME] = EOL; /* ensure it is null terminated */
  l = strlen(buffer);
  repl_nl(buffer,l);
  strcpy(dbe->name.last,buffer); /* save it in the dbentry */

  printf("First name: ");
  fgets(buffer,MAXNAME,stdin); /* get line from standard input */
  buffer[MAXNAME] = EOL; /* ensure it is null terminated */
  l = strlen(buffer);
  repl_nl(buffer,l);
  strcpy(dbe->name.first,buffer); /* save it in the dbentry */

  printf("Middle name: ");
  fgets(buffer,MAXNAME,stdin); /* get line from standard input */
  buffer[MAXNAME] = EOL; /* ensure it is null terminated */
  l = strlen(buffer);
  repl_nl(buffer,l);
  strcpy(dbe->name.middle,buffer); /* save it in the dbentry */
}
```

Working with Data: Files, Structures, and Storage

```c
void get_addr(dbe)
struct dbentry *dbe;
{
  char buffer[MAXNAME+1]; /* input buffer - MAXNAME big enough */
  int l; /* for length of string in buffer */

  printf("City: ");
  fgets(buffer,MAXNAME,stdin); /* get line from standard input */
  buffer[MAXNAME] = EOL; /* ensure it is null terminated */
  l = strlen(buffer);
  repl_nl(buffer,l);
  strcpy(dbe->address.city,buffer); /* save it in the dbentry */

  printf("State: ");
  fgets(buffer,MAXNAME,stdin); /* get line from standard input */
  buffer[MAXNAME] = EOL; /* ensure it is null terminated */
  l = strlen(buffer);
  repl_nl(buffer,l);
  /* save state index */
  dbe->address.state_index = st_index(buffer);

  printf("House number: ");
  fgets(buffer,MAXNAME,stdin); /* get line from standard input */
  buffer[MAXNAME] = EOL; /* ensure it is null terminated */
  l = strlen(buffer);
  repl_nl(buffer,l);
  dbe->address.number = atoi(buffer); /* save number */

  printf("Street: ");
  fgets(buffer,MAXNAME,stdin); /* get line from standard input */
  buffer[MAXNAME] = EOL; /* ensure it is null terminated */
  l = strlen(buffer);
  repl_nl(buffer,l);
  strcpy(dbe->address.street,buffer); /* save it in the dbentry */

  printf("Zip code: ");
  fgets(buffer,MAXNAME,stdin); /* get line from standard input */
  buffer[MAXNAME] = EOL; /* ensure it is null terminated */
  l = strlen(buffer);
  repl_nl(buffer,l);
  dbe->address.zip = atol(buffer); /* save number */
}
```

Chapter 10

```
void get_phone(dbe)
struct dbentry *dbe;
{
    char buffer[MAXNAME+1]; /* make sure it's big enough */
    int l;   /* for length of string in buffer */

    printf("Area code (3 digits): ");
    fgets(buffer,MAXNAME,stdin);  /* get line from standard input */
    buffer[3] = EOL;  /* only look at first three characters */
    l = strlen(buffer);
    repl_nl(buffer,l);
    dbe->number.area = atoi(buffer);

    printf("Exchange (3 digits): ");
    fgets(buffer,MAXNAME,stdin);  /* get line from standard input */
    buffer[3] = EOL;
    l = strlen(buffer);
    repl_nl(buffer,l);
    dbe->number.exch = atoi(buffer);

    printf("Number (4 digits): ");
    fgets(buffer,MAXNAME,stdin);  /* get line from standard input */
    buffer[4] = EOL;  /* ensure it is null terminated */
    l = strlen(buffer);
    repl_nl(buffer,l);
    dbe->number.num = atoi(buffer);
}
```

In general, you can see that for each field in a structure (for name, address, or phone number), a prompt is given, and **fgets** is called to fill the buffer with the input from the user. **repl_nl** is called to overwrite the newline left in the buffer by **fgets**, and the buffer is then processed. This usually amounts to copying it into the appropriate field of the **dbentry** pointed to by the **dbe** parameter to the function. However, in the case of the state and the numeric fields (house number, zip code, phone numbers), other functions are called.

Notice that there is very little error checking or handling of the input strings in these functions. For example, if the user types in a response with blank spaces at the beginning or the end, these spaces will become part of the input. In the case of a name, the spaces would be counted by the program as part of the name. A modification you might want to make is to trim spaces from the beginning and end of the input buffer after **repl_nl** is called.

To handle the cases of house numbers, zip codes, and phone numbers, either **atoi** is called to convert the buffer from a string into the number represented by that string, or **atol** is called (for the zip code) to convert the buffer into a long integer.

Working with Data: Files, Structures, and Storage

For state names, the function `st_index` is called to return the index in `state_names[]` where the given state name is found. `st_index` is coded as follows:

```c
st_index(s)
char *s;   /* string */
{
  int i, j;
  char buffer[MAXNAME];

  /* Convert the string to upper case */
  for (i = 0; i < strlen(s); i++)
      s[i] = toupper(s[i]);

  for (i = 0; i < NUM_STATES; i++)
  {
    /* Make a copy of the state name to play with */
    strcpy(buffer,state_names[i]);
    for (j = 0; j < strlen(buffer); j++)  /* convert to upper */
        buffer[j] = toupper(buffer[j]);
    if (strcmp(buffer,s) == 0)  /* found a match */
        return(i);
  }

  /* return index of last entry in array */
  return(NUM_STATES - 1);
}
```

First, the buffer passed (via a pointer) to `st_index` is converted to uppercase. Next, `st_index` loops through the `state_names[]` array and converts each string it finds to uppercase in a temporary buffer. It then compares the temporary buffer to the (converted) input. If a match is found, the index of the matching string is returned. If no match is found, the index of the last entry in `state_names[]` is returned, and this will be the index of the "UNKNOWN STATE" string. The conversion to uppercase is performed so that oddities in what the user types in (in terms of case) may be ignored (for example, "Arizona", "ARIZONA", "ARizona"). The program does not recognize abbreviations of state names, so this is a feature you might want to add.

Finally, after the *get* functions are called, `add_entry()` calls `add_dbe` to add this entry to the list.

Sorting the Data Base and Searching for an Entry Because the data base contains many different types of information (names, addresses, and phone numbers), you might want to search it for any of these different types of information. To simplify matters in the example, however, a search routine is implemented for full names only. You can modify the program to generalize this if you like.

Chapter 10

The code that implements `case '4'` of the `switch` statement is as follows:

```
case '4': /* Search */
    if (dbfirst == NULL)
       {
        if (name_tree != NULL)
           {
            dbfirst = make_list(name_tree);
            dblast = find_last(dbfirst);
           }
        else
           {
            printf("Data base is empty\n");
            pause();
            break;
           }
       }
    puts("\nName to search for:\n\n");
    get_name(&dbent);
    if ((flags & NAME_SORTED) == 0)
       /* data base not currently sorted */
       name_sort();
    parent = NULL; /* no parent of top node */
    ln = name_search(&dbent.name,name_tree,&parent);
    if (ln == NULL)
       {
        puts("Name not found\n");
        pause();
        break;
       }
    printf("\nFound entry:\n\n");
    disp_entry(stdout,ln->dbe);
    pause();
    break;
```

First, a check is made to be sure that there is a data base to search. If `dbfirst` is NULL, but `name_tree` is non-NULL (this happens if there was a deletion prior to the search), `make_list` is called to remanufacture the linked list from the newly sorted tree. `find_last` is then called to find its last element. `make_list` is discussed below in the discussion of `case '6'`.

If there is a list, `get_name` is called to prompt for and record the name to search for. In order to search the data base, you must first be sure that it is sorted (ordered) in the proper way. The `NAME_SORTED` flag is set if the data base is currently sorted.

Working with Data: Files, Structures, and Storage

If it is not, **name_sort( )** is called to sort it. The **name_sort** function is as follows:

```
name_sort()
{
  LIST_NODE *ln;   /* pointer to node in linked list */
  LIST_NODE *tn;   /* pointer to node in tree */
  LIST_NODE *tmp, *next;  /* used for tree search */

  if (name_tree != NULL) /* there is an existing name tree */
     free_tree(name_tree);  /* wipe it out */

  ln = dbfirst;
  while (ln != NULL)
  {
   if ((tn = lnalloc()) == NULL)  /* allocate tree node */
      {
      free_tree();  /* free nodes already allocated */
      return(0);
      }
   tn->dbe = ln->dbe;  /* point to same dbentry as list node */
   if (name_tree == NULL) /* this is the first node encountered */
      name_tree = tn;
  else /* need to see where tn goes in name_tree */
      {
      next = name_tree; /* start at top of tree */
      while (next != NULL)  /* stop at bottom of tree */
         {
         if (name_cmp(&(tn->dbe->name),&(next->dbe->name)) < 0)
            /* tn's name prior to next's */
            {
            if (next->u.c.left == NULL)
               {
               next->u.c.left = tn;
               break;
               }
            else
               next = next->u.c.left; /* go down left branch */
            }
         else if (name_cmp(&(tn->dbe->name),&(next->dbe->name)) > 0)
               /* next's name prior to tn's */
            {
            if (next->u.c.right == NULL)
               {
               next->u.c.right = tn;
               break;
               }
            else
               next = next->u.c.right; /* go down right branch */
            }
```

Chapter 10

```
            else /* names compare as equal -- put it on left */
                {
                if (next->u.c.left == NULL)
                    next->u.c.left = tn;
                else
                    {
                    tmp = next->u.c.left;  /* old left child of next */
                    next->u.c.left = tn;   /* tn becomes new left child */
                    /* old left child becomes tn's left child */
                    tn->u.c.left = tmp;
                    }
                break;
                }
            } /* end of while (next != NULL) */
        } /* end of else */
    ln = ln->u.next;
    } /* end of while ln != dblast */

    /* set flag to indicated sort is up to date */
    flags |= NAME_SORTED;
}
```

The `name_sort()` function takes the list pointed to by **dbfirst** and sorts it into a binary tree pointed to by **name_tree**. The type of sort employed here is sometimes referred to as a *tree sort* for obvious reasons. The algorithm used to create the tree is similar to the algorithm used to search the tree after it is created. This is easier to understand if you think in items of sorting numbers.

Think of a sequence of numbers that will be placed at nodes in the tree, for example,

> 15, 9, 17, 12, 5, 7, 16

To sort this list into a tree, go through the following steps:

1. Pick the next number in the list.
2. Start at the top of the tree. If there is no tree yet, the number becomes the root node in the tree.
3. If the number is less than the one in the tree node you are looking at, look at the left child node.
4. If your number is greater than the one in the tree node, look at the right child node.
5. Repeat steps 3 and 4 until you reach a NULL node; place your number there.
6. Go back to step 1.

In the sequence of numbers being considered, the stages (iterations) you go through and the final tree are shown in **Figure 10.9**.

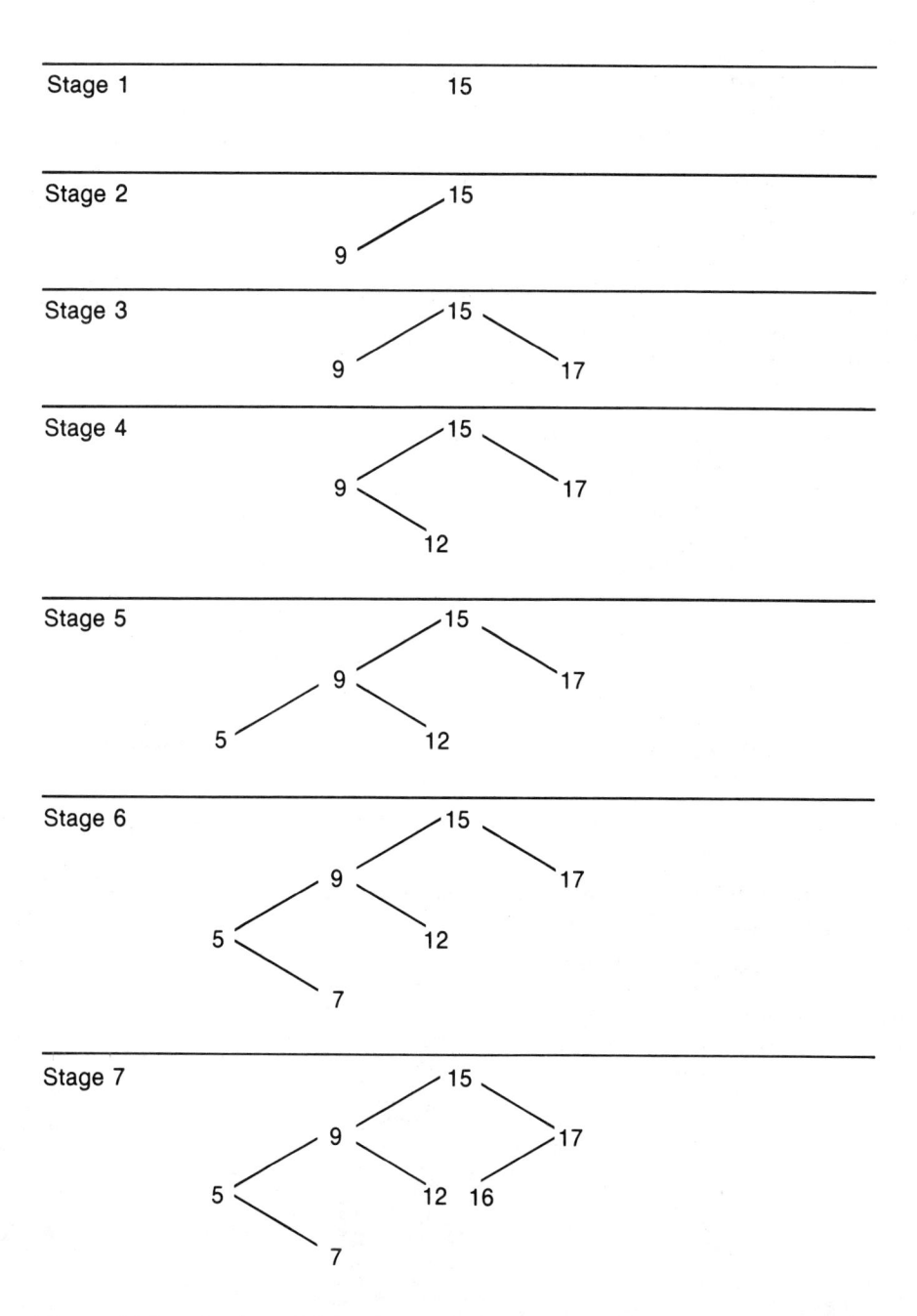

Working with Data: Files, Structures, and Storage

Stage 1   15

Stage 2
```
      15
     /
    9
```

Stage 3
```
      15
     /  \
    9    17
```

Stage 4
```
      15
     /  \
    9    17
     \
      12
```

Stage 5
```
        15
       /  \
      9    17
     / \
    5   12
```

Stage 6
```
        15
       /  \
      9    17
     / \
    5   12
     \
      7
```

Stage 7
```
         15
        /  \
       9    17
      / \   /
     5  12 16
      \
       7
```

Figure 10.9 Sorting a List into a Tree

Chapter 10

You can see that `name_sort()` implements precisely this kind of sorting algorithm. Instead of comparing numbers, `fullname` structures are being compared, and the function `name_cmp` is used to do this:

```
name_cmp(name1,name2)
struct fullname *name1;   /* pointer to first fullname */
struct fullname *name2;   /* pointer to second fullname */
{
   int r;  /* result of comparison */

   /* First compare surnames */
   if ((r = strcmp(name1->last,name2->last)) != 0)
       return(r);

   /* Surnames are the same -- compare first names */
   if ((r = strcmp(name1->first,name2->first)) != 0)
       return(r);

   /* Surnames and first are the same - compare middle names */
   return(strcmp(name1->middle,name2->middle));
}
```

In this function, surnames are more significant than first and middle names, and first names are more significant than middle names. One name is said to be *less* than another if it precedes the other in normal alphabetic ordering. `name_cmp` returns a number less than zero if the name pointed to by its first parameter is *less than* that pointed to by its second. It returns zero if both are *equal*, and it returns a number greater than zero if the second name is *less than* the first.

The variable `name_tree` points to the sorted tree and the `NAME_SORTED` flag is set to indicate that the data base is now sorted.

Once the data base has been sorted, it can be searched, and the function `name_search` is called to do the searching:

```
LIST_NODE * name_search(fn,tree,parent)
struct fullname *fn;   /* name being sought */
LIST_NODE *tree;   /* tree (or sub-tree) to be searched */
LIST_NODE **parent;   /* will point to parent LIST_NODE */
                     /* note double indirection - ptr to ptr */
```

Working with Data: Files, Structures, and Storage

```
{
  LIST_NODE *t;

  if (tree == NULL)
     return(NULL);
  if (name_cmp(fn,&(tree->dbe->name)) == 0) /* this one matches */
     return(tree);
  *parent = tree;   /* tree is now the prospective parent */
  if ((t = name_search(fn,tree->u.c.left,parent)) != NULL)
     return(t);
  if ((t = name_search(fn,tree->u.c.right,parent)) != NULL)
     return(t);
  return(NULL);
}
```

If the top node pointed to by the **tree** parameter matches the **fullname** parameter, **name_search** returns a pointer to that node. Otherwise, it searches the left subtree of that node, returning a pointer to the matching node if one is found. Next, if the left subtree search is not successful, the right subtree is searched and a pointer to the matching node (if one is found) is returned. Finally, if the complete search results in no match, a NULL pointer is returned.

name_search takes a **fullname** structure that is to be searched for and a pointer to a binary tree where it is to begin its search. You might wonder why **name_search** is not defined with just a single parameter pointing to the name to be sought, if the only tree here is **name_tree**. The reason the second parameter is used is that **name_search** is most naturally written as a recursive function where it is called by itself to search subtrees. Thus, although the **main()** function calls **name_search** with **name_tree** as the second parameter, **name_search** calls itself recursively with subtrees of the one pointed to by its second parameter. Each time **name_search** is called, the search process becomes *simpler*. In other words, the alternatives for the search are progressively narrowed down. The point of the recursion is to proceed through calls to **name_search** until the search is terminated by reaching the end of the tree or successfully finding the entry being searched for.

The third parameter of **name_search** comes into play when you implement the deletion of entries. When an entry is to be deleted, you need to have not only a pointer to its **LIST_NODE**, but a pointer to the **LIST_NODE** of its parent as well so that any children can be attached to the parent nodes of the node to be deleted. A pointer to the parent node will be returned in the parameter **parent**, which should be passed by the calling function as the address of a **LIST_NODE** pointer.

Chapter 10

In the code for `case '4'`, a message is displayed if the search is a failure. If it is successful, the function `disp_entry` is called to display the `dbentry` at the matching node:

```
void disp_entry(fp,dbe)
FILE *fp;   /* file pointer for output file */
struct dbentry *dbe;
{
fprintf(fp,"%s %s %s\n",dbe->name.first,dbe->name.middle,
                        dbe->name.last);
fprintf(fp,"%d %s\n%s, %s %ld\n",dbe->address.number,
                        dbe->address.street,
                        dbe->address.city,
                        state_names[dbe->address.state_index],
                        dbe->address.zip);
fprintf(fp,"(%d) %d-%d\n",dbe->number.area,dbe->number.exch,
                        dbe->number.num);
}
```

This function uses some of the formatting capabilities of `fprintf` to format the information in the `dbentry`. Note in particular that `db->address.number` is formatted as an `int` while `dbe->address.zip` is formatted as a `long`. This function is used here both for the `search` selection and (later) for the `list` option where the data base is printed to an output file. In the `search` case, the file is *standard output* or `stdout`.

Deleting an Entry from the Data Base   The code to implement deletion of an entry from the data base is similar to that for searching for an entry, but a deletion function rather than a display function is called:

```
case '5': /* Delete */
        if (dbfirst == NULL)
           {
           printf("Data base is empty\n");
           pause();
           break;
           }
        puts("\nName to delete:\n\n");
        get_name(&dbent);
        if ((flags & NAME_SORTED) == 0)
           /* data base not currently sorted */
           name_sort();
        parent = NULL;   /* no parent of top node */
        ln = name_search(&dbent.name,name_tree,&parent);
        if (ln == NULL)
           {
           puts("Name not found\n");
           pause();
           break;
           }
```

Working with Data: Files, Structures, and Storage

```
              del_dbe(ln,parent); /* delete it */
              printf("\nEntry deleted:\n\n");
              pause();
              break;
```

Here the function **del_dbe** is called with the node to delete and that node's parent. It is coded as follows:

```
void del_dbe(node,parent)
LIST_NODE *node;
LIST_NODE *parent;
{
LIST_NODE *p, *next;

if (parent == NULL || node == parent->u.c.left)
   /* node is top node (name_tree) or node is left child of parent */
   {
   if (node->u.c.left == NULL) /* has no left child of its own */
      {
      if (parent == NULL) /* node is name_tree */
         name_tree = node->u.c.right;
      else
         /* Make its right child the left child of the parent */
         parent->u.c.left = node->u.c.right;
      }
   else /* node has a left child */
      {
      if (parent == NULL)  /* node is top node (name_tree) */
         /* left child of top becomes top */
         name_tree = parent = node->u.c.left;
      else
         /*
          * Make node's left child the left child of the parent
          * and attach node's right subtree (if there is one)
          * as the farthest right subtree of node's left child.
          */
         parent->u.c.left = node->u.c.left;

      /* Find the farthest right node of left child */
      for (p = node, next = node->u.c.right;
         next != NULL; next = next->u.c.right)
            p = next; /* save pointer to parent of next node */
      /* p is now farthest right node of left child */
      /* splice right child to it */
      p->u.c.right = node->u.c.right;
      }
   }
   else /* node is right child of parent */
   {
   if (node->u.c.left == NULL) /* has no left child of its own */
      /* Make its right child the right child of the parent */
      parent->u.c.right = node->u.c.right;
```

Chapter 10

```
    else /* node has a left child */
      {
      /*
       * Make node's left child the right child of the parent
       * and attach node's right subtree (if there is one)
       * as the farthest right subtree of node's left child.
       */
      parent->u.c.right = node->u.c.left;
      /* Find the farthest right node of left child */
      for (p = node, next = node->u.c.right;
           next != NULL; next = next->u.c.right)
          p = next; /* save pointer to parent of next node */
      /* p is now farthest right node of left child */
      /* splice right child to it */
      p->u.c.right = node->u.c.right;
      }
    }

/* Reset LIST_OK flag since reordering has taken place */
flags &= ~LIST_OK;
free_list(dbfirst,0);  /* free the list nodes */
free(node->dbe); /* free the dbentry of the node */
free(node); /* free the tree node */
}
```

Fundamentally, given a node and its parent node, **del_dbe** does the following:

1. If there is a left child
    a. replace node to be deleted by it

    b. if there is right subtree (to the node to be deleted),
        splice it to rightmost node of the left child that replaced the deleted node.

2. If there is no left child, the node to be deleted is replaced by its right child.

Working with Data: Files, Structures, and Storage

Some complications are introduced if you want to delete the very top or root node in the tree, but in general, these two fundamental guidelines are followed.

In terms of the numeric tree example used previously, if you start with the tree

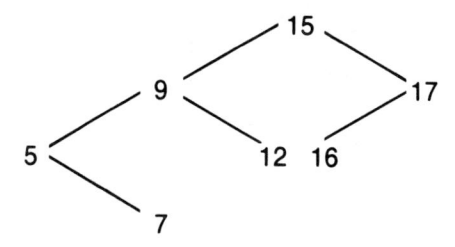

```
            15
          /    \
         9      17
        / \    /
       5  12  16
        \
         7
```

and want to delete the node 9, you end up with

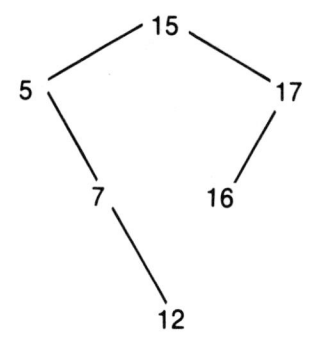

```
            15
          /    \
         5      17
          \    /
           7  16
            \
             12
```

Chapter 10

However, if instead you wanted to delete 17, the final tree looks like this:

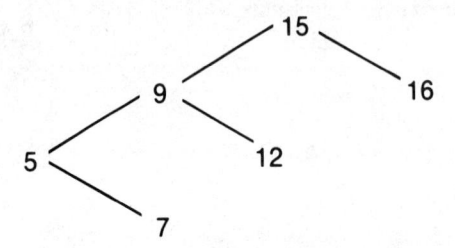

```
            15
           /  \
          9    16
         / \
        5   12
         \
          7
```

Again, you may want to step through this code with a debugger, if one is available to you.

Saving the Data Base to a File   The code to implement `case '6'` for saving the data base to the current file is

```
case '6': /* Save */
        if ((flags & LIST_OK) == 0)
            {
            free_list(dbfirst,0);  /* free list nodes */
            dbfirst = make_list(name_tree);
            flags |= LIST_OK;
            }
        if (dbwrite(dbfp) != 0)  /* no error */
            {
            fclose(dbfp);
            free_tree(name_tree,1);
            free_list(dbfirst,1);
            flags &= ~FILE_LOADED;
            dbfirst = dblast = name_tree = NULL;
            printf("Data base saved to file %s\n",dbfname);
            }
        break;
```

The first thing `case '6'` does is check to see if the linked list is up to date. It might not be if an entry has been deleted from the tree and the tree has not been transformed back into the list since that deletion. If the list is not up to date (in other words, the `LIST_OK` flag is not set), `make_list` is called to perform this transformation:

```
LIST_NODE * make_list(tree)
LIST_NODE *tree;  /* tree to be turned into list */
{
  LIST_NODE *left;   /* points to head of list of left subtree */
  LIST_NODE *right;  /* points to head of list of right subtree */
  LIST_NODE *node;   /* points to list node for 'tree' */
  LIST_NODE *last;   /* points to last node in a list */
```

Working with Data: Files, Structures, and Storage

```
   if (tree == NULL)
      {
      fprintf(stderr,"Error: attempt to list non-existent tree\n");
      pause();
      return(NULL);
      }

/*
 * If there is a left child of this node, recursively
 * append its subtree to the list.
 */
   if (tree->u.c.left != NULL)
      left = make_list(tree->u.c.left);
   else
      left = NULL;   /* no left subtree */

   /* Make a list node for the dbentry pointed to by 'tree' */
   if ((node = lnalloc()) == NULL)
      return(NULL);

   node->dbe = tree->dbe;   /* place dbentry at that node in list */

/*
 * If there is a right child of this node, recursively
 * append its subtree to the list.
 */
   if (tree->u.c.right != NULL)
      right = make_list(tree->u.c.right);
   else
      right = NULL;

/* The top of the list starting at the node pointed to by
 * 'tree' will be the node pointed to by 'left' if there
 * was a left subtree.  Otherwise it will be the node
 * pointed to by 'node'.
 */
   if (left == NULL) /* no left subtree */
      {
      node->u.next = right;   /* attach list from right subtree */
      return(node);
      }

   last = find_last(left);   /* find end of list from left subtree */
   last->u.next = node;      /* attach node to it */
   node->u.next = right;     /* append list from right subtree */
   return(left);
}
```

Chapter 10

This function *walks* the tree in what is sometimes referred to as *inorder* traversal. Inorder traversal recursively walks the tree as follows:

1. go left
2. "visit" the node
3. go right.

As a result, the list will be constructed in alphabetical order. For example, recall the numeric example used earlier. Using the inorder method, then, the tree is traversed in the following order:

5 7 9 12 15 16 17

For more information on traversing trees, see "tree sorts" in an advanced computer science text.

Before making a new list, the **LIST_NODE**s for the old list are freed (but not the data base entries they point to because you still need these, just in a different order). A pointer to the new list is returned, and it is assigned to **dbfirst**. It is not necessary to assign the last entry to **dblast** because **dbwrite** does not make use of that information.

After it is determined that the list is up to date, **dbwrite** is called to write the list out to the file that was originally created or loaded:

```
dbwrite(fp)
FILE *fp;  /* FILE pointer for data base file */
{
  LIST_NODE *ln;
  int wsize;

  fseek(fp,0L,0);  /* seek to beginning of file */
  for (ln = dbfirst; ln != NULL; ln = ln->u.next)
      if ((wsize = fwrite((char *)ln->dbe,1,DBESIZE,fp)) != DBESIZE)
          {
          fprintf(stderr,"Error writing data base record\n");
          pause();
          return(0);
          }
  return(1);
}
```

In writing out the linked list of data base entries, **fseek** is first called to seek (return the file pointer) to the beginning of the file. If a new data base file has been created, this is not necessary, but if an existing data base file is being updated, the file pointer would be at the end of the file after the call to **dbread**.

Other than this call to **fseek**, the **dbwrite** function is the inverse of the **dbread** function. **dbwrite** goes through the linked list, writing out each **dbentry** until it

Working with Data: Files, Structures, and Storage

reaches the end of the list. If some non-`DBESIZE` number of bytes is written, it is regarded as an error.

If no error has been encountered, the current data base file is closed, and the current list and `name_tree` are freed. The `FILE_LOADED` flag is reset to indicate that a file is no longer loaded, and `dbfirst`, `dblast`, and `name_tree` are reinitialized to NULL.

Listing the Data Base The data base may be listed to a file (for example, for use as a mailing list) by selecting option 7, which is implemented as follows:

```
    case '7': /* List */
        if (dbfirst == NULL)
            {
            printf("Data base is empty\n");
            }
        else
            {
            if ((flags & LIST_OK) == 0)
                {
                free_list(dbfirst,0);   /* free list nodes */
                dbfirst = make_list(name_tree);
                flags |= LIST_OK;
                }
            if (dblist())
                printf("Data base listed to file\n");
            }
        pause();
        break;
```

First, the usual checks and actions are taken to be sure there is a data base list and that it is up to date. Then the function `dblist()` is called to prompt for a filename and print the data base information to that file. `dblist()` is coded as follows:

```
dblist()
{
  FILE *fp;   /* file pointer for text file */
  char buffer[MAXNAME+1];   /* buffer for filename */
  int code;
  LIST_NODE *ln;

  printf("Name of output file: ");
  fgets(buffer,MAXNAME,stdin);   /* get name from input */
  buffer[MAXNAME] = EOL;         /* make sure it's terminated */
  repl_nl(buffer,strlen(buffer));   /* replace newline with EOL */

  if ((fp = dbcreate(buffer,"wa",&code)) == NULL)
     {
     fprintf(stderr,"File %s already exists\n",buffer);
     return(0);
     }
```

Chapter 10

```
    /* File has been opened successfully */

    for (ln = dbfirst; ln != NULL; ln = ln->u.next)
        {
        disp_entry(fp,ln->dbe);   /* print that entry to the file */
        fprintf(fp,"\n");         /* add a line for space */
        }
    fclose(fp);   /* close the output file */
    return(1);
    }
```

The user is not permitted to write the information to an existing file. You might want to liberalize this restriction by allowing the user to specify that an existing file is to be overwritten.

The **dbcreate** function is called to create the file and open it in the proper mode (which, in this case, is text mode because you want to list the file). If the open is successful, the data base information is written to the file, the file is closed, and 1 is returned. If file creation fails, 0 is returned.

Abandoning the Current Data Base   The user may wish to abandon the current data base. This would happen if one data base had just been read but another data base was needed without updating the first. Since the program does not permit the loading of a data base file if one is currently loaded, selection 8 on the menu provides a way of abandoning the current data base so that another one may be loaded or created. The code for this case is:

```
case '8': /* Abandon */
        if (flags & FILE_LOADED)
            {
            fclose(dbfp);
            dbfp = NULL;  /* reinitialize */
            free_tree(name_tree,1);
            free_list(dbfirst,1);
            flags = 0;  /* reset all flags */
            dbfirst = dblast = name_tree = NULL;
            printf("Data base abandoned\n");
            }
      else
            printf("No data base currently loaded\n");
        pause();
        break;
```

If there currently is a data base loaded, its file is closed, and its list and tree (if these exist) are freed. All flags are set to 0, and **dbfirst**, **dblast**, and **name_tree** are reinitialized to NULL. If no data base currently is loaded, no action is taken.

302

Working with Data: Files, Structures, and Storage

Quitting the Program The last selection on the menu is to quit the program. In this case an `exit(0)` call is executed. (`exit()` is a standard C function that ensures all output buffers are written, files are closed, and so on, upon program termination.)

```
case '9': /* Quit */
    exit(0);
```

To forestall unintended exits, you might want to insert code prompting for confirmation that the user really wants to terminate the program at this time.

Module 23 Summary

In this module, you built a data base program step-by-step to illustrate the use of several C features as well as introduce basic concepts about data structures.

New C Tools

Concepts	Code
data structure	`malloc`
data base	`free`
data base operations	`exit`
dynamic memory allocation	
linked list	
binary tree	
node	
recursion	

Chapter Summary

In this chapter you have completed a complex and useful C program. Take the time to really work through this example until you understand each section of code. If you do, you will be well on your way to becoming a C programmer.

In the next and last chapter of the tutorial, some of the most common (and sometimes frustrating) programming bugs are listed and examples are given.

Chapter 11
Helpful Hints

Chapter 11

CONTENTS

Introduction 307
Correcting C Code - Common Mistakes 307

Introduction

By now, you have a good idea of what it means to program in C. You probably also realize that a lot of programming time can be spent tracking down and correcting errors (or bugs) in your program, even if it is syntax error-free after the compile step. So, before you take your new C skills out into the world, take a look at some of the more common (and sometimes hard to find) mistakes people make using C.

The format of this chapter is different from previous chapters. This chapter is designed to serve as a quick reference, so the material is presented in list form. Common mistakes are described and helpful examples are provided to illustrate less obvious program consequences.

This chapter concludes the tutorial portion of the Student Compiler. You are now ready to apply your C skills. You could start by incorporating many of the examples in this book into one system by using the menu structure provided in Chapter 5. You can also expand and rewrite many of the examples to meet your own software needs.

The remaining chapters (the User's Guide) serve as a reference guide for the Student Compiler software. In them you will find additional programming and software development hints. Good luck and happy C programming.

Correcting C Code - Common Mistakes

1. Misplacing a ;
   Placing a ; immediately following the condition statement in a `for`, `while`, `switch`, or `if` makes the conditional part of the statement a null statement. For example, the following code just prints the message "The value of i is now 10."

   ```
   for ( i = 0; i < 10; i++ );
       printf( "The value of i is now %d.\n", i );
   ```

2. Forgetting to initialize variables
   Forgetting to initialize a variable can cause unexpected results. Many languages assign the value 0 to any variable not explicitly given a value. Except for uninitialized `statics` and `externs` (which are assigned 0), C does not guarantee that a variable has any specific initial value. An uninitialized pointer is a frequently committed error. Before you explicitly assign a value to a pointer, it simply points to some random area of memory. For example, in the following code:

   ```
   struct list_node start;
   search()
   {
      struct list_node *next;
      while (next != NULL)
   ```

Chapter 11

```
        {
            if (strcmp(next->name,text) == 0)
                return (1);
            next = next ->node;
        }
        return (0);
    }
```

Since the variable **next** starts without a value, the attempt to dereference it (in **next->name**) will lead to a run-time error (unless, by chance, the value that happens to be in storage points to something valid). What is really needed in place of the **while** loop is the following:

```
for (next = &start; next != NULL; next = next->node)
  if (strcmp (next-> name, text) == 0)
    return (1);
```

where **next** is first initialized to the address of **start**.

3. Referencing an array element beyond the end of the array
   C does not make checks at run-time to make sure that all references to an array occur inside the bounds of the array. For example, when using the Student Compiler, the code below will print the message "The value of i is 11."

```
#include <stdio.h>

main()
{
    int arr[10];
    int i = 0;
    int j;

    for ( j = 0; j <= 10; j++ )
        {
        arr[j] = 11;
        }

    printf( "The value of i is %d.\n", i );
    return 0;
}
```

Other compilers may generate different results for this code.

4. Misusing **unsigned** types
   There are times when an **unsigned** type can cause an entire expression to be unsigned, for example:

   ```
   unsigned u;
   int i;
       .
       .
       .
   if (i + u < 0 )   /* This will always be false. */
       .
       .
       .
   ```

5. Missing end of comment (*/)
   Leaving off the end of a comment can cause subsequent code to be treated as comments and not be executed. A related problem occurs when comments are nested. Some compilers allow nesting of comments. Most do not, however, so the practice should be avoided. In the following code, the second assignment statement is not executed because the comment on the first line is never closed.

   ```
   start = 1;          /* Set initial value.
   terminal = 10;      /* Set termination value. */
   ```

6. Missing **#endif**
   An **#if** or **#ifdef** that is not matched with an **#endif** causes subsequent code to be treated as part of the preprocessing step.

7. Using **char** as the return value for **getchar()**
   A common misconception is that the **getchar()** function returns a **char** type when it actually returns an **int**. Because the standard library EOF value can be outside the range representable for a **char** value, the following code can cause an infinite loop. This happens because the assignment ch = **getchar()** is an implicit cast to **char**. In this case, that value will never be equal to EOF because EOF is outside the range of a **char** value.

   ```
   #include <stdio.h>

   char ch;
       .
       .
       .
   while ( ( ch = getchar() ) != EOF )
      {
          .
          .
          .
      }
       .
       .
       .
   ```

8. Using /n instead of \n

    Using a slash (/) instead of a backslash (\) can cause unexpected results, especially when used in a character constant. Using '/n' instead of '\n' on most compilers will return an error mentioning "character constant too long." (The Student Compiler will generate the error "invalid lexical token.")

9. Using = instead of ==

    The use of = instead of == is an especially tricky error because it is easy to miss and sometimes causes very subtle problems. For example, the following code will always print "i equals 2," because the if statement sets the value of i to 2 instead of comparing i to 2. Because the expression for the if statement has a nonzero value (specifically it is always 2), the printf() statement is executed.

    ```
    .
    .
    .
    if ( i = 2 )
       printf( "i equals 2\n" );
    .
    .
    .
    ```

10. Forgetting the \0 (null byte) in terminating strings

    Forgetting to terminate a string with a null byte causes the library routines that rely on the \0 to continue to process the string regardless of where the actual string ends. This error generally happens when you are building a string in a loop.

11. Forgetting to allow space for the \0 (null byte) in arrays

    An array must be big enough to hold your string and the null byte. When defining a character array to hold a string or dynamically allocating memory for this purpose, you should always make the size one character more than the anticipated length of the string (for example, strlen(s) + 1) to ensure space for the null byte.

12. Confusing single and double quotes

    Many beginning C programmers use single and double quotes for the wrong type of operation. Just remember that single quotes delimit a single character and return the ASCII value of that character as the value of the character constant. Double quotes are used in C to represent a null terminated string of characters, and the string is of type "pointer to char."

13. Using getchar() to input a single character

    Many beginning users forget that the getchar() function uses buffered input/output. This means that when getchar() is called, the entire input line is read into the program, including all characters typed and the \n character.

Helpful Hints

For example, assuming that the user types an uppercase "A" followed by return, the following code will print "A 'newline'".

```
main()
{
   char ch;

   printf( "Enter an 'A' : " );
   printchar( getchar() );
   printchar( getchar() );
}
printchar( ch )
int ch;
{
   if ( ch == EOF )
      {
      printf( "EOF encountered.\n" );
      exit( 1 );
      }
   if ( ch == '\n' )
      printf( "\"newline\"\n" );
   else
      putchar( ch );
}
```

14. **Declaring functions with an incorrect type**
    Functions that do not return `int` must always be declared before they are used. Declarations for library functions are in the header file, but user-written functions need to be declared according to the type of value they return.

15. **Passing an incorrect parameter type**
    Passing the wrong type of parameter to a function (in the absence of a prototype) can cause unexpected results (for example, passing an `int` to a function expecting a `long`).

16. **Hiding external definitions with local ones**
    If you use a local variable with the same name as a global or external variable, the global or external variable becomes unreachable, for example,

```
char buffer[10];

main()
{
   char buffer[10];     /* This hides the external variable. */
   .
   .
   .
   puts( buffer );      /* This prints the contents of the
                           local buffer, not the global one. */
   .
   .
   .
```

311

Chapter 11

```
        }
        miscfunc()
        {
            .
            .
            .
            puts( buffer );         /* This prints the value of the global
                                       buffer, not the one in main. */
            .
            .
            .
        }
```

17. Confusing Boolean and bitwise operators
    Using logical operators instead of Boolean operators often gives misleading errors.

    ```
        .
        .
        .
        val = 1 & 2;        /* bitwise -> val = 0 */
        val = 1 && 2;       /* Boolean -> val = 1 */
        .
        .
        .
        if ( i && ( j > 20 ) )  /* true if i is nonzero and j greater than 20 */
        .
        .
        .
        if ( i & ( j > 20 ) )   /* true if j greater than 20 and i is odd */
                                /* If j > 20, that expression
                                   evaluates to 1 so, for the bitwise
                                   AND to be true, the low bit of i must
                                   be 1, thus making i odd */
        .
        .
        .
    ```

18. Improper or ambiguous evaluation of expressions
    In general, avoid depending on a default order of evaluation of expressions within statements. Always use parentheses, the comma operator, or break the statement down into its component expressions, for example,

    ```
        .
        .
        .
        i = 1;
        i = ( j = i++ ) + i++;  /* Depending on the order of evaluation of the
                                   operands, j will be assigned the value 1 or 2. */
        .
        .
        .
    ```

Helpful Hints

19. **Using automatic variables incorrectly**
    Recall that automatic variables do not retain their value from one call to the function containing them to the next. A `static` declaration must be used to force this behavior. For example, the following code:

    ```
    main()
    {
       int i;

       for ( i = 0; i < 10; i++ )
          dumb_func();
    }
    dumb_func()
    {
       int a = 0;
       static int b = 0;

       a++; b++;
       printf( "a = %d    b = %d\n" );
    }
    ```

    produces the following output:

    ```
    a = 1  b = 1
    a = 1  b = 2
    a = 1  b = 3
      .
      .
      .
    ```

20. **Returning pointers to automatic variables**
    Automatic variables are only valid during the execution of the function that defines them, so returning pointers to an automatic variable has undefined results. For example, when using the Student Compiler, the following code will print only the string "What happened?":

    ```
    main()
    {
       char *str;
       char *create_str();

       str = create_str();
       print_str( str );
    }
    create_str()
    {
       char init_val[80];

       strcpy( init_val, "Help.\n" );
       return( init_val );
    }
    ```

Chapter 11

```
print_str(str)
char *str;
{
   char dummy[80];

   strcpy( dummy, " What happened?\n" );
   printf( str );
}
```

Other compilers may generate different results for this code.

21. **Calling a function that returns a pointer to a `static` buffer, without first saving the old value**
Each call to a function using a `static` variable may overwrite the value of the variable, so that any previous value is lost, unless it is saved by the calling function. The following code prints the message "call 2 call 2":

```
main()
{
   char *copy();

   printf( "%s %s\n", copy("call 1"), copy("call 2") );
}
char *copy(str)
char *str;
{
   static buffer[80];

   strcpy( buffer, str );
   return( buffer );
}
```

22. **Comparing array names to see if strings are identical**
Remember, if you compare array names, you are comparing pointer values to the first element of the array rather than the contents of the array. To compare array elements, use the `strcmp` function, which takes two string pointers as arguments.

```
char *str1 = "hello";
char *str2 = "hello";
   .
   .
   .
   if ( str1 == str2 )
```
instead of
```
   if ( strcmp( str1, str2 ) == 0 )
```

314

Helpful Hints

23. Using `#define` for types instead of `typedef`
    Remember that `typedef`s are processed by the compiler versus the preprocessor for `#define`s. In the following example, the second line expands to

    ```
    char *a,b;
    ```

    causing `a` to be a pointer and `b` to be a character.

    ```
    #define CHARP char *
    typedef char *charp;
    charp a,b;   /* a and b are pointers. */
    CHARP a,b;   /* a is a pointer, b is a character. */
    ```

24. Failing to `#include` the proper header file
    Failure to `#include` the proper header (`.h`) file needed for the functions you are using will cause errors.

25. Trying to assign identical structures that have different names
    Even though two structures have identical members, if you define two different names or templates, the compiler treats them as unique, separate objects, for example:

    ```
    typedef struct { int part1; int part2; } struct1;
    typedef struct { int part1; int part2; } struct2;
    .
    .
    .
    struct1 temp;
    struct2 hold;
    .
    .
    .
    temp = hold;  /* This fails even though struct1 and struct2 contain
                     identical types, because each named structure is
                     given a unique structure type. */
    ```

26. Using a semicolon at the end of a `#define`
    Using a semicolon at the end of a `#define` statement can lead to a syntax error where no error is immediately obvious to you. In the following code, the preprocessor expands the definition to `char buff[100;]`, which contains an invalid semicolon before the right bracket.

    ```
    #define MAX_SIZE  100;
    .
    .
    .
    char buff[MAX_SIZE];   /* This causes an error. */
    .
    .
    .
    ```

Chapter 11

27. **Assuming that passing a `struct` passes the structure and not a pointer**
    Many new compilers do this correctly; however, older compilers do not allow `struct` passing and pass a pointer instead, making this one case a call by reference instead of a call by value. Assuming that changes made by the function will not be seen by the program is a bad assumption.

28. **Reading characters into integer variables**
    Reading characters into an integer field can cause many unexpected results.

    ```
    unsigned short a = 0xffff;
       .
       .
       .
    fread((char *)&a, 1, 1, stdin);
    printf( "a = %hx\n", a );
       .
       .
       .
    ```

    Assuming that the input is 'A' followed by return, the above code will print ff41 when run on the PC. However, other machines may generate a different result, the next most common result being 41ff.

29. **Failing to set the `include` environment variable for the Student Compiler**
    If the value of this environment variable does not contain the directory where the standard header files (`stdlib.h`, `stdio.h`, and so on) are to be found, the compiler will be unable to find these files when processing `#include` statements.

Part II: User's Guide for the SAS/C™ Compiler, Student Edition

Chapter 12
Introduction to the User's Guide for the SAS/C™ Compiler, Student Edition

Chapter 12

CONTENTS

Introduction 321
Using the Student Compiler User's Guide 321
Your Program and the Student Compiler 323
    Programs 323
    Compiling Your Source Program 324
    Writing a Program: The Software Development Cycle 325

Introduction to the User's Guide for the SAS/C Compiler, Student Edition

Introduction

Welcome to Part II, the User's Guide of the **SAS/C Compiler, Student Edition**. Part II of this book shows you how to create and run C language programs using this compiler, editor, and debugger. This chapter is an introduction to the Student Compiler (SC), as it is often called. To get you started, the first section describes how Part II is organized and suggests how you might want to use it, depending on your background and experience. The following topics are covered:

- how to use the Student Compiler User's Guide
- your program and the Student Compiler.
    - What is a computer program?
    - What does it mean to compile a program?
    - How is a program developed?

Using the Student Compiler User's Guide

This User's Guide is divided into seven chapters and two appendices, as described below.

Chapter 12   "Introduction to the User's Guide for the SAS/C Compiler, Student Edition"
explains how the User's Guide is organized and where to turn for help if you need it. If you are new to programming, there is also a section explaining what a program is and what a compiler does. You should read this section if you feel that you need more background information on compilers before learning how to install and use the Student Compiler.

Chapter 13   "Installing the Student Compiler"
describes how to prepare the Student Compiler to work on your IBM personal computer. This chapter explains the hardware needed, how to install the compiler on a hard disk or double-floppy disk system, how to set the CONFIG.SYS and AUTOEXEC.BAT files, and how to execute your first sample C program.

Chapter 14   "Using the Student Compiler and Editor"
teaches you to use the compiler and editor so that you can develop and run your own C language programs. This chapter shows you the editing and program screens and the commands you will use to write, run, and debug your program.

Chapter 15   "Programming Environment for the Student Compiler"
explains the compiler's programming environment. This chapter describes more about what goes on behind the scenes when a program is compiled and run. This information includes how the compiler uses your personal computer to process your program, a look at some

Chapter 12

common operating system errors you may encounter, and a description of some C language components that are particularly relevant to the Student Compiler.

Chapter 16 "Standard Function Library for the Student Compiler"
describes the ANSI Standard functions provided with the Student Compiler. You can think of functions as self-contained sets of C language code that help you perform certain tasks in your program. For example, there are functions that read and write data, get the time of day, and compare two character strings. Each function description includes its syntax, #include files, and how the function is used in your C programs.

Chapter 17 "Graphics and Screen Management Functions for the Student Compiler"
explains the background information needed to set the characteristics of your display screen and to create simple line drawings. This chapter then describes the functions that let you change the screen's color, set the cursor's size, and make drawings. Each function description includes its syntax, #include files, and how the function is used in your C programs.

Chapter 18 "Source-Level Debugger for the Student Compiler"
describes the Student Compiler's source-level debugger, which lets you monitor your source program for execution errors. As in Chapter 14, this chapter shows the screens and commands you can use to debug and execute your program.

Appendix 1 "Error Messages for the Student Compiler"
lists the error messages that you may receive while compiling your program, for example, syntax errors or invalid arguments. This chapter lists and explains each message and often includes information to correct the error.

Appendix 2 "ASCII Character Set"
includes a table of the ASCII character set, which is the collating sequence most frequently used with C language implementations. Each ASCII character is listed with its decimal, hexadecimal, and octal values.

If you are new to programming and the C language, you should read Chapters 1 through 7, the C Tutorial, which is in the beginning of this book. If you are familiar with C but new to the Student Compiler, read Chapter 13 to install the compiler and Chapters 14 and 15 to learn how to use the compiler and editor. Chapter 16, the function library, can be used as a reference.

Good luck and welcome to the world of C programming!

Introduction to the User's Guide for the SAS/C Compiler, Student Edition

Your Program and the Student Compiler

This section provides some background information on programs and compilers. You will find this description particularly helpful if you are just starting to learn to write programs. If you are already familiar with the programming process and compilers, go on to the next chapter.

In reading about computers and their uses, the word *program* is often encountered. The term program can be confusing because it is often used to mean many different things. For example, people talk about "running a program," "writing a program," "compiling a program," "testing a program," and "debugging a program." You may wonder how it is possible for the computer to run something that is written. Can the computer read what you write? How does it know what you mean? Why is it necessary to compile your program before running it, and what does the compiler do to the program? The purpose of this section is to answer these and related questions, and to provide you with a basic understanding of what a compiler is and what it does.

This section covers the following topics:

- describing a computer program
- compiling your program
- developing your program.

Programs

The difficulty with the word *program* is that it has several distinct but related meanings, and people frequently are not careful to distinguish among these meanings. A simple definition of **program** is

> a series of steps (or operations) intended to solve a
> certain problem or to produce certain results.

So when people talk of writing a computer program, they have in mind some problem they wish to solve or some task they wish the computer to perform. The program, in this sense, tells the machine what to do.

A **source program** is a description of what you want the computer to do to solve the problem or perform the task. The source program is written in a *source language*, also called a *programming language*. There are quite a number of programming languages, and it is possible to write a program to do the same thing but in several different languages. In other words, you can write several different source programs (each in a different programming language) that describe the same series of steps (program) to be performed by the computer. In this sense, you could write the same abstract program in either Basic or C, but the two source programs would be different because they are written in different languages.

Once you have written your source program, you want the computer to execute or *run* it. This requires that the computer understand your program. But here is a real problem: the computer cannot understand your program when it is in its source

Chapter 12

language form. In fact, the computer does not understand anything because, in reality, it is just a complicated arrangement of very small switches and circuits. The program that the computer can run is actually just a particular arrangement of these switches and circuits. This version of the program is written in *machine language* and is therefore called the **machine program** or the executable program.

You need to change the source program (that you can read and understand) into the machine program (that the computer can understand and execute). The way to do this is to use another program called a compiler.

Compiling Your Source Program

The **compiler** is really a translator. It translates your source program into a machine program, as illustrated in **Figure 12.1**.

```
┌──────────┐             ┌──────────┐
│  SOURCE  │  compiler   │ MACHINE  │
│ PROGRAM  │ ──────────▶ │ PROGRAM  │
└──────────┘             └──────────┘
```

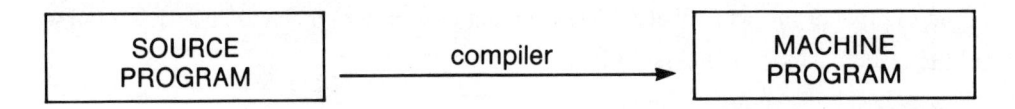

Figure 12.1   Translating Your Program

Compilers are machine-specific; that is, they are designed to run on a certain kind of computer because each kind of computer has its own machine language. For example, the Student Compiler can produce a machine program on an IBM PC (or one of its compatibly designed computers) that corresponds to your C language source program.

In the 1940s, when computers were programmed by turning on and off a series of switches, there were no high-level programming languages that you could write a program in to solve a given problem. The programmer had to sketch out (in English) a solution to the problem and then think of how this solution could be translated into primitive instructions for the computer, which then set the correct switches. As you can imagine, this was a very time-consuming, difficult task that was error prone. Compilers and high-level programming languages were developed as tools to simplify this process.

Once your source program is compiled into a machine program, the computer can be told to run the program. This is done by giving a command to your computer's operating system, which then performs whatever actions are necessary to execute the program. The Student Compiler simplifies this process even further. It is known as a **compile, load**, and **go** compiler. This means that immediately after the Student Compiler finishes compiling your source program, it loads the machine program into the computer and runs it as well.

Introduction to the User's Guide for the SAS/C Compiler, Student Edition

Writing a Program: The Software Development Cycle

Creating a program involves several steps, some of which may need to be repeated until the program acts the way you want it to. This process is called the **software development cycle**, and it consists of the following steps:

1. Identify the goal or problem.
2. Design a solution.
3. Create a C source file containing your solution coded in the C programming language.
4. Compile the source file. The Student Compiler is designed to be used with single-source file applications, so you never have to worry about *linking* separately compiled source files.
5. If there are errors in the compilation phase, review the error messages, modify your C source program, and return to step 4.
6. Test your program by running it. (This step is done automatically by the Student Compiler.)
7. If your program compiled successfully but did not accomplish the goal you intended for it, use the debugging features of the compiler to see what went wrong, modify the source program as necessary, and return to step 4.

If your program performs as you expected it to, you have completed the development of your program.

The Student Compiler provides an integrated environment in which each of the steps 3 through 7 can be accomplished. The first two design steps do not directly involve the use of the C programming language. In step 1, try to write a clear and precise description of the problem you want to solve or the goal you want your program to accomplish. In step 2, try to write a clear, simple English description of the steps that will make up your program. Then go on to step 3 and translate your English description of the program into C source code.

In the next chapter, you will learn how to install the compiler on your IBM personal computer (PC) so that you can start developing and running your own programs.

Chapter 13
Installing the Student Compiler

Chapter 13

CONTENTS

Introduction **329**
Recommended Computer Systems **329**
Copying and Installing the Student Compiler **330**
    Installing the Student Compiler on a Hard Disk System **330**
    Installing the Student Compiler on a Floppy-Disk Drive System **331**
Creating a Path to Your SC Directory **333**
    Creating an AUTOEXEC.BAT File **333**
    Editing an Existing AUTOEXEC.BAT File **334**
    The PATH and SET Commands **334**
Running the "Hello.C" Program **334**
Chapter Summary **335**

Installing the Student Compiler

Introduction

This chapter shows you how to make the Student Compiler, editor, and debugger a part of your personal computer system. This process of making a software package available for use on your computer is called **installing** the software (software in this case means the contents of the SC diskettes). The following sections take you through the steps involved in this process:

- recommending computer systems for the Student Compiler
- copying the diskettes and installing the compiler
- creating or editing the AUTOEXEC.BAT file.

Recommended Computer Systems

To run the Student Compiler successfully, you need to be sure that the microcomputer you will be using has the recommended physical components or **hardware**. This compiler is designed to work on the following IBM personal computers: PC, PC XT,™ PC AT,™ and the Personal System 2 (PS/2™), or on IBM compatible microcomputers; the PC must have a hard disk drive or a double-floppy disk drive system. It runs under the PC DOS or MS-DOS® operating system, Version 2.1 or later. (The operating system is the software that controls your microcomputer's resources and processes.) Because PC DOS and MS-DOS are so similar, they are referred to in this manual as DOS.

The operating system needs to know certain characteristics about the Student Compiler. When you install MS-DOS or PC DOS, you will be asked to respond to questions about the CONFIG.SYS file. This file contains commands that modify the way DOS works. (The CONFIG.SYS file is described in detail in your DOS manual.) For the Student Compiler, add the BREAK command to the CONFIG.SYS file and set it to ON, so that you can interrupt the compiler during execution, if necessary.

Your PC must have 512 kilobytes (KB) of Random Access Memory (RAM) available. In some cases, other software (called memory resident programs) may take up some of this space. You can check how much space is available on the current disk drive by using the DOS DIR command. (Type DIR to display a list of your directories and the number of bytes free on the drive.) For some of the graphics functions (see Chapter 17), your PC also needs special hardware called a color display adapter card.

Your PC salesperson or an experienced programmer can help you locate this information if it is not included in your computer's documentation.

PC XT, PC AT, and PS/2 are trademarks of IBM Corp.
MS-DOS is a registered trademark of Microsoft Corp.

Chapter 13

Copying and Installing the Student Compiler

The Student Compiler is distributed on two 360-kilobyte (KB) double-sided, double-density diskettes. These diskettes contain the compiler in the form of several **files**, which are collections of program statements or data. The diskettes contain the following files:

1. first diskette
contains the Student Compiler's executable file, its header files, the Help facility and a file called `read.me`. The `sc.exe` executable file is the actual compiler; that is, when you invoke the compiler, you invoke this file. The header files (those that end with the extension `.h`) are used in compiling the C language programs; Chapter 15 lists and describes them. The Help facility (`sc.hlp`) gives you online information about the Student Compiler's functions and error messages. See the Help command description in Chapter 14 for more information. The `read.me` file contains additional information and important notices. Read this file.

2. second diskette
contains the sample programs that are to be used with the C Tutorial, in Part I of this book, and with the Student Compiler's graphics and screen management functions.

Finally, after you install the Student Compiler, you need to tell DOS how to find it on your system. This is explained in **Creating a Path to Your Student Compiler Directory**, following the installation instructions.

The installation instructions are divided into two parts because they depend on whether your PC has a hard disk drive or two floppy-disk drives. If you have a double-floppy disk drive system, skip to the next section.

Installing the Student Compiler on a Hard Disk System

To install the compiler on a hard disk system, take the following steps:

1. Create a directory into which you want to load the Student Compiler files. For example, from the root directory (\) on the C: drive, type the following:

    ```
    C > MKDIR \SC <enter>
    ```

    To verify that the directory was created, type DIR and press the <enter> key to list the directories in the root directory. Then type the following to move to the new directory:

    ```
    C > CD SC <enter>
    ```

2. Insert the first SC diskette into the disk drive. Type the following to copy the files on the first SC diskette into the SC directory on the C: drive:

    ```
    C > COPY A:*.*  C:\SC   <enter>
    ```

Installing the Student Compiler

The file for the Help facility (`sc.hlp`) must appear in the same directory as the compiler's executable file (`sc.exe`) or in the directory in which you are currently working. If you copy the files as directed here, `sc.hlp` will be in the same directory. Otherwise, you will not be able to bring up the Help facility; see Chapter 14 for more information on the Help facility.

3. When the screen displays a message that all the files are copied, remove the diskette, insert the second diskette, and repeat step 2 for the second SC diskette.

Screen 13.1 illustrates the steps described above.

```
C > \          <enter>
C > MKDIR \SC  <enter>
C > DIR        <enter>

Directory of C:\

COMMAND    COM     22677    9-01-87   09:15a
DOS        <DIR>            9-01-87   09:20a
SC         <DIR>            6-22-87   12:54p

           3 File(s) 19261440 bytes free

C >  CD SC              <enter>
C >  COPY  A:*.*  C:\SC <enter>

SC.EXE
SC.HLP
BIOS.H
CTYPE.H
   .
   .
   .

18 File(s) copied
```

Screen 13.1 Installing the Student Compiler on a Hard Disk System

The copying continues until all the files on the SC diskette are listed in the specified directory.

Installing the Student Compiler on a Floppy-Disk Drive System

Installing a double-floppy disk drive system involves two steps: formatting blank diskettes and copying the SC diskettes onto the newly formatted diskettes. Because you use the copied SC diskettes to invoke the compiler, putting the SC diskettes into the disk drives installs the Student Compiler.

Chapter 13

You should make copies of your Student Compiler diskettes and store the original diskettes. Then, if something should damage your copies, you will have the original diskettes as a back-up. To do this, you need to **format** two (or more) new blank diskettes. Formatting prepares the diskettes to receive and store the files you are going to copy. To format a diskette you need the DOS commands diskette, which contains the formatting program, and a *blank* (unformatted) diskette. Caution: if you re-format a used diskette, its current contents are wiped out. The steps involved are as follows:

1. Type "A:" and press the <enter> key to display the A > prompt on the screen. Insert the DOS diskette into drive A: and an unformatted diskette into drive B:. Type the following to format the diskette in drive B:

    ```
    A > FORMAT B:  <enter>
    ```

2. A message is displayed on the screen when formatting is completed. The system then asks if you have another diskette to format. If you type "y" (for yes), you need to remove the formatted diskette, insert an unformatted diskette, and press <enter> to repeat the formatting steps.

3. Repeat step 2 until you have formatted all the diskettes you need. It is recommended that you format extra diskettes to have them available later, in case you run out of disk space while editing a file and need to add a new diskette. If you have no formatted diskettes, you may lose the entire file.

After you have formatted the diskettes, copy the Student Compiler diskettes onto the new diskettes. Take the following steps to copy the SC diskettes:

1. Type "A:" and press the <enter> key to display the A > prompt on the screen. Insert your DOS diskette in drive A: and a newly formatted diskette in drive B:. Then, type the following:

    ```
    A > DISKCOPY A:  B:  <enter>
    ```

    The DOS command DISKCOPY makes an exact copy of one floppy disk to another. When DISKCOPY begins, it displays the following message:

    ```
    Insert SOURCE disk in drive A:    <enter>

    Insert TARGET disk in drive B:    <enter>

    Press any key when ready ...
    ```

    Put the first Student Compiler diskette in drive A: and a newly formatted diskette in drive B:. Press a key to begin copying.

2. When the copy is complete, a message is displayed on the screen asking if you want to copy another diskette. Enter "y" (for yes) to copy the next set of diskettes. Put the second SC diskette in drive A: and the second newly formatted diskette in drive B: and follow the DISKCOPY prompts.

The file for the Help facility (`sc.hlp`) must appear in the same directory as the SC executable file (`sc.exe`) or in the directory in which you are currently working. If you copy the files as directed here, `sc.hlp` will be in the same directory. Otherwise,

Installing the Student Compiler

you will not be able to bring up the Help facility; see Chapter 14 for more information on this facility.

When you have copied all the SC diskettes, remove the original diskettes and store them in a safe place. Put the first and second (copied) SC diskettes in drives A: and B:, respectively, to *install* the Student Compiler. You must then set the Student Compiler path so that DOS can find the compiler on your system.

Creating a Path to Your SC Directory

You need to specify a destination path so that DOS can always find the Student Compiler. The destination path lists the disk drive (hard disk or diskette) and directory that contain the compiler. Specify the destination path by adding it to the DOS batch file AUTOEXEC.BAT. This file enables DOS to find your path when it loads and executes programs. AUTOEXEC.BAT is included in the root directory of most DOS commands diskettes and is automatically executed whenever DOS is started. You can edit this file to add your compiler's destination path or, if your system does not have an AUTOEXEC.BAT file, you can create one and add your path to it.

You can create the AUTOEXEC.BAT file from the DOS command line, or you can edit an existing AUTOEXEC.BAT file using the Student Compiler's Screen Editor, the DOS EDLIN utility, or any other editor you may have online. The contents of the AUTOEXEC.BAT file (the PATH and SET commands) are described after the file creation and editing sessions are explained. The following sections tell you how to tailor your own AUTOEXEC.BAT file.

Creating an AUTOEXEC.BAT File

To create an AUTOEXEC.BAT file from the DOS command line, go to the root directory and use the DOS command, COPY. This command lets you copy all the characters on the console screen (CON) to a file by the name of AUTOEXEC.BAT. Be careful when typing in this file because you cannot return to a previous line to correct an error once you have pressed the <enter> key. To create an AUTOEXEC.BAT file on your hard disk or double-floppy disk drive system, type the lines listed in **Table 13.1**.

Table 13.1   Creating an AUTOEXEC.BAT File

Hard Disk System	Floppy-Disk System
C > cd \ <enter>	A > cd \ <enter>

C > COPY CON AUTOEXEC.BAT <enter>
    path C:\SC <enter>
    set INCLUDE=C:\SC <enter>
    CTRL-Z <enter>
	A > COPY CON AUTOEXEC.BAT <enter>
	    path A:\ <enter>
	    set INCLUDE=A:\ <enter>
	    CTRL-Z <enter>

C > AUTOEXEC <enter>	A > AUTOEXEC <enter>

Chapter 13

To exit from the AUTOEXEC.BAT file back to the DOS command line, hold down the CTRL key while pressing the "z" key, release them, and then press the <enter> key. The CTRL-Z key combination serves as a DOS end-of-file indicator on IBM PCs.

To establish the new destination path for the compiler, type the word "AUTOEXEC" and press the <enter> key. You only need to type this once because DOS will now call this file automatically in the future.

Editing an Existing AUTOEXEC.BAT File

You should add the same information to an existing AUTOEXEC.BAT file (described above in the COPY CON example) and type "AUTOEXEC" when you have finished editing. This establishes the compiler's new destination path.

You can use any text editor to edit an existing AUTOEXEC.BAT file, including the Student Compiler's editor, described in Chapter 14. If you want to use the SC editor and do not know how, you can specify the destination path when you invoke the compiler for the first time; you can then edit the existing AUTOEXEC.BAT file once you have learned how to use the SC editor. See **Invoking the Student Compiler** in Chapter 14 for more information and examples.

The PATH and SET Commands

The PATH command defines the destination path that DOS is to follow. The default paths for the Student Compiler are listed above in **Table 13.1**. If your Student Compiler is not in the current directory when you run it, DOS searches each of the path directories.

The compiler uses the SET command to locate header files that are fetched via the `#include` operation. It refers to the destination path and to any other directories in which you keep header files. (In the Student Compiler, you usually keep your header files in the directory that contains the `sc.exe` file.) The default settings for this compiler are listed above in **Table 13.1**.

If you want to add other directories to this setting, list and separate them with a semicolon. For example,

```
SET INCLUDE=C:\SC; C:\HDRS
```

directs the compiler to look for header files in the C:\SC and C:\HDRS directories.

Running the "Hello.C" Program

After installing the Student Compiler, you would probably like to see if everything works! To do this, the Student Compiler comes with a program that you can run to be sure the compiler is correctly installed on your PC. To execute the program on a hard disk system, type

```
C > CD C:\SC   <enter>
C > SC HELLO.C   <enter>
```

Installing the Student Compiler

To execute the program on a double-floppy disk system, type

```
A > B: <enter>
B > SC HELLO.C  <enter>
```

When the `hello.c` program is displayed on your screen, press the function key F7. You will see a number of messages about the compilation and execution on your screen. Press <enter> when you get the prompt for arguments. The following output will be displayed on your screen:

```
Hello World!
```

Now you know that you have successfully installed the Student Compiler software. (Press the function key F4 to exit the Student Compiler.)

Chapter Summary

This chapter has shown you how to make the Student Compiler a part of your personal computer system. The following sections took you through the steps involved in this process:

- recommending computer systems for the Student Compiler
- copying the SC diskettes and installing the compiler on an IBM PC
- creating or editing the AUTOEXEC.BAT file.

You are now ready to write and run your own C programs. The next chapter shows you how to do this.

Chapter 14
Using the Student Compiler and Editor

Chapter 14

CONTENTS

Introduction	**341**
Using the Editing Screen and the Program Screen	**341**
Invoking the Student Compiler	341
The Editing Screen	342
Using the Menu System	344
Getting Started: Creating and Editing Programs	**350**
Introduction	350
Edit Menu	352
Delete Line	353
Erase to End	353
Join Line	354
Split Line	355
Block Menu	355
Select Line	356
Undo Select	357
Copy	358
Move	359
Delete	360
Left Shift	360
Right Shift	362
Search Menu	363
Search	364
Next	366
First Error	366
Query Replace	368
Replace All	369
Compiling and Running Programs	**370**
Introduction	370
File Menu	370
Help	371
Save	374

Using the Student Compiler and Editor

File	**375**
Quit	**376**
Run	**376**
New File	**378**
Print	**379**
Debug	**380**
Function Keys and Key Combinations	**382**
Using the C Language Templates	**383**
Introduction	**383**
Program	**385**
C-Function	**385**
If-Else	**386**
Switch	**386**
For Loop	**386**
While Loop	**387**
Do While Loop	**387**
Chapter Summary	**388**

Chapter 14

Using the Student Compiler and Editor

Introduction

This chapter shows you how to use the editor and compiler provided with the SAS/C Compiler, Student Edition, to build and run C programs. Topics covered include:

- creating and editing files
- saving and printing source code
- compiling and executing programs
- debugging programs
- using the C language templates.

Using the Editing Screen and the Program Screen

The Student Compiler is designed to help you perform many common programming tasks in an easy, straightforward way. It is menu-driven and provides a full-screen editor. This section covers the Student Compiler's screens and menus. After reviewing the entire chapter, you should understand how to get started and keep things going using the Student Compiler.

The Student Compiler has two major screen displays: the Editing Screen and the Program Screen.

- The Editing Screen allows you to create, edit, and execute your C program. This screen contains a menu bar, an editing window, a status/input line, and a message line.
- The Program Screen displays messages from the compiler and output from your program while they are running.

Invoking the Student Compiler

To invoke the Student Compiler, go to the directory that contains the compiler (the one containing the **sc.exe** file). You can then invoke the compiler and be prompted for a filename or you can invoke the compiler and specify a file to edit.

To invoke the compiler and be prompted for a filename, type the initials SC from your DOS command line and press the <enter> key. To invoke SC when you have installed it on a hard disk system, type the following from the \SC directory:

```
C > SC   <enter>
```

Or, to invoke the compiler from a double-floppy disk system, type the following from the \SC directory:

```
A > SC   <enter>
```

Chapter 14

A **Source:** prompt is displayed on your screen. To respond to it, enter the name of the source file that you want to edit or the name of a new file that you want to create. For example:

    Source: hello.c   <enter>

You should always include the `.c` extension on source files that contain C language programs.

In some cases you will need to give the **Source:** prompt additional information about the source file that you want to create or edit. Enter the filename's disk drive and directory path if you have not set the compiler's destination path in the AUTOEXEC.BAT file or if you are not currently in the directory that contains the SC compiler. For example:

    Source: c:\autoexec.c   <enter>

or

    Source: c:\sc\hello.c   <enter>

See Chapter 13, "Installing the Student Compiler," for information on setting the destination path with the AUTOEXEC.BAT file.

To invoke the compiler and specify a file in one step, type SC *filename.c* from your DOS command line and press the <enter> key. For example, to invoke SC with the `hello.c` file, type

    C > sc hello.c   <enter>

Once you have invoked the Student Compiler, the first display you see is the Editing Screen. Whenever this screen is visible, you are in the SC editor.

To exit the Student Compiler, press the function key F4. The system asks if you want to save your file and then lets you exit back to the PC DOS or MS-DOS environment. See the Quit command, later in this chapter, for more information.

The Editing Screen

The Editing Screen contains the editing window, menu bar, input/status line, and message line. The **editing window** is a display area for your source file that encompasses most of your screen. It is 20 lines high and 77 columns (or characters) wide. See **Getting Started: Creating and Editing Programs**, later in this chapter, for more information on editing text.

The cursor is associated with a single character position in the source file called the **current cursor position** or sometimes just the **current line**. A cursor's position is described by its line and column coordinates in the editing window, and it is represented in the screen examples as an underline (_) character. **Screen 14.1** shows the Editing Screen, where the editing window contains the "Hello World" C program. Note that the cursor is located at the end of the `printf` function and its position is described (line 5, column 28) on the line below the window.

Using the Student Compiler and Editor

```
 File      Edit     Block    Search    Templates    (MENU BAR)

 ==== Top of file ====
 #include <stdio.h>

 main()
    {
    printf("Hello World!\n");_ (CURSOR)
    }
 ==== Bottom of file ====




                                               
 Line 5    Column 28    Replace   hello.c       (STATUS/INPUT LINE)
 (MESSAGE LINE) . . . . . . . . . . . . . . . . . . . . .
```

Screen 14.1 Editing Screen

Menu Bar The menu bar is a list of the SC menu names along the top of the editing window. You can choose to use the File, Edit, Block, Search, or Templates menu. The File menu helps you save, run, and debug your program. The Edit, Block, Search, and Templates menus help you create and modify your program. These menus are described in detail later in this chapter.

Press the function key F10 and the <enter> key to move from the editing window to the menu bar, where one of the menus will be displayed. Press the ESC (escape) key twice to move the cursor from the menu bar back to the editing window. See **Screen 14.1** for the menu bar display.

Status Line The status line is located below the source window. It lists where the cursor is in your source file (by the line and column numbers), the cursor mode (that is, whether you can insert or overwrite/replace text), and the name of the source file being edited.

Input Line The input line replaces the status line when you begin to type on it. It is used to input information to the editor commands. For example, a prompt appears on this line so that you can type in the search string argument for the Search command.

Chapter 14

Message Line The message line is the last line on the screen and it displays all the SC editor messages. Messages are always highlighted, that is, displayed in reverse video. For example, if you enter an invalid search string (in response to the prompt on the input line), the system tells you so from this line.

Using the Menu System

The best way to learn how to use the Student Compiler's editor is to experiment with it. The editor is designed to be very flexible, so that you can select menus and commands in a number of ways. The brief description that follows introduces you to one way of selecting menus and commands, but there are others. See **Tables 14.2–14.4** for the exact instructions. Remember, you cannot break this editor or compiler, so play with it. If you get stuck, press the ESC key once or twice to release your cursor or cancel a command.

Each SC menu listed on the menu bar is known as a **pull-down menu.** In this compiler, a pull-down menu is a box that overlays part of the editing window and its contents. The menu itself does not modify the contents of your editing window, although you can use the commands in each menu to create, modify, run, and debug your program. When you exit from the pull-down menu (by pressing the ESC key), the editing window's contents will not be changed unless you have done so with the menus' commands.

As an overview, each Student Compiler menu and its commands are displayed in **Table 14.1.** Some commands can also be executed by pressing a function key or CTRL key combination; these **fast path** keys are listed where available and are described later in this chapter. See **Table 14.5** for an alphabetic list of the commands by their function keys or key combinations.

Table 14.1   Summary of Commands in Each SC Menu

File Menu	Edit Menu	Block Menu
Help (F1)	Delete Line (F5)	Select Line (CTRL-L)
Save (F2)	Erase to End (F6)	Undo Select (CTRL-U)
File (F3)	Join Line	Copy (CTRL-Z)
Quit (F4)	Split Line	Move (CTRL-M)
Run (F7)		Delete (CTRL-D)
New File (F8)		Left Shift (CTRL ←)
Print		Right Shift (CTRL →)
Debug		

(continued)

344

Table 14.1 (*continued*)

Search Menu	Templates Menu
Search (CTRL-S)	Program
Next (CTRL-N)	C-Function
First Error (CTRL-F)	If-Else
Query Replace (CTRL-R)	Switch
Replace All (CTRL-A)	For Loop
	While Loop
	Do While Loop

Making a Menu Selection When you invoke the Student Compiler, the Editing Screen appears and the file you specified is displayed in the editing window. The word File appears in a highlighted bar (that is, reverse video) because it is the default pull-down menu choice.

To display the File menu, press function key F10 and the <enter> key. This moves your cursor to the menu bar and displays the File menu over part of the editing window. (Press F10 and <enter> to display whichever pull-down menu name is highlighted.) If you want to display a menu other than the highlighted one, press F10 and the initial letter of the menu you want to display; for example, F10 S displays the Search menu.

Each pull-down menu contains entries representing Student Compiler commands. One command on each menu is highlighted as the default choice for that menu; in the File menu, the Help command is highlighted. To make a selection, use the up and down arrow keys to choose the command you want and press the <enter> key. Once you have displayed a pull-down menu, you can use only the commands in that menu.

When you are in a pull-down menu, each command with a fast path key has it listed next to the command. It is here for your information. You can only use a fast path key to execute that command if no pull-down menus are displayed. Using the fast path keys is described in **Table 14.4**.

When one pull-down menu is displayed, you can use the left and right arrow keys to move to and display another menu; the cursor (as a highlighted bar) jumps from one displayed menu to another. Press the ESC key once to return to the menu bar and a second time to return to the editing window. **Screen 14.2** shows the File menu displayed over the "Hello World" program in the editing window.

Chapter 14

```
┌─────────────────────────────────────────────────────────────────────┐
│   File      Edit     Block    Search    Templates    (MENU BAR)     │
│ ┌─────────────┐─────────────────────────────────────────────────────│
│ │ Help    F1 │                                                      │
│ │ Save    F2 │                                                      │
│ │ File    F3 │              (FILE MENU)                             │
│ │ Quit    F4 │                                                      │
│ │ Run     F7 │World!\n");_                                          │
│ │ New File F8│                                                      │
│ │ Print      │                                                      │
│ │ Debug      │                                                      │
│ └────────────┘                                                      │
│                                                                     │
│                                                                     │
│                                                                     │
│                                                                     │
│                                                                     │
│─────────────────────────────────────────────────────────────────────│
│   Line 5    Column 28    Replace    hello.c                         │
└─────────────────────────────────────────────────────────────────────┘
```

Screen 14.2 Display of the SC Default Menu

You can use the Student Compiler in different ways depending on your level of expertise.

- If you are just learning to use the Student Compiler, it offers pull-down menus to remind you of its editing and execution commands. You can execute the commands in one menu at a time (described in **Table 14.2** and **Table 14.3**).

- If you are familiar with the Student Compiler but need an occasional reminder, it offers a shortcut approach to the pull-down menus (described in **Table 14.3**). Again, you can execute the commands in one menu at a time.

- If you are an experienced Student Compiler user, it offers the fast path. This allows you to select a pull-down menu or to execute menu commands directly from anywhere in the Editing Screen, as long as a menu is not displayed. The fast path is described in **Table 14.2** for menus and in **Table 14.4** for commands.

The following tables describe these three levels. **Table 14.2** describes how to select a menu and how to change between menus quickly. Note that once you have selected and displayed a pull-down menu, you can use only the commands in that one menu. If you want to use commands in another menu, you must select another menu.

Table 14.2 Selecting a Menu

From the Menu

1. Press function key F10 and the <enter> key to move the cursor to the menu bar (at the top of the editing window) and to display whichever menu name is highlighted. If you have just invoked the compiler, the default menu name, File, is highlighted.

   When you press F10, a dark character box marks your cursor's position in the editing window.

2. Use the left or right arrow keys to highlight the desired pull-down menu, which is then displayed automatically over part of the text in the editing window. The default command within the menu is highlighted.

   Once a pull-down menu is displayed, use the left and right arrow keys to display other menus.

3. Or, press the ESC key to return to the menu bar and use the left or right arrow keys to move the highlighted bar to the menu you want. Press <enter>. The menu you select is displayed and the default command is highlighted.

4. Press the ESC key twice to cancel the menu display and to return to the editing window. The cursor returns to its previous position.

Fast Path

1. Press function key F10 and the initial letter of the menu name to select and display that menu. For example, press F10 and B to display the Block menu over part of the text in the editing window.

2. Or, use the ALT key plus the initial letter of the SC pull-down menu you want to select:

ALT-F	File menu
ALT-E	Edit menu
ALT-B	Block menu
ALT-S	Search menu
ALT-T	Templates menu

   This initial letter can be typed in lowercase or uppercase. Pressing this key combination automatically displays the specified pull-down menu. You can use this key combination from anywhere in the editing window to change menus.

3. Press the ESC key twice to cancel the menu display and to return to the editing window. The cursor returns to its previous position.

Chapter 14

Table 14.3 describes the two methods that can be used to select and execute a command once you have displayed the SC pull-down menu. The benefits and limitations of using these methods versus the fast path method are described following this table. The method outlined below assumes that you are working within one menu. To select commands directly from within the editing window, see **Table 14.4**.

Table 14.3   Executing a Command Within a Menu

Command Selection

1. Move the cursor to the line in your file on which you want to act (the action line). For example, if you want to delete a line, move your cursor to the line to be deleted. This step varies some with each command, so see the individual command descriptions.

2. Use function key F10, the <enter> key, and the left/right arrow keys to select a menu. Note that once you press F10, a dark character box is left on the action line in the window.

3. Use the up/down arrow keys to select a command in the pull-down menu and press the <enter> key to execute the command.

   Once the command has been executed, the cursor returns to its previous position in the editing window.

Command Selection Shortcut

1. Move the cursor to the line in your file on which you want to act (the action line). For example, if you want to delete a line, move your cursor to the line to be deleted. This step varies some with each command, so see the individual command descriptions.

2. Use function key F10, the <enter> key, and the left/right arrow keys to select a menu. Note that once you press F10, a dark character box is left on the action line in the window.

   Then type the initial letter of the command you want to select, for example, type D for Delete Line in the Edit menu.

3. Pressing this letter key automatically executes the command. The cursor returns to its previous position in the editing window.

There are two benefits of using commands within a single menu. First of all, the commands are displayed on the screen to prompt you. This is especially helpful as you are learning to use the Student Compiler. Secondly, this method allows you to select any command in the menus, whether or not the command also has a fast path key. Some users would rather not have to remember function keys or other key combinations.

Using the Student Compiler and Editor

The main limitation of using commands within a single menu is that you can use only the commands in that one menu at any one time. This means that you have to exit from one menu to use commands in another menu, which some users prefer not to do.

Table 14.4 describes the fast path method of selecting and executing a command. Unlike the two methods listed above, the fast path enables you to use function key and CTRL key combinations to execute commands directly from the editing window if an SC pull-down menu is not currently displayed.

The fast path function key and CTRL key combinations are summarized in **Tables 14.1** and **14.5** and are listed in each menu command description. You should not select a pull-down menu first with this method. The benefits and limitations of the fast path method are described following **Table 14.4**.

Table 14.4 Fast Path Method of Executing Commands

Fast Path

1. Move the cursor to the line in your file on which you want to act (the action line). For example, if you want to delete a line, move your cursor to the line to be deleted. This step varies some with each command, so see the individual command descriptions.

2. Press the function key or CTRL key combination listed for the command you want. This executes the command and leaves the cursor on the same line in the editing window. For example, press CTRL-L for Select Line. Remember, you cannot use the fast path if a pull-down menu is displayed.

The main benefit of using the fast path method is that you can execute most of the commands directly, without having to switch between pull-down menus. This is quick and takes few keystrokes.

The main limitation of this method is that not all commands have fast path keys. You still have to access certain menus to execute certain commands, as listed in **Table 14.1**. Also, if you have not learned the function keys or CTRL key combinations, you may press the wrong key and modify your file in an undesirable way.

Now that you have seen the various methods of selecting menus and commands, experiment with them to see which method you like best. You may begin with one execution method and later choose another as you become familiar with the menus and commands. Or, you may like using the function keys in the File menu to run your programs but the commands in the pull-down menus for entering text. Again, play with the editor and compiler to find the methods that suit you best.

The next section explains how to edit text using the control cursor keys and how to use the Edit menu commands. This pull-down menu helps you create and modify your program. The Block, Search, File, and Templates menus also help you develop a program, and are described in subsequent sections.

Chapter 14

Getting Started: Creating and Editing Programs

Introduction

Once you are familiar with the menu system, you can begin to create and edit text. This section describes how to do this and how to use the Edit menu.

If you want to create a new, empty source file or edit an existing one, enter the name of the file when you invoke the Student Compiler or in response to the **Source:** prompt. (See **Invoking the Student Compiler** section earlier in this chapter for more information on this process.) In each case, SC positions the cursor at line one, column one, of the editing window. You can then begin to enter or edit text.

Once in the editing window, press function key F10 and <enter> to select and display the Edit menu, or use the ALT-E key combination to select this menu. You can then use the Edit menu and control cursor keys to edit your file. (See **Table 14.2** for more information on selecting a menu.)

The editing window is where you input and edit the text in your source file. All characters typed are added to your source file once you have saved your file (using the Save command described below). Press the <enter> key to add new lines to the file or to split an existing line into two lines. Source lines are limited to 77 characters in width and the end of a source line is its last nonblank character. Once a source line is full, SC discards any additional characters that you type and displays the message

```
Line is full
```

If you edit an existing file that has source lines exceeding 77 characters, SC tries to split the line at a blank space and automatically appends the C language continuation character, a backslash (\), at the end of the split line.

The cursor moves as you type in new characters. You can type in either replace mode or insert mode. The current cursor mode is displayed below the editing window on the status line.

In **replace mode**, the character at the cursor position is overwritten or replaced as you type in new characters. Replace mode is the default cursor mode.

In **insert mode**, the cursor and all the characters to its right are shifted right as you type in new characters. Use the INS key to switch between insert mode and replace mode.

You can move the cursor either by typing in new characters or by using the cursor control keys. For example, the TAB key can be used to move the cursor quickly to the next tab stop. A tab stop is associated with every eight characters of the editing window. The first tab stop is in column 1, the next in column 9, and so on. Use the cursor control keys to move the cursor within the editing window and to scroll the source file up or down in this window.

The Student Compiler provides a set of cursor control keys to help you move around in the edit window.

Key	Function
Left Arrow	moves the cursor one position to the left (does not move if the cursor is in column 1).
Right Arrow	moves the cursor one position to the right (does not move if the cursor is in column 77).
Up Arrow	moves the cursor one position upwards (does not move if the cursor is on the first line of the source file). This key scrolls the source file upwards by one line if the cursor is on the first line of the editing window.
Down Arrow	moves the cursor one position downwards (does not move if the cursor is on the last line of the source file). This key scrolls the source file downwards by one line if the cursor is on the last line of the editing window.
PgUp	scrolls the source file upwards by one page.
PgDn	scrolls the source file downwards by one page.
HOME	moves the cursor to the start of the current source line.
END	moves the cursor to the end of the current source line.
CTRL-HOME	moves the cursor to the first line of the source file.
CTRL-END	moves the cursor to the last line of the source file.
CTRL-PgUp	moves the cursor to the first line of the editing window.
CTRL-PgDn	moves the cursor to the last line of the editing window.
TAB	moves the cursor to the next tab stop to the right.
SHIFT TAB	moves the cursor to the next tab stop to the left.
BACKSPACE	deletes the character to the left of the cursor and moves the cursor back one space (does not move if the cursor is in column 1).
CTRL-BACKSPACE	deletes the current line.
DEL	deletes the character at the current cursor position. This key also joins two lines; if you position the cursor at the end of the line and press DEL, that line is joined with the line below it.
INS	switches back and forth between insert mode or replace mode.

Once you have created a source file, use the SC Edit, Block, and Search menus to help modify the text quickly and easily. These three menus and their commands are described next.

Chapter 14

Edit Menu

The Edit menu allows you to delete a line, erase to the end of a line, join two lines, or split a line in your source file. You can access this menu using three methods (see **Table 14.2**), but the fastest way is to press the ALT-E key combination. The Edit menu is then displayed over part of the editing window (see **Screen 14.3**).

Each command in the Edit menu is described below. In most cases, move the cursor to the line that you want to act on (for example, to delete a line) and use the arrow keys and <enter> to select the command you want or press the appropriate function key (fast path). At the end of each command description, the fast path method is described.

Remember, if you do not use the fast path method of executing commands, use only the commands in the currently displayed menu. If you want to use commands in another menu, you have to move to that menu.

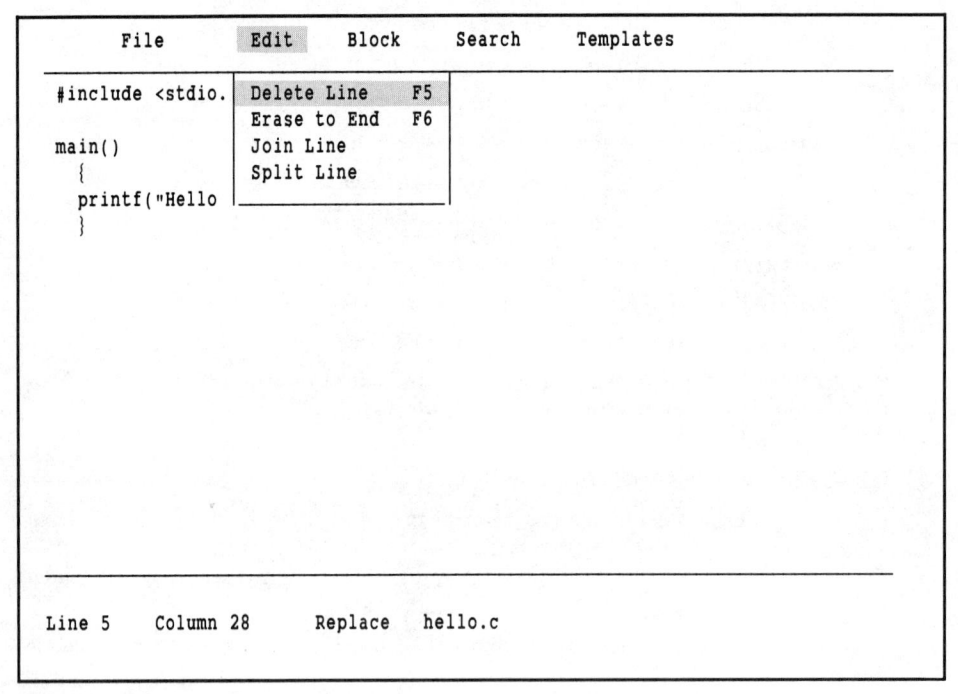

```
         File      Edit     Block    Search    Templates
  #include <stdio.| Delete Line    F5 |
                  | Erase to End   F6 |
  main()          | Join Line         |
   {              | Split Line        |
    printf("Hello |_____|
   }




     Line 5    Column 28    Replace    hello.c
```

Screen 14.3 The Edit Menu

352

Using the Student Compiler and Editor

Delete Line   To delete a source line, position the cursor on the line you want to delete. Then press F10 and the letter E to display the Edit menu. You can then either select Delete Line and press <enter> or type the initial letter D (for Delete Line). The source lines below the deleted line scroll up by one line position and the cursor remains in the same position (in the same column) as the line directly below the deleted line. For example:

before

```
if (c > 0)
   {
_  a = z - c;                        current line
   printf("Input is valid \n");
   }
```

after

```
if (c > 0)
   {
_  printf("Input is valid \n");      current line
   }
```

If you need more information on selecting a menu or command, see **Making a Menu Selection** earlier in this chapter.

Fast Path

Function key: F5

Position the cursor on the line you want to delete and press function key F5. This deletes the selected line. The source lines below it scroll up by one position and the cursor remains in the same position (in the same column) as the line directly below the deleted line.

Note that you can also use the control cursor key CTRL-BACKSPACE to delete a line of text.

Erase to End   To erase all the characters from the current cursor position to the end of the source line, position the cursor on the line and character you want to erase. Press function key F10 and the letter E to display the Edit menu. You can then either select Erase to End and press <enter> or type the initial letter E (for Erase to End). Either action erases all the characters to the right of the cursor,

Chapter 14

including the character at the cursor position. For example:

before

```
if (c > 0)
   {
   printf("Input is valid \n");        current line
   }       (cursor)
```

after

```
if (c > 0)
   {
   printf("In_                         current line
   }
```

If you need more information on selecting a menu or command, see **Making a Menu Selection** earlier in this chapter.

Fast Path

Function key: F6

To erase all the characters from the current cursor position to the end of the current source line, press function key F6. This deletes all of the characters from the cursor to the end of the current line.

Join Line   To join a source line with the line below it, position the cursor at the end of the line you want to join. Press function key F10 and the letter E to display the Edit menu. You can then either select Join Line and press <enter> or type the initial letter J (for Join Line). For example:

before

```
if (c > 0) {
   z = z - c;_                         current line
   printf("Input is valid \n");
   }
```

after

```
if (c > 0) {
   z = z - c;_  printf("Input is valid \n");   current line
   }
```

SC limits the width of a source line to 77 columns, so it will not join lines that would exceed this width. If the lines are too long to be joined, the following message is displayed on the message line:

   Line(s) are too long to join

If you need more information on selecting a menu or command, see **Making a Menu Selection** earlier in this chapter.

Using the Student Compiler and Editor

> **Fast Path**

You can also join two lines by moving the cursor to the end of the first line and pressing the DEL key. The same line-length limit message noted above applies.

Split Line To split a source line into two lines, position the cursor to where you want to split the line. Press function key F10 and the letter E to display the Edit menu. Then either select Split Line and press <enter> or type the initial letter S (for Split Line). This splits the line, moving the characters to the right of the current cursor position to the next line. For example:

before

```
if (c > 0) {
   z = z - c;
   printf_("Input is valid \n");      current line
        (cursor)
   }
```

after

```
if (c > 0) {
   z = z - c;
   printf
_("Input is valid \n");               current line
(cursor)
   }
```

If you need more information on selecting a menu or command, see **Making a Menu Selection** earlier in this chapter.

> **Fast Path**

You can also split a line by moving the cursor to where you want to split the line and pressing <enter>. This moves the characters to the right of the current cursor position to column one of the next line.

Block Menu

The Block menu allows you to select a block of lines to copy or move to another place in your source file, delete the block, or shift it left or right in the file. You can access this menu using three methods (see **Table 14.2**), but the fastest way is to press the ALT-B key combination. The Block menu is then displayed over part of the editing window.

Each command in the Block menu is described below. In most cases, select one or more contiguous source lines (a block) and use the other commands to manipulate (for example, move) the block. You can execute the commands by pressing the appropriate

Chapter 14

CTRL key combination (fast path) or by pressing F10 and the letter B to display the Block menu and then selecting the command you want.

Remember, if you do not use the fast path method of executing commands, you can use only the commands in the currently displayed menu. If you want to use commands in another menu, you will have to move to that menu.

When you select Block on the menu bar, the Block menu appears as shown in **Screen 14.4.**

The Block menu commands are described in the following sections.

```
         File      Edit     Block      Search      Templates

    #include <stdio.h>     Select Line      CTRL-L
                           Undo Selection   CTRL-U
    main()                 Copy             CTRL-Z
    {                      Move             CTRL-M
       printf("Hello World!| Delete         CTRL-D
    }                      Left  Shift      CTRL ←
                           Right Shift      CTRL →




    Line 5    Column 28    Replace   hello.c
```

Screen 14.4 The Block Menu

Select Line   A block of text is one or more contiguous source lines. You select a block of text so that you can copy, move, delete, or shift (left or right) it. (These commands are described following this one.)

You define a block of text by selecting the first and last source lines of the block. To select the first source line, position the cursor on the line you want and press the F10 function key and the letter B to display the Block menu. You can then either choose Select Line and press <enter> or type the initial letter S (for Select Line). The selected source line is displayed in reverse video and, on some consoles, in a different

Using the Student Compiler and Editor

color. Selecting a single line is equivalent to selecting a block that contains only one line.

To select multiple lines, move the cursor to another source line and choose Select Line again; the second selected line is the last line of your block. All the source lines within the block will be displayed in reverse video.

Here is an example of how you would select a block containing the entire `main` function:

```
#include <stdio.h>

main()                                First select this line.
  {
  printf("Hello World!\n");
  }                                   Then select this line.
```

SC allows only one block to be selected at a time. If you have already selected a block of text and try to perform the Select Line command again, SC displays this message on the message line:

```
Selected block already exists
```

First, you must undo the selection (see the **Undo Select** command below) or delete or move the block before you can select another block.

Fast Path

Control key combination: CTRL-L

To select one or more source lines, position your cursor on the first line to be selected and press CTRL-L. Repeat this step to select a block of lines. The selected source line(s) will be displayed in reverse video. Then copy, move, delete, or shift them, as noted above.

Undo Select If you want to undo your source line selection (those in reverse video), position the cursor on any line in the selected block. Press F10 and the letter B to display the Block menu. Then either choose Undo Select and press <enter> or type the initial letter U (for Undo Select). This changes the entire block displayed in reverse video back to normal text and allows you to select another block.

Fast Path

Control key combination: CTRL-U

To undo one or more selected source lines, position your cursor on a line in the selected block and press CTRL-U. This changes the block displayed in reverse video back to normal text and allows you to select another block.

Chapter 14

Copy   The Copy command takes a selected block of text and duplicates it elsewhere in your source file, without affecting or deleting the original block of text. The Copy command works only if you have already selected one or more source lines using the Select Line command.

To copy the selected block to another part of the file, move the cursor to the source line that you want the block copied after. Press function key F10 and the letter B to display the Block menu. You can then either choose Copy and press <enter> or type the initial letter C (for Copy). A copy of the selected block will be inserted after the current source line, making the lines below it scroll down.

The original block of text remains selected, so you can repeat these steps to copy the same block again. When you finish copying, you can undo the selected block using the Undo Select command.

Here is an example of how you could copy the entire `main` function:

```
#include <stdio.h>

main()
 {
 printf("Hello World!\n");
 }
```
                          First select this line
                          (using Select Line).

                          Then select this line.

```
/* Copy this function after this comment */
_
```
                          Move cursor here and select
                          the Copy command.

The result looks like this:

```
#include <stdio.h>

main()
 {
 printf("Hello World!\n");
 }

/* Copy this function after this comment */
_
main()
 {
 printf("Hello World!\n");
 }
```
                                      The cursor position does not change.

If you need more information on selecting a menu or command, see **Making a Menu Selection** earlier in this chapter.

> **Fast Path**

Control key combination: CTRL-Z

To copy the selected block to another part of the source file, move the cursor to the source line you want the block copied after and press CTRL-Z. A copy of the selected

358

Using the Student Compiler and Editor

block is inserted after the current source line, making the lines below it scroll down. The block of text remains selected, so that you can repeat these steps to copy it again. To undo the selection, use the Undo Select (CTRL-U) command.

Move   The Move command takes a selected block of text and moves it elsewhere in your source file, thereby removing it from its original location. This command works only if you have already selected one or more source lines using the Select Line command.

To move the selected block, move the cursor to the source line that you want the block moved after. Press function key F10 and the letter B to display the Block menu. You can then either select Move and press <enter> or type the initial letter M (for Move). The current cursor position does not move.

Here is an example of how you could move the `#include` statement before the `main` function:

```
_                                       Move cursor here and select
                                        the Move command.
main()
  {
  printf("Hello World!\n");
  }

/* Move the #include statement before main() */

#include <stdio.h>                      Select this line
                                        (using Select Line).
```

The result looks like:

```
_
#include <stdio.h>
main()
  {
  printf("Hello World!\n");
  }

/* Move the #include statement before main() */
```

Notice that the cursor position does not change during the command execution.

If you need more information on selecting a menu or command, see **Making a Menu Selection** earlier in this chapter.

Fast Path

Control key combination: CTRL-M

To move the selected block, move the cursor to the source line that you want the block moved after and press CTRL-M. The current cursor position does not move.

Chapter 14

Delete   The Delete command takes a selected block of text and removes it from your source file. This command works only if you have already selected one or more source lines using the Select Line command.

To delete the selected block of lines, press the function key F10 and the letter B to display the Block menu. You can then choose Delete and press <enter> or type the initial letter D (for Delete). The current cursor position does not move.

Here is an example of how you could delete the entire `main` function:

```
#include <stdio.h>

main()                          First select this line (using Select Line).
 {
  printf("Hello World!\n");
_ }                             Then select this line and choose
                                the Delete command.
```

The result looks like this:

```
#include <stdio.h>
_
```

If you need more information on selecting a menu or command, see **Making a Menu Selection** earlier in this chapter.

Fast Path

Control key combination: CTRL-D

To delete the selected block, press CTRL-D.

If you are deleting a block of text that is only one or two lines long, it is faster to delete the lines using the Delete Line command in the Edit menu. The fast path way of using this command is to move your cursor to the line(s) to be deleted and press function key F5.

Left Shift   The Left Shift command moves a selected block of text one space left in your source file. This command works only if you have already selected one or more source lines using the Select Line command.

The lines within the same selected block may shift differently, depending on the block's current position in the source file. Shifting a block to the left has the same effect as deleting the first character of each line in the block, as long as that character is a blank space. In the example below, the entire `main` function is indented three spaces, so one execution of the Left Shift command moves the entire block one space left.

If the first character in a selected line is already in column one of the editing window, that line of the block does not shift left; this prevents text in column one from being deleted. Lines in the block that are not in the first column, however, will continue to

Using the Student Compiler and Editor

shift left one space with each execution of the command until they are in the first column. In the second example below, `main()` does not shift left because it is in the first column, but the indented `printf` function and the curly brackets do shift one space left with each execution of the Left Shift command.

To shift the text within the selected block left, press the function key F10 and the letter B to display the Block menu. You can then either select Left Shift and press <enter> or type the initial letter L (for Left Shift). The current cursor position does not change as you shift the block of text.

The original block of text remains selected, so you can repeat these steps to shift the same block again. When you finish shifting it, undo the selected block using the Undo Select command.

Here is an example of how you shift the entire `main` function one space to the left:

```
#include <stdio.h>

  main()                           First select this line
  {                                (using Select Line).
    printf("Hello World!\n");
  }_                               Then select this line.
```

The result looks like this:

```
#include <stdio.h>

 main()
 {
 printf("Hello World!\n");
 }_
```

Notice that the `main` function was lined up under the letter `c` of `#include`, and it is now lined up under the letter `n`.

In this example, the `main` function line does not shift but the other indented lines in the selected block shift one space to the left:

```
#include <stdio.h>

main()
  {                                First select this line
    printf("I love programming.\n"); (using Select Line ).
  } _                              Then select this line.
```

The result looks like this:

```
#include <stdio.h>

main()
 {
 printf("I love programming.\n");
 } _              The cursor remains in the same position.
```

Chapter 14

Notice that the curly braces and `printf` function were lined up under the letter n of `main` and they are now lined up under the letter i.

If you need more information on selecting a menu or command, see **Making a Menu Selection** earlier in this chapter.

> **Fast Path**
>
> Control key combination: CTRL ←
>
> To shift the selected block left, press the CTRL and left arrow (←) keys. The current cursor position does not change as you shift the block of text. The lines within a selected block may shift differently, as described above.

Right Shift   The Right Shift command moves a selected block of text one space right in your source file. This command works only if you have already selected one or more source lines using the Select Line command.

The lines within the same selected block may shift differently, depending on the block's current position in the source file. Shifting a block to the right has the same effect as inserting a space character to the left of each line in the block. In the example below, the entire `main` function shifts one space right with one execution of the Right Shift command.

If shifting a selected line right would cause the line to exceed the 77 character limit, the line is not shifted and the following message is displayed on the message line:

```
Line(s) too long to be shifted right
```

Lines within the same selected block that are shorter than 77 characters will shift one space right, whether or not all the lines move right, until they reach the SC line-length limit.

To shift the text within the selected block right, press function key F10 and the letter B to display the Block menu. You can then either select Right Shift and press <enter> or type the initial letter R (for Right Shift). The current cursor position does not change as you shift the block of text.

The original block of text remains selected, so you can repeat these steps to shift the same block again. When you finish shifting it, undo the selected block using the Undo Select command.

Here is an example of how you shift the entire `main` function one space to the right:

```
#include <stdio.h>

  main()                          First select this line
  {                               (using Select Line).
  printf("Hello World!\n");
  } _                             Then select this line.
```

Using the Student Compiler and Editor

The result looks like this:

```
#include <stdio.h>

    main()
      {
      printf("Hello World!\n");
      }_
```

Notice that the `main` function was lined up under the letter `c` of `#include` and it is now lined up under the letter `l`.

If you need more information on selecting a menu or command, see **Making a Menu Selection** earlier in this chapter.

Fast Path

Control key combination: CTRL →

To shift the selected block right, press the CTRL and right arrow (→) keys. The current cursor position does not change as you shift the block of text. The lines within a selected block may shift differently, as described above.

Search Menu

The Search menu allows you to search for a character string or syntax errors in your source file and to replace or correct them. You can access this menu using three different methods (see **Table 14.2**), but the fastest way is to press the ALT-S key combination. The Search menu is displayed over part of the editing window, as shown in **Screen 14.5**.

Each command in the Search menu is described in the following sections. Remember, if you do not use the fast path method of executing commands, you can use only the commands in the currently displayed menu. If you want to use commands in another menu, you will have to move to that menu.

Chapter 14

```
 File        Edit       Block      Search       Templates
─────────────────────────────────────────────────────────────
 #include <stdio.h>                Search      CTRL-S
                                   Next        CTRL-N
 main()                            First Error CTRL-F
 {                                 Query Replace CTRL-R
 _ printf("Hello World!\n");       Replace All CTRL-A
 {
─────────────────────────────────────────────────────────────
 Line 5      Column 1     Replace   hello.c
```

Screen 14.5 The Search Menu

Search   The Search command allows you to search for a character string in your source file. The direction of the search is always from the current cursor position to the end of the source file. The Search command is not case sensitive; that is, a search on the string "ABC" is equivalent to a search on the string "abc".

To search for a string in the source file, press function key F10 and the letter S to display the Search menu. Then choose Search and press <enter> or type the initial letter S (for Search). A prompt, **Search String:**, appears on the input line, requiring you to follow these three steps:

1. Type in the string you are searching for between the double quotes after the **Search String:** prompt. You can search for any character, including double quotes, because the double quotes on the screen are provided as part of the input line. The maximum length of a search string is limited to 50 characters.

2. Use the backspace key, not the left arrow key, to correct any mistakes made while typing in the search string.

3. Press the <enter> key to perform the search command or the ESC key to cancel it and to return to the editing window.

Screen 14.6 shows the editing window during a search for the string `printf`.

Using the Student Compiler and Editor

```
File      Edit       Block      Search      Templates
─────────────────────────────────────────────────────────

  #include <stdio.h>

  main()
   {
  _ printf("Hello World!\n");
   }











─────────────────────────────────────────────────────────

  Search string:   "printf"
```

Screen 14.6 Searching for a String

If the string is found, the cursor is placed on the first character of the found string.

```
#include <stdio.h> _            old current line

main()
 {
 printf("Hello World!\n");      new current line
 }
```

If the string is not found, the cursor position remains unchanged and the following message is displayed on the message line:

```
Not found
```

If you need more information on selecting a menu or command, see **Making a Menu Selection** earlier in this chapter.

Fast Path

Control key combination: CTRL-S

To search for a character string in the source file, press CTRL-S to display the **Search String:** prompt. Then follow the steps described above.

Chapter 14

Next The Next command allows you to search for and stop at every instance of a particular string in your source file. This command works only if you have already searched for a character string or syntax error using the Search, First Error, or Query Replace commands.

To repeat the last string or error search, press function key F10 and the letter S to display the Search menu. Then select Next and press <enter> or type the initial letter N (for Next). The cursor moves to the first character of the next instance of the search string in the source file.

If SC cannot find the search string, the **Not found** message appears on the message line and the cursor remains on the most recent instance of the search string. If you want to search the file again for the specified string, press the CTRL-HOME cursor key to return the cursor to the top line of the file. You can then use the fast path key (CTRL-N) or the menu command to search for the next instance of the search string.

If you need more information on selecting a menu or command, see **Making a Menu Selection** earlier in this chapter.

Fast Path

Control key combination: CTRL-N

To repeat the last character string or error search, press the CTRL-N keys. The cursor moves to the first character of the next instance of the search string in the source file. If SC cannot find the search string, the **Not found** message appears on the message line.

First Error If there are any syntax errors in your program after you have run it, you can use the First Error and Next commands to help you find and correct compilation errors quickly.

To search for the first syntax error, press function key F10 and the letter S to display the Search menu. You can then either select First Error and press <enter> or type the initial letter F (for First Error). The Student Compiler keeps track of all the syntax errors that have occurred during the compilation of your source file, placing them in a list. Using the Next command allows you to proceed through this list, one error at a time, making the necessary changes to your source file.

If you exit SC without correcting the syntax errors, the error list will be lost and you will need to recompile and execute the First Error command to re-create the list.

For example, suppose you tried to run the following program:

```
#include <stdio.h>

main()
  {
  printf("Hello the first time.\n")
  printf("Hello the second time.\n");
```

Using the Student Compiler and Editor

```
printf("Hello the third time.\n");
printf("Hello the fourth time.\n";
}
```

A semicolon is missing from the first `printf` statement and a right parenthesis is missing from the last `printf`. The compilation results displayed on the Program Screen indicate two kinds of errors (**Screen 14.7**).

```
SAS/C Compiler, Student Edition, Version 1.00
Copyright 1988 SAS Institute Inc.

Compiling hello.c
hello.c  5  Error 57:  semicolon expected
hello.c  7  Error 16:  invalid function argument

Failed to compile

<Press F9 to return to the previous screen>
```

Screen 14.7 Program Screen

When you return to the Editing Screen, notice that the first error message is displayed on the message line and the cursor is positioned on the line following the first syntax error. When you select the Next command, the second error message is displayed and the cursor is positioned at the next syntax error, and so on, until you have looped through the entire error list and corrected all the errors. To return to the first error, select the First Error option again; you can do this from anywhere in the error list.

If you need more information on selecting a menu or command, see **Making a Menu Selection** earlier in this chapter.

Chapter 14

> **Fast Path**

Control key combination: CTRL-F

To search for the first syntax error, press the CTRL-F keys. This search assumes that you have already run your program and SC has created a list of compilation errors for your source file. When you return to the SC Editing Screen, the first error message is displayed on the message line and the cursor is positioned on the line following the first syntax error. Use the Next command fast path (CTRL-N) to display the next error message, and so on. See the description and example above for detailed information.

Query Replace   The Query Replace command searches for a character string in a source file and replaces it with another string. The direction of the search and replace is always from the current cursor position to the end of the source file. The Query Replace command replaces only the first instance of the string found in the source file; to replace all instances of the string, see the Replace All command below. The Query Replace command is not case sensitive; that is, a search on the string "ABC" is equivalent to a search on the string "abc".

To search and replace a string in your source file, press function key F10 and the letter S to display the Search menu. Then select Query Replace and press <enter> or type the initial letter Q (for Query Replace). A prompt, **Search String:**, appears on the input line, requiring you to follow these five steps:

1. Type in the string that you are searching for between the double quotes after the **Search String:** prompt. You can search for any character, including double quotes, because the double quotes on the screen are provided as part of the input line. The maximum length of a search string is limited to 50 characters.

2. Use the backspace key, not the left arrow key, to correct any mistakes made while typing in the search string.

3. Press the <enter> key to perform the search command or the ESC key to cancel it.

4. Type in the replace string between the double quotes after **Replace String:** prompt. The same rules apply to the replace string as apply to the search string. Use the backspace key to correct any typing mistakes. The replace string is case-sensitive, so it will replace the search string exactly as you have typed it.

5. Press the <enter> key to execute the replace command. You will be prompted to confirm the replace request (described below). To cancel the request, press the ESC key to return to the editing window.

Using the Student Compiler and Editor

If the search string is found, the cursor is placed on the first character of the string. For example, suppose you wanted to replace the string "World!" by the string "Out There!"

```
#include <stdio.h>                  old current line

main()
 {
 printf("Hello World!\n");          new current line
 }
```

SC asks you to confirm the replace command by displaying the following message on the message line:

```
Replace? Type y or n
```

Type "y" (for yes) if you want the "World!" string to be replaced by the "Out There!" string, and type "n" (for no) if you do not. Typing "y" results in

```
#include <stdio.h>

main()
 {
 printf("Hello Out There!\n");
 }
```

The original search string remains selected, so you can repeat the search using the Next command; see its description earlier in this chapter.

If the string is not found, the cursor position does not change and the following message is displayed on the message line:

```
Not found
```

If you need more information on selecting a menu or command, see **Making a Menu Selection** earlier in this chapter.

Fast Path

Control key combination: CTRL-R

To search and replace a character string in a source file, press CTRL-R to display the **Search String:** prompt. Then follow the steps described above.

Replace All   The Replace All command searches for a character string in a source file and replaces all instances of that string with another string. The direction of the search and replace is always from the current cursor position to the end of the source file. A search by this command is not case sensitive.

To search and replace a string in your source file, press function key F10 and the letter S to display the Search menu. You can then select Replace All and press <enter> or type the initial letter R (for Replace All).

Chapter 14

From this point on, the Replace All command works exactly like the Query Replace command, except that the Replace All command replaces all instances rather than the first instance of a particular string with another string. See the previous description of Query Replace for more information.

The Replace All command also asks you to confirm the replace command by displaying the following message on the message line:

```
Are you sure? Type y or n
```

If you type "y", the cursor is placed on the first character of the last instance of the replacement string. If no instance of the string is found, the cursor position does not change and the `Not found` message is displayed on the message line.

If you need more information on selecting a menu or command, see **Making a Menu Selection** earlier in this chapter.

Fast Path

Control key combination: CTRL-A

To search for a character string in a source file and to replace every instance of it with another string, press CTRL-A (for All) to display the **Search String:** prompt. Then follow the steps described in the Query Replace command.

Compiling and Running Programs

Introduction

After you have created or edited a source file, you will want to save the file and perhaps compile or print it. In the File menu, the Student Compiler provides commands that handle the files themselves and not their contents.

File Menu

The File menu contains all the commands you can perform on the current source file. Use this menu to create a new file, switch between existing source files, and then to save, file, quit, run, debug, and print a source file. The File menu also lets you access the Help screens, which are an online information system.

When you first enter the Student Compiler, the File menu is highlighted as the default menu. To display this menu, press the function key F10 and the letter F **(Screen 14.8)**. See **Table 14.2** for information on other ways to access the SC pull-down menus.

Each command in the File menu is described below. Remember, if you do not use the fast path method of executing commands, you can use only the commands in the currently displayed menu. If you want to use commands in another menu, you will have to move to that menu.

Using the Student Compiler and Editor

```
 File      Edit      Block     Search    Templates
┌─────────────────┐
│ Help       F1   │
│ Save       F2   │
│ File       F3   │
│ Quit       F4   │
│ Run        F7   │ World!\n");_
│ New File   F8   │
│ Print           │
│ Debug           │
└─────────────────┘




       Line 5    Column 28    Replace   hello.c
```

Screen 14.8 The File Menu

File menu commands are useful as you develop your source programs. These commands enable you to switch between files without exiting SC, save the changes you make to your file, or save the file and quit SC with the one-step command, File. You can compile and execute your program with a single command, Run. If your program compiles but does not perform the task you thought it would, you can use the Debug command to monitor the program's execution. You can then select the File Menu command Print to get a printed copy of your source code.

In using the commands on the File menu, notice that the Editing Screen disappears while your program is compiling. The Program Screen replaces the Editing Screen in order to display compilation messages and your program's output. After results are displayed, press function key F9 to return to the Editing Screen. The commands in the File menu are described in the following sections.

Help   The Help command displays information on your screen about two topic areas: the syntax and use of the ANSI Standard, graphics, and screen management functions and explanatory information on the Student Compiler error messages (accessed by their error number).

Chapter 14

To get this help information, press F10 and the letter F to display the File menu. You can then select Help and press the <enter> key or type the initial letter H (for Help). A prompt, **Help On:**, appears on the input line, requiring you to follow these three steps:

1. Between the double quotes, type the name of the function or the number of the error message on which you want information.
2. Use the backspace key, not the left arrow key, to correct any typing mistakes.
3. Press the <enter> key to get help information on the specified function or error message. Press the ESC key to cancel the command and return to the editing window.

If you do not know which topic to request or if you just want to see the available topics, press the <enter> key when the **Help On:** prompt appears.

Once you have pressed <enter>, a help window replaces the editing window. The two topic areas (functions and error messages) and an example of each is displayed in the window (**Screen 14.9**).

```
                          HELP
Help is available on functions and compiler error messages.

Functions by name            (for example, Help On: "isprint")

Error messages by number     (for example, Help On: "25")




_____

Help On: " "
Press the ESC key to return to the previous screen.
```

Screen 14.9 Help Window Display

Using the Student Compiler and Editor

Information on the topic you request is displayed on the screen as shown. For example, in **Screen 14.10** information on the `isprint` function has been requested.

```
isprint - Test for a printable character

#include <ctype.h>

int isprint(c);
    int c;        character to test

A printing character is any character that prints and is
not a control character (ASCII decimal codes 32 through 126).




















Help On: "isprint"
Press the ESC key to return to the previous screen.
```

Screen 14.10 Help Window—Function Display

To get more information on the ANSI functions, see Chapter 16; to get more information on the graphics and screen management functions, see Chapter 17. The error messages are described in Appendix 1.

Fast Path

Function key: F1

To get online information, press function key F1. You can request this information from anywhere in the SC Editing Screen. Enter the topic after the **Help On:** prompt and press the <enter> key. Or, after the prompt, press <enter> to see the available topics. Press the ESC key to return to the editing window. See the description above for details.

Chapter 14

Save   The Save command saves the contents of the current source file onto the computer's hard disk or onto a diskette (on floppy disk systems). See the File command below to save a source file and quit SC with a single command.

It is recommended that you save the contents of your source files regularly. If your computer system goes down or the disk is full when you attempt to save your file, the changes you have made since the last save operation will be lost. However, changes made to the file before that save operation remain unaltered.

To save the contents of the current file, press function key F10 and the letter F to display the File menu. Then select Save and press <enter> or type the initial letter S (for Save). A prompt—including the name of the file—appears on the message line.

    Save File: "hello.c"

Press the <enter> key to save the file with its current name. If you want to rename the file or to rename it and save it to a disk drive other than the current one, you can type the new drive and filename after the **Save File:** prompt. (Use the backspace key to erase the current name after the prompt.) For example, to rename the `hello.c` program and move it to the second drive on your floppy-disk system, you should type `b:\newpgms\test.c` after the prompt.

If you have not named your file, you must type a name after the **Save File:** prompt in order to save it. If you exit the Student Compiler without naming your file, DOS deletes that file from your directory.

If SC cannot save your file, the following message is displayed on the message line:

    Error in opening file (file not saved)

If SC fills up your disk while it is trying to save your source file, the following message is displayed on the message line:

    Disk is full (file not saved)

If this happens, try saving the file to another disk drive (as described above) or to a new diskette. Insert a formatted diskette and try to save the file to that diskette. (On a hard disk system, save the file to `a:\`*dirname*`\hello.c` and on a floppy system, to `b:\`*dirname*`\hello.c`.) If you have not named the file at all, you can save the file to a diskette or different disk drive by naming it, for example, `a:\newpgms\test.c`.

If you do not have an extra formatted diskette, cancel this command by pressing the ESC key, edit the file down to a smaller size, and try again to save it. If you still cannot save the file, exit the compiler (using the Quit command) and copy or delete files to provide more disk space. You will lose changes to the source file that you have made since the last save operation, but the file saved earlier remains unchanged.

If you need more information on selecting a menu or command, see **Making a Menu Selection** earlier in this chapter.

Using the Student Compiler and Editor

Fast Path

Function key: F2

To save the contents of the current source file to disk, press F2. The same cautions and messages apply, as described above.

File   The File command is a combination of the Save and Quit commands. It allows you to save the contents of the current source file to disk and to quit the Student Compiler and return to the PC DOS or MS-DOS environment. See the Save and Quit commands for more detailed information.

To save the contents of the current file and to quit SC, press function key F10 and the letter F to display the File menu. Then select File and press <enter> or type the initial letter F (for File).

If SC cannot save your file, the following message is displayed on the message line and you will not be allowed to exit the system:

`Error in opening file (file not saved)`

If SC fills up your disk while it is trying to save your source file, the following message is displayed on the message line and you will not be allowed to exit the system:

`Disk is full (file not saved)`

If this happens, cancel the File command (by pressing the ESC key) and try to save the file to another disk drive or to a new diskette. To save the file to a disk drive other than the current one, type the new drive and filename after the **Save File:** prompt. (Use the backspace key to erase the current name after the prompt.) For example, to rename the `hello.c` program and move it to the second drive on your floppy-disk system, you should type `b:\newpgms\test.c` after the prompt.

You can also save the file to a diskette, if you have one available. Insert a formatted diskette and try to save the file to that diskette. (On a hard disk system, save the file to `a:\`*dirname*`\hello.c` and on a floppy system, to `b:\`*dirname*`\hello.c`.) If you have not named the file at all, you can save the the file to a diskette or different disk drive by naming it (for example, `a:\newpgms\test.c`).

If the above alternatives do not work, cancel the File command, edit the file down to a smaller size, and try again to save it. If you still cannot save the file, use the Quit command to exit the compiler. You will lose changes to the source file that you have made since the last save operation, but the file saved earlier remains unchanged.

If you need more information on selecting a menu or command, see **Making a Menu Selection** earlier in this chapter.

Chapter 14

Fast Path

Function key: F3

To save the contents of the current source file to disk and to quit SC, press F3. The same cautions and messages, described above and in the Save and Quit commands, apply.

Quit   The Quit command allows you to exit from the Student Compiler and return to the PC DOS or MS-DOS environment. To do this, press function key F10 and the letter F to display the File menu. You can then select Quit and press <enter> or type the initial letter Q (for Quit).

If you have modified the current source file and have not saved your changes (using the Save command), the following message is displayed on the message line:

    Your changes aren't saved. Do you want to exit SC?   Type y or n

This message prevents you from accidentally quitting SC and losing all of your changes. Type "y" (for yes) if you want to exit and type "n" (for no) if you do not. DOS deletes any unnamed file once you exit the compiler; see the Save command for details.

If you need more information on selecting a menu or command, see **Making a Menu Selection** earlier in this chapter.

Fast Path

Function key: F4

To exit from the Student Compiler, press F4. If you have not saved changes to your source file, you will be asked if you really want to quit SC. Answering yes allows you to exit, although your changes will not be saved.

Run   The Run command allows you to save, compile, and execute (run) your current source program. To do this, press function key F10 and the letter F to display the File menu. You can then select Run and press <enter> or type the initial, uppercase letter R (for Run). Before the run begins, you will be prompted to save your current file, if it has been modified since the last run:

    Save file: "hello.c"

Press the <enter> key to save the file with its current name. (See the Save command for ways to save the file to other names or disk drives.) Saving your file at this point prevents any changes from being lost, due to programming, disk, or system errors.

Using the Student Compiler and Editor

Once you have saved your file, the program's compilation and execution begins and their results are displayed on the Program Screen. You must use this command or the Debug command to re-run your program, even if you have not modified it between executions.

This command enables you to test your program and return to your source file to correct any syntax errors. Any errors in your program are displayed on the Program Screen as the program runs. See the First Error command for information on finding and correcting these syntax errors.

Once you have corrected any errors, select the Run command again. If the compile is successful, the Student Compiler pauses so that you can enter any command line arguments (that is, parameters you may want to pass to your program from the console screen). If you do not want to enter command line arguments, simply press the <enter> key after the program has finished compiling. This executes your program (**Screen 14.11**).

```
SAS/C Compiler, Student Edition, Version 1.00
Copyright 1988 SAS Institute Inc.

Compiling hello.c

Compiled OK

Executing hello.c

Arguments: _  <enter>

Hello World!


<Press F9 to return to the previous screen>
```

Screen 14.11 Executing a Program

Press the function key F9 to return to the Editing Screen or F7 to run the program again.

Chapter 14

If you want to enter command line arguments, type them after the **Arguments:** prompt and press the <enter> key. Separate the arguments with commas (,) and use the backspace key to correct any typing mistakes. If the command line arguments do not fit on one line, SC automatically wraps them around to the next line. Press the <enter> key to execute the program (with the argument list) or press the CTRL-BREAK key combination to cancel it.

The example above displays a compilation and execution session using the Student Compiler. If you have not modified your source file since the last successful compile, SC displays only the execution results in your Program Screen. In other words, SC does not recompile your program unless you have modified it.

If you need more information on selecting a menu or command, see **Making a Menu Selection** earlier in this chapter.

| Fast Path |

Function key: F7

To compile and execute the current source program, press F7. The results of the program's compilation and execution are displayed on the Program Screen. If there are any syntax errors, they are also displayed on the Program Screen; you can use the First Error (fast path, CTRL-F) command to correct your program. Once corrected, press F7 to run your program again.

If your program compiles successfully, you are prompted for command line arguments. Either enter an arguments list and press the <enter> key or press the CTRL-BREAK key combination to cancel the session. Pressing <enter> executes your program and displays it on the Program Screen. See the Print command if you want to print your program's output.

New File   The New File command allows you to edit a new source file without exiting the Student Compiler. Use this command to switch between existing source files or to create a new, empty source file.

To edit or create a new file, press function key F10 and the letter F to display the File menu. You can then select New File and press <enter> or type the initial letter N (for New File). A prompt, **New File:**, appears on the input line, requiring you to follow these three steps:

1. Type the name of the file you want to edit between the double quotes; the quotes are provided as part of the input line. A filename is limited to eight characters plus a three-character extension, for example, `myfilenm.bat`. If you want the file to be in a different directory, use the full destination path, such as `a:\sasc\promos.c`.

2. Use the backspace key, not the left arrow key, to correct any typing mistakes.

3. Press the <enter> key to edit the new file or the ESC key to cancel it.

Using the Student Compiler and Editor

If you are currently editing a file when you execute New File, SC asks you if you want to save your changes to the current source file. If you have not named the file yet, it waits for you to enter the name; DOS discards any unnamed files once you exit the compiler. The name of the current file is included on the message line:

```
Save file "hello.c" first?  Type y or n
```

Type "y" (for yes) if you want to save your changes. If you type "n" (for no), all of your changes since the last save operation will be discarded; see the Save command for more information. SC then switches you to the specified new file.

If you need more information on selecting a menu or command, see **Making a Menu Selection** earlier in this chapter.

Fast Path

Function key: F8

This command enables you to edit or create a new source file without exiting the Student Compiler. To do this, press F8. You are prompted for the new filename and then asked if you want to save the changes in your current file before switching files. See the description above for details.

Print The Print command enables you to print a copy of your current source file. To print a copy of your program output, see the DOS printing instructions in **Printing Program Output** below.

To print your source file, press function key F10 and the letter F to display the File menu. Then select Print and press <enter> or type the initial letter P (for Print). The Student Compiler assumes that the printer is attached to the PRN device. If the printer is not attached or becomes disconnected during the print operation, the following message is displayed on the message line:

```
Printer error (file not printed)
```

If a printer error occurs, the print operation is aborted and you must select the Print command again to print your file.

If you need more information on selecting a menu or command, see **Making a Menu Selection** earlier in this chapter.

The Print command has no fast path keys.

Chapter 14

Printing Program Output You can print your program's output in two ways. You can use the DOS print commands to dump the output to a DOS file; see your DOS manual for more information. Or, you can run your program and print your output using the following key combinations:

Shift-PrtSc sends the output on your Program Screen to the printer specified as PRN. Press this key combination after your program has run, that is, once the following message is displayed on your Program Screen:

```
<Press F9 to return to the previous screen>
```

Shift-PrtSc prints everything on the current Program Screen, including the compile and execute statements.

CTRL-PrtSc performs exactly as Shift-PrtSc, except that it continues to print any SC program output or DOS commands/output until you turn it off by pressing CTRL-PrtSc again. Use this command to print your screen's output from anywhere in the the Student Compiler or while you are in DOS.

Debug The Debug command enables you to compile and execute (run) the current source program in debugger mode. This means that you can enter the debugger between the compilation and execution steps to monitor the program as it executes. You can then use the debugger to detect runtime errors, that is, errors that occur while your program is executing. To detect errors that occur during compilation, see the First Error command.

This command works almost like the Run command, except that the Debug command allows you to enter the debugger directly after your source program has successfully compiled. See the Run command for more information and examples.

To compile and execute your program in debugger mode, press F10 and the letter F to display the File menu. You can then select Debug and press <enter> or type the initial letter D (for Debug). Before the compilation begins, you will be prompted to save your current file, if it has been modified since the last compilation:

```
Save File: "hello.c"
```

Press the <enter> key to save the file with its current name. (See the Save command for ways to save the file to other names or disk drives.) Saving your file at this point prevents any changes from being lost, due to programming, disk, or system errors.

Once you have saved your file, the program's compilation begins and their results, including any compile-time errors, are displayed on the Program Screen. A message is then displayed that the Student Compiler is debugging your program.

When the compilation is successful, SC pauses so that you can enter any command line arguments (that is, parameters you may want to pass to your program from the console screen). See **Screen 14.12**.

Using the Student Compiler and Editor

```
SAS/C Compiler, Student Edition, Version 1.00
Copyright 1988 SAS Institute Inc.

Compiling hello.c

Compiled OK

Debugging hello.c

Arguments: _  <enter>
```

Screen 14.12 Program Screen While Debugging

If you do not want to enter command line arguments (at the **Arguments:** prompt), press the <enter> key to enter the SC debugger. The debugger's source and output windows appear on your screen and your program begins to execute; the results of your program's execution are displayed on the Program Screen.

If you want to enter command line arguments, type them after the **Arguments:** prompt and press the <enter> key. Separate the arguments with commas (,) and use the backspace key to correct any typing mistakes. If the command line arguments do not fit on one line, SC automatically wraps them around to the next line.

Press the <enter> key to execute the program (with the argument list) and to enter the SC debugger. The debugger's source and output windows appear on your screen and your program begins to execute; the results of your program's execution are displayed on the Program Screen.

Use function key F9 to go back and forth between the debugger and the Program Screen. To exit the debugger and to return to the compiler's Editing Screen, press the function key F4. See Chapter 18 for more information and examples of debugging sessions.

If you have not modified your source file since the last successful compile, SC displays only the execution results in your Program Screen. In other words, SC does not recompile your program unless you have modified it.

Chapter 14

If you need more information on selecting a menu or command, see **Making a Menu Selection** earlier in this chapter.

The Debug command has no fast path keys.

Function Keys and Key Combinations

In developing your program, you may find that it is faster or easier to execute a command by pressing its function key or key combination, rather than moving the cursor to the pull-down menu selection. These keys are listed in each command's fast path description. Note that you can use these keys only when a Student Compiler pull-down menu is not displayed.

As you use the keys, you will notice that they are divided into three groups:

- ALT keys are used for switching between SC menus. The ALT key is combined with the initial letter of the menu's name.

- CTRL keys manipulate the contents of source files, that is, they enable you to move, copy, and delete the text of source files. In most cases, the CTRL key is combined with the initial letter of the first or second word in the command's name.

- Function keys manipulate the files themselves, enabling you to save, run, or print them. In some cases, these keys are also used in editing.

Earlier in this chapter, **Table 14.1** summarized the SC pull-down menus and the list of commands under each menu, including its key combination (if it had one). **Table 14.5** lists the available function keys and key combinations in sequential or alphabetical order. You may want to keep this list next to your computer terminal as a quick reminder.

Table 14.5 Student Compiler Key Combinations

Keys for Switching Between Menus		Fast Path Editing Keys	
ALT-B	Block	CTRL-A	Replace All
ALT-E	Edit	CTRL-D	Delete
ALT-F	File	CTRL-F	First Error
ALT-S	Search	CTRL-L	Select Line
ALT-T	Templates	CTRL-M	Move
		CTRL-N	Next
		CTRL-R	Query Replace
		CTRL-S	Search
		CTRL-U	Undo Select
		CTRL-Z	Copy
		CTRL ←	Left Shift
		CTRL →	Right Shift

(continued)

Table 14.5 (*continued*)

Function Keys and Cancelling Keys	
F1	Help
F2	Save
F3	File
F4	Quit
F5	Delete Line
F6	Erase to End
F7	Run
F8	New File
F9	Move between the Editing Screen and Program Screen (compiler)
	Move between the Source Screen and Program Screen (debugger)
F10	Move the cursor to the menu bar and display the highlighted menu name.
ESC	To *escape* from a location or to cancel a command. Use ESC to
	- cancel an F10 move to the menu bar
	- press ESC to resume editing
	- move from the menu bar to the editing window
	- move from a pull-down menu to the menu bar
	- cancel a move from a pull-down menu (sometimes a command execution) to the editing window
	- cancel a command's execution
	- cancel an input string
	- cancel a string search or replace.
	If you cannot resume editing (that is, your cursor is stuck) press the ESC key once or twice.
CTRL-BREAK	Cancels a Run command, once you have begun the compilation.

Using the C Language Templates

Introduction

The Student Compiler provides you with one more set of commands to make it easier for you to program in the C language. The Templates menu is used to insert certain C language statement templates into your source file. Whether you are just learning C or are an experienced C programmer, this feature can help speed the coding process and reduce the chance of syntax errors.

You can access this menu using three methods (**Table 14.2**), but the fastest way is to press the ALT-T key combination. The Templates menu is then displayed over part of the editing window. Remember, you can use only the commands in the currently displayed menu. If you want to use commands in another menu, you have to move to that menu.

When you select the **Templates** menu on the menu bar, the following commands appear, as seen in **Screen 14.13**. This menu uses no fast path key combinations.

Chapter 14

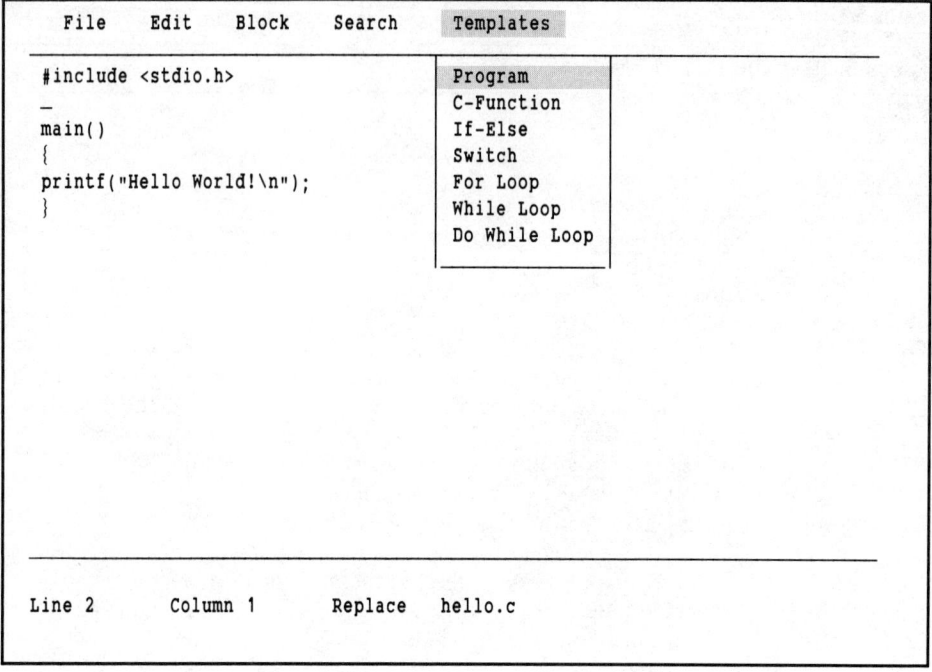

```
    File      Edit     Block     Search    Templates
   #include <stdio.h>                      Program
   _                                       C-Function
   main()                                  If-Else
   {                                       Switch
   printf("Hello World!\n");               For Loop
   }                                       While Loop
                                           Do While Loop




    Line 2        Column 1       Replace   hello.c
```

Screen 14.13 The Templates Menu

C language templates are inserted on the line following the current cursor position. All templates are indented so that they line up with the indentation of the current line. For example, inserting the If-Else template after the `printf` statement gives the following:

```
#include <stdio.h>

main()
{
  printf("Hello World!\n");          old current position
  if (_)                             new current position
    {
    }
  else
    {
    }
}
```

Notice that the cursor moves to the first significant position after the conditional expression of the `if-else` statement.

Each of the template types is described in the following sections.

Program   The Program template contains the shell of a standard C language program:

```
#include <stdio.h>

int
main(argc,argv)
int argc;
char *argv[];
{_
return 0;
}
```

The cursor is positioned after the `main` function.

To insert a `main` program definition into your source file, position the cursor on the line where you want to insert the template. Press F10 and the letter T to display the Templates menu. Then select Program and press <enter> or type the initial letter P (for Program).

If you need more information on selecting a menu or command, see **Making a Menu Selection** earlier in this chapter.

This command does not have a fast path key.

C-Function   The C-Function template contains the declaration of a standard C language function called `f` with an integer parameter called `parm`:

```
int
f(parm)
int parm;
{
}
```

The cursor is positioned on the function return type, `int`.

To insert a function declaration into your source file, position the cursor on the line where you want to insert the template. Press F10 and the letter T to display the Templates menu. Then select C-Function and press <enter> or type the initial letter C (for C-Function).

If you need more information on selecting a menu or command, see **Making a Menu Selection** earlier in this chapter.

This command does not have a fast path key.

Chapter 14

If-Else   The If-Else template contains the shell of a standard C language `if-else` statement:

```
if(_)
  {
  }
else
  {
  }
```

The cursor is positioned on the conditional expression of the `if-else` statement.

To insert an `if-else` statement into your source file, position the cursor on the line where you want to insert the template. Press F10 and the letter T to display the Templates menu. Then select If-Else and press <enter> or type the initial letter I (for If-Else).

If you need more information on selecting a menu or command, see **Making a Menu Selection** earlier in this chapter.

This command does not have a fast path key.

Switch   The Switch template contains the shell of a standard C language `switch` statement:

```
switch(_)
  {
  case 0:
          break;
  default:
          break;
  }
```

The cursor is positioned on the conditional expression of the `switch` statement.

To insert a `switch` statement into your source file, position the cursor on the line where you want to insert the template. Press F10 and the letter T to display the Templates menu. Then select Switch and press <enter> or type the initial letter S (for Switch).

If you need more information on selecting a menu or command, see **Making a Menu Selection** earlier in this chapter.

This command does not have a fast path key.

For Loop   The For Loop template contains the shell of a standard C language `for` statement:

```
for (_; ; )
  {
  }
```

Using the Student Compiler and Editor

The cursor is positioned on the initialization expression of the `for` statement.

To insert a `for` statement into your source file, position the cursor on the line where you want to insert the template. Press F10 and the letter T to display the Templates menu. Then select For Loop and press <enter> or type the initial letter F (for For Loop).

If you need more information on selecting a menu or command, see **Making a Menu Selection** earlier in this chapter.

This command does not have a fast path key.

While Loop   The While Loop template contains the shell of a standard C language `while` statement:

```
while(_)
  {
  }
```

The cursor is positioned on the conditional expression of the `while` statement.

To insert a `while` statement into your source file, position the cursor on the line where you want to insert the template. Press F10 and the letter T to display the Templates menu. Then select While Loop and press <enter> or type the initial letter W (for While Loop).

If you need more information on selecting a menu or command, see **Making a Menu Selection** earlier in this chapter.

This command does not have a fast path key.

Do While Loop   The Do While Loop template contains the shell of a standard C language `do-while` statement:

```
do
  {
  }
while(_);
```

The cursor is positioned on the conditional expression of the `do-while` statement.

To insert a `do-while` statement into your source file, position the cursor on the line where you want to insert the template. Press F10 and the letter T to display the Templates menu. Then select Do While Loop and press <enter> or type the initial letter D (for Do While Loop).

If you need more information on selecting a menu or command, see **Making a Menu Selection** earlier in this chapter.

This command does not have a fast path key.

Chapter 14

Chapter Summary

This chapter has described how you prepare and run C programs. The major topics that were covered are

- how to create and edit a source file
- how to compile a program, interpret messages about syntax errors, and correct the errors
- how to print a source file
- how to compile and execute (run) a program
- how to debug a program while it is executing
- how to use the SC C code templates.

The next chapter provides information on the Student Compiler itself, including how the compiler implements the C language and other information, such as descriptions of variable types and header files.

Chapter 15
Programming Environment for the Student Compiler

Chapter 15

CONTENTS

Introduction 391
How the Student Compiler Uses Memory 391
      The extern Declarations 393
      Data Sizes and Formats 393
Handling DOS Error Messages 394
The #include Files 396
Chapter Summary 398

Programming Environment for the Student Compiler

Introduction

This chapter decribes the Student Compiler's features and restrictions. These are important as you compile and execute programs. The following sections describe

- how the compiler uses memory
- the data types the compiler supports
- how to get more information when you see an MS-DOS error message
- the `#include` (header) files provided by the compiler.

How the Student Compiler Uses Memory

The Student Compiler compiles your program directly into memory, thereby providing a very fast and efficient development environment. (Memory is where information is stored for subsequent use or retrieval.) Your program compiles and runs quickly so that you can make changes to your source file and see the results of your changes in just a few seconds.

To promote speed and simplicity, this compiler is designed for use with single source file programs. This means that you can compile and run only one source file at a time. Although this feature enables you to focus on the programming aspects of a problem, it also means that you cannot combine (or *link*) several separately compiled source files.

Figure 15.1 is a diagram of the way the Student Compiler uses memory to compile and run a program.

Chapter 15

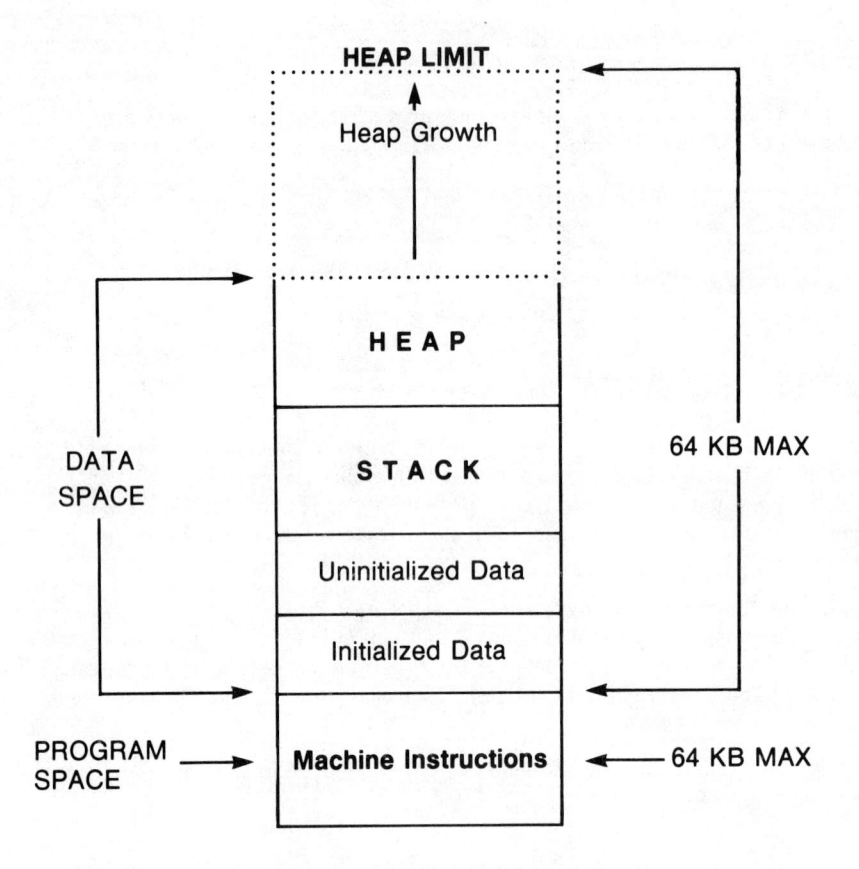

Figure 15.1 Model of the Student Compiler's Memory Organization

Programming Environment for the Student Compiler

With the Student Compiler, your program and data can each use 64 kilobytes (KB) of space. (These numbers represent maximum values because the real values are limited by the actual amount of physical memory on your PC.) As **Figure 15.1** shows, the compiler organizes memory so that it contains information of different types.

The **program space** contains all of the machine instructions that carry out your program operations. The **data space** contains all of the data items, including variables, literals, and constants.

The data space also contains the stack and the heap. (Stack and heap are types of storage structures. See the "Glossary" at the end of this book for definitions.) The **stack** is used to store all the automatic variables that are declared inside functions. These variables are placed on the stack when the function is called and taken off the stack when the function returns.

The **heap** contains all of the dynamically allocated memory. You can allocate memory dynamically using the `malloc` and `calloc` functions. Dynamically allocated memory is used for dynamic data structures, for example, linked lists and binary trees. You can release dynamic memory using the `free` function.

It is helpful to know how the Student Compiler uses memory if you need to keep track of the space used by data items or the amount of memory used by your program for stack and heap space.

The extern Declarations

In the C language, the `extern` declaration is often used to enable the code in one source file to access variables that are defined in another source file. However, the Student Compiler is designed for use with single source file applications. For this reason, you should never need to use an `extern` declaration in any of your programs, provided that you have the proper `#include` statements for any library functions you are calling (see **The #include Files** section later in this chapter).

If you are referencing or converting a C program that uses external variables defined in another source file, you must do one of two things in the Student Compiler. You must either merge all the source files together into one file, or you must drop the `extern` class and provide the complete definition of the variable in your program.

Data Sizes and Formats

The Student Compiler maintains data in forms that can be used efficiently by your IBM personal computer or compatible machine. **Table 15.1** gives the sizes of the Student Compiler's C language data types.

Chapter 15

Table 15.1 Student Compiler's Data Type Characteristics

Type	Bits	Range
`char`	8	Min: -128 Max: $+127$
`unsigned char`	8	Min: 0 Max: 255
`short int`	16	Min: $-32,768$ Max: $+32,767$
`unsigned short int`	16	Min: 0 Max: 65,535
`int`	16	Min: $-32,768$ Max: $+32,767$
`unsigned int`	16	Min: 0 Max: 65,535
`long int`	32	Min: $-2,147,483,648$ Max: $+2,147,483,647$
`unsigned long int`	32	Min: 0 Max: 4,294,987,295
`float`	32	Small: $+/-10E-37$ Large: $+/-10E+38$
`double`	64	Small: $+/-10E-307$ Large: $+/-10E+308$
`pointer`	16	Low: 0 High: 0xFFFF

Handling DOS Error Messages

Your source program executes in the PC DOS and MS-DOS environments. Therefore, you can encounter errors not only from the way you have coded C, but also from the way your program interacts with the operating system. For example, a common error on both operating systems is noted with the message "Insufficient memory." This means you do not have enough space on your disk to hold the output file that you are trying to write to. If your program fails to run because of a PC DOS or MS-DOS error, you can get more information about the error by using a special variable called `errno`.

The variable `errno` is an external integer that is initialized to zero at start-up time. If an error is detected by one of the standard library functions, a nonzero value is placed in `errno`. To use `errno`, either include the header file `error.h` or define `errno` as an integer before or outside of any function. The values that `errno` can contain are listed in **Table 15.2**.

Table 15.2   `errno` Codes and Their Definitions

Symbol	Code	Meaning
EOSERR	−1	Operating system error
EPERM	01	User is not owner
ENOENT	02	No such file or directory
ESRCH	03	System error
EINTR	04	Interrupted system call
EIO	05	I/O error
ENXIO	06	System error
E2BIG	07	System error
ENOEXEC	08	System error
EBADF	09	Bad file number
ECHILD	10	System error
EAGAIN	11	System error
ENOMEM	12	No memory available
EACCES	13	Access denied
EFAULT	14	Bad address
ENOTBLK	15	Bulk device required
EBUSY	16	Resource is busy
EEXIST	17	File already exists
EXDEV	18	System error
ENODEV	19	No such device
ENOTDIR	20	Is not a directory
EISDIR	21	Is a directory
EINVAL	22	System error
ENFILE	23	No more files (system)
EMFILE	24	No more files (process)
ENOTTY	25	System error
ETXTBSY	26	Text file is busy
EFBIG	27	File is too large
ENOSPC	28	No space left
ESPIPE	29	System error
EROFS	30	Read-only file system
EMLINK	31	System error
EPIPE	32	System error
EDOM	33	Math function argument error
ERANGE	34	Math function result is out of range

Often, you use the information provided in `errno` in two ways. In some cases, it is appropriate to check `errno` after a long sequence of operations, and abort if any error occurred along the way. In other cases, you might check `errno` periodically to see if it

Chapter 15

is nonzero and then take appropriate corrective action. In the latter case, you would reset `errno` before beginning another processing phase.

All that `errno` provides is a number, as listed in **Table 15.2**. If you want additional information, you can use the `perror` function to print the messages that correspond to the codes found in `errno`. For example, if you think that you may be trying to open a file that does not exist, use the following example to check for an operating system error:

```
#include <stdio.h>
#include <error.h>

main()
{
FILE *f;
f = fopen("myfile", "r");
if (f == NULL)
   perror("Error opening myfile:");
}
```

If `myfile` does not exist, the following message is displayed on the Program Screen:

```
Error opening myfile:  No such file or directory
```

The message that corresponds to the `errno` number is printed only if you call `perror`.

The #include Files

This section describes the files (often called *header files*) that you need to include in your program with a `#include` statement to access the external names defined in the Student Compiler's function libraries.

Many users who are not familiar with the C language tend to include all of the header files, just to be safe. However, including unnecessary header files slows down the compiler and can possibly cause it to run out of memory. In general, try to minimize the number of header files that you include.

You can type or print each header file to see its contents. You can also modify header files, if you ever need to, by using the Student Compiler's editor. However, be careful when altering a header file. A change to a header file may cause unexpected results in other areas. For example, changing a variable definition from `float` to `int` for one function's use could affect the results of another function using the same header file. Many functions call another function as part of their definition, so changing the header file may cause the first function to abort.

Programming Environment for the Student Compiler

Here is a list of header files for library functions that may be specified using the `#include` statement:

```
<bios.h>    /* screen management and graphics functions */
<dos.h>     /* DOS-dependent definitions */
<error.h>   /* symbolic definitions for errno codes */
<ctype.h>   /* character check macros */
<float.h>   /* floating point constants */
<limits.h>  /* system limits */
<math.h>    /* SC math library */
<setjmp.h>  /* setjump function */
<stdio.h>   /* standard input/output functions */
<stdlib.h>  /* other standard library definitions */
<string.h>  /* string function definitions */
<time.h>    /* time functions */
```

The individual function descriptions in Chapters 16 and 17 list which header file you should include with each function in your program.

bios.h should be included whenever you use any of the Student Compiler's graphics or screen management functions.

ctype.h defines the macro forms of the various character checking and conversion operations. For example, if you include this file and use the **isalpha** operation, the check is handled by in-line code rather than a function call. (This is called *in-line* replacement, because the code to perform the operation is produced directly in the program that has invoked the operation: no function call and return processing is done.)

dos.h contains a large number of definitions needed by the operating system. It is used primarily with MS-DOS functions such as **int86** (system interrupt generator).

error.h contains the definitions of the error codes that are placed into **errno** by the standard library functions. (A list of these codes is provided in **Table 15.2**.)

float.h contains symbolic constants that are used by the SC math library for floating point operations. For example, **FLT_ROUNDS** is a constant indicating how numbers are to be rounded during computation. **HUGE_VAL** defines a large double value. Other constants refer to the maximum and minimum values for decimal digits, exponents, and so on.

limits.h defines the limits for data types other than for **float** and **long** for the particular operating system that you are using with the compiler. For example, **CHAR_MAX** defines the maximum value for a **char** variable. **INT_MIN** defines the minimum value for an integer.

math.h provides definitions that should be included whenever you are calling any of the floating point functions from the SC math library. For example, the **sin** function returns a **double**.

Chapter 15

                    Note: if a definition is not provided for the return value, C assumes that the value is an integer. Leaving out the header file in this case could cause a serious computational error.

`setjmp.h`   contains the definitions needed when you use the `setjump` and `longjmp` functions.

`stdio.h`   contains information for standard input and output operations such as `fopen`, `getchar`, and `putchar`. Sometimes these operations are defined as macros rather than functions. This header file also contains the definition of `NULL`, which represents a null pointer (a pointer containing the value zero). Usually, you will want to include this header file in your program.

`stdlib.h`   contains definitions and function declarations associated with a variety of memory management and sort functions. Also included are declarations for general purpose functions such as `atoi` and `exit`.

`string.h`   should be included whenever you use any of the string functions, such as `strcpy` or `strlen`.

`time.h`   is used with any of the time functions, such as `ctime` or `asctime`.

Keep in mind that you can list or print a particular header file if you need more information about its contents.

Chapter Summary

This chapter has covered topics related to the features and restrictions of the Student Compiler's programming environment. The primary areas described were

- how the compiler uses memory
- data types supported by the compiler
- obtaining information about MS-DOS errors
- Student Compiler header files.

The next chapter describes the Draft ANSI Standard functions provided with the Student Compiler.

Chapter 16
Standard Function Library for the Student Compiler

Chapter 16

abs

abs - Absolute value macro Class: ANSI

NAME

abs Absolute value macro.

SYNOPSIS

```
#include <math.h>

int abs(x);

int x;    argument
```

DESCRIPTION

The `abs` macro computes the absolute value of an integer. This macro accepts any data type as its argument and generates in-line code to perform the conversion. The definition is:

```
#define abs(x) ((x)<0?-(x):(x))
```

RETURN VALUE

This macro returns the absolute value of its argument. Both the result and the argument are of type `int`.

SEE ALSO

`fabs, labs`

EXAMPLE

```
/* This example uses the abs macro. */

#include <stdio.h>
#include <math.h>

main()
{
int x, r;
float xf,rf;

x = -10;

r = abs(x);

printf("The return of %d is %d.\n", x, r);
xf = 10.4;
rf = abs(xf);
printf("The return of %lf is %lf.\n", xf, rf);
}
```

abort

abort - Abnormally terminate the current process　　　　　　**Class: ANSI**

NAME
       `abort`　　　　Abnormally terminate the current process.

SYNOPSIS
```
#include <stdlib.h>

void abort();
```

DESCRIPTION

    The **abort** function ends the current process abnormally. Open files are closed before termination, and the standard I/O buffers are flushed. The function returns a completion code of 3 to the Student Compiler.

RETURN VALUE

    Control is never returned to the caller of **abort**.

SEE ALSO
    exit

EXAMPLE
```
/* This example uses the abort function. */

#include <stdlib.h>
#include <stdio.h>

main()
{

printf("This line will go to the screen.\n");

abort();

printf("This line will never print.\n");
}
```

access

access - Test for file accessibility   **Class: ANSI**

NAME
    `access`   Test for file accessibility.

SYNOPSIS
```
#include <stdio.h>

int access(name,mode);

char *name;     filename
int mode;       access mode
```

DESCRIPTION
The `access` function queries if the file pointed to in `name` exists and whether the given type of access (specified by `mode`) is allowed. Access can be the sum of one or more of the following mode types:

```
0  => Check if file exists.
2  => Check if file is writable.
4  => Check if file is readable.
6  => Check if file is readable and writable.
```

Since all MS-DOS files are readable, modes 0 and 4 are identical, as are modes 2 and 6.

RETURN VALUE
A return value of zero indicates that access is allowed. If access is denied or the file cannot be found, -1 is returned. Additional error information can be found in `errno`.

SEE ALSO
    `perror`

EXAMPLE
```
/* This example uses access to test a given file for accessibility. */

#include <stdio.h>

main()
{
int r;

r = access("MYFILE",0);
    /* If the return code is 0, MYFILE exists */
if (r == 0)
   print("Myfile exists.\n");
else
   printf("Myfile does not exist.\n");
}
```

403

asctime

---

asctime - Convert time to a character string. **Class: ANSI**

NAME
    asctime   Convert time to a character string.

SYNOPSIS
```
#include <time.h>

char *asctime(t);

struct tm *t;     points to time structure
```

DESCRIPTION

The `asctime` function converts a time structure (pointed to by `t`) into a printable ASCII character string of exactly 26 characters having the form:

```
DDD MMM dd hh:mm:ss YYYY\n\0
```

where `DDD` is the day of the week, `MMM` is the month, `dd` is the day of the month, `hh:mm:ss` is the hour:minute:seconds, and `YYYY` is the year. An example is

```
Wed Sep 04 15:03:22 1988\n\0
```

The time structure argument `t` is usually returned by the `gmtime` or `localtime` function.

RETURN VALUE

This function returns a pointer to the first character of the formatted date and time string.

CAUTION

The pointer returned by the function refers to `static` storage that is shared by `asctime`, `ctime`, `gmtime`, and `localtime`, and a call to one of these functions overwrites the results of a previous call.

SEE ALSO

`ctime`, `gmtime`, `localtime`, `time`

atof

atof - Convert a string to floating point   Class: ANSI

NAME

    atof   Convert a string to floating point.

SYNOPSIS

```
#include <math.h>

double atof(p);

char *p;      input string pointer
```

DESCRIPTION

The `atof` function converts a character input string (pointed to by `p`) into a double-precision, floating-point number. The input string may contain leading white space (such as blanks, tabs, and newlines), although `atof` usually skips over it before performing the conversion. The conversion stops at the first unrecognized character.

The string may contain a decimal point and may be followed by an `e` or `E` and a signed integer exponent; that is, a valid floating-point number in normal or scientific notation. A plus or minus sign may be added to indicate a positive or negative number. White space is not allowed between the plus/minus sign and the floating-point number or between the number and the exponent.

For example, the following is a valid number in scientific notation:

```
123.456e-53
```

RETURN VALUE

The `atof` function returns the value of the converted string as a double.

CAUTIONS

No indication of overflow or underflow is returned to the program if the string represents a number outside the hardware range of floating-point numbers.

No indication is returned to the program to specify if the string contained a valid number.

atof

EXAMPLE

```
/* This program illustrates the atof function. */

#include <stdio.h>
#include <math.h>

main()
{
char buff[80];
double d;

while(1){
   printf("\nEnter a number: ");
   if(gets(buff) == NULL) exit(0);
   if(buff[0] == '\0') exit(0);
   d = atof(buff);
   printf("%e\n",d);
   }
}
```

atoi, atol - Convert strings to integers   Class: ANSI

NAME

    `atoi`   Convert a string to an integer.
    `atol`   Convert a string to a long integer.

SYNOPSIS

```
#include <stdlib.h>

int  atoi(str);
long atol(str);

char *str;    character string
```

DESCRIPTION

The `atoi` function converts a character string (pointed to by `str`) to an integer. The `atol` function converts a character string (pointed to by `str`) to a long integer. Each string must have the form:

    `[white space][sign]digits`

where:

- `white space` indicates optional leading white space.
- `sign` indicates an optional + or − sign character.
- `digits` is a contiguous string of decimal digit characters.

Once the decimal digit portion is reached, the conversion continues until a nondigit character is reached.

RETURN VALUE

Each function returns the integer value represented by the character string, up to the first nondigit character. If no initial segment of the string is a valid integer, the return value is zero.

CAUTION

No indication of integer overflow or other error is returned, so it is recommended that you validate the string before calling either function.

SEE ALSO

    `atof`

atoi, atol

EXAMPLE
```
/*
 * This program demonstrates atoi, which
 * converts ASCII strings to integers.
 */

#include <stdlib.h>

main()
{
char inputline[20];

gets(inputline);

printf ("%d\n", atoi(inputline));
}
```

See also, the example under the `strcat` function.

calloc - Allocate and clear memory   **Class: ANSI**

NAME
calloc   Allocate and clear memory.

SYNOPSIS
```
#include <stdlib.h>

void *calloc(nelt,esize);

size_t nelt;      number of elements
size_t esize;     element size
```

DESCRIPTION
The `calloc` function allocates a block of dynamic memory that is large enough to hold an array of `nelt` elements, each of size `esize`. The block of memory is then cleared to zeros. The memory block is suitably aligned for the storage of any type of data.

The `calloc` function allocates a block whose size in bytes is

```
n = nelt * esize
```

where `n` may be a long integer.

RETURN VALUE
If successful, `calloc` returns a pointer to the first element in the block of memory allocated. If the block cannot be allocated, `calloc` returns a NULL pointer.

SEE ALSO
`free`, `malloc`, `realloc`

calloc

EXAMPLE

```
/* Initialize two arrays using calloc and malloc. */

#include <stdio.h>
#include <stdlib.h>

main()
{
double *carray, *marray;
int r;

   /* Allocate two arrays of 1000 elements. */

carray = (double *) calloc((size_t)1000, sizeof(double));

marray = (double *) malloc((size_t)1000);

   /* Print element from each array. */

printf("Element from carray: %.*f\n",1,carray[0]);

printf("Element from marray: %.*f\n",1,marray[4]);

   /* Free a block allocated by calloc. */

r = free((char*) carray);

r = free((char*) marray);
}
```

ceil

ceil - Round a floating-point number up   **Class: ANSI**

NAME

    `ceil`   Round a floating-point number up.

SYNOPSIS

```
#include <math.h>

double ceil(y);

double y;     argument
```

DESCRIPTION

    The `ceil` function rounds a decimal number up to the next higher integer and returns this value as a double-precision, floating-point number.

RETURN VALUE

    This function returns its argument as type `double`.

CAUTION

    Note that even though this function returns an integral value, the result is still a real number.

SEE ALSO

    `floor`

EXAMPLE

```
/* This example tests the floor and ceil functions. */

#include <math.h>
#include <stdio.h>

main()
{
double r;

   /* R will be 524.00 */

r = ceil(523.96);

printf("r is %f \n", r);

   /* R will be 523.00 */

r = floor(523.96);

printf("r is %f \n", r);
}
```

cos, acos, cosh - Cosine functions   **Class: ANSI**

NAME

    cos   Compute the cosine in radians.
    acos   Compute the arccosine.
    cosh   Compute the hyperbolic cosine.

SYNOPSIS

```
#include <math.h>

double cos(x);
double acos(x);
double cosh(x);

double x;    argument
```

DESCRIPTION

Each cosine function performs the computation as indicated:

- The `cos` function computes the cosine of value `x`, where `x` is expressed in radians.

  Because `cos` is periodic, only the value of `x mod` 2π is used to compute the cosine. If `x` is very large, only a limited precision is left to represent `x mod` 2π.

- The `acos` function computes the arccosine of `x` and returns the result in radians. This is the inverse of the `cos` function and is expressed by the relation

  $$r = \cos^{-1}(x)$$

  where `x` is in the closed interval [-1.0, 1.0].

- The `cosh` function computes the hyperbolic cosine of the value `x` and returns the result in radians. This relation can be expressed as

  $$r = (e^x + e^{-x}) / 2$$

RETURN VALUE

The `cos` function returns the principal value of the cosine of `x` (of type `double`), provided that this value is defined and computable.

If `x` is outside the range of what can be handled numerically, `cos` returns 0.0 and the `errno` parameter is set to `EDOM`.

The `acos` function returns a double-precision, floating-point number in the closed interval [0,π] radians. If `x` is less than -1.0 or greater than 1.0, 0.0 is returned and the `errno` parameter is set to `EDOM`.

The `cosh` function returns the principal value of the hyperbolic cosine of `x` (of type `double`), provided that this value is defined and computable.

cos, acos, cosh

If `x` has an absolute value that is too large to be represented, `cosh` returns the largest positive floating-point number that can be represented, `HUGE_VAL`, and the `errno` parameter is set to `ERANGE`.

SEE ALSO

`asin, sin, sinh`

EXAMPLES

```
/* This example uses the cos function. */

#include <stdio.h>
#include <math.h>

main()
{
double angle, result;

angle = PI;

result = cos(angle);

printf("The result is: %f\n", result);
}


/* This example uses the acos function. */

#include <stdio.h>
#include <math.h>

main()
{
double value, result;

value = 0;

result = acos(value);

printf("The result is: %f\n", result);

value = 1;

result = acos(value);

printf("The result is: %f\n", result);
}
```

ctime

ctime - Convert a time value to local time   Class: ANSI

NAME

    ctime   Convert a time value to a string.

SYNOPSIS

```
#include <time.h>

char *ctime(t);

time_t *t;     pointer to time value
```

DESCRIPTION

The `ctime` function converts a Greenwich Mean Time time value (pointed to in `t`) to a printable ASCII character string of exactly 26 characters having the form:

```
DDD MMM dd hh:mm:ss YYYY\n\0
```

where `DDD` is the day of the week, `MMM` is the month, `dd` is the day of the month, `hh:mm:ss` is the hour:minute:seconds, and `YYYY` is the year. An example is

```
Wed Sep 04 15:13:02 1988\n\0
```

The time value argument `t` must point to a long integer that is the number of seconds since 00:00:00 Greenwich Mean Time, January 1, 1970. Normally this value is obtained from the `time` function.

`ctime(t)` is implemented as `asctime(localtime(t))`.

RETURN VALUE

This function returns a pointer to the first character in the formatted local date and time string.

CAUTIONS

Note that `t` is a pointer to a `time_t` object. A common error is to pass the integer itself instead of the pointer. Observe the use of the ampersand (`&`) operator in the example below.

The pointer returned by the function refers to `static` storage that is shared by `ctime`, `asctime`, `gmtime`, and `localtime`; a call to one of these functions will overwrite the results of a previous call.

SEE ALSO

`asctime, gmtime, localtime, time`

EXAMPLE

```
#include <time.h>
#include <stdio.h>

main()
{
time_t t;

time(&t);

printf("Current time is %s\n",ctime(&t));
}
```

exit

exit - Terminate program execution normally   **Class: ANSI**

NAME
        exit   Terminate execution normally.

SYNOPSIS

```
#include <stdlib.h>

void exit(code);

int code;    code
```

DESCRIPTION

        The **exit** function terminates execution of the current program normally and returns control to the parent program. Use **exit** to write to all pending output buffers and to close all files explicitly.

        The **code** argument is a value from 0 to 255 that gets passed back to the Student Compiler. By convention, a value of zero indicates success and other values indicate failure.

RETURN VALUE

        Control does not return from the **exit** function.

EXAMPLE

```
/*
 * This example shows how you would exit a program
 * if it is not called with a valid input filename.
 */

#include <stdio.h>

main(argc, argv)

int argc;
char *argv[];
{
FILE *f;

if (argc > 1) {
   f = fopen(argv[1], "r");
   if (f == NULL) {
      fprintf(stderr, "Can't open file\"%s\"\n", argv[1]);
      exit(1);
      }
   }
else {
   fprintf(stderr, "No file specified\n");
   exit(1);
   }
}
```

416

exp

exp - Compute the exponential function   **Class: ANSI**

NAME
    `exp`   Compute the exponential function.

SYNOPSIS
```
#include <math.h>

double exp(x);

double x;    argument
```

DESCRIPTION
The `exp` function computes the exponential function of its argument `x`. The result is `e` to the power `x`, where `e` is the base of the natural logarithm 2.71828....

The exponential function is the inverse of the natural logarithm and is as expressed in the relation

```
r = exp(x)
```

The argument `x` is a double-precision, floating-point number.

RETURN VALUE
The `exp` function returns the exponential function of its argument `x`, as expressed as a double-precision, floating-point number.

If the argument is too large and its result so large that it cannot be represented, `exp` returns the largest positive floating-point number that can be represented, which is 1.797693e+308 or `HUGE_VAL`.

If an overflow error occurs, `exp` returns the constant `HUGE_VAL` and the variable `errno` is assigned the value `ERANGE`.

EXAMPLE
```
/* This example demonstrates the exp function. */

#include <stdio.h>
#include <math.h>

main()
{
double x, r;

x = 0.0;

r = exp(x);
printf("e to the x is: %f\n",r);
r = exp(1.0);
printf("e to the x is: %f\n", r);
}
```

fabs

fabs - Floating-point absolute value function   Class: ANSI

NAME
    `fabs`   Floating-point absolute value function.

SYNOPSIS
```
#include <math.h>

double fabs(d);

double d;           argument
```

DESCRIPTION
The `fabs` function computes the absolute value of a double-precision floating-point number. The argument `d` is defined as a double because of the rule that all function arguments of type `float` are converted to type `double` before the call is made.

The most general approach is to use the `abs` macro, which is defined in the `math.h` header file. This macro accepts any data type as its argument and generates in-line code to perform the conversion. The definition is

```
#define abs(x) ((x)<0?-(x):(x))
```

To minimize code size, you can use the `fabs` function call instead of the `abs` macro.

RETURN VALUE
The `fabs` function returns the absolute value of its argument. Both the result and the argument are of type `double`.

SEE ALSO
    `abs, labs`

fabs

EXAMPLE

```
/* This example uses the fabs function. */

#include <stdio.h>
#include <math.h>

main()
{
double x, r;

x = -100000000.4;

r = fabs(x);

printf("The return of fabs(%f) is %f.\n", x, r);

x = 100000000.4;

r = fabs(x);

printf("The return of fabs(%f) is %f.\n", x, r);
}
```

fclose

fclose - Close a standard I/O file   **Class: ANSI**

NAME
    `fclose`   Close a standard I/O file.

SYNOPSIS

```
#include <stdio.h>

int fclose(fp);

FILE *fp;
```
    `FILE *fp;`   pointer for the file to be closed

DESCRIPTION

The `fclose` function completes the processing of a standard I/O file and releases all related resources, such as buffers that remain allocated while the file is open. If the file was being written, any data that have accumulated in the buffer is written to the file and the buffer are freed.

The `fclose` function is called automatically for all open files when the `exit` function is called or when your program terminates. However, it is good programming practice to close your own files explicitly. The last buffer is not written until `fclose` is called, so data may be lost if an output file is not properly closed.

RETURN VALUE

If successful, `fclose` returns zero. If an error occurs, it returns -1 and places additional error information in `errno`.

If `fclose` fails, you will be unable to use the `FILE` pointer. The file will be closed and you will have to reopen it (using the `freopen` function).

SEE ALSO

    `fopen, freopen, perror`

EXAMPLE

See the example under the `fopen` function.

feof - Check for a standard I/O end-of-file   Class: ANSI

NAME
    feof   Check for a standard I/O end-of-file.

SYNOPSIS
```
#include <stdio.h>

int feof(fp);

FILE *fp;    file pointer
```

DESCRIPTION
The `feof` macro is an error-handling macro that tests for an end-of-file (EOF) indication for the standard input file addressed by `fp`.

RETURN VALUE
This macro returns a nonzero value if it finds an EOF condition and a zero if it does not.

CAUTION
This macro does not check whether `fp` is a valid file pointer.

EXAMPLE
```
/* Use feof to determine the end of a file opened for reading. */

#include <stdio.h>

main()
{
FILE *fp;
char c;
int count;

fp = fopen("MYFILE","r");

count = 0;

while (!feof(fp) && !ferror(fp)) {
   c = fgetc(fp);
   ++count;
   }

printf("The count was %d and the last character was %c\n",count,c);
}
```

ferror

ferror - Check for a standard I/O error Class: ANSI

NAME
    `ferror` — Check for a standard I/O error.

SYNOPSIS
```
#include <stdio.h>

int ferror(fp);

FILE *fp;    file pointer
```

DESCRIPTION
The `ferror` macro indicates whether the error flag has been set for the standard I/O file addressed by `fp`. This flag is set whenever an I/O function fails for some reason. The file's error flag remains set after an error until it is cleared using the `clearerr` function.

RETURN VALUE
This macro returns a nonzero value if it finds a standard I/O error for the specified file and a zero if it finds no error.

CAUTION
This macro does not check whether `fp` is a valid file pointer.

SEE ALSO
    `clearerr`

EXAMPLES
See the examples under the `feof` and `fread` functions.

fflush

fflush - Flush a standard output buffer Class: ANSI

NAME
    `fflush`   Flush a standard output buffer.

SYNOPSIS
```
#include <stdio.h>

int fflush(fp);

FILE *fp;      file pointer
```

DESCRIPTION

The `fflush` macro forces buffered output to be written to the file addressed by `fp` if the file was opened for output. Without the use of `fflush`, the output is only written when a buffer becomes full, when a file is closed normally, or when `fflush` is called.

RETURN VALUE

If successful, `fflush` returns a zero. If an error occurs, the return value is end-of-file (EOF), and the appropriate error code is placed into `errno`.

SEE ALSO

`fclose`, `fopen`, `perror`

EXAMPLE

```
/*
 * This example creates a new file buffer using the setbuf
 * function and uses fflush to flush the output buffer.
 */

#include <stdio.h>

main()
{
FILE *fp;
char *buff;
int x, r;

buff = (char *) calloc(1000, sizeof(char));

fp = fopen("MYFILE","w");      /* Open MYFILE for writing. */
setbuf(fp, buff);
for (x = 0; x != 50; ++x)
   fprintf(fp,"a");
r = fflush(fp);
printf("Return value: %d\n",r);
}
```

fgetc

fgetc - Read a character from a file **Class: ANSI**

NAME
fgetc   Read a character from a file.

SYNOPSIS
```
#include <stdio.h>

int fgetc(fp);

FILE *fp;      file pointer
```

DESCRIPTION
The `fgetc` function reads the next single character from the standard I/O file addressed by `fp` and returns the character. It is implemented as a function call rather than a macro, so it will be slower than `getc`.

RETURN VALUE
This function returns the next input character or EOF (end-of-file) if no character could be read.

In the event of an EOF return, error information can be found in `errno`. Most programmers treat any EOF return as an indication of end-of-file. However, if you want to distinguish errors from ends-of-file, you should reset `errno` before calling the function and then analyze its contents when you receive an EOF return.

SEE ALSO
`fopen`, `getc`, `perror`

EXAMPLE
```
/*
 * This example reads a file and counts its characters.  The
 * total number of characters is printed to the screen.
 */

#include <stdio.h>
main()
{
FILE *fp;
int c,i;
i = 0;
fp = fopen("MYFILE","r");       /* Open file MYFILE to read. */
while ((c = fgetc(fp)) != EOF)  /* Count characters. */
    ++i;
printf("Number of characters is %d.",i);
fclose(fp);
}
```

fgets - Read a string from a standard I/O file   Class: ANSI

NAME

    `fgets`   Read a string from a standard I/O file.

SYNOPSIS

```
#include <stdio.h>

char *fgets(buffer,length,fp);

char *buffer;      buffer pointer
int length;        buffer length in bytes
FILE *fp;          file pointer
```

DESCRIPTION

The `fgets` function reads a string from the standard file addressed by `fp`, which must be open for input. Characters (that is, bytes) are read from the file to the buffer until one of the following: the number of characters read exceeds `length` -1; a newline ('\n') is read; an end-of-file (EOF) is reached; or an I/O error occurs. The string is then terminated with a null character ('\0').

In the EOF case, a null character is placed into the buffer after the last character that was read. If the EOF is reached before any characters are read, a NULL pointer is returned.

RETURN VALUE

This function returns the `buffer` argument unless an EOF or an I/O error occurs, in which case a NULL pointer is returned.

SEE ALSO

    `feof`, `ferror`, `fopen`, `fgetc`, `getc`, `gets`, `perror`

fgets

EXAMPLE

```
/* This example uses fgets to read a line from a file to an array. */

#include <stdio.h>
#define LENGTH 80

main()
{
char *array;
FILE *f;

array = malloc(LENGTH);

f = fopen("MYFILE","r");      /* Open file "MYFILE" for reading. */

fgets(array,LENGTH,f);    /* Read 80 char string into "array". */

printf("The file line was:\n");

printf("%s",array);

fclose(f);
}
```

floor - Round a floating-point number down Class: ANSI

NAME
> `floor`   Round a floating-point number down.

SYNOPSIS
> ```
> #include <math.h>
> 
> double floor(y);
> 
> double y;    argument
> ```

DESCRIPTION
> The `floor` function rounds a decimal number down to the next lower integer and returns this value as a double-precision floating-point number.

RETURN VALUE
> This function returns its argument as type `double`.

CAUTION
> Note that even though this function returns an integral value, the result is still a real number.

SEE ALSO
> `ceil`

EXAMPLE
> ```
> /* This example tests the floor and ceil functions. */
> 
> #include <math.h>
> #include <stdio.h>
> 
> main()
> {
> double r;
> 
>    /* R will be 524.00 */
> r = ceil(523.96);
> 
> printf("r is %f \n", r);
> 
>    /* R will be 523.00 */
> r = floor(523.96);
> printf("r is %f \n", r);
> }
> ```

fmod

fmod - Compute a floating-point modulus   **Class: ANSI**

NAME
    `fmod`   Compute a floating-point modulus.

SYNOPSIS
```
#include <math.h>

double fmod(y,z);

double y,z;     arguments
```

DESCRIPTION

The `fmod` function computes and returns the floating-point remainder of `y` divided by `z` to produce an integer `i`. This function satisfies the following relationship, where `i` is an integer:

```
y = (i * z) + x
```

This function performs the same modulus (%) operation for double and float arguments.

RETURN VALUE

The `fmod` function returns the floating-point remainder. If `z` is zero, `fmod` returns the value of `y`.

SEE ALSO

    `modf`

EXAMPLE

```
/* This example uses the fmod and modf functions. */

#include <math.h>
#include <stdio.h>

main()
{
double r,ff,fi;
r = fmod(5.7,1.5); /* r contains 1.2 */
printf("r is %f\n", r);
ff = modf(r,&fi);  /* ff contains 0.2 */
                   /* fi contains 1.0 */
printf("ff is %f\n",ff);
printf("fi is %f\n",fi);
}
```

fopen

fopen - Open a standard I/O file **Class: ANSI**

NAME

    `fopen`   Open a standard I/O file.

SYNOPSIS

```
#include <stdio.h>

FILE *fopen(name, mode);

char *name;     filename
char *mode;     access mode
```

DESCRIPTION

The `fopen` function opens a standard I/O file for buffered access. The `name` string can be any valid filename and may include a device code and directory path. The `mode` string indicates how the file is to be processed, as follows:

MODE	CREATE	TRUNC	READ	WRITE	APPEND	TRANSLATE
`"r"`	No	No	Yes	No	No	Default
`"w"`	Yes	Yes	No	Yes	No	Default
`"a"`	Yes	No	No	No	Yes	Default
`"r+"`	No	No	Yes	Yes	No	Default
`"w+"`	Yes	Yes	Yes	Yes	No	Default
`"a+"`	Yes	No	Yes	No	Yes	Default
`"ra"`	No	No	Yes	No	No	Mode A
`"wa"`	Yes	Yes	No	Yes	No	Mode A
`"aa"`	Yes	No	No	No	Yes	Mode A
`"ra+"`	No	No	Yes	Yes	No	Mode A
`"wa+"`	Yes	Yes	Yes	Yes	No	Mode A
`"aa+"`	Yes	No	Yes	No	Yes	Mode A
`"rb"`	No	No	Yes	No	No	Mode B
`"wb"`	Yes	Yes	No	Yes	No	Mode B
`"ab"`	Yes	No	No	No	Yes	Mode B
`"rb+"`	No	No	Yes	Yes	No	Mode B
`"wb+"`	Yes	Yes	Yes	Yes	No	Mode B
`"ab+"`	Yes	No	Yes	No	Yes	Mode B

CREATE — Yes

    The file will be created if it does not already exist.

fopen

CREATE — No

 The function will fail if the file does not already exist.

TRUNC — Yes

 If the file exists, it will be truncated, that is, marked as empty.

TRUNC — No

 If the file exists, its current contents will not be changed.

READ — Yes

 The file can be read via functions such as `fread` and `fgetc`. Also, `fseek` can be used to position the file before reading.

READ — No

 The file cannot be read.

WRITE — Yes

 The file can be written via functions such as `fwrite` and `fputc`. Also, `fseek` can be used to position the file before writing.

WRITE — No

 The file cannot be written, but see APPEND below.

APPEND — Yes

 The file can be written, but it is automatically positioned to the current end-of-file before each write operation. This effectively prevents existing data from being changed.

APPEND — No

 Automatic positioning to the end-of-file is not done before a write operation. Also, writes are not allowed unless WRITE is Yes.

TRANSLATE — Mode A

 On a read operation, each carriage return character ('\r') is deleted and the CTRL-Z character is treated as a logical end-of-file mark. On a write operation, each line feed character ('\n') is expanded to a carriage return followed by a line feed.

TRANSLATE — Mode B

 The data are unchanged as they are read or written.

If the file is successfully opened, the function returns a pointer to a buffered I/O control block, which is defined in the header file `stdio.h`. Normally, you do not need to access any information in the control block directly, but you should be very careful not to disturb the block. A common C programming error is to modify one of these control blocks accidentally, which can write invalid data to a file.

fopen

RETURN VALUE

A NULL pointer is returned if the file cannot be opened. Consult `errno` for detailed error information.

SEE ALSO

`fclose, fgetc, fgets, fputc, fputs, fread, freopen, fwrite`

EXAMPLE

```
/*
 * This example opens and reads a file and counts the
 * characters it contains.  The total number of characters is
 * printed to the screen and then the file is closed.
 */

#include <stdio.h>

main()
{
FILE *f;
int c,i;

i = 0;

f = fopen("MYFILE","r");          /* Open file MYFILE to read. */

while ((c = fgetc(f)) != EOF)++i;  /* Count characters. */

printf("Number of characters is %d.",i);

fclose(f);
}
```

See also the example under the `fread` function.

fprintf, printf, sprintf

fprintf, printf, sprintf — Write formatted print **Class: ANSI**

NAME

    `fprintf`   Write formatted print to a file.
    `printf`   Write formatted print to stdout.
    `sprintf`   Write formatted print to storage.

SYNOPSIS

```
#include <stdio.h>

int fprintf(fp,fmt,arg1,arg2,...);
int printf(fmt,arg1,arg2,...);
int sprintf(s,fmt,arg1,arg2,...);

char *fmt;      format string
FILE *fp;       file pointer
char *s;        storage pointer
```

See below for `arg1`, `arg2`, and so on.

DESCRIPTION

These functions generate a stream of ASCII characters by analyzing the format string and performing various conversion operations on the remaining arguments.

The `printf` function writes the output data to the standard output file, `stdout`, which is usually the user's screen. The `fprintf` function is similar to `printf`, but it writes the data to the standard I/O file addressed by `fp`.

Finally, the `sprintf` function writes the output characters into the storage area whose address is given by `s`. This area must be large enough to hold the maximum number of characters that may be generated. Note that `sprintf` also generates a null character ('\0') to terminate the stored string.

The `fmt` argument points to a string consisting of ordinary characters and conversion specifications. The ordinary characters are simply copied to the output, but each conversion specification is replaced by the results of the conversion. These results come from operating sequentially upon the arguments that follow `fmt`. Thus, the first conversion specification operates upon `arg1`, the second operates upon `arg2`, and so on. In some cases, as described below, a conversion specification may process more than one argument.

Each conversion specification must begin with a percent sign (%). If you want to write an ordinary percent sign into the output stream, precede it with another percent sign in the `fmt` string; for example, typing %% will write a single percent character to the output stream. If the percent sign is not preceded by another percent sign, then a conversion specification is

fprintf, printf, sprintf

introduced, as follows:

```
%[flags][width][.precision][l]type
```

where the brackets [...] indicate optional fields and the fields have the following definitions:

- **flags** — Control output justification and the printing of signs, blanks, decimal places, and hexadecimal prefixes.
- **width** — Specifies the field width, which is the minimum number of characters to be generated for this format item.
- **precision** — Specifies the field precision, which is the required precision of numeric conversions or the maximum number of characters to be copied from a string, depending on the **type** field.
- **l** — Specifies the large size modifier, which indicates that the argument is 32 bits long.
- **type** — Specifies the type of argument conversion to be done.

Flags

If any flag characters are used, they must appear after the **percent** sign and can be any of the following:

- Minus (−) — This causes the result to be left-adjusted within the field specified by **width** or within the default width.
- Plus (+) — This flag is used with the various numeric conversion types to place a plus or minus sign before the result. If it is absent, the sign character is generated only for a negative number.
- Blank — This flag is similar to the plus, but it places a leading blank for a positive number and a minus sign for a negative number. If both the plus and the blank flags are present, the plus takes precedence.
- Sharp (#) — This flag causes special formatting. With the **o**, **x**, and **X** types, the sharp flag prefixes any nonzero output with 0, 0x, or 0X, respectively. With the **f**, **e**, and **E** types, the sharp flag forces the result to contain a decimal point. With the **g** and **G** types, the sharp flag forces the result to contain a decimal point and prevents the elimination of trailing zeros.

Width

The **width** is a nonnegative number that specifies the minimum field width. If fewer characters are generated by the conversion operation, the result is padded on the left or right (depending on the minus flag described above). A blank is used as the padding character unless **width** begins with a zero. In that case, zero padding is performed. Note that **width** specifies the

fprintf, printf, sprintf

minimum field width, and it will not cause lengthy output to be truncated. Use the `precision` specifier for that purpose.

If you do not want to specify the field width as a constant in the format string, you can code it as an asterisk (*), with or without a leading zero. The asterisk indicates that the width value is an integer in the argument list. See the examples for more information on this technique.

Precision

The meaning of the `precision` item depends on the field type, as follows:

Type c
> The precision item is ignored.

Types d, o, u, x, and X
> The precision is the minimum number of digits to appear. If fewer digits are generated, leading zeros are supplied.

Types e, E, and f
> The precision is the number of digits to appear after the decimal point. If fewer digits are generated, trailing zeros are supplied.

Types g and G
> The precision is the maximum number of significant digits.

Type s
> The precision is the maximum number of characters to be copied from the string.

As with the width item, you can use an asterisk (*) for the precision to indicate that the value should be picked up from the next argument.

Conversion Type

The conversion type can be any of the following:

- c Single character conversion
  The associated argument must be an integer. The single character in the rightmost byte of the integer is copied to the output.

- d Decimal integer conversion
  The associated argument must be an integer, and the result is a string of digit characters preceded by a sign. If the plus and blank flags are absent, the sign is produced only for a negative integer. If the large size modifier l is present, the argument is taken as a long integer.

- e Double conversion ±d.dde-ddd
  The associated argument must be a double, and the result has the form

  ±d.dde-ddd

fprintf, printf, sprintf

where **d** is a single decimal digit, **dd** is one or more digits, and **ddd** is an exponent of exactly three digits. The first minus sign is omitted if the floating point number is positive and the second minus sign is omitted if the exponent is positive.

The plus and blank flags dictate whether there will be a sign character omitted if the number is positive. The large size modifier **l** is ignored.

E   Double conversion ±d.ddE-ddd
This is exactly the same as type **e** except that the result has the form

     ±d.ddE-ddd

f   Double conversion ±dd.dd
The associated argument must be a double, and the result has the form

     ±dd.dd

where **dd** indicates one or more decimal digits. The minus sign is omitted if the number is positive, but a sign character will still be generated if the plus or blank flag is present.

The number of digits before the decimal point depends on the magnitude of the number, and the number after the decimal point depends on the requested precision. If no precision is specified, the default is six decimal places. If the precision is specified as 0 or if all digits to the right of the decimal point are zero, then the decimal point is omitted.

g   Double conversion, general form
The associated argument must be a double, and the result is in the **e** or **f** format, depending on which gives the most compact result. The **e** format is used only when the exponent is less than -4 or greater than the specified or default precision. Trailing zeros are eliminated, and the decimal point appears only if any nonzero digits follow it.

G   Double conversion, general form
This is identical to the **g** format, except that the **E** type is used instead of **e**.

o   Octal integer conversion
The associated argument is taken as an unsigned integer, and it is converted to a string of octal digits. If the large size modifier **l** is present, the argument must be a long integer.

p   Pointer conversion
The associated argument is taken as a data pointer and is converted to hexadecimal representation. The pointer is presented as four hexadecimal digits with leading zeros if

fprintf, printf, sprintf

necessary. 0x is placed in front of the output if the # flag is present.

p   Pointer conversion
This is the same as the **p** format except that uppercase letters are used as hexadecimal digits.

s   String conversion
The associated argument must point to a null-terminated character string. The string is copied to the output, but the null character is not copied.

u   Unsigned decimal integer conversion
The associated argument is taken as an unsigned integer and is converted to a string of decimal digits. If the large size modifier (**l**) is present, the argument must be a long integer.

x   Hexadecimal integer conversion
The associated argument is taken as an unsigned integer and is converted to a string of hexadecimal digits with lowercase letters. If the large size modifier (**l**) is present, the argument is taken as a long integer.

X   Hexadecimal integer conversion
This is the same as the **x** format, except that uppercase letters are used for hexadecimal digits.

RETURN VALUES

Each function returns the number of output characters generated. For **sprintf**, this number does not include the terminating null character ('\0').

EXAMPLES

```
/* This example uses fprintf to write output to a file. */

#include <stdio.h>

main()
{
FILE *output;
int i, places;
double sum;

i = 27;

places = 5;

sum = 47.3284;

output = fopen("MYOUT","w");

fprintf(output, "iterations = %d, sum = %.*g\n",i, places, sum);

fclose(output);
}
```

fprintf, printf, sprintf

```c
/*
 * This program demonstrates printf, which writes
 * formatted output to the screen.
 */

#include <stdio.h>

main()
{
int id = 5409;
double score = 98.5;

printf("id = %d, score = %.1f%%\n", id, score);
}


/*
 * This program demonstrates the functions
 * sprintf and sscanf. The format of a name
 * is changed from "first, middle, last" to
 * "last, first, middle." Then "last, first,
 * middle" is written to the string lfm_name.
 */

#include <stdio.h>

main()
{
char first[30], middle[30], last[30];
char *fml_name;
char lfm_name[91];

fml_name = "Joan Q. Public";

sscanf(fml_name, "%s %s %s", first, middle, last);

printf ("%s %s %s\n", first, middle, last);

if (!*last) {
   strcpy(last,middle);
   *middle = '\0';
   }

sprintf(lfm_name,"%s %s %s", last, first, middle);

printf ("%s\n", lfm_name);
}
```

fputc

fputc - Write a character to a standard I/O file   **Class: ANSI**

NAME
    fputc   Write a character to a standard I/O file.

SYNOPSIS
```
#include <stdio.h>

int fputc(c,fp);

int c;        character to be output
FILE *fp;     file pointer
```

DESCRIPTION

The **fputc** function writes a single character (**c**) into the standard I/O file addressed by **fp** and returns the character as a value of type **int**. The file must be opened for output. Successive calls to **fputc** write the given characters sequentially to the output file.

RETURN VALUE

If successful, **fputc** writes the given character. An end-of-file (EOF) is written if an error occurs.

For disk files, an EOF return usually means that the disk is full. However, this type of return can also occur if the device is write protected or if a write error occurs. In any case, additional error information can be found in **errno**.

SEE ALSO

    fopen, perror, putc, putchar

EXAMPLE

```
/*
 * This program opens MYFILE for reading and YOURFILE for
 * writing.  Characters are read from MYFILE and written to
 * YOURFILE.
 */

#include <stdio.h>

main()
{
int c;
FILE *m, *y;

if ((m = fopen("MYFILE", "r")) == NULL) {
   fprintf(stderr, "Open failure on MYFILE\n");
   exit(1);
   }
```

fputc

```
      if (( y = fopen("YOURFILE", "w"))  == NULL) {
         fprintf(stderr, "Open failure on YOURFILE\n");
         exit(1);
         }

      while ((c = fgetc(m)) != EOF)
         if (fputc(c, y) == EOF)
            break;

      fclose(m);
      }
```

fputs

fputs - Write a string to a standard I/O file   **Class: ANSI**

NAME
    `fputs`   Write a string to a standard I/O file.

SYNOPSIS
```
#include <stdio.h>

int fputs(str,fp);

char *str;      string pointer
FILE *fp;       file pointer
```

DESCRIPTION

The `fputs` function writes all the characters of a null-terminated string (pointed to by `str`), except for its null-terminated character ('\0'), to the specified standard I/O file. The file must already be open for output.

If the output file has a buffer, the characters are saved in memory and then sent to the file in blocks. If the file is unbuffered, the characters are sent there immediately.

RETURN VALUE

If successful, this function returns zero. If an error occurs, the return value is -1. Additional error information can be found in `errno`.

SEE ALSO

    `ferror`, `fopen`, `fputc`, `perror`, `puts`

EXAMPLE

```
/*
 * This example writes the following two lines to stdout:
 * Esse quam videri.
 * To be rather than to seem.
 */

#include <stdio.h>

main ()
{
fputs("Esse quam videri.", stdout);
fputs("To be rather than to seem.", stdout);
}
```

fread

fread - Read blocks from a standard I/O file   Class: ANSI

NAME
fread   Read blocks from a standard I/O file.

SYNOPSIS
```
#include <stdio.h>

size_t fread(blk,bsize,n,fp);

void *blk;       pointer to first block
size_t bsize;    size of block in bytes
size_t n;        maximum number of blocks
FILE *fp;        file pointer
```

DESCRIPTION
The `fread` function reads blocks of data from the standard I/O file addressed by `fp`. Although this function can be used to read characters, it is oriented toward binary I/O. The pointer `blk` points to the first item in the buffer. It is described as `void *`, although it is usually a pointer to some other sort of data that have been converted to `void *` via a cast.

Each block contains `bsize` bytes of type `size_t`; `size_t` is the unsigned integral result of the `sizeof` operator.

Up to `n` blocks are stored into contiguous memory locations beginning at location `blk`. Blocks are read until `n` have been stored, an error has occurred, or the end-of-file (EOF) is reached. If `n` is less than 1, no input is done and the buffer is left unmodified. If the EOF is reached in the middle of a block, that partial block will be stored in the `blk` array, but it will not be included in the function return value. In other words, the return value indicates the number of complete blocks that were read.

RETURN VALUE
The function returns the number of complete blocks that were read. If an error occurs while reading, the file position is unpredictable; you can read or set the position using `fseek`, `ftell`, or `rewind`.

If `fread` returns 0, an error or an EOF could have occurred; use the `ferror` or `feof` functions to tell which situation it is.

SEE ALSO
`fclose`, `feof`, `ferror`, `fgetc`, `fopen`, `fputc`, `fseek`, `fwrite`

fread

EXAMPLE

```c
/* This program demonstrates the function fread, which reads blocks
   from a standard I/O file. */

#include <stdio.h>

main()
{
FILE *inf, *outf;
int data[100];
size_t count;

if ( (inf=fopen("FILEREAD", "r")) == NULL ) {
   fprintf(stderr, "Can't open FILEREAD\n");
   exit(1);
   }

if ( (outf=fopen("FILEWRITE", "w")) == NULL ) {
   fprintf(stderr, "Can't open FILEWRITE\n");
   exit(1);
   }

while ( !ferror(inf) && !ferror(outf) ) {

   /* Test for error. */
   /* Read items from FILEREAD and store the */
   /* number of items read in count. */

   count = fread((void*)data, sizeof(data[0]), (size_t)100, inf);

   if (count == (size_t)0)
      break;

   /* Write items to FILEWRITE and store the  */
   /* number of items written in count. */

   count = fwrite((void*)data, sizeof(data[0]), count, outf);

   if (count < (size_t)100)
      break;
   }

fclose(inf);

fclose(outf);
}
```

free - Free a block of memory

Class: ANSI

NAME
free — Free a block of memory.

SYNOPSIS
```
#include <stdlib.h>

void free(blk);

void *blk;      block pointer
```

DESCRIPTION
The `free` function releases a block of memory (pointed to by `blk`) that was previously obtained using `calloc`, `malloc`, or `realloc`. The block is not actually returned to the free space pool until the next time you call `calloc`, `malloc`, `realloc`, or `free`; until that time, the memory block's contents are left undisturbed.

If the next call is to the `realloc` function and the block being reallocated is the one that was just freed, `realloc` proceeds correctly. In other words, you can ask `realloc` to reallocate a block that was freed as long as you have not called `calloc`, `malloc`, or `realloc` in the meantime.

RETURN VALUE
This function has no return value.

SEE ALSO
`calloc`, `malloc`, `perror`, `realloc`

EXAMPLE
See the example under the `malloc` function.

freopen

freopen - Reopen a standard I/O file   Class: ANSI

NAME
    freopen   Reopen a standard I/O file.

SYNOPSIS

```
#include <stdio.h>

FILE *freopen(name, mode, fp);

char *name;      file name
char *mode;      access mode
FILE *fp;        current file pointer
```

DESCRIPTION

The `freopen` function reopens a standard I/O file pointed to by `fp`. It attaches a new file to a previously-used file pointer. The previous file is automatically closed before the file pointer is reused. The `name` and `mode` arguments are the same as those for `fopen`.

RETURN VALUE

If the file is reopened successfully, a pointer is returned to it. If not, a NULL is returned. Check the return code for NULL because the same errors as defined for `fopen` may occur.

CAUTION

For complete portability, do not assume that the returned file pointer (`fpr`) and `fp` are identical because this is not true on all systems and all compilers. In other words, use `fpr` to access the reopened file, not `fp`.

SEE ALSO

    fopen

EXAMPLE

```
/* This example uses freopen to reopen stdin for reading. */

#include <stdio.h>
main()
{
FILE *yf;
int c;
yf = fopen("YOURFILE","w");        /* Open YOURFILE for write. */
freopen("MYFILE","r",stdin);       /* Reopen stdin.            */
while((c = getchar()) != EOF)      /* Read character from MYFILE. */
    fputc(c, yf);                  /* Copy character to YOURFILE. */
}
```

frexp

frexp - Split a float into a fraction and exponent **Class: ANSI**

NAME
      `frexp`   Split a float into a fraction and exponent.

SYNOPSIS

```
#include <math.h>

double frexp(v,xp);

double v;      value
int *xp;       exponent pointer
```

DESCRIPTION

      The `frexp` function separates a floating-point value `v` into a fraction and an integer exponent of 2.

RETURN VALUE

      This function returns a `double` whose absolute value is equal to or greater than 0.5 and less than 1.0 or zero. The exponent of 2 is stored in the location addressed by `xp`; its absolute value must be less than 1024. If `v` is zero, the return value and `xp` will both be zero.

SEE ALSO

      `fmod, ldexp, modf`

EXAMPLE

```
/* This example uses frexp and ldexp. */

#include <math.h>
#include <stdio.h>

main()
{
double f, v, q;
int x, *xp = &x;

q = 0.0;
v = 234.6;

    /* Split floating-point value V. */
f = frexp(v, xp);
printf("X is %d and F is %lf\n", x, f);
    /* Perform the reverse operation. Q = V now. */
q = ldexp(f, x);
printf("Q is %f\n",q);
}
```

fscanf, scanf, sscanf

fscanf, scanf, sscanf - Read formatted input　　　　　　　　**Class: ANSI**

NAME
- **fscanf**　　Read formatted data from a standard I/O file.
- **scanf**　　Read formatted data from the standard input file.
- **sscanf**　　Read formatted data from a string.

SYNOPSIS

```
#include <stdio.h>

int fscanf(fp,fmt,arg1,arg2,...);
int scanf(fmt,arg1,arg2,...);
int sscanf(ss,fmt,arg1,arg2,...);

FILE *fp;      file pointer (fscanf only)
char *ss;      input string (sscanf only)
char *fmt;     format string
void *argx;    pointers to input data areas
```

DESCRIPTION

These functions perform formatted input conversions on text obtained from a specified standard I/O file, the standard input file (**stdin**), or a specified character string.

For **fscanf**, input characters are read from the standard I/O file addressed by **fp**. The input data are then checked against the format string that **fmt** points to.

For **scanf**, input characters are read from the standard input file **stdin**. The input data are then checked against the format string that **fmt** points to.

For **sscanf**, input characters are read from the string addressed by **ss**. The input data are then checked against the format string that **fmt** points to.

In each of these functions, the format string **fmt** may contain any of the following:

White space
: Any number of spaces, horizontal tabs, or newline characters cause input to be read up to the next character that is not white space.

Ordinary characters
: Any character that is not white space and is not the percent sign (%) must match the next input character. Use two percent signs (%%) in the format string to match a single percent sign in the input. If there is not an exact match, scanning stops and the function returns.

Conversion specification
: This is a multi-character sequence that indicates how the next input characters are to be converted. The form is

    ```
    "%*nlt"
    ```

fscanf, scanf, sscanf

where the various fields are defined as follows:

% A percent sign introduces a conversion specifier. If you want to match a percent sign in the input, use two percent signs (%%) in the format string.

* The asterisk is optional. If present, it means that the conversion should be performed, but the result should not be stored. There should be no value pointer in the argument list for a suppressed conversion.

n This is an optional decimal number that specifies the maximum input field width. This is used only with the s (string) format.

l The letter l is optional. If present, it indicates that a long conversion should be performed.

t The t stands for one of the following format characters: c, d, e, f, g, i, n, o, s, u, x. These are described below.

If the conversion is successful and assignment is not suppressed, the result is placed into the corresponding argument. The argument list must contain a pointer to an appropriate data item for each conversion specification that does not suppress assignment.

The function returns the number of conversion values that were assigned. This can be less than the number expected if the input characters do not agree with the format string. If an end-of-file (EOF) is reached before any values are assigned, the return value is EOF.

The format characters listed above specify how the input characters are to be converted. Leading white space is skipped in all cases except the c conversion.

c character
The corresponding argument must point to a character. The next input character is moved to that destination. No white space is skipped.

d decimal number
The corresponding argument must point to an integer or to a long integer. The latter applies if the d is preceded by an l. The input characters should be decimal digits, optionally preceded by a plus or minus sign.

e, f, g floating point
These three types are identical. The corresponding argument must point to a float or a double. The latter applies if the

fscanf, scanf, sscanf

letter is preceded by an l. The input characters must consist of the following sequence:

1. Optional leading white space.
2. An optional plus (+) or minus (−).
3. A sequence of decimal digits.
4. An optional decimal point followed by zero or more decimal digits.
5. An optional exponent, consisting of the letter e or E followed by an optional plus or minus sign and by one or more decimal digits. This general form is shown below, where [...] indicates an optional part:

   [white space][sign]digits[.digits][exponent]

n   character count
No input characters are read. The corresponding argument must point to an integer into which is written the number of input characters read so far.

o   octal number
An octal number is expected. The corresponding argument should point to an integer or to a long integer if the o is preceded by an l.

s   string
A character string is expected. The corresponding argument should point to a character array large enough to hold the string and a terminating null character. The input string is terminated by white space or the end-of-input. Also, if a maximum field width is specified, the output array size should be at least that width plus 1 because the reading of input characters stops at the field width even if no white space has been reached.

u   unsigned number
An unsigned decimal number is expected. The corresponding argument should point to an unsigned integer or to an unsigned long integer if the u is preceded by an l.

x   hexadecimal number
A hexadecimal number is expected. The corresponding argument should point to an integer or to a long integer if the x is preceded by an l. The hexadecimal number can begin with the characters 0x or 0X, and case is not significant for the hexadecimal letters.

RETURN VALUE

These functions return the number of assignments that were made. For example, a return value of 3 indicates that conversion results were assigned to `arg1`, `arg2`, and `arg3`.

fscanf, scanf, sscanf

CAUTION

All of the result arguments (`arg1`, `arg2`, and so on) must be pointers. Also, you should not supply a pointer for any conversion specification that uses the * to suppress assignment.

EXAMPLES

```
/* This program reads a floating point number and a "unit name." */

#include <stdio.h>

main ()
{
float amount;
char unit[8];
FILE *inf;

inf=fopen("IN_FILE", "r");

fscanf(inf,"%f %s", &amount, &unit);

printf("%f %s\n", amount, unit);
}


/*
 * This program reads a number of type
 * integer and a name (char) type to demonstrate
 * the function scanf.
 */

#include <stdio.h>

main()
{
int account;
char *name;

printf("Please specify account number and name\n");

scanf("%d %s", &account, name);

printf("%d %s\n", account, name);
}
```

See also the example using `sscanf` under the `fprintf` function.

fseek, ftell

fseek, ftell - Set or read a standard I/O file position   **Class: ANSI**

NAME

       `fseek`   Set a standard I/O file position.
       `ftell`   Read a standard I/O file position.

SYNOPSIS

```
#include <stdio.h>

int fseek(fp,rpos,mode);
long ftell(fp);

FILE *fp;       file pointer
long rpos;      relative file position
int mode;       seek mode
```

DESCRIPTION

The `fseek` function moves the byte cursor of a standard I/O file to a new position. The new position determines the place in the file where the next input or output operation will occur. This repositioning is sometimes referred to as random access.

The file pointed to by `fp` must be open for input or output.

The arguments `rpos` and `mode` determine the new file position. The `ftell` function returns the value of `rpos`. The argument `mode` must be one of the following values:

    0   The (signed) `rpos` argument is the number of bytes from the beginning of the file. This value must be positive.

    1   The (signed) `rpos` argument is the number of bytes relative to the current position. This value can be positive or negative.

    2   The (signed) `rpos` argument is the number of bytes relative to the end of the file. This value must be negative or zero.

When a file is opened for both input and output, the call `fseek(f, 0L, 1)` can be used to switch between reading and writing without changing the file position.

The `fseek` function clears the end-of-file indicator (EOF) and undoes any effects of the `ungetc` function; that is, it erases all memory of pushed-back characters from the file. After a call to `fseek`, the next operation on a file opened for writing can be either input or output.

The `ftell` function returns a long value that is the current byte position in the file, relative to the file's beginning. The standard file must already be open for input or output. The position returned by `ftell` can be passed to `fseek` to restore the file position at the time of the call to `ftell`.

fseek, ftell

RETURN VALUE

If successful, these functions return zero. If an error occurs, `fseek` returns a value of −1 and `ftell` returns a value of −1L. In either case, `errno` contains additional error information.

SEE ALSO

`fopen, perror, rewind, ungetc`

EXAMPLE

```
/* This example demonstrates the fseek function. */

#include <stdio.h>

main()
{
FILE *fp;
int error, c;

   /* Open the file and read the first character. */

fp = fopen("myfile","r");

c = fgetc(fp);

printf("%c",c);

   /* Move the position four units
      relative to the current position. */

error = fseek(fp, 4, 1);

   /* Read the 6th character in the file. */

c = fgetc(fp);

printf("%c",c);

fclose(fp);
}
```

fwrite

fwrite - Write blocks of data to a standard file Class: ANSI

NAME
fwrite   Write blocks of data to a standard file.

SYNOPSIS
```
#include <stdio.h>

size_t fwrite(blk,bsize,n,fp);
```

`void *blk;`	pointer to first block
`size_t bsize;`	size of block in bytes
`size_t n;`	maximum number of blocks
`FILE *fp;`	file pointer

DESCRIPTION
The `fwrite` function writes blocks of data to the standard I/O file addressed by `fp`. Although this function can be used to write characters, it is oriented toward binary I/O. The argument `blk` is a pointer to the first item to be written. It is described above as `void *`, although it is usually a pointer to some other sort of data that have been converted to `void *` via a cast.

Each block contains `bsize` bytes of type `size_t`; `size_t` is the unsigned integral result of the `sizeof` operator.

Up to n blocks are stored into contiguous memory locations beginning at location `blk`. If n is less than 1, no output is written. Blocks are written until n has been sent or until the output file cannot accept any more. If the output file becomes full in the middle of a block, a partial block will be written, but it will not be included in the function return value. In other words, the return value indicates the number of complete blocks that were written.

The parameter `fp` is a pointer to the input file. Calls to `fwrite` frequently have the following form:

```
fwrite((void *)&X,sizeof(X) ...);
```

RETURN VALUE
The function returns the number of complete blocks that were written. If an error or end-of-file occurs, `fwrite` returns zero and the buffer is not modified. If an error occurs while writing, the file position is unpredictable; see the `ftell`, `fseek`, and `rewind` functions to read or set the file position.

SEE ALSO
`fclose, feof, ferror, fgetc, fopen, fputc, fread, fseek`

EXAMPLE
See the example under the `fread` function.

getc, getchar

getc, getchar - Read a character   **Class: ANSI**

NAME

    `getc`   Read a character from a standard file.
    `getchar`   Read a character from the standard input file, stdin.

SYNOPSIS

```
#include <stdio.h>

int getc(fp);
int getchar();

FILE *fp;     file pointer
```

DESCRIPTION

The `getc` macro reads the next single character from the standard I/O file addressed by `fp`. The `getchar` macro reads the next single character from the standard input file, `stdin`. These are implemented as macros in order to maximize execution speed.

RETURN VALUE

These macros return the next input character or end-of-file (EOF) if no character could be read.

In the event of an EOF return, error information can be found in `errno`. Most programmers treat any EOF return as an indication of EOF. However, if you want to distinguish errors from EOF, you should reset `errno` before calling the function, and then analyze its contents when you receive an EOF return.

SEE ALSO

`fgetc`, `fgetchar`, `fopen`, `perror`

EXAMPLES

```
/*
 * This program copies one file to another using the
 * functions getc and putc.
 */

#include <stdio.h>

main()
{
FILE *inf, *outf;
int c;

inf = fopen("COPYME", "r");

outf = fopen("HERE", "w");
```

getc, getchar

```
   if (inf == NULL)
     printf ("Couldn't open file for reading.\n");
   else {

     if (outf == NULL)
       printf ("Could not open file for writing.\n");
     else {
       while ((c=getc(inf)) != EOF)
         putc(c, outf);
       printf ("File has been copied.\n");
       }
     }
   }


/*
 * This program reads a character from standard input and writes
 * the character to standard output.
 */

#include <stdio.h>

main()
{
int c;

while ((c = getchar()) != EOF)
  putchar(c);
}
```

gets

gets - Read a string from stdin   **Class: ANSI**

NAME

gets   Read a string from the standard input file, stdin.

SYNOPSIS

```
#include <stdio.h>

char *gets(buffer);

char *buffer;      buffer pointer
```

DESCRIPTION

The `gets` function reads a line of characters from the standard input file, `stdin`, until a newline or end-of-file is reached. The argument `buffer` points to the beginning of the line of characters. The newline is not read into the buffer and a null character ('\0') is put there in its place.

CAUTION

You should make sure that your `gets` buffer can hold the largest line that it will encounter while reading `stdin` because the function does not check for a maximum length. In the Student compiler, the maximum is 127 characters for `stdin`.

RETURN VALUE

This function returns the `buffer` argument unless an end-of-file or an I/O error occurs, in which case a NULL pointer is returned. If an error occurs while reading, the buffer may be left unmodified, partially modified, or filled with invalid data.

SEE ALSO

`feof`, `ferror`, `fgetc`, `fgets`, `fopen`, `getc`, `perror`

gets

EXAMPLE

```
/* This example uses gets to read a string from the screen. */

#include <stdio.h>
#define  MAXLINE 128

main()
{
char line [MAXLINE];

for (;;){

   /* Type up to MAXLINE characters. */

   printf("Enter a line of data (up to %d characters)\n",
          MAXLINE);

   /* Read data into string from stdin. */

   if(gets(line) != NULL){

      /* Write string to stdout, check for error. */

      if(puts(line) == EOF) break;}
      }
   else break;
   }
}
```

gmtime

gmtime - Separate GMT into its components   **Class: ANSI**

NAME
    `gmtime`   Separate Greenwich Mean Time into its components.

SYNOPSIS
```
#include <time.h>

struct tm *gmtime(t);

time_t *t;    pointer to time value
```

DESCRIPTION

The **gmtime** function coverts a `time_t` value (pointed to by `t`) into Greenwich Mean Time (GMT), separating it into its components. The time value represents the number of seconds since 00:00:00, January 1, 1970, GMT, without adjustment for local time zones.

RETURN VALUE

This function returns a pointer to `struct tm` that contains the results of the conversion, that is, the broken down GMT value. The `struct tm` structure is defined as follows:

```
struct tm
    {
    int tm_sec;    /* seconds after the minute (0-59) */
    int tm_min;    /* minutes after the hour (0-59)   */
    int tm_hour;   /* hours since midnight (0-23)     */
    int tm_mday;   /* day of the month (1-31)         */
    int tm_mon;    /* month of the year (0-11)        */
    int tm_year;   /* years since 1900                */
    int tm_wday;   /* days since Sunday (0-6)         */
    int tm_yday;   /* day of the year (0-365)         */
    int tm_isdst;  /* Is it daylight savings time?    */
    }
```

CAUTION

Note that this function expects a pointer as the argument. A common error is to pass the actual time value instead of the pointer.

The pointer returned by the function refers to `static` storage that is shared by `asctime`, `ctime`, `gmtime`, and `localtime`; a call to one of these functions will overwrite the results of a previous call.

SEE ALSO
    `asctime, ctime, localtime, time`

gmtime

EXAMPLE

```
#include <time.h>
main()
{
struct tm *p;
time_t t;
time(&t);
p = gmtime(&t);
printf("GMT is %s\n",asctime(p));
}
```

int86, intdos

int86, intdos - Generate an interrupt   Class: MS-DOS

NAME
```
        int86           Generate an interrupt.
        int86s          Generate an interrupt (segments in/out).
        int86x          Generate an interrupt (segments in).
        intdos          Generate a DOS interrupt.
        intdoss         Generate a DOS interrupt (segments in/out).
        intdosx         Generate a DOS interrupt (segments in).
```

SYNOPSIS
```
        #include <dos.h>

        int int86(intnum,in,out);
        int int86s(intnum,sin,sout);
        int int86x(intnum,in,out,segs);

        int intdos(in,out);
        int intdoss(sin,sout);
        int intdosx(in,out,segs);

        int intnum;              interrupt number

        struct REGS *in;         input registers without segments
        struct REGS *out;        output registers without segments
        struct SREGS *segs;      input segment registers

        union REGSS *sin;        input registers with segments
        union REGSS *sout;       output registers with segments
```

DESCRIPTION

These functions generate iAPX86 software interrupts. For those functions beginning with `int86`, specify the interrupt number; for functions in the `intdos` set, use interrupt 0x21. In either case, the operation is as follows:

1. The current machine register contents are saved, as required by the assembly language interface. Specifically, the segment registers saved are the base pointer (BP), data segment (DS), and extra segment (ES).

2. All the machine registers are loaded from the specified input structure, except for BP, CS, SS, and SP, which retain their current operational values. The interrupt routines will preserve the values of these four registers.

3. An interrupt number (`intnum`) generates the specified interrupt. The interrupt routine is expected to return to the next instruction indicated by the stack pointer, as the stack pointer was at the time of the call. You cannot use the `int86` functions to invoke interrupts that do not follow this convention, such as the MS-DOS interrupts 0x25 and 0x26.

int86, intdos

4. When the interrupt returns, the machine registers are saved in the specified output structure. Again, the contents of BP, CS, SS, and SP are not passed back in the output structure.

5. The original machine register contents are restored.

6. The machine flags returned by the interrupt are passed back as the function return value.

The various register storage structures are defined in `dos.h` as follows:

```
struct XREG /* 16-bit registers, no segs */
   {
   short ax,bx,cx,dx,si,di;
   };

struct XREGS /* 16-bit registers, with segs */
   {
   short ax,bx,cx,dx,si,di,ds,es;
   };

struct HREG /* 8-bit registers */
   {
   byte al,ah,bl,bh,cl,ch,dl,dh;
   };

struct SREGS /* segment registers */
   {
   short es,cs,ss,ds;
   };

union REGS
   {
   struct XREG x;
   struct HREG h;
   };

union REGSS
   {
   struct XREGS x;
   struct HREG h;
   };
```

Note that `int86` and `intdos` do not change the contents of the segment registers before generating the interrupt, nor do they pass back the values returned in the segment registers by the interrupt.

You can use `int86x` and `intdosx` for cases where the interrupt routine needs different DS and ES segment register values from those normally placed there by the run-time support system. These functions load the DS and ES registers from the `segs` structure before generating the interrupt, but they do not pass back the values placed in these registers by the interrupt routine.

int86, intdos

Finally, for the most general cases you should use `int86s` and `intdoss` because they pass and return all registers that the interrupt might use for its input and output values, including the DS and ES registers.

RETURN VALUE

Each function returns the processor status flags that were passed back by the interrupt routine. Bit 0 is the carry flag (CF), which is used by many MS-DOS interrupt routines to indicate that an error has occurred. A complete description of the other processor status flags can be found in *The iAPX86 Programmer's Reference Manual*; see References in Part III of this book.

CAUTION

Because MS-DOS and iAPX86 do not provide a protected operating environment, you can easily cause a system crash by passing invalid data to an interrupt routine. Therefore, you should be thoroughly familiar with IBM's *Disk Operating System Technical Reference* before using any of these functions.

isalnum, isalpha

isalnum, isalpha - Test for an alpha character   Class: ANSI

NAME
    `isalnum`   Test for an alphanumeric character.
    `isalpha`   Test for an alphabetic character.

SYNOPSIS
```
#include <ctype.h>

int isalnum(c);
int isalpha(c);

int c;    character to test
```

DESCRIPTION
The `isalnum` macro tests an integer value c to determine if it is an alphabetic (upper- or lowercase) or numeric character. The `isalpha` macro tests an integer value c to determine if it is an alphabetic (upper- or lowercase) character.

RETURN VALUES
These macros return zero if the character does not meet the test (for example, if the character is not alphabetic) and a nonzero value if it does. If the argument is EOF, zero is returned.

CAUTION
You can use either characters or integers as arguments, but the macros are defined only over the integer range -1 to 255.

The -1 is included as a valid argument to avoid a nonsense result if you give the end-of-file (EOF) value to one of the macros. EOF can be returned by `getchar` and other I/O functions; if you pass it to any of the character test macros, the resulting truth value is zero.

SEE ALSO
    `getchar`

EXAMPLE
```
#include <stdio.h>
#include <ctype.h>

main()
{
int c;

while((c = getchar()) != EOF)
  printf("\n%c %s alpha.\n",c,
     isalpha(c) ? "is" : "is not");
}
```

iscntrl - Test for a control character   Class: ANSI

NAME
    `iscntrl`   Test for a control character.

SYNOPSIS
```
#include <ctype.h>

int iscntrl(c);

int c;    character to test
```

DESCRIPTION
The `iscntrl` macro tests an integer value `c` to determine if it is a control character. In the standard ASCII 128-character set, the control characters are those with decimal codes between 0 through 31 (hex 0x00 through 0x1F), plus code 127 (hex 0x7F).

RETURN VALUE
This macro returns a nonzero value if it is a control character and a zero if it is not. If the argument is EOF, zero is returned.

CAUTION
You can use either characters or integers as arguments, but the macro is defined only over the integer range -1 to 255.

The -1 is included as a valid argument to avoid a nonsense result if you give the end-of-file (EOF) value to this macro. EOF can be returned by `getchar` and other I/O; if you pass it to `iscntrl`, the resulting truth value is zero.

EXAMPLE
```
/* Test for a control character using the iscntrl function. */

#include <stdio.h>
#include <ctype.h>

main()
{
int c, n;

for (n=1; n<=5; n=n+1){
   c=getchar();
   printf("\n%c is a control character\n",c,
          iscntrl(c) ? "is" : "is not");
   getchar();     /* Read the return character. */
   }
}
```

isdigit, isxdigit

isdigit, isxdigit - Test for a decimal or hex digit   Class: ANSI

NAME
    isdigit   Test for a decimal digit.
    isxdigit   Test for a hexadecimal digit.

SYNOPSIS
```
#include <ctype.h>

int isdigit(c);
int isxdigit(c);

int c;     character to test
```

DESCRIPTION
These functions test if an integer value c is a numeric character, either a decimal or hexadecimal digit.

RETURN VALUES
These macros return a nonzero value if the character meets the test (for example, if the character is a digit) or a zero if it does not. If the argument is EOF, zero is returned.

CAUTIONS
You can use either characters or integers as arguments, but the macros are defined only over the integer range −1 to 255.

The −1 is included as a valid argument to avoid a nonsense result if you give the end-of-file (EOF) value to one of the macros. EOF can be returned by `getchar` and other I/O functions; if you pass it to either character test macros, the resulting truth value is zero.

EXAMPLE
```
/* Tests for a decimal digit using the isdigit function. */

#include <stdio.h>
#include <ctype.h>

main()
{
int c, n;

for (n=1; n<=5; n=n+1){
  c=getchar();
  printf("\n%c %s a digit.\n",c,
    isdigit(c) ? "is" : "is not");
  getchar();   /* Read the return character. */
  }
}
```

isgraph

isgraph - Test for a graphics character   Class: ANSI

NAME
    isgraph   Test for a graphics character.

SYNOPSIS
```
#include <ctype.h>

int isgraph(c);

int c;    character to test
```

DESCRIPTION

The `isgraph` macro tests if an integer value `c` is a graphics character. A graphics character is any printable character, including digits and letters, other than a blank space. In the standard ASCII 128-character set, graphics characters are those with decimal codes 33 through 126.

RETURN VALUE

This macro returns a nonzero value if `c` is a graphics character and a zero if it is not. If the argument is EOF, zero is returned.

CAUTION

You can use either characters or integers as arguments, but the macro is defined only over the integer range -1 to 255.

The -1 is included as a valid argument to avoid a nonsense result if you give the end-of-file (EOF) value to this macro. EOF can be returned by `getchar` and other I/O functions; if you pass it to `isgraph`, the resulting truth value is zero.

EXAMPLE

```
/* Test for a graphics char using the isgraph function. */

#include <stdio.h>
#include <ctype.h>

main()
{
int c, n;

for (n=1; n<=5; n=n+1){
   c=getchar();
   printf("\n%c %s a graphics character\n",c,
          isgraph(c) ? "is" : "is not");
   getchar();      /* Read the return character. */
   }
}
```

islower, isupper

islower, isupper - Test for a lower- or uppercase character   **Class: ANSI**

NAME
        `islower`   Test for a lowercase character.
        `isupper`   Test for an uppercase character.

SYNOPSIS
```
#include <ctype.h>

int islower(c);
int isupper(c);

int c;    character to test
```

DESCRIPTION

These macros test if an integer value c is a lowercase or an uppercase character. In the standard ASCII 128-character set, lowercase characters are those with decimal codes 97 through 122, and uppercase codes are 65 through 90.

RETURN VALUES

These macros return a nonzero value if the character meets the test (for example, if the character is uppercase) or a zero if it does not. If the argument is EOF, zero is returned.

CAUTION

You can use either characters or integers as arguments, but the macros are defined only over the integer range -1 to 255.

The -1 is included as a valid argument to avoid a nonsense result if you give the end-of-file (EOF) value to one of the macros. EOF can be returned by `getchar` and other I/O functions; if you pass it to any of the character test macros, the resulting truth value is zero.

SEE ALSO
        `tolower, toupper`

islower, isupper

EXAMPLE

```
/* Test for a lowercase character using the islower function. */

#include <stdio.h>
#include <ctype.h>

main()
{
int c, n;

for (n=1; n<=5; n=n+1){
   c=getchar();
   printf("\n%c %s a lowercase character\n",c,
          islower(c) ? "is" : "is not");
   getchar();      /* Read the return character. */
   }
}
```

isprint

isprint - Test for a printable character Class: ANSI

NAME
isprint   Test for a printable character.

SYNOPSIS
```
#include <ctype.h>

int isprint(c);

int c;     character to test
```

DESCRIPTION
The `isprint` macro tests if an integer value `c` is a printable character. A printable character is any character that prints and is not a control character. In the standard ASCII 128-character set, printable characters are those with decimal codes 32 through 126.

RETURN VALUES
This macro returns a nonzero value if the character is a printable character or a zero if it is not. If the argument is EOF, zero is returned.

CAUTION
You can use either a character or an integer as an argument, but the macro is defined only over the integer range from −1 to 255.

The −1 is included as a valid argument to avoid an invalid result, if you give the end-of-file (EOF) value to the macro. EOF can be returned by `getchar` and other I/O functions; if you pass it to any of the character test macros, the resulting truth value will be zero.

EXAMPLE
```
/* Test for a printable character using the isprint function. */

#include <stdio.h>
#include <ctype.h>

main()
{
int c, n;

for (n=1; n<=5; n=n+1)
  {
  c=getchar();
  printf("\n%c %s a printable character\n",c,
         isprint(c) ? "is" : "is not");
  getchar();     /* Read the return character. */
  }
}
```

ispunct

ispunct - Test for a punctuation character   Class: ANSI

NAME

    ispunct   Test for a punctuation character.

SYNOPSIS

```
#include <ctype.h>

int ispunct(c);

int c;     character to test
```

DESCRIPTION

The `ispunct` macro tests if an integer value `c` is a punctuation character. This includes any character that is not alphanumeric and is not a control character. In the standard ASCII 128-character set, punctuation characters are those with decimal codes 32 through 47, 58 through 64, 91 through 96, and 123 through 126. This list includes the following characters:

```
! " # $ & ' ( ) * + , - . / : ; <

= > ? @ [ \ ] ^ _ ` { | } ~
```

RETURN VALUE

This macro returns a nonzero value if the character is a punctuation character or a zero if it is not. If the argument is EOF, zero is returned.

CAUTION

You can use either a character or an integer as an argument, but the macro is defined only over the integer range from −1 to 255.

The −1 is included as a valid argument to avoid an invalid result, if you give the end-of-file (EOF) value to the macro or function. EOF can be returned by `getchar` and other I/O functions; if you pass it to any of the character test macros, the resulting truth value will be zero.

ispunct

EXAMPLE

```
/* Test for a punctuation character using the ispunct function. */

#include <stdio.h>
#include <ctype.h>

main()
{
int c, n;

for (n=1; n<=5; n=n+1)
  {
  c=getchar();
  printf("\n%c %s a punctuation character\n",c,
         ispunct(c) ? "is" : "is not");
  getchar();     /* Read the return character. */
  }
}
```

isspace

isspace - Test for a white space character　　　　　　　　　　**Class: ANSI**

NAME

    isspace　　　　Test for a white space character.

SYNOPSIS

    #include <ctype.h>

    int isspace(c);

    int c;　　character to test

DESCRIPTION

    The `isspace` macro tests if an integer value `c` is printable white space. The following and their decimal ASCII code are included: a single space (blank, 32), tab (9), newline (line feed, 10), carriage return (13), form feed (12), or vertical tab character (11).

RETURN VALUE

    This macro returns a nonzero value if the character is a space character or a zero if it is not. If the argument is EOF, zero is returned.

CAUTION

    You can use either a character or an integer as an argument, but the macro is defined only over the integer range from −1 to 255.

    The −1 is included as a valid argument to avoid an invalid result, if you give the end-of-file (EOF) value to the macro or function. EOF can be returned by **getchar** and other I/O functions; if you pass it to any of the character test macros, the resulting truth value will be zero.

EXAMPLE

```
/* Test for a space character using the isspace function. */

#include <stdio.h>
#include <ctype.h>

main()
{
int c, n;

for (n=1; n<=5; n=n+1)
  {
  c=getchar();
  printf("\n%c %s a space character\n",c,
         isspace(c) ? "is" : "is not");
  getchar();     /* Read the return character. */
  }
}
```

labs

labs - Long integer absolute value function   **Class: ANSI**

NAME
: labs   Long integer absolute value function.

SYNOPSIS
```
#include <math.h>

long labs(l);

long l;    argument
```

DESCRIPTION

The **labs** function computes the absolute value of a long integer (l).

The most general approach is to use the **abs** macro, which is defined in the **math.h** header file. This macro accepts any data type as its argument and generates in-line code to perform the conversion. The definition is

```
#define abs(x) ((x)<0?-(x):(x))
```

To minimize code size, you can use the **labs** function call instead of the **abs** macro.

RETURN VALUE

The **labs** function returns the absolute value of its argument. Both the result and the argument are of type **long**.

SEE ALSO
: **abs, fabs**

EXAMPLE
```
/* This example uses the labs function. */

#include <math.h>
#include <stdio.h>

main()
{
long al, l;

l = -500000;
al = labs(l);
printf("L is %ld and AL is %ld\n", l, al);
}
```

ldexp - Load an exponent   Class: ANSI

NAME
    `ldexp`   Load an exponent.

SYNOPSIS
```
#include <math.h>

double ldexp(frac,x);

double frac;    fraction
int x;          exponent
```

DESCRIPTION
The `ldexp` function adds the integer `x` to the exponent in `frac`, which is the same as computing

    $v = frac * 2^x$

where `v` is a value of type `double`. Note that if `frac` and `x` are the results of `frexp`, `ldexp` performs the reverse operation, that is, it takes the components parts (from `frexp`) and builds a number of type `double`.

RETURN VALUE
This function returns a double whose value is the result of the above calculation.

SEE ALSO
`fmod`, `frexp`, `modf`

EXAMPLE
```
/* This example uses frexp and ldexp. */

#include <math.h>
#include <stdio.h>

main()
{
double f, v, q;
int x, *xp = &x;

q = 0.0;
v = 234.6;

    /* Split floating point value V. */
f = frexp(v, xp);
printf("X is %d and F is %lf\n", x, f);
    /* Perform the reverse operation. Q = V now. */
q = ldexp(f, x);
printf("Q is %f\n",q);
}
```

localtime

localtime - Separate local time into its components Class: ANSI

NAME
localtime   Separate local time into its components.

SYNOPSIS
```
#include <time.h>

struct tm *localtime(t);

time_t *t;      pointer to time value
```

DESCRIPTION
The `localtime` function converts a `time_t` value (pointed to by `t`) into local time, separating it into its components. The time value represents the number of seconds since 00:00:00, January 1, 1970, Greenwich Mean Time, with adjustment for the local time zone.

RETURN VALUE
This function returns a pointer to `struct tm` that contains the results of the conversion, that is, the broken down local time value. See the header file `time.h` for a listing of the components in `struct tm`.

CAUTIONS
Note that this function expects a pointer as the argument. A common error is to pass the actual time value instead of the pointer.

The pointer returned by the function refers to `static` storage that is shared by `asctime`, `ctime`, `gmtime`, and `localtime`; a call to one of these functions will overwrite the results of a previous call.

SEE ALSO
asctime, ctime, gmtime, time

localtime

EXAMPLE
```
/*
 * Converts time to local time using the localtime function.
 * The local time is then printed using the asctime function.
 */

#include <stdio.h>
#include <time.h>

main()
{
struct tm *p;
time_t t;

time(&t);
p = localtime(&t);
printf("The local time is %s\n", asctime(p));
}
```

log, log10

log, log10 - Compute a logarithm   **Class: ANSI**

NAME
    `log`   Compute a natural logarithm.
    `log10`   Compute a common logarithm.

SYNOPSIS
```
#include <math.h>

double log(x);
double log10(x);

double x;     argument
```

DESCRIPTION
The `log` function computes the natural logarithm of its argument `x`, which must be a positive double-precision, floating-point number. The natural logarithm is the inverse of the exponential function, `exp`.

The `log10` function computes the common (base 10) logarithm of its argument `x`, which must be a positive double-precision, floating-point number.

RETURN VALUE
The `log` function returns the natural log of `x` as type `double`. The `log10` function returns the common log of `x` as type `double`.

If `x` is less than or equal to zero, the function returns the smallest floating point number, which is the negative of `HUGE_VAL`, and the `errno` parameter is set to `EDOM`.

SEE ALSO
    `exp`

EXAMPLE
```
/* This example demonstrates both the log and the log10 functions. */

#include <stdio.h>
#include <math.h>

main()
{
double r, x;

x = 2.0;
r = log(x);
printf("Log result is: %f\n");
r = log10(x);
printf("Log10 result is: %f\n");
}
```

malloc

malloc - Allocate memory   Class: ANSI

NAME

    `malloc`   Allocate memory.

SYNOPSIS

```
#include <stdlib.h>

void *malloc(esize);

size_t esize;     element size
```

DESCRIPTION

The `malloc` function allocates a block of dynamic memory of the size requested by `esize`. The block is not initialized in any particular way, so you should assume it is filled with invalid data. The memory block is suitably aligned for the storage of any type of data.

RETURN VALUE

If successful, `malloc` returns a pointer to the first element in the block of memory allocated. If the block cannot be allocated, `malloc` returns a NULL pointer.

SEE ALSO

    `calloc, free, realloc`

EXAMPLES

```
/*
 * This program builds linked lists of text strings obtained from
 * the standard input file.
 */

#include <stdio.h>
#include <stdlib.h>

    /*
     * These elements are linked together to form
     * the text string list.
     */

struct LIST{
    struct LIST *next;   /* forward linkage */
    char text[2];        /* minimum text string */
 };

    /* Main program. */
main()
{
struct LIST *p,*q,*list = NULL;
char b[256];
size_t x;
```

malloc

```c
      /* Build the list. */
   while(1){
      printf("\nBegin new group...\n");
      for(q = (struct LIST *)(&list);;q = p){
         printf("Enter a text string: ");
         if(gets(b) == NULL) break;
         if(b[0] == '\0') break;
         x = sizeof(struct LIST) - (size_t)2 + strlen(b) + (size_t)1;
         p = (struct LIST *) malloc(x);
         if(p == NULL) {
            printf("No more memory\n");
            break;
            }
         p->next = q->next;
         strcpy(p->text,b);
         }

      /* Print list. */
      printf("\n\nTEXT LIST...\n");

      for(p = list; p != NULL; p = p->next){
         printf("%s",p->text);
         free(p);
         }
      }
   }


/* Initialize two arrays using calloc and malloc. */

#include <stdio.h>
#include <stdlib.h>

main()
{
double *carray, *marray;
int r;

   /* Allocate two arrays of 1000 elements. */
carray = (double *) calloc((size_t)1000, sizeof(double));

marray = (double *) malloc((size_t)1000);

   /* Print element from each array. */
printf("Element from carray: %.*f\n",1,carray[0]);

printf("Element from marray: %.*f\n",1,marray[4]);
```

malloc

```
    /* Free a block allocated by calloc. */
r = free((char*) carray);

r = free((char*) marray);
}
```

See also the examples under the **fgets** function.

memory

memory - **Memory block operations**   **Class: ANSI**

NAME
    memchr   Find a character in a memory block.
    memcmp   Compare two memory blocks.
    memcpy   Copy a memory block.
    memset   Set a memory block to a value.

SYNOPSIS
```
#include <string.h>

void *memchr(blk1,c,n);
int   memcmp(blk1,blk2,n);
void *memcpy(dest,source,n);
void *memset(dest,c,n);

char *dest;            destination pointer
char *source;          source pointer
size_t n;              number of bytes
int c;                 character value
char *blk1,*blk2;      block pointers
```

DESCRIPTION

    These functions manipulate blocks of memory in various ways.

    The **memchr** function returns a pointer to the first occurrence of the specified character (**c**) in the initial **n** characters of the memory block addressed by **blk1**. If the character is not found, **memchr** returns a null pointer.

    The **memcmp** function performs a character-by-character comparison of the two memory blocks pointed to by **blk1** and **blk2**. The **n** argument is the number of characters to be compared. A null character ('\0') is treated like any other character. The character comparison is performed using the standard ASCII collating sequence.

    The **memcmp** function returns the following integral values:

    NEGATIVE => first memory block is less than the second.
    POSITIVE => first memory block is greater than the second.
    ZERO   => first memory block equals the second.

    The **memcpy** function copies the number of characters specified by **n** from one area of memory (pointed to by **source**) to another (pointed to by **dest**). All characters, including the null character, are copied. If successful, **memcpy** returns a pointer to **dest**.

    The **memset** function copies the value of **c** into each of the first **n** characters of the memory block (pointed to by **dest**). If successful, **memset** returns a pointer to the **dest** block; if not, it returns a null pointer.

memory

RETURN VALUE

The return values are noted above for most of the functions.

CAUTION

Remember that these functions neither recognize nor produce the null character ('\0') usually found at the end of strings. A common mistake is to assume that `memcpy`, just like `strcpy`, automatically places a null character at the end of the block. It does not.

EXAMPLES

```
/*
 * This program demonstrates the function memchr by locating
 * every "t" in the input string and replacing with the
 * letter "m."
 */

#include <string.h>
#include <stdio.h>

main()
{
static char tmp_str[] = "hat, tan, tom, tingle, toss";
char *stop;

printf ("%s\n", tmp_str);
while (stop = memchr(tmp_str, 't', sizeof(tmp_str))){
  *stop = 'm';
  }
printf ("%s\n", tmp_str);
}

/*
 * This program demonstrates the memcmp function which compares two
 * blocks of memory specified by str1 and str2. If equal, memcmp returns
 * zero. If the first block is less than the second, memcmp returns a
 * negative value. If the first block is greater than zero, memcmp
 * returns a positive value.
 */

#include <string.h>
#include <stdio.h>

main ()
{
struct large{
  int month;
  int day;
  int year;
  };
struct large day1, day2, *first, *second;
```

memory

```c
        day1.month = 7;
        day1.day = 10;
        day1.year = 1987;
        day2.month = 7;
        day2.day = 11;
        day2.year = 1987;

        first = &day1;
        second = &day2;
        if (memcmp((char *) first,(char *) second,
              sizeof(struct large)))
           puts("structures not equal\n");
        }


/* This program demonstrates the memcpy function which copies
 * a specified number of characters from one area of memory to
 * another.  The function returns a pointer to the area copied "to."
 */

#include <string.h>
#include <stdio.h>

main ()
{
struct large{
  int month;
  int day;
  int year;
  };
static struct large day1 = {7,10,1987};
static struct large day2 = {7,11,1987};
struct large *first = &day1;
struct large *second = &day2;
memcpy((char *) first,(char *) second, sizeof(struct large));
printf ("day1 is now %d/%d/%d.\n", day1.month, day1.day,
        day1.year % 100);
printf ("day2 remains %d/%d/%d.\n", day2.month,
        day2.day,day2.year % 100);
}
```

modf

modf - Split a floating-point value Class: ANSI

NAME
    modf   Split a floating-point value.

SYNOPSIS
```
#include <math.h>

double modf(y,p);

double y,*p;    arguments
```

DESCRIPTION

The `modf` function separates an argument (`y`) of type **double** into its fractional and integral parts. This function returns the fraction and writes the integer into the double-precision, floating-point number pointed to by `p`. Both parts have the same sign as `y`. Note that the fraction is the number that would be obtained by calling the `fmod` function in the following way:

```
x = fmod(y,1.0);
```

RETURN VALUE

This function returns a fraction of type **double**.

CAUTION

Make sure that the second argument of `modf` is a pointer to a double. A common error is to use a pointer to an integer.

SEE ALSO

    fmod

EXAMPLE

```
/* This example uses fmod and modf. */

#include <math.h>
#include <stdio.h>

main()
{
double r,ff,fi;
r = fmod(5.7,1.5);    /* r contains 1.2. */
printf("r is %f\n", r);
ff = modf(r,&fi);     /* ff contains 0.2 and fi contains 1.0. */
printf("ff is %f\n",ff);
printf("fi is %f\n",fi);
}
```

perror

perror - Map errno to an error message   **Class: ANSI**

NAME

    `perror`   Map the external variable errno to an error message.

SYNOPSIS

```
#include <stdio.h>

void perror(str);

char *str;    message prefix
```

DESCRIPTION

The `perror` function checks `errno` and, if it is nonzero, writes an error message to the standard error file, `stderr`. The external variable `errno` is initialized to zero at start-up time; if an error is detected by a standard library function, a nonzero value is stored there.

The error message is preceded by the prefix string (pointed to by `str`), a colon (:), and a blank space. It is followed by a newline ('\n').

RETURN VALUE

This function does not return a value.

SEE ALSO

See Chapter 15 for a list of the `errno` messages and more information on `perror`.

EXAMPLE

See the examples under the `remove` and `rename` functions.

pow

pow - Compute the value of the power function Class: ANSI

NAME

    pow   Compute the value of the power function.

SYNOPSIS

```
#include <math.h>

double pow(x,y);

double x,y;     arguments
```

DESCRIPTION

The **pow** function computes the value of **x** raised to a power of **y**, as expressed in the relation

$$r = x^y$$

If **x** is a negative number, **y** must be an integer.

RETURN VALUE

The **pow** function returns the value of **x** raised to the power of **y**, as expressed in a double-precision, floating-point number.

If an error occurs, **pow** takes the following actions:

- If the arguments are so large that x^y cannot be represented, **pow** returns the largest positive floating-point number that can be represented, **HUGE_VAL** and the **errno** parameter is set to **ERANGE**.

- If **x** is a negative number or **y** is a noninteger, the function returns 0.0 and the **errno** parameter is set to **EDOM**.

- If **x**=0.0 and **y** is negative, the function returns **HUGE_VAL** and sets the **errno** parameter to **ERANGE**.

EXAMPLE

```
/* This example demonstrates the pow function. */

#include <stdio.h>
#include <math.h>

main()
{
double x, y, r;

x = 10.0;
y = 2.0;
r = pow(x, y);
printf("R is: %f\n", r);
}
```

putc, putchar - Write a character Class: ANSI

NAME

putc — Write a character to a standard I/O file.
putchar — Write a character to **stdout**.

SYNOPSIS

```
#include <stdio.h>

int putc(c,fp);
int putchar(c);

int c;        Character to be output
FILE *fp;     file pointer
```

DESCRIPTION

The `putc` macro writes a single character (c) to the standard I/O file addressed by `fp`. The `putchar` macro writes a single character to the standard output file, `stdout`. `putchar` is a macro that expands into `putc(c, stdout)`. Note that these are implemented as macros in order to maximize execution speed.

RETURN VALUE

If successful, the character is written. An end-of-file (EOF) is returned if an error occurs.

For disk files, an EOF return usually means that the disk is full. However, this type of return can also occur if the device is write protected or if a write error occurs. In any case, additional error information can be found in `errno`.

SEE ALSO

`fopen`, `fputc`, `getc`, `getchar`, `perror`,

EXAMPLES

See the examples under the `getc` and `ungetc` functions.

puts

puts - Write a string to stdout **Class: ANSI**

NAME

    puts   Write a string to the standard output file, stdout.

SYNOPSIS

```
#include <stdio.h>

int puts(str);

char *str;         string pointer
```

DESCRIPTION

    The `puts` function writes the entire string (pointed to by `str`) to the standard output file, `stdout`. The string's terminating null character ('\0') is not written, but a newline is written after the string.

RETURN VALUE

    If an error occurs, the return value is -1; otherwise, it is zero. Additional error information can be found in `errno`.

SEE ALSO

    `ferror, fopen, fprintf, fputc, fputs, perror,`

EXAMPLE

    See the example under the `gets` function.

qsort

qsort - Sort a data array   **Class: ANSI**

NAME

    qsort   Sort a data array.

SYNOPSIS

```
#include <stdlib.h>

void qsort(darray,n,size,cmp);

    void *darray;                data array pointer
    size_t n;                    number of elements in array
    size_t size;                 element size in bytes
    int (*cmp)(void *, void *);  pointer to comparison function
```

DESCRIPTION

The `qsort` function sorts the data array pointed to by `darray`, using the ACM 271 algorithm popularly known as Quicksort.

During its operation, `qsort` calls the comparison routine `cmp` with pointers to the two array elements of the block being compared. `cmp` compares the two elements and determines which is larger or smaller or if they are equal. The `cmp` function thereby defines the ordering relation for the elements to be sorted. The precise comparison technique depends on the type of data being compared and on the application.

The comparison routine (`cmp`) should return an integral result as follows:

    NEGATIVE => first of two elements is less than the second
    POSITIVE => first of two elements is greater than the second
    ZERO   => two elements are equal

If the two elements are equal, their order after sorting is arbitrary.

You can pass a third argument, `size`, which can be ignored but must be included. The argument `size` is of type `size_t`, which is an unsigned integer in the Student compiler.

RETURN VALUE

This function has no return value.

qsort

EXAMPLE

```
/* This example demonstrates the qsort function. */

#include <stdlib.h>
#include <stdio.h>

chrcmp(a,b)
char *a, *b;
{

if (*a<*b)
   return(-1);
else if (*a==*b)
   return(0);
else
   return(1);
}

main()
{
char a[20];

strcpy(a,"hiiiiffkdlslddkjflkj");

qsort(a, strlen(a), (size_t)1, chrcmp);

printf("%s",a);
}
```

rand

rand - Generate a random number   **Class: ANSI**

NAME
rand   Generate a random number.

SYNOPSIS
```
#include <stdlib.h>

int rand();
```

DESCRIPTION
The `rand` function returns pseudorandom numbers in the range from zero to the maximum positive integer value, 32,767. See the `srand` function to initialize or reset the seed value for `rand`.

RETURN VALUE
The `rand` function returns a pseudorandom number as described above.

SEE ALSO
srand

EXAMPLE
```
/* This example tests the rand and srand functions. */

#include <stdlib.h>
#include <stdio.h>
#include <time.h>

main()
{
char card, suit;
unsigned seed;
time_t t;

/* Seed the generator with the system time. */
time(&t);
seed = (unsigned) t;
srand(seed);

/* Assign a random value to card and suit. */
card = "A23456789TJQK"[rand()%13];
suit = "CDHS"[rand()%4];
printf("Your card: %c %c\n", card, suit);
}
```

realloc

realloc - Reallocate memory   **Class: ANSI**

NAME
    `realloc`   Reallocate memory.

SYNOPSIS
```
#include <stdlib.h>

void *realloc(blkptr,n);

char *blkptr;      block pointer
size_t n;          number of bytes
```

DESCRIPTION

The `realloc` function obtains a new block of dynamic memory whose size is n bytes. It copies the old memory block addressed by `blkptr` to a new block and releases the old block. If n is greater than the old block size, the extra space is cleared to zeros. If it is less than the old block size, only the first n bytes are copied.

If a block of memory has just been released using the `free` function and your next call is to `realloc`, `realloc` proceeds correctly. In other words, `realloc` can reallocate a block that was freed as long as you have not called `calloc` and `malloc` in the meantime.

RETURN VALUE

If successful, `realloc` returns a pointer to the first element in the new block of memory. If the block cannot be allocated, `realloc` returns a NULL pointer.

SEE ALSO
    `calloc`, `free`, `malloc`

remove

remove - Delete a standard I/O file   **Class: ANSI**

NAME
       remove   Delete a standard I/O file.

SYNOPSIS
```
#include <stdio.h>

int remove(name);

char *name;    filename
```

DESCRIPTION

The `remove` function deletes the standard I/O file pointed to in `name` from the system. The filename argument can include a path, but it cannot include wild card characters, such as * or ?. You can remove only one file at a time.

RETURN VALUE

This function returns zero if the file is deleted. If a nonzero value is returned, an error has occurred and you can find additional information in `errno`. The most common errors occur when you try to delete a file that does not exist or that is marked as read-only.

SEE ALSO
       `perror`

EXAMPLE
```
/*
 * This program removes all files specified in the
 * argument list.  It does not allow wild card
 * characters in the filenames.
 */
#include <stdio.h>

main(argc,argv)

int argc;
char *argv[];
{
int i;  /* loop counter */
int ret = 0; /* exit code, non-zero if error */
for(i = 1; i < argc; i++) if(remove(argv[i])){
  perror("RMV");
   ret = 1;
   }
exit(ret);
}
```

rename

rename - Change a standard I/O filename   **Class: ANSI**

NAME

    `rename`   Change a standard I/O filename.

SYNOPSIS

```
#include <stdio.h>

int rename(old,new);

char *old;      old filename
char *new;      new filename
```

DESCRIPTION

The `rename` function changes the name of the standard I/O file pointed to by `old`, if possible. The old name can include a path, but the new name must include a path. A failure occurs if the old file cannot be found or if the new name is the same as an existing file.

This function allows you to move a file quickly from one directory to another. For example, given the old name `\old\file1` and the new filename `\new` in the current directory `\now`, the renamed path and filename would be `\now\new`, not `\old\new`.

RETURN VALUE

If successful, this function returns zero. If the function fails, it returns -1 and places additional error information into `errno`.

EXAMPLE

```
/*
 * This is a version of the MS-DOS rename function
 * that prompts for the old and new names.
 */

#include <stdlib.h>
#include <stdio.h>
#include <dos.h>

main(argc,argv)
int argc;
char *argv[];
{
char old[FMSIZE],new[FMSIZE];
char *pold,*pnew;
```

rename

```
        if(argc < 2){ /* Get old filename. */
           printf("OLD FILE: ");
           if(gets(old) == NULL) exit(1);
           pold = old;
           }
        else pold = argv[1];

        if(arc < 3){
           printf("NEW FILE: ");
           if(gets(new) == NULL) exit(1);
           pnew = new;
           }
        else pnew = argv[2];

        if(rename(pold,pnew)){
           perror("RENAME");
           exit(1);
           }
        }
```

rewind - Reset the file position   **Class: ANSI**

NAME
        `rewind`   Reset the file position.

SYNOPSIS
```
#include <stdio.h>

void rewind(fp);

FILE *fp;     file pointer
```

DESCRIPTION

The `rewind` macro resets the specified standard I/O file to its first byte. The file must already be open. A `rewind` call is equivalent to the following `fseek` call:

```
int fseek(fp,0L,0);
```

In fact, `rewind` is implemented as a macro that simply calls `fseek` in the above way.

RETURN VALUE

This function has no return value.

SEE ALSO

`fopen`, `fseek`, `ftell`, `perror`

setbuf, setvbuf

setbuf, setvbuf - Set buffer mode for a file   Class: ANSI

NAME
　　setbuf　　　　Set buffer mode for a standard I/O file.
　　setvbuf　　　Set varying-length buffer for a standard I/O file.

SYNOPSIS
```
#include <stdio.h>

void setbuf(fp,buff);
int setvbuf(fp,buff,type,size);
```

```
FILE *fp;        file pointer
char *buff;      buffer pointer
int type;        type of buffering
size_t size;     buffer size in bytes
```

DESCRIPTION

The `setbuf` function sets the buffer mode for a standard I/O file. The `setvbuf` function sets a varying-length buffer for a standard I/O file. You should call these functions after calling `fopen` and before calling any other standard I/O functions. If you fail to follow this rule, the file may become corrupted.

The standard I/O system automatically allocates a buffer using `malloc` when you perform the first read or write operation. The data being read or written are then passed through this buffer to improve I/O efficiency.

If you would rather use your own buffer instead of having one allocated for you, call `setbuf` with a non-null buffer pointer. The buffer size must be at least as large as the value given in the external integer `_bufsiz`, which defaults to the value of the symbol `BUFSIZ` as defined in `stdio.h`.

You can eliminate buffered I/O by calling `setbuf` with a null buffer pointer. When this is done, physical I/O occurs whenever your program performs a standard read or write operation, even if only one byte is being transferred. This is very inefficient for disk files but is often desirable for terminal or communication ports.

The `setvbuf` function can do everything that `setbuf` can do. It can also set "line buffered" mode and attach a buffer of nonstandard size. `setvbuf` does this by flushing the buffer after each line, so that the buffer varies in size.

The `type` argument must be one of the following symbols, defined in `stdio.h`:

```
_IOFBF => Fully buffered
_IOLBF => Line buffered
_IONBF => Non-buffered
```

For `_IOFBF` and `_IOLBF`, the specified buffer is attached to the file unless `buff` is null, in which case a buffer will be automatically allocated on the

setbuf, setvbuf

first read or write operation. For the __IONBF case, the **buff** and **size** arguments are ignored.

The line-buffered mode is useful for interactive applications. In this mode, the buffer is flushed whenever a newline is sent, the buffer is full, or input is requested. Note, however, that you must use the **fputc** and **fputchar** functions instead of the **putc** and **putchar** macros for line buffering to work correctly. The macros do not check if line-buffered mode is active, so they behave as if the file were fully buffered.

RETURN VALUES

If successful, **setvbuf** returns a zero. If not, the error code is nonzero if **type** or **size** is invalid. **setbuf** returns no value.

CAUTION

These functions must be used only after **fopen** and before any other standard I/O file operations. A common error is to allocate a buffer on the stack within a function, attach it to a file, and then return from the function. This will corrupt the stack.

SEE ALSO

fopen

EXAMPLE

```
/* This example creates a new file buffer using the setbuf function. */

#include <stdio.h>

main()
{
FILE *fp;
char *buff;
int x;

buff = (char *) calloc(1000, sizeof(char));
fp = fopen("MYFILE","w");     /* Open MYFILE for writing. */
_bufsiz = 1000;
setbuf(fp, buff);
/* Proceed to write the file. */
   .
   .
   .
}
```

setjmp, longjmp

setjmp, longjmp - Setup or perform a nonlocal goto   **Class: ANSI**

NAME
    setjmp   Define a label for a nonlocal goto.
    longjmp   Perform a nonlocal goto.

SYNOPSIS
```
#include <setjmp.h>

int setjmp(save);
void longjmp(save,value);

int value;        return value
jmp_buf *save;    address of saved area
```

DESCRIPTION

The `setjmp` function defines a target for a nonlocal goto. It saves its stack environment in `save` (whose type `jmp_buf` is defined in `setjmp.h`) so that it can come back to that point. The value of `save` is also used by the `longjmp` function. Setjmp then returns the value zero.

The `longjmp` function restores the stack environment saved by the last call to `setjmp` with the corresponding `save` argument. After `longjmp` is completed, program execution continues as if the corresponding call of `setjmp` has just returned the value of `value`; `setjmp` must not have returned in the interim between these two calls.

The `longjmp` function cannot cause `setjmp` to return the value 0. If `longjmp` is invoked with a second argument of 0, `setjmp` returns 1. All accessible data have values as of the time `longjmp` was called. This mechanism is useful for quickly popping back up through multiple layers of function calls under exceptional circumstances, but is not recommended because it can disrupt the system. See CAUTIONS below.

These functions are useful for dealing with errors and interrupts encountered in a low-level subroutine of a program.

RETURN VALUES

A return code of zero from `setjmp` indicates that the `setjmp` call is the initial call to save the stack. When control returns from `setjmp` (that is, due to the use of `longjmp`), the return value is nonzero. Control does not return from `longjmp`.

CAUTIONS

Calling `longjmp` with an invalid save area can cause serious and unpredictable results. One common error is to use `longjmp` after the function calling `setjmp` has returned to its caller. This cannot possibly succeed because the stack frame for that function no longer exists.

setjmp, longjmp

Variables of the storage classes `auto` and `register` whose values have been changed between the `setjmp` and `longjmp` calls may or may not be restored to the value they had when `setjmp` was called.

EXAMPLE

```
/*
 * This shows how to use setjmp and longjmp to force
 * an orderly exit from a user program.
 */

#include <stdio.h>
#include <setjmp.h>

jmp_buf env;

void main()
{
int ret;
void dummy();

if ((ret = setjmp(&env)) != 0) {
   fprintf(stderr, "Long jump called with value %d\n", ret);
   exit(1);
   }
dummy();
}

void dummy()
{
printf("Entering dummy routine\n");
longjmp(&env, 3);
printf("Never reached\n");
}
```

sin, asin, sinh

sin, asin, sinh - Sine functions   Class: ANSI

NAME
    sin   Compute sine in radians.
    asin   Compute arcsine.
    sinh   Compute hyperbolic sine.

SYNOPSIS
```
#include <math.h>

double sin(x);
double asin(x);
double sinh(x);

double x;    argument
```

DESCRIPTION
Each sine function performs the computation indicated as follows:

- The `sin` function computes the sine of its argument x, where x is expressed in radians.

  Because `sin` is periodic, only the value of $x \bmod 2\pi$ is used to compute the sine. If x is very large, only a limited precision is left to represent $x \bmod 2\pi$.

- The `asin` function computes the arcsine of x and returns the result in radians. This is the inverse of the `sin` function and is expressed by the relation:

  $$r = \sin^{-1}(x)$$

  where x is in the closed interval $[-1.0, 1.0]$.

- The `sinh` function computes the hyperbolic sine of the value x and returns the result in radians. This relation can be expressed as

  $$r = (e^x + e^{-x}) / 2$$

RETURN VALUES
The `sin` function returns the principal values of the sine of x (of type `double`), provided that this value is defined and computable.

If x is outside the range of what can be handled numerically, `sin` returns 0.0 and the `errno` parameter is set to `EDOM`.

The `asin` function returns a double-precision, floating-point number in the closed interval $[0, \pi]$ radians. If x is less than -1.0 or greater than 1.0, 0.0 is returned and the `errno` parameter is set to `EDOM`.

The `sinh` function returns the principal values of the hyperbolic sine of x (of type `double`), provided that this value is defined and computable.

sin, asin, sinh

If `x` has an absolute value that is too large to be represented, `sinh` returns the largest positive floating-point number that can be represented, `HUGE_VAL`, and the `errno` parameter is set to `EDOM`.

SEE ALSO

`acos`, `cos`, `cosh`

EXAMPLES

```
/* This example uses the sin function. */

#include <stdio.h>
#include <math.h>

main()
{
double angle, result;

angle = PID2;

result = sin(angle);

printf("The result is: %f\n", result);
}

/* This example uses the asin function. */

#include <stdio.h>
#include <math.h>

main()
{
double value, result;

value = 0;

result = asin(value);

printf("The result is: %f\n", result);

value = 1;

result = asin(value);

printf("The result is: %f\n", result);
}
```

sqrt

sqrt - Compute the square root   **Class: ANSI**

NAME

    `sqrt`   Compute the square root.

SYNOPSIS

```
#include <math.h>

double sqrt(x);

double x;      argument
```

DESCRIPTION

The `sqrt` function computes the square root of its argument `x`, which must be a double-precision, floating-point number.

RETURN VALUE

The `sqrt` function returns the square root of `x` as type double.

If `x` is a negative number, `sqrt` returns 0.0 and the `errno` parameter is set to `EDOM`.

EXAMPLE

```
/* This example demonstrates the sqrt function. */

#include <stdio.h>
#include <math.h>

main()
{
double r, x, l;

x = 100;

r = sqrt(x);

l = sqrt(225.0);

printf("R is: %f\n", r);

printf("L is: %f\n", l);
}
```

srand - Set the seed for rand function Class: ANSI

NAME
srand   Set the seed for the rand function.

SYNOPSIS
```
#include <stdlib.h>

void srand(seed);

unsigned seed;     random number seed
```

DESCRIPTION
The **srand** function initializes or resets the pseudorandom number generator used to generate values for the **rand** function. The initial default **seed** is 1. After calling **srand**, successive calls to **rand** will produce a series of pseudorandom numbers. Calling **srand** again with a different **seed** causes **rand** to produce a different series of numbers.

RETURN VALUE
The **srand** function has no return values.

SEE ALSO
rand

EXAMPLE
```
/* This example tests the rand and srand functions. */

#include <stdlib.h>
#include <stdio.h>

main()
{
char card, suit;
long seed;

   /* Seed the generator with the system time. */
time(&seed);
srand(seed);

   /* Assign a random value to card and suit. */
card = "A23456789TJQK"[rand()%13];
suit = "CDHS"[rand()%4];
printf("Your card: %c %c\n", card, suit);
}
```

strcat, strncat

strcat, strncat - Concatenate two strings   Class: ANSI

NAME
    strcat   Concatenate two null-terminated strings.
    strncat   Concatenate two null-terminated strings (limited).

SYNOPSIS
    #include <string.h>

    char *strcat(dest,source);
    char *strncat(dest,source,n);

    char *dest;   destination string pointer
    char *source;   source string pointer
    size_t n;   maximum source length

DESCRIPTION

The `strcat` function adds characters from the second argument string (pointed to by `source`) to the end of the first argument string (pointed to by `dest`) until a terminating null character ('\0') is found; this null character is then added to the output string.

The `strncat` function works like `strcat` does except that it adds characters until a null character is found or until the number of characters specified by `n` has been added. After the maximum number has been reached, a terminating null character is added to the output string.

RETURN VALUES

Both functions return a pointer that matches the `dest` argument.

CAUTIONS

The following cautions apply to both functions. No check is made that the `dest` string is long enough for all the characters of both strings. Characters are added until a null character is reached or until a protection/addressing exception occurs. You can check if the `dest` string is not properly terminated by adding such a check to your program. If the `dest` and `source` strings overlap, the effect is undefined.

For `strncat`, if the n value is zero, no characters will be copied.

Because a null terminating character is always appended to the `dest` string, n+1 characters are added if the length of the `source` string is greater than n.

SEE ALSO
    strcpy

strcat, strncat

EXAMPLE
```
#include <stdio.h>
#include <string.h>

main()
{
char a[256],b[256],temp[256];
size_t n;

while(1) {
   printf("\nEnter string A: ");
   if (gets(a) == NULL)
      exit(0);
   printf("Enter string B: ");
   if (gets(b) == NULL)
      exit(0);
   printf("Enter maximum length N: ");
   gets(temp);
   n = (size_t)atoi(temp);
   printf("strcat(A,B):     \"%s\"\n",strcat(a,b));
   printf("strncat(A,B,N): \"%.*s\"\n",n,strncat(a,b,n));
   }
}
```

strchr, strrchr

---

strchr, strrchr - Find a character in a string　　　　　　　　**Class: ANSI**

NAME
        strchr   Find the first occurrence of a character in a string.
        strrchr   Find the last occurrence of a character in a string.

SYNOPSIS
```
#include <string.h>

char *strchr(str,c);
char *strrchr(str,c);

char *str;      input string pointer
int c;          character to be located
```

DESCRIPTION

The **strchr** function searches the null-terminated input string (pointed to by **str**), including the null-terminating character ('\0'), for the first occurrence of the character specified by **c** (converted to type **char**). Similarly, the **strrchr** function searches for the last occurrence of the character **c**.

RETURN VALUES

If successful, these functions return a pointer to the first or last occurrence of the character in the string. **strchr** returns a NULL pointer if the input string is empty or if the specified character is not found; **strrchr** returns a NULL pointer if the input string is empty or does not contain the character **c**.

EXAMPLE
```
/* This program demonstrates strchr, which finds a character in a string. */

#include <stdio.h>
#include <string.h>

main()
{
char p[256],s[256];

while (1) {
   printf("\nEnter test string: ");
   if (gets(s) == NULL)
      exit(0);
   printf("\nEnter character: ");
   gets(p);
   printf("strchr: %s\n",strchr(s,p[0]));
   }
}
```

strcmp, strncmp - Compare two strings   Class: ANSI

NAME
    strcmp   Compare two null-terminated strings.
    strncmp   Compare portions of two null-terminated strings.

SYNOPSIS
```
#include <string.h>

int strcmp(str1,str2);
int strncmp(str1,str2,n);

char *str1,*str2;     strings being compared
size_t n;             comparison result
```

DESCRIPTION
The `strcmp` function compares two null-terminated ('\0') character strings using a case-sensitive ASCII collating sequence. It returns an integer value that is less than, equal to, or greater than zero, indicating that the string pointed to by `str1` is lexicographically less than, equal to, or greater than the string pointed to by `str2`. The integral value is returned as follows:

    NEGATIVE => first string is less than the second
    ZERO   => strings are equal
    POSITIVE => first string is greater than the second

The `strncmp` function works in the same way, except that it compares the strings only up to **n** characters or until the null-terminating character is reached.

These functions compare characters one charcter at a time. If efficiency is a prime concern, use another method of comparison, such as `memcmp`.

RETURN VALUE
These functions each return an integer value that is less than, equal to, or greater than zero, as described above.

SEE ALSO
memcmp

strcmp, strncmp

EXAMPLE

```
/* This example demonstrates the strcmp and related functions. */

#include <stdio.h>
#include <string.h>

main()
{
char a[256],b[256],temp[256];
int x;
size_t n;
void result();

while(1) {
   printf("Enter string A: ");
   if (gets(a) == NULL)
      exit(0);
   printf("Enter string B: ");
   if (gets(b) == NULL)
      exit(0);
   printf("Enter maximum compare length: ");
   gets(temp);
   n = atoi(temp);

   result("strcmp:  ",strcmp(a,b));
   result("strncmp: ",strncmp(a,b,n));
   }
}

result(name,r)
char *name;
int r;
{
char *p;

if (r == 0)
   p = "is equal to";
if (r < 0)
   p = "is less than";
if (r > 0)
   p = "is greater than";
printf("%s String A %s string B\n",name,p);
}
```

strcpy, strncpy

strcpy, strncpy - Copy one string to another   **Class: ANSI**

NAME
        `strcpy`   Copy one null-terminated string to another.
        `strncpy`   Copy a portion of a null-terminated string.

SYNOPSIS
```
#include <string.h>

char *strcpy(dest,source);
char *strncpy(dest,source,n);

char *dest;        destination pointer
char *source;      source pointer
size_t n;          number of bytes to be copied
```

DESCRIPTION

The `strcpy` function copies characters from the second argument string (pointed to by `source`) to the first argument string (pointed to by `dest`) until a null terminating character is ('\0') found. This null character is then also copied to the `dest` string.

The `strncpy` function always writes exactly n characters to the `dest` string. If the null terminator is reached before n characters are copied from the `source` string, the `dest` string is filled with null characters. If the `source` string contains n or more non-null characters, the `dest` string will not be null-terminated.

RETURN VALUES

If successful, both functions return a pointer that matches the `dest` argument.

CAUTIONS

If the `dest` and `source` strings overlap, the effect is undefined.

For `strncpy`, if the n value is zero, no characters will be copied.

strcpy, strncpy

EXAMPLE

```
/* This example should print: Hello, my name is Susan Johnston. */

#include <string.h>

main()
{
char b[256],*p;

p = strcpy(b,"Hello, ");
p = strcpy(p,"my name is");
p = strcpy(p,"Susan Johnston.");

puts(b);
}
```

strcspn, strspn - Measure characters in/not in a set Class: ANSI

NAME
strcspn   Measure a span of characters not in a set.
strspn   Measure a span of characters in a set.

SYNOPSIS
```
#include <string.h>

size_t strcspn(str,set);
size_t strspn(str,set);

char *str;      points to string being scanned
char *set;      points to character set string
```

DESCRIPTION
These functions measure the number of characters at the beginning of an input string that are either in or not in the specified set of characters.

The **strcspn** function searches the null-terminated string pointed to by **str** for the first occurrence of a character that is included in the null-terminated string pointed to by **set**, ignoring characters that are not in the **set** string. The second string, **set**, is considered to be a set of characters; it does not matter how the characters are ordered or if there are duplicates.

The **strspn** function performs a similar action. It searches for the first occurrence of a character in the **s** string that is not in the **set** character set, ignoring other characters that are in the **set** set.

RETURN VALUES
The **strcspn** function returns the length (in bytes) of the longest initial segment of the **str** string that consists of characters not found in the **set** character set. If no character of **str** appears in **set**, the total length of **str** (excluding the null terminator, '\0') is returned. This same action occurs if **str** is an empty string.

The **strspn** function returns the length (in bytes) of the longest initial segment of the **str** string that consists of characters found in the **set** characater set. If every character of **str** appears in **set**, the total length of **str** (excluding the null terminator) is returned. If **str** is an empty string, **strspn** returns a zero.

strcspn, strspn

EXAMPLE

```
/* This example demonstrates the strcspn function. */

#include <stdio.h>
#include <string.h>

main()
{
char a[80], b[80];
int length;

printf("Enter string a: \n");

gets(a);

printf("Enter string b: \n");

gets(b);

length = strcspn(a,b);

printf("Number of leading characters: %d\n", length);
}
```

strlen

strlen - Measure the length of a string   **Class: ANSI**

NAME
    `strlen`   Measure the length of a null-terminated string.

SYNOPSIS
    `size_t strlen(str);`

    `char *str;`   character string

DESCRIPTION
    The `strlen` function returns the number of characters (in bytes) in the string (pointed to by `str`) preceding the null-terminating character ('\0'). An empty string causes `strlen` to return a zero.

RETURN VALUE
    This function returns the number of characters in the string, as described above.

EXAMPLE

```
/* This example demonstrates the strlen function. */

#include <stdio.h>
#include <string.h>

main()
{
size_t x;

x = strlen("abc");       /* x is 3 */

printf("%d\n",x);

x = strlen("");          /* x is 0 */

printf("%d\n",x);
}
```

strpbrk

strpbrk - Find the first character of a set in a string Class: ANSI

NAME
strpbrk   Find the first character of a set in a string.

SYNOPSIS
```
#include <string.h>

p = strpbrk(str,brk);

char *str;      string to be scanned
char *brk;      break characters
```

DESCRIPTION
The `strpbrk` function searches the null-terminated string pointed to by `str` for the first occurrence of one of the characters included in the null-terminated string pointed to by `brk`, ignoring characters that are not in the `brk` string. The second string, `brk`, is considered to be a set of characters. It does not matter how the characters are ordered or if there are duplicates.

RETURN VALUE
This function returns a pointer to the character found. If no character from `brk` is found in `str`, `strpbrk` returns a NULL pointer.

SEE ALSO
strcspn, strspn

EXAMPLE
```
/*
 * This example demonstrates the strpbrk function.  The string is
 * searched until the next break character is encountered.  The tail
 * of the string is displayed after each break character.
 */

#include <stdio.h>
#include <string.h>

main()
{
char *s, *b;

s = "Hoc opus, hic labor est";
for (b = s; (b = strpbrk(b, ",. ")) != NULL; ++b)
    printf("%s\n",b);
}
```

strtok

strtok - Get a token   **Class: ANSI**

NAME

    `strtok`   Get a token.

SYNOPSIS

```
#include <string.h>

char *strtok(str,brk);

char *str;      input string pointer or NULL
char *brk;      break character string pointer
```

DESCRIPTION

The `strtok` function regards the input string (pointed to by `str`) as a sequence of one or more text tokens separated by spans of one or more characters from the break string (pointed to by `brk`). By making a sequence of calls to `strtok`, you can obtain the tokens in a left-to-right order.

The first call with pointer `str` returns a pointer to the first (leftmost) character of the first token, having written a null character into `str` immediately following the returned token. The function keeps track of its position in the string between separate calls. To get the next tokens, call the function repeatedly with a NULL pointer for `str`, until you get a NULL return pointer to indicate that there are no more tokens. The break string can be changed from one call to another.

Each time it is entered, `strtok` takes the following steps:

- If the input string is NULL, obtain the string pointer that was used on the preceding call. Otherwise use the new input string pointer.

- Scan forward through the string to the next non-break character. If it is a null character, return a value of NULL to indicate that there are no more tokens.

- Scan forward through the string to the next break character or the null terminator ('\0'). In the former case, write a null character into the string to terminate the token, and then scan forward until the next non-break is found. In either case, save the final value of the string pointer for the next call, and return the token pointer.

Note that the input string gets changed as the scan progresses. Specifically, a null character is written at the end of each token.

RETURN VALUE

The `strtok` function returns a pointer to the first character of a token or a NULL pointer when there are no more tokens.

SEE ALSO

    `strcspn, strspn`

strtok

EXAMPLE

```c
/* This example demonstrates the strtok function. */

#include <stdio.h>
#include <string.h>

main()
{
char *test;
char *token;

test = "first, second third, fourth";

token = strtok(test, ", ");

while (token != NULL) {
   printf("%s\n",token);
   token = strtok(NULL,", ");
   }
}
```

strtol - Convert a string to a long integer   Class: ANSI

NAME

    `strtol`   Convert a string to a long integer.

SYNOPSIS

```
#include <string.h>

long strtol(p,np,base);

char *p;        input string pointer
char **np;      receives new input string pointer
int base;       conversion base
```

DESCRIPTION

This function converts an ASCII input string (pointed to by `p`) to a long integer. The string is expected to contain an integer in the base `base`. The `base` argument may contain integers in the range from 0 to 36, excluding 1; if `base` is larger than 10, letters a through z (upper- or lowercase) are interpreted as digits greater than 9. The highest allowable character is determined by the conversion base. For example, if the base is 17, then the string can contain digits from 0 to 9, a to g, and A to G.

The function ignores initial white space and then checks for an initial plus or minus sign. In the latter case, the result of the conversion is negated before it is returned. The conversion stops at the first invalid character, and a pointer to that invalid character is returned in `np` if the `np` argument is not NULL. If `np` is NULL, it is not modified. Note that if the entire string is converted, `np` will contain a pointer to the null-terminating character ('\0').

If `base` is 0, the input string is analyzed to see if it is octal, decimal, or hexadecimal, as follows:

Base 16

    If the string begins with 0x or 0X, base 16 (hexadecimal) conversion is performed. If a leading 0x is present in the string, it is ignored.

Base 8

    Otherwise, if the string begins with 0, base 8 (octal) conversion is performed.

Base 10

    If neither of the above applies, base 10 (decimal) conversion is performed.

RETURN VALUE

This function returns the long integer value represented by the input character string, up to the first invalid character. If no initial segment of the string can be interpreted as an integer of the appropriate base, 0L is returned.

strtol

CAUTION

No check for overflow is returned if the string represents a number larger than the maximum `long` value.

SEE ALSO

`atol`

EXAMPLE

```c
/* This program tests the strtol function. */

#include <stdio.h>
#include <string.h>

main()
{
char *p,buff[80];
int base;
long x;

while(1){
 printf("\nEnter number base (0 to 36): ");
 if(gets(buff) == NULL) exit(0);
 if(buff[0] == '\0') exit(0);
 base = atoi(buff);
 if((base < 0) || (base > 36) || (base == 1)) continue;

 printf("Enter number: ");
 if(gets(buff) == NULL) exit(0);
 if(buff[0] == '\0') exit(0);
 x = strtol(buff,&p,base);
 printf("Decimal result = %ld\n",x);
 if(*p != '\0') printf("Residual = %s\n",p);
 }
}
```

tan, atan, atan2, tanh - Tangent functions   Class: ANSI

NAME

`tan`	Compute the tangent in radians.
`atan`	Compute the arctangent.
`atan2`	Compute the arctangent of a quotient.
`tanh`	Compute the hyperbolic tangent.

SYNOPSIS

```
#include <math.h>

double tan(x);
double atan(x);
double atan2(x,y);
double tanh(x);

double x,y;      arguments
```

DESCRIPTION

Each tangent function performs the computation as indicated:

- The `tan` function computes the trigonometric tangent of its argument `x` expressed in radians.

  Because `tan` is periodic, only the value of `x mod` 2π is used to compute the tangent. If `x` is very large, only a limited precision is left to represent `x mod` 2π.

- The `atan` function computes the arctangent of `x` and returns the result in radians. This is the inverse of the `tan` function and is expressed by the relation:

  $r = \tan^{-1}(x)$

  where `x` is in the open interval $(-\pi/2, \pi/2)$ radians.

- The `atan2` function computes the angle defined by the positive x-axis and a line through the point (`x`, `y`) to the point (0,0). The signs of both `x` and `y` are used to determine the quadrant of the result in a Cartesian system. The result (in radians) is the inverse trigonometric tangent of `y/x`, if `x` is not zero.

- The `tanh` function computes the hyperbolic tangent of the value `x` and returns the result in radians. This relation can be expressed as the following:

  $r = (e^x - e^{-x}) / (e^x + e^{-x})$

RETURN VALUES

The `tan` function returns the principal values of the tangent of `x`, provided that this value is defined and computable. The return value is a double-precision, floating-point number.

tan, atan, atan2, tanh

If `tan(x)` is such a large negative number that it cannot be represented, `tan` returns the largest negative double-precision, floating-point number that can be represented.

For a very large or small argument (`x` > 6.7465e9) or (`x` < −6.7465e9), `tan` returns 0.0. If an error occurs in `tan`, an error number is placed in `errno`, and control returns to the user.

The `atan` function returns the principal value of the arc tangent of `x`, provided that this value is defined and computable. The return value is a double-precision, floating-point number in the open interval ($-\pi/2, \pi/2$) radians. If an error occurs in `atan`, an error number is placed in `errno`, and control returns to the user.

Provided that it is defined and computable, the `atan2` function returns the angular position of the point (`x,y`). This return value is a double-precision, floating-point number that lies in the half-open interval (-π,π] radians. For input values (0.0, y), the return value will be either $\pi/2$ or -$\pi/2$ if `y` does not equal zero.

If `x` and `y` are both zero, `atan2` returns the value 0.0. If an error occurs, the `errno` parameter is set to `EDOM` and control returns to the user.

The `tan(x)` function returns the principal value of the hyperbolic tangent of `x`, provided that this value is defined and computable. The return value is a double-precision, floating-point number in the closed interval [−1.0,1.0].

If `tanh(x)` has an absolute value that is too large to be represented, `tanh` returns the largest positive floating-point number that can be represented and writes a message to `stderr`. If an error occurs, the `errno` parameter is set to `ERANGE` and and control returns to the user.

SEE ALSO

    `acos, asin, cos, cosh, sin, sinh`

EXAMPLES

```
/* This example uses the tan function. */

#include <stdio.h>
#include <math.h>

main()
{
double angle, result;

angle = PID2;
result = tan(angle);
printf("The result is: %lf\n", result);
}
```

```c
/* This example uses the atan function. */

#include <stdio.h>
#include <math.h>

main()
{
double value, result;

   /* This should return 0. */
result = atan2(0.0, 2.0);

printf("The result is: %f\n", result);

   /* This should return pi/4. */
value = 1;

result = atan(value);

printf("The result is: %f\n", result);
}
```

time

time - Get the current time in seconds **Class: ANSI**

NAME
time   Get the current time in seconds.

SYNOPSIS
```
#include <time.h>

time_t time(timeptr);

time_t *timeptr;     pointer to time value storage
```

DESCRIPTION
The `time` function returns the current time expressed as the number of seconds since 00:00:00 Greenwich Mean Time, January 1, 1970. If `timeptr` pointer is not NULL, this time value is also stored in the storage addressed by `timeptr`.

RETURN VALUE
This function returns the current time expressed in the number of seconds, as described above. If the time cannot be determined, `(time_t)` −1 is returned.

SEE ALSO
asctime, ctime, gmtime, localtime

EXAMPLE
```
/*
 * Find the correct time using the time function. This is the era time or
 * number of seconds since the start of an era.
 */

#include <time.h>
#include <stdio.h>

main()
{
long t;
time(&t);

printf("The era time is %ld\n", t);
}
```

tmpnam

tmpnam - Generate a unique filename   **Class: ANSI**

NAME

    tmpnam   Generate a unique filename.

SYNOPSIS

```
#include <stdio.h>

char *tmpnam(buff);

char *buff;      buffer for filename or NULL
```

DESCRIPTION

The **tmpnam** function creates a file with a unique name and returns a pointer to the name.

If **buff** is NULL, **tmpname** puts its results in a static internal buffer and returns a pointer to it. This internal buffer (and thus the filename) is changed on every call to **tmpnam**, even if **buff** is not NULL.

If **buff** is not NULL, **tmpnam** places the filename in that buffer and returns the buffer's name. If you reuse the buffer, the name changes with each call to **tmpnam**. The buffer must be large enough to hold the filename; 16 bytes is a safe size for MS-DOS.

RETURN VALUE

If successful, **tmpnam** returns the unique filename. A NULL return indicates that the unique file could not be created.

CAUTION

This function is only available for MS-DOS Version 3.00 and later.

SEE ALSO

    tmpfile

EXAMPLE

```
/*
 * This program demonstrates the function tmpnam which creates a file
 * with a unique name and returns a pointer to the name.
 */

#include <stdio.h>

main()
 {
char name[16];
tmpnam(name);
printf( "%s\n", name );
 }
```

tolower, toupper

tolower, toupper – Convert characters to lower- or uppercase **Class: ANSI**

NAME

    `tolower`   Convert a character to lowercase.
    `toupper`   Convert a character to uppercase.

SYNOPSIS

```
#include <ctype.h>

int tolower(c);
int toupper(c);

int c;     character to convert
```

DESCRIPTION

The `tolower` macro tests if c is an uppercase alphabetic character and if so, converts it to lowercase. The `toupper` function tests if c is a lowercase alphabetic character and if so, converts it to uppercase.

RETURN VALUE

If successful, these macros return the converted character; otherwise, the argument value is returned.

SEE ALSO

`islower`, `isupper`

EXAMPLE

```
/* The following program changes a character to lowercase. */

#include <stdio.h>
#include <ctype.h>

main()
{
int c, cc, n;

for (n=1; n <= 5; ++n){
   c=getchar();
   cc=tolower(c);
   printf("\nThe lowercase of %c is %c.\n",c,cc);
   getchar();     /* Read the return character. */
   }
}
```

ungetc - Undo the effect of getc

Class: ANSI

NAME
ungetc — Undo the effect of `getc`.

SYNOPSIS
```
int ungetc(c, fp);

int c;        character to be pushed back
FILE *fp;     file pointer
```

DESCRIPTION

The `ungetc` function undoes the effect of `getc`. The `ungetc` function verifies that `c` is the input character most recently read, and backs up the file pointer `fp` so that the next call to an input function will read `c` again. The process is often referred to as "pushing a character back" to the standard input file.

Before calling `ungetc`, you must have read at least one character via `fgetc` or one of the other standard input functions. The character pushed need not be the same as the one that was most recently read.

Note that you can push back only one character. If you call `ungetc` more than once between input functions, the results are undefined.

RETURN VALUE

Normally, `ungetc` returns the character that was pushed back. However, if the end-of-file has been reached or if no characters have been read yet, the value end-of-file (EOF) is returned.

SEE ALSO

`fgetc`, `fscanf`, `getc`, `perror`, `putc`, `putchar`, `scanf`

ungetc

EXAMPLE

```
/* This example uses the ungetc function. */

#include <stdio.h>

main()
{
FILE *fp;
int x, d;
char c;

   /* Open file and read five characters. */

fp = fopen("MYFILE","r");

for(x = 0; x != 5; x++)
  c = fgetc(fp);

printf("This is character 5: %c\n",c);

   /* Push fifth character onto stack and read it again. */

d = ungetc(c,fp);

c = fgetc(fp);

printf("This is character 5 read again: %c\n",c);
}
```

Chapter 17
Graphics and Screen Management Functions for the Student Compiler

Chapter 17

CONTENTS

Introduction 529
Introduction to Graphics on the Student Compiler 529
Screen Interface 529
      Display Modes 531
      Color and Text Attributes 534
Screen Management and Graphics Functions 537

Graphics and Screen Management Functions for the Student Compiler

Introduction

This chapter describes the Student Compiler's graphics and screen management functions. It describes how you use these functions to create graphics and colors on your screen. The following sections describe

- the hardware needed to use the Student Compiler screen management and graphics functions
- how the computer creates characters on the display screen
- how the screen's text and appearance is modified
- the screen management and graphics functions
- sample graphics programs for you to compile and execute.

Introduction to Graphics on the Student Compiler

Chapter 13 described some of the hardware you need to run the Student Compiler on your microcomputer. This section describes the hardware you need to control your display screen.

In Chapter 13, we noted that you would need a Color/Graphics Adapter (CGA) card if you planned on using the Student Compiler's graphics functions. This optional **display adapter card** and its extended version, the Enhanced Graphics Adapter (EGA) card, can be purchased from your microcomputer dealer. If your display screen is a color other than gray or black, a color display adapter card has probably already been added to your computer. If you have this card, the documentation that comes with your computer states whether you have a CGA or EGA card.

The CGA and EGA cards are actually small printed circuit boards that each store a set of alphabetic, numeric, and graphics characters. You can use the screen management and graphics functions to modify how the text looks on your screen (for example, you can make the letters taller and broader), to change the color of the screen itself or the characters on it, and to produce simple line drawings.

If your computer does not contain a CGA or EGA, it contains a Monochrome Adapter (MA) card. This card produces high-resolution text characters in one color (usually gray), but not graphics. Having an MA card allows you to use the Student Compiler's screen management functions to change the text or appearance of the screen, but it ignores calls to the graphics functions.

Screen Interface

This section describes how the display adapter cards, such as an EGA, work with the computer's software to manage the screen's appearance. This is known as a **screen interface** because this compiler's screen management and graphics functions provide a C language interface to the routines (stored on the display adapter card) that control

Chapter 17

the display screen. These routines are mapped from memory to a **display buffer**, where your C programs and the SC functions can access and modify the routines. You can modify these routines by setting a video mode with the `setvideomode` function. Video modes are described below.

The video mode determines how text characters and graphics appear on your display screen, that is, whether the characters are bold, narrow and tall, broad and short, and so on. The display on your screen is produced by one of two types of video modes: graphics and text. In **graphics video mode**, you can produce simple drawings and text characters, while **text video mode** allows only text characters to be displayed. If you have a CGA or EGA card, your computer can produce displays using either the graphics or text video mode; if your computer has an MA card, you can use only the text video mode. Although they look the same on the screen, these two video modes store and produce text characters and graphics differently.

Graphics Video Mode The display buffer in graphics video mode is a rectangular grid of pixels that is translated into a rectangular grid of dots on a display screen. **Pixels**, or picture elements, are represented as the dots of light on your screen. The system encodes each pixel with one to four bits, depending on your PC's display adapter card and the value given to the `setvideomode` function. The higher the number of bits per pixel, the greater the resolution (or clarity) of the character on the screen and the greater the number of shades a color may have. In graphics video mode, each text character and drawing is stored on a bit-by-bit basis, and each is drawn on the display screen one pixel at a time.

A single pixel is the smallest unit you can work with in graphics video mode. Because each pixel in the display buffer corresponds to a point in a positive integer coordinate system, refer to a pixel in terms of its (X,Y) coordinates. In the Student Compiler, the X (row) values are horizontal and increasing from left to right. The Y (column) values are vertical and increasing from top to bottom. The numbering for the coordinates (0,0) begins at the top left corner of the screen.

Text Video Mode The display buffer in text video mode is a rectangular grid of character boxes that is translated into a rectangular grid of boxes on a display device. A character box, not a pixel, is the smallest element you can work with in text video mode.

In text video mode, each character is contained in a **character box**, which is a small grid composed of pixels. The size of the character box depends on the PC's display adapter card: on a CGA, a character box is 8 by 8 pixels and on an MA or EGA, a box is 9 pixels wide and 14 pixels high. **Figure 17.1** displays a character box for an uppercase letter and one for a lowercase letter.

Graphics and Screen Management Functions for the Student Compiler

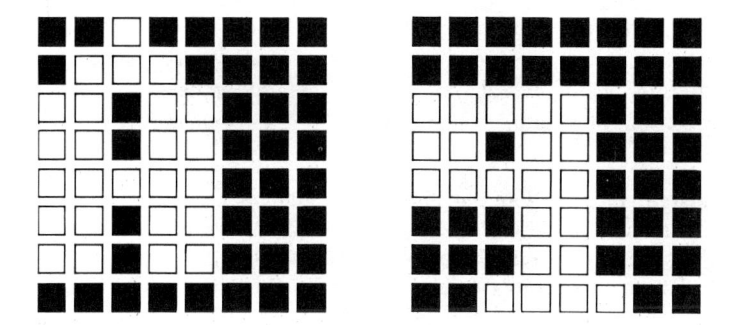

Figure 17.1 Character Boxes for an Uppercase A and Lowercase Q

In text video mode, the ASCII value of the character is stored in the display buffer, rather than an image of the character itself. (ASCII is a standard character encoding scheme in which each character has a numeric value; see the Glossary.) This ASCII value acts as the argument for the character generator that actually draws the character on the screen; the character generator is part of the display adapter card.

The graphics and text video modes each have certain attributes that are pre-set by the routines stored on the display adapter cards. The following section describes how to use the screen management and graphics functions to modify the pre-set video mode, color, and appearance of the text.

Display Modes

Every display monitor has certain default display characteristics that define what the characters look like, the resolution (or clarity) of the graphics, text, and colors, and the amount of text per screen that can be displayed. On IBM PCs and their compatible microcomputers, the default setting is a text video mode. This section describes how you can use the graphics and text video modes to re-define your screen's display characteristics.

You can use the graphics and text video modes to create eleven different display modes, as described in **Table 17.1** and **Table 17.2** below. Each **display mode** is assigned a value, listed in the Display Mode column, that serves as the argument to the `setvideomode` function. You use this function to re-set your display monitor's default display characteristics. For example, if your computer has a CGA card and you want to specify display mode 4, you include the following in your program:

```
#include <bios.h>
setvideomode(4);
```

This allows you to produce text characters and graphics, sets your screen size to 320 by 200 pixels, and enables the screen to display up to four colors simultaneously. You can then select the four colors from a palette of sixteen colors using the `setpalette` and `setcolor` functions. See the descriptions of these functions in the **Screen Management and Graphics Functions** section later in this chapter.

Chapter 17

Display Modes that Use the Text Video Mode When you select display mode 0, 1, 2, or 3 (using `setvideomode`), you limit your display adapter cards to producing text characters only, even though the adapter cards listed are capable of displaying graphics as well. For this reason, display modes 0-3 and 7 are often referred to as the **text display modes**.

Table 17.1 lists the text display modes. Note that the display adapter card in your PC must be able to support the display mode you select or unpredictable results may occur. For example, if your computer has a Monochrome Adapter card, you can specify only display mode 7 because an MA card is listed under the Adapter Card column.

Table 17.1 Text Display Modes

Display Mode	Constant	Video Type	Colors	Dimensions*	Adapter Card
0	BW40	Text	16 gray	40x25	CGA, EGA
1	CO40	Text	16 foreground 8 background	40x25	CGA, EGA
2	BW80	Text	16 gray	80x25	CGA, EGA
3	CO80	Text	16 foreground 8 background	80x25	CGA, EGA
7	MONO	Text	2 b/w	80x25	MA, EGA

* Dimensions are defined in columns (that is, character boxes) and rows for the text video modes. The higher the number of columns, the greater the character and color resolution.

Text display modes 0 through 3 allow you to set up to sixteen **foreground** colors (the color of the text) and up to eight **background** colors (the color of the screen). After you have selected a text mode with `setvideomode`, you set the character and screen colors using the `writechar` function. The color choices are listed in **Tables 17.3** and **17.4** later in this chapter.

Originally, text modes 0 and 2 produced only black and white displays (actually 16 shades of gray) because they were designed for PCs that were connected to composite display monitors. Now almost all PCs are connected to RGB (red-green-blue) display monitors, which produce high-quality characters and graphics in color. RGB monitors always display color, even in the black/white modes 0 and 2. Now in most cases, modes 0 and 1 are identical and modes 2 and 3 are identical. The two sets of modes vary only in their level of resolution.

Display mode 7 also allows the display of text characters only. If your computer has an MA card and is connected to a monochrome display monitor, display mode 7 is its default setting. If your computer has an EGA card with a monochrome monitor, mode

Graphics and Screen Management Functions for the Student Compiler

7 is the default text mode setting. In mode 7, the two colors allowed by the MA card are white text (the foreground color) on a black screen (the background color).

The include file **<bios.h>** provides the constants to set the text display modes in your program. To set one of the text display modes using **setvideomode**, you can specify either the constant or its display mode number (as listed in **Table 17.1**) as the function's argument. For example, the following function calls produce the same result:

```
setvideomode(3);
    or
setvideomode(C080);
```

Note that the constants are case-sensitive and must be entered in uppercase. To set the colors for text display mode 3, see the **writechar** function. See the **setcurpos** function description below for another example using these constants.

Display Modes that Use the Graphics Video Mode Display modes 4 through 6 and 13 through 16 allow the display of both text characters and graphics, and are therefore referred to as the **graphics display modes**. Choose these modes if you have a computer with a CGA or EGA card. You can select the screen's level of resolution and the number of colors you want by referring to **Table 17.2**.

Table 17.2 lists the graphics display modes. Note that the display adapter card in your PC must be able to support the display mode you select or unpredictable results may occur. For example, if your computer has a CGA card, you can use the graphics display modes 4 through 6 but not 13 through 16. A more thorough description of the graphics display modes follows this table.

Table 17.2 Graphics Display Modes

Display Mode	Video Type	Colors	Dimensions*	Adapter Card
4	Graphics	4	320x200	CGA, EGA
5	Graphics	4 gray	320x200	CGA, EGA
6	Graphics	2	640x200	CGA, EGA
13	Graphics	16	320x200	EGA
14	Graphics	16	640x200	EGA
15	Graphics	2 b/w	640x350	EGA**
16	Graphics	4	640x350	EGA

* Dimensions are defined in pixels for the graphics video modes. The higher the number of pixels, the greater the character, color, and graphics resolution.

** Graphics display mode 15 works differently than the other graphics display modes. Mode 15 requires the use of an EGA card in a PC connected to a monochrome display monitor. This setting lets you create black and white graphics as well as text, but it is rarely used.

Chapter 17

As with the text display modes, use the `setvideomode` function to set the graphics modes. You specify the display mode number as the function argument, that is, 4 through 6 and 13 through 16. Graphics mode 5, like text display modes 0 and 2, was originally a black/white mode, but it now works like mode 4 on most PCs. The graphics modes do not have constants that you can substitute for the display mode number in `setvideomode`. Instead, use constants to specify the colors on your display screen, as described in the **Color and Text Attributes** section later in this chapter.

Choosing the Best Display Mode for You Your choice of display mode setting depends on your PC's adapter card and on your own preferences. You may be happy with your computer's default setting and rarely use the `setvideomode` function. If you do re-set the display characteristics, your choice will be determined by the following:

- if you want to produce graphics as well as text characters

- the level of resolution you want in your text and graphics (the higher the number of pixels or character boxes per line, the sharper or clearer the image is on your screen)

- the number of colors you want to choose from for your text or graphics and screen. (For more information on choosing colors for the graphics display modes, see the `setpalette` and `setcolor` functions; for the text display modes, see the `writechar` function.)

Finally, you need to think about how you want to use the screen management and graphics functions in your programs. The task you want to accomplish with your program determines how you will set your display characteristics.

Color and Text Attributes

On IBM PCs and their compatible computers, a color is composed of four elements: three primary colors (red, green, and blue) and an intensity (or brightness) component. These components blend to make up the sixteen colors available through the Student Compiler's screen management and graphics functions. The graphics and text display modes use the same colors, but combine them in different ways to produce their display screens.

The graphics display modes use a single pixel to define its color and intensity. The color of a pixel is encoded using one to four bits, depending on your computer's display adapter card and on the display mode selected using `setvideomode`. The number of colors that each graphics mode can display is listed in the Colors column of **Table 17.2**.

By using the graphics and screen management functions in the graphics display modes, you can turn pixels on or off to produce colors and shapes on the display screen. On the bit level, a 1 bit is the *on* bit or foreground color and 0 is the *off* bit or background color. On a typical color display screen, the text character in yellow is the foreground color and the background color of the screen is brown. See the `setpalette` and `setcolor` functions for more information on setting colors in the graphics display modes.

In the text display modes, the character box is the smallest unit you can use. Each text character takes two bytes of memory, one for the character's ASCII value (defined above) and the other for the attributes that set each character's foreground and background colors, intensity, and blinking characteristics. This second byte is called the character's **attribute byte**, illustrated in **Figure 17.2**. As in the graphics display modes, bits are turned on and off to draw the character within the box, according to the attribute byte's definition.

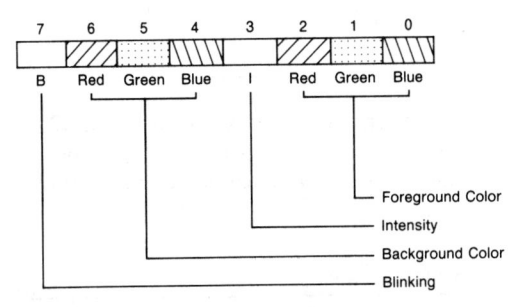

Figure 17.2 Attribute Byte for a Character Box

See also **Figure 17.1** for examples of character boxes with on and off pixels.

In the text display modes, you set a character's ASCII value and attribute byte using the `writechar` function. The constants that specify the colors and other attributes, such as reverse video, are described in the tables in the next section.

Constants Used to Set Colors and Attribute Bytes For both the graphics and text display modes, the include file `<bios.h>` provides constants that you can use in your programs to set the colors and the character attribute byte.

The Student Compiler screen management and graphics functions enable you to specify constants in your programs in a number of ways. You can use the constant, its hexadecimal number, or its decimal number. For example, you can set the color of a foreground character using `YELLOW`, `0x0E`, or `14`. This constant would produce characters on the screen in the color yellow (provided you had a color adapter card). To help you read or debug your programs later, specify the constant itself (such as the name of the color or `BRIGHT`).

In computers with a CGA or EGA card, you can use the constants listed in **Table 17.3** to set the background (BG) color for the text display modes. The `BLINK` constant controls the blinking of the foreground character for the text display modes.

Chapter 17

Table 17.3 Background Colors and Blinking Characteristic for Text Display Modes

Constant	Hex Number	Decimal Number
BLINK	0x80	128
BLACK_BG	0x00	0
BLUE_BG	0x10	16
GREEN_BG	0x20	32
CYAN_BG	0x30	48
RED_BG	0x40	64
MAGENTA_BG	0x50	80
BROWN_BG	0x60	96
LIGHTGRAY_BG	0x70	112

In computers with a CGA or EGA card, you can use the constants listed in **Table 17.4** to set the colors for both display modes. These constants can be used to specify the foreground colors for the text and graphics modes and the background colors for the graphics display modes.

Table 17.4 Colors for Graphics and Text Display Modes

Constant	Hex Number	Decimal Number
BLACK	0x00	0
BLUE	0x01	1
GREEN	0x02	2
CYAN	0x03	3
RED	0x04	4
MAGENTA	0x05	5
BROWN	0x06	6
LIGHTGRAY	0x07	7
DARKGRAY	0x08	8
LIGHTBLUE	0x09	9
LIGHTGREEN	0x0A	10
LIGHTCYAN	0x0B	11
LIGHTRED	0x0C	12
LIGHTMAGENTA	0x0D	13
YELLOW	0x0E	14
WHITE	0x0F	15

Graphics and Screen Management Functions for the Student Compiler

In a PC with an MA or EGA card that is connected to a monochrome display monitor, you can use the constants listed in **Table 17.5** to control the intensity of the foreground character and the appearance of the text.

Table 17.5 Foreground Intensity and Text Appearance

Constant	Hex Number	Decimal Number
BLINK	0x80	128
BRIGHT	0x08	8
NORMAL	0x07	7
UNDERLINE	0x01	1
REVERSEVIDEO	0x70	112
INVISIBLE	0x00	0

In the next section, the screen management and graphics functions are described in greater detail. Sample programs are included with `setpalette` and other functions so that you can see how several of the graphics functions work together to produce simple, color line drawings.

Screen Management and Graphics Functions

The Student Compiler has screen management and graphics functions to control your screen's display settings and characteristics. These functions can be divided into the following categories:

Screen Management Functions

`setvideomode`	Set the display mode.
`getvideomode`	Get the display mode.
`setcurpos`	Set the cursor position.
`getcurpos`	Get the cursor position.
`setcursize`	Set the cursor size.
`getcursize`	Get the cursor size.
`writechar`	Write the character and attribute.
`readchar`	Read the character and attribute.
`scrollup`	Scroll window up.
`scrolldown`	Scroll window down.
`setborder`	Set the border color.

Chapter 17

Graphics Functions

`setpalette`	Set the color palette.
`setcolor`	Set the current color.
`setpixel`	Set the color of the pixel.
`getpixel`	Get the color of the pixel.
`drawline`	Draw a line.
`drawrect`	Draw a rectangular outline.
`fillrect`	Fill a rectangle.

If your computer contains a Monochrome Adapter (MA) card, you can use only the screen management functions. If your computer has a Color/Graphics Adapter (CGA) or Enhanced Graphics Adapter (EGA) card, you can use both sets of functions. See the **Screen Interface** section earlier in this chapter for more information on these display adapter cards and setting your computer's display mode. Note: the Student Compiler debugger cannot be used for screen management or graphics functions.

In the following section, each screen management and graphics function is described. (Diskette 2 contains the screen management and graphics function examples.)

setvideomode, getvideomode - Set or get the display mode   Class: BIOS

NAME

    `setvideomode`   Set the display mode.
    `getvideomode`   Get the display mode.

SYNOPSIS

```
#include <bios.h>

void setvideomode(mode);
int  getvideomode(mode);

int mode;       display mode
```

DESCRIPTION

The `setvideomode` function sets the screen's display characteristics, that is, the way characters (text and graphics) look on the screen, the screen's colors, level of resolution, and the number of lines displayed per screen. You can use this function to re-set your screen's default setting or a previous setting.

The system's display buffer is cleared when the mode is set, so that you can also use this function to clear the screen.

The `mode` argument can be a display mode number or, for the text display modes only, a constant. The display mode numbers and constants are provided in the header file `<bios.h>` and are described below in **Table 17.6**. (This table is a combined version of **Tables 17.1** and **17.2** and is repeated here for easy reference.)

setvideomode, getvideomode

Table 17.6 Display Modes and Constants

Display Mode	Constant	Video Type	Colors	Dimensions*	Adapter Card
0	BW40	Text	16 gray	40x25	CGA, EGA
1	CO40	Text	16 foreground 8 background	40x25	CGA, EGA
2	BW80	Text	16 gray	80x25	CGA, EGA
3	CO80	Text	16 foreground 8 background	80x25	CGA, EGA
4		Graphics	4	320x200	CGA, EGA
5		Graphics	4 gray	320x200	CGA, EGA
6		Graphics	2	640x200	CGA, EGA
7	MONO	Text	2 b/w	80x25	MA, EGA
13		Graphics	16	320x200	EGA
14		Graphics	16	640x200	EGA
15		Graphics	2 b/w	640x350	EGA**
16		Graphics	4	640x350	EGA

* Dimensions are defined in columns (that is, character boxes) and rows for the text video modes and in pixels for the graphics video modes. For both video modes, the higher the number of columns or pixels, the greater the character and color resolution.

** Graphics display mode 15 works differently than the other graphics modes. Mode 15 requires the use of an EGA card in a PC connected to a monochrome display monitor. This setting lets you create black and white graphics as well as text, but it is rarely used.

Because you can use either the display mode number or the constant name (in the second column of **Table 17.6**) to set a text display mode, the following examples produce the same result:

```
setvideomode(0);
    or
setvideomode(BW40);
```

Note that these constants are case-sensitive and should be typed in uppercase letters.

The `getvideomode` function returns the value (that is, the number) of the current display mode.

setvideomode, getvideomode

RETURN VALUE

The **setvideomode** function has no return value. The **getvideomode** function returns one of the display mode numbers listed in **Table 17.6**.

EXAMPLE

```
/* The following program turns on a high resolution graphics mode
   for an EGA card. */

#include <stdio.h>
#include <bios.h>

main()
   {
   setvideomode(16);
   }



/* The following program clears the screen. */

#include <stdio.h>
#include <bios.h>

main ()
   {
   setvideomode (getvideomode());
   }
```

setcurpos, getcurpos

setcurpos, getcurpos - Set or get the cursor position　　　　**Class: BIOS**

NAME
    setcurpos   Set the cursor position.
    getcurpos   Get the cursor position.

SYNOPSIS

```
#include <bios.h>

void setcurpos(row,col);
void getcurpos(row,col);

int row;            row of the cursor position
int col;            column of the cursor position

int *row;           pointer to row of the cursor position
int *col;           pointer to column of the cursor position
```

DESCRIPTION

    The `setcurpos` function sets the cursor position using its (X,Y) (row/column) coordinates. The `getcurpos` function indicates the current cursor position using its (X,Y) coordinates. The numbering for the coordinates (0,0) begins in the top left corner of the screen.

RETURN VALUES

    These functions have no return values.

EXAMPLE

```
/* This example uses setcurpos and getcurpos.  Note: you must reset
   the screen's display mode after execution. */

#include <stdio.h>
#include <bios.h>

void
printstring(str)
char *str;
{
int row, col;

   /* Change foreground and background colors for text
      and move cursor to a new position on the screen. */
for(;*str; str++) {
   writechar(*str, (unsigned char) (GREEN_BG | RED), 1);
   getcurpos(&row, &col);
   setcurpos(row, col + 1);
   }
}
```

setcurpos, getcurpos

```
main()
{

   /* Change the monitor to a new graphics mode and
      move the cursor to the center of the screen. */
   setvideomode(CO40);
   setcurpos(10,15);
   printstring("This is it!");
}
```

SEE ALSO

setcursize, getcursize

setcursize, getcursize - Set or get the cursor size   **Class: BIOS**

NAME
    `setcursize`   Set the cursor size.
    `getcursize`   Get the cursor size.

SYNOPSIS

```
#include <bios.h>

void setcursize(start,end);
void getcursize(start,end);

int start;       starting scan line of the cursor
int end;         ending scan line of the cursor

int *start;      pointer to starting scan line of the cursor
int *end;        pointer to ending scan line of the cursor
```

DESCRIPTION

The `setcursize` function sets the the size of the blinking cursor that appears on display screens set with the text display modes. (Because of the IBM PC design, a cursor cannot be displayed when your screen is set with a graphics display mode; if you call this function from a graphics mode, the system ignores it.)

The `getcursize` function indicates the number of scan lines that make up the cursor's size.

The `setcursize` function allows you to change the height of the cursor by changing the number of scan lines that are displayed. A cursor is defined as one character box, where the box can be one to fourteen scan lines high, depending on your computer's display adapter card; the width of the cursor's character box is counted in pixels. Scan lines are not to be confused with a line of text characters. Any single text character (or cursor) is made up of a number of scan lines.

By default, the standard cursor appears as one or two blinking scan lines. The computer's display adapter card determines the number of scan lines per character box. You can use one scan line or the full character box as the cursor.

Adapter Card	Character Box Size (Cursor Size Limit)
CGA	8 scan lines numbered from the top, from 0 through 7; the box is eight pixels wide
EGA	14 scan lines numbered from the top, from 0 through 13; the box is nine pixels wide
MA	14 scan lines numbered from the top, from 0 through 13; the box is nine pixels wide

setcursize, getcursize

The cursor's size (height) is defined by specifying its starting and ending scan lines. If the starting scan line is less than or equal to the ending scan line, the cursor is displayed in one part:

```
0
1
2
3   -----------   starting scan line
4   -----------
5   -----------
6   -----------   ending scan line
7
```

If the starting scan line is greater than the ending scan line, the cursor is displayed in two parts:

```
0   -----------
1   -----------
2   -----------   ending scan line
3
4
5
6   -----------   starting scan line
7   -----------
```

The latter example makes your cursor look like an equals sign (=) on the display screen.

You can set or change only the height of a cursor, not its width.

RETURN VALUES

These functions have no return values.

SEE ALSO

`getcurpos, setcurpos`

EXAMPLE

```
/* This example demonstrates setcursize and getcursize. */

#include <stdio.h>
#include <bios.h>
#include <dos.h>

void main()
{
int start, end;
int i, j;
long tmp;

getcursize(&start, &end);

printf("Notice that the cursor changes size as you watch.\n");
printf("Press any key to exit:");
```

setcursize, getcursize

```
      i = 0;
      j = 0;

      while ( !kbhit() )
         {
         setcursize( i, j );
         i = ( i + 1 ) % 8;
         if ( i == 0 )
            j = ( j + 1 ) % 8;
            for ( tmp = 0; tmp < 5000; tmp++ );
         }

      getch();

      setcursize(start, end);
      }

   kbhit()
   {
      union REGS regs;

      regs.h.ah = 1;
      regs.h.al = 0;

      int86( 0x16, &regs, &regs );

      return (int)( regs.h.al );
   }

   getch()
   {
      union REGS regs;

      regs.h.ah = 0;
      regs.h.al = 0;

      int86( 0x16, &regs, &regs );

      return ( regs.x.ax );
   }
```

writechar, readchar

writechar, readchar - Write or read the character and attribute   **Class: BIOS**

NAME

    `writechar`   Write the character and attribute.
    `readchar`   Read the character and attribute.

SYNOPSIS

```
#include <bios.h>

void writechar(character,attr,number);
void readchar(character,attr);

char character;              character to be written out
unsigned char attr;          attribute byte of characters to be written out
int number;                  number of times to write character and attribute

char *character;             pointer to character to be read
unsigned char *attr;         pointer to attribute byte of characters to be read
```

DESCRIPTION

The `writechar` function writes a text character with an attribute byte at the current cursor position (without moving the position). You can use this function to define colors and other attributes (such as reverse video or underlining) for the text display modes. To define a color in the text modes, you must use a computer containing a CGA or EGA card.

The `character` argument is any ASCII character (or its ASCII value) that you want to write at the current position. When using alphabetic characters, `writechar` is case-sensitive. The `character` argument is enclosed in single quotes (').

The `attr` argument is the constant you specify to describe or modify the character's appearance, for example, to make a character blink or the color blue. These attribute constants are listed in **Table 17.3** for the background color, **Table 17.4** for the foreground color, and **Table 17.5** for attributes if your computer has a Monochrome Adapter card. In the `attr` argument, you can specify the constant by its name (for example, YELLOW) or by its hexadecimal or decimal number. It is recommended that you use the constant itself because it is easier to read and debug your program later.

To represent a single argument, the attributes are grouped using parentheses; each attribute is separated using a vertical bar, for example,

```
writechar(*s, (unsigned char)(GREEN_BG | RED), 5);
```

You should add the data type for the `attr` argument to your C code, as shown above, because the Student Compiler has to cast the constant's type from an `int` to an `unsigned char`.

writechar, readchar

You use the `number` argument to set the number of times that you want to write the character. If the specified number is greater than one, duplicate characters are written to the right of the current cursor position. In the text display modes, the duplicated characters are wrapped around from line to line.

The `readchar` function reads the character and the attribute at the current cursor position into the specified parameters. This function does not move the current cursor position.

RETURN VALUES

These functions have no return values.

EXAMPLE

```
/* This example shows the writechar function in a multicolor display.
   Do not use this example if your computer has an MA card. */

#include <stdio.h>
#include <bios.h>

main()
{
    int row, col;

    setvideomode(getvideomode());

    for (row = 0; row < 16; row++)
       for (col = 0; col < 16; col++)
       {
       setcurpos(row+1, (col*5)+1);
       writechar('*', (unsigned char)((row << 4) | col), 4);
       }

    return(0);
}
```

scrollup, scrolldown

scrollup, scrolldown - Scroll the window up or down　　　　　　　**Class: BIOS**

NAME
scrollup　　　Scroll up the window.
scrolldown　　Scroll down the window.

SYNOPSIS
```
#include <bios.h>

void scrollup(rmin,cmin,rmax,cmax,attr,number);
void scrolldown(rmin,cmin,rmax,cmax,attr,number);

int rmin;              row number of upper-left corner
int cmin;              column number of upper-left corner
int rmax;              row number of lower-right corner
int cmax;              column number of lower-right corner
unsigned char attr;    character attribute of blank lines
int number;            number of blank lines to scroll the window up
                          or down by
```

DESCRIPTION
The `scrollup` and `scrolldown` functions allow you to create a text-window and then to scroll it up or down by a specified number of lines. The scrolled window is defined using the (X,Y) (row/column) coordinates of its upper-left and lower-right corners. The numbering for the coordinates (0,0) begins in the top left corner of the screen.

The scrolled lines are replaced by blank lines (lines without text) having the attribute specified in `attr`; this attribute usually has the same characteristics as your display screen. For example, if your screen is specified with **BROWN_BG**, the number of lines you scroll will also be brown.

You should add the data type for the `attr` argument to your C code, as shown in the example below, because the Student Compiler has to cast the constant's type from an `int` to an `unsigned char`.

RETURN VALUES
These functions have no return values.

EXAMPLE
```
/* This example demonstrates the scrollup and scrolldown functions. */

#include <stdio.h>
#include <bios.h>
```

scrollup, scrolldown

```c
main()
{
int i;

/* Clear the screen and position the cursor for first demo. */
setvideomode(getvideomode());
setcurpos(7,0);

/* Print demonstration text to the screen. */
for(i = 0;i != 10;++i)
   printf("Demo Text Demo Text Demo Text Demo Text\n");

scrolldown(5, 5, 40, 75, (unsigned char)(RED_BG), 10);

/* Prepare screen for the next example. */
setcurpos(1,1);
printf("Type <enter> to continue:");
getchar();

setvideomode(getvideomode());
setcurpos(9,0);

/* Print demonstration text. */
for(i = 0;i != 3;++i)
   printf("Demo Text Demo Text Demo Text Demo Text\n");

scrollup(5, 5, 20, 75, (unsigned char)(RED_BG), 2);
setcurpos(1,1);
}
```

setborder

setborder - Set the border color　　　　　　　　　　　　　　　　　**Class: BIOS**

NAME

setborder　　　Set the border color.

SYNOPSIS

```
#include <bios.h>

void setborder(color);

int color;      border color
```

DESCRIPTION

The `setborder` function sets the color of the border around the text, if your computer contains a CGA or EGA card. You can select the color from the full color palette listed below. This function can be used only with the text display modes.

The include file `<bios.h>` provides constants that you can use to set the border color. In your programs, you can specify the color using the constant or by using either of its numbers, although using the name of the constant is considered the best programming practice.

Constant	Hex Number	Decimal Number
BLACK	0x00	0
BLUE	0x01	1
GREEN	0x02	2
CYAN	0x03	3
RED	0x04	4
MAGENTA	0x05	5
BROWN	0x06	6
LIGHTGRAY	0x07	7
DARKGRAY	0x08	8
LIGHTBLUE	0x09	9
LIGHTGREEN	0x0A	10
LIGHTCYAN	0x0B	11
LIGHTRED	0x0C	12
LIGHTMAGENTA	0x0D	13
YELLOW	0x0E	14
WHITE	0x0F	15

setborder

RETURN VALUE

This function has no return value.

SEE ALSO

`setpalette, setcolor`

EXAMPLE

```
/* This example uses setborder to show different text options. */

#include <stdio.h>
#include <bios.h>

main()
{
setvideomode(getvideomode());
setborder((unsigned char)(RED));

setcurpos(2,0);
printf("Here's a Red Border.\n");
}
```

setpalette

setpalette - Set the color palette Class: BIOS

NAME

setpalette   Set the color palette.

SYNOPSIS

```
#include <bios.h>

void setpalette(background,palette);

int background;     background color
int palette;        color palette
```

DESCRIPTION

The `setpalette` function controls the colors displayed on your screen. You can use this function only with the graphics display modes; to set colors in the text display modes, see the `writechar` function. See **Table 17.6** for a list of the graphics and text display modes. **Color and Text Attributes** describes how colors are formed using these display modes.

Rather than describing `setpalette` with each of the seven display modes, this function is described in terms of display modes 4, 5, and 6. These graphics display modes allow the use of computers with a CGA or EGA card, and produce colors or shades of gray, as follows:

Display Mode	Video Type	Colors	Resolution	Dimensions (in pixels)
4	Graphics	4	Medium	320x200
5	Graphics	4 (gray)	Medium	320x200
6	Graphics	2	High	640x200

See **Table 17.6** for information on the other display modes.

Display Mode 4   In display mode 4, the screen can display four colors simultaneously. You define the four colors by specifying the `background` and `palette` arguments. The background color you specify is described first.

The background color sets the color of your display screen. It is a constant and can be any color that the color adapter card is capable of displaying. These constants are included in the header file `<bios.h>` and are repeated here from **Table 17.4**. In your programs, you can specify the background color by the constant, its hexadecimal number, or its decimal number, although it is recommended that you use the constant's name.

setpalette

Constant	Hex Number	Decimal Number
`BLACK`	0x00	0
`BLUE`	0x01	1
`GREEN`	0x02	2
`CYAN`	0x03	3
`RED`	0x04	4
`MAGENTA`	0x05	5
`BROWN`	0x06	6
`LIGHTGRAY`	0x07	7
`DARKGRAY`	0x08	8
`LIGHTBLUE`	0x09	9
`LIGHTGREEN`	0x0A	10
`LIGHTCYAN`	0x0B	11
`LIGHTRED`	0x0C	12
`LIGHTMAGENTA`	0x0D	13
`YELLOW`	0x0E	14
`WHITE`	0x0F	15

Once you have specified the `background` argument, you must specify the `palette` argument, which lets you choose the other three colors for display mode 4.

Palettes are specified by their number, 0 to 3. Each palette contains four colors, including the background color you have already selected. Each palette acts as a separate, noninterchangeable group. You cannot switch colors between palettes, and the only color you can choose within each palette is the background color. **Table 17.7** lists the four palettes and the colors that each includes.

setpalette

Table 17.7 Color Palette

Palette 0	Color Number for `setcolor`	Real Color
	0	**background** color
	1	**GREEN**
	2	**RED**
	3	**BROWN**
Palette 1	Color Number	Real Color
	0	**background** color
	1	**CYAN**
	2	**MAGENTA**
	3	**LIGHTGRAY**
Palette 2	Color Number	Real Color
	0	**background** color
	1	**LIGHTGREEN**
	2	**LIGHTRED**
	3	**YELLOW**
Palette 3	Color Number	Real Color
	0	**background** color
	1	**LIGHTCYAN**
	2	**LIGHTMAGENTA**
	3	**WHITE**

In each palette, the default background color is listed first and the default foreground color is listed last. So in the following example, choosing a background color **GREEN** with palette 2

```
setpalette(GREEN,2);
```

results in a green display screen with yellow characters.

The Color Number column in **Table 17.7** lists the number given as the argument to the `setcolor` function. This function selects the current color for all the graphics drawing operations, if you have set your screen using a graphics display mode. The `setcolor` and `setpalette` functions work together to specify the colors for your drawings as well as your foreground and background colors.

setpalette

If you plan to produce drawings with your program, you should call the `setpalette` function before calling the `setcolor` function. For example, if you want your drawing to appear in light red, specify

```
setpalette(GREEN,2)
setcolor(2)
```

This results in a green screen, yellow text, and light red drawings. For more information, see the EXAMPLE below and the `setcolor` function description.

Display Mode 5 Display mode 5 operates in the exact same way as mode 4 on PCs with an EGA card and on recently made PCs with a CGA card. On some older PCs that are connected to composite display monitors, the color is suppressed in mode 5. The screen display appears to be black and white although it is actually composed of four shades of gray. Modes 4 and 6 are used more often than mode 5.

Display Mode 6 In display mode 6, the screen can display two colors. One of the colors is always black and the other can be any of the 16 colors (from **Table 17.4**) that the color adapter card is capable of producing. The other color is specified by the `background` color argument, as described above in **Display Mode 4**.

The `palette` argument has no significance in this mode because there is only one palette. You should set `palette` to 0. If you specify a palette number other than 0, the compiler ignores it. For example, if you specify a background color `CYAN` with palette 0, the screen displays a cyan background with black text.

Color Number for `setcolor`	Real Color
0	Black
1	Background color

Setpalette with Text Display Modes If you mistakenly use `setpalette` while your screen is set to a text display mode (modes 0-3 and 7), the background color you specify is displayed as a border color.

RETURN VALUE

This function returns no value.

SEE ALSO

`setcolor`

setpalette

EXAMPLE

```
#include <stdio.h>
#include <dos.h>
#include <bios.h>

/* This program draws the French flag on the screen. */

void
main() {
   int oldvideomode;

/* Set the display to a color graphics video mode. */
oldvideomode = getvideomode(); /* Save the current video mode */
setvideomode(4);               /* 320 x 200 with 4 colors */

/* Set your color palette so that colors 0, 1, 2, and 3 have
   the following meaning:

   Color Number        Real Color

        0              blue (background)
        1              light cyan
        2              light magenta
        3              white

   You can do this by selecting palette 3 with a blue
   background color */

setpalette(BLUE, 3);

/* Select light magenta as the current color. */
setcolor(2);         /* 2 is the color number */
                     /* for light magenta. */

/* Paint the left portion of the screen light magenta. */
fillrect(0,0(319/3), 199);

/* Select white as the current color. */
setcolor(3);         /* 3 is the color number */
                     /* for white. */

/* Paint the middle portion of the screen white. */
fillrect((319 / 3), 0, (2 * (319/3), 199);

/* Select blue as the current color. */
setcolor(0);         /* 0 is the color number */
                     /* for blue. */

/* Paint the right portion of the screen blue. */
fillrect((2 * (319/3)), 0, 319, 199);
```

setpalette

```
            /* Draw a thin light cyan border around the flag. */
            setcolor(1);            /* 1 is the color number */
                                    /* for light cyan. */

            drawrect(0,0,319,199);

            /* Wait for the user to type a character. */
            getch();
            setvideomode(oldvideomode);   /* Restore old video mode. */
            }
```

setcolor

setcolor - Set the current color   **Class: BIOS**

NAME
    setcolor   Set the current color.

SYNOPSIS
    #include <bios.h>

    void setcolor(color);

    int color;   current color

DESCRIPTION

The `setcolor` function selects the current color for all the graphics drawing operations and can therefore be used only while your screen is set to a graphics display mode.

The `setcolor` function is always used in conjunction with `setpalette`: the value of the argument `color` is derived from the Color Number column in the palettes' list in **Table 17.7**.

The value of the `color` argument depends on the color adapter card your computer has. As in the `setpalette` description, `setcolor` is described here in terms of the graphics display modes 4, 5, and 6.

CGA Card   In most graphics display modes, the `color` argument is a number, 0 to 3, as defined in the color palette table (**Table 17.7**).

Display mode 6 has only two colors, specified as 0 or 1, that can be displayed. For more information on mapping the color numbers to real colors, see `setpalette`.

EGA Card   The value for the `color` argument follows the numbers of the color constants (0 to 15) listed in **Table 17.4** and repeated below for reference; these numbers actually refer to the EGA card's color registers. These color constants are included in the header file `<bios.h>`. You can specify the `color` argument using the constant's name, its hexadecimal number, or its decimal number.

setcolor

Constant	Hex Number	Decimal Number
`BLACK`	0x00	0
`BLUE`	0x01	1
`GREEN`	0x02	2
`CYAN`	0x03	3
`RED`	0x04	4
`MAGENTA`	0x05	5
`BROWN`	0x06	6
`LIGHTGRAY`	0x07	7
`DARKGRAY`	0x08	8
`LIGHTBLUE`	0x09	9
`LIGHTGREEN`	0x0A	10
`LIGHTCYAN`	0x0B	11
`LIGHTRED`	0x0C	12
`LIGHTMAGENTA`	0x0D	13
`YELLOW`	0x0E	14
`WHITE`	0x0F	15

RETURN VALUE

This function has no return value.

SEE ALSO

`setpalette`

EXAMPLE

See the example under the `setpalette` function.

setpixel, getpixel - Set or get the color of the pixel   **Class: BIOS**

NAME
      `setpixel`   Set the color of the pixel.
      `getpixel`   Get the color of the pixel.

SYNOPSIS

```
#include <bios.h>

void setpixel(x,y);
int  getpixel(x,y);

int x,y;       pixel coordinates
int color;     color of the pixel
```

DESCRIPTION

The `setpixel` function sets the color of the pixel at the specified (`x,y`) location. The color is set to the current color, as defined by the `setcolor` function. The `getpixel` function returns the color of the specified pixel. Pixel locations are defined by their row and column (X,Y) location on a coordinate grid, where (0,0) is at the top left corner of the screen. These functions can be used only in a graphics display mode.

RETURN VALUE

The `setpixel` function returns no value. The `getpixel` function returns a color argument, as described in `setcolor`.

SEE ALSO

    `setcolor`

EXAMPLE

```
/* This example demonstrates the setpixel and getpixel functions
   and draws the letter "V".
   NOTE: The color set below is not necessarily the color that
   will appear on your display.  Do not use this with a monochrome
   display. */

#include <stdio.h>
#include <bios.h>

void main()
{
int x, y, color, oldmode;

/* Set to graphics mode. Save previous mode. */
oldmode = getvideomode();
setvideomode(4);

/* Set color and draw the "V" using two loops. */
setcolor((unsigned char)2);
```

setpixel, getpixel

```
    x = 20;
    for(y = 20; y != 140; y++){
       ++x;
       setpixel(x,y);
    }

    x = 139;
    for(y = 139; y != 19; y--){
       ++x;
       setpixel(x,y);
    }

    /* Report color at cursor position. */
    color = getpixel(20,20);
    setcurpos(19,0);
    printf("The color is %d\n", color);

    /* Prompt user before resetting to original mode. */
    printf("Press <enter> to continue:");
    getchar();
    setvideomode(oldmode);
}
```

drawline, drawrect

drawline, drawrect - Draw a line Class: BIOS

NAME
    drawline   Draw a line.
    drawrect   Draw an outline of a rectangle.

SYNOPSIS
    #include <bios.h>

    void drawline(x1,y1,x2,y2);
    void drawrect(x1,y1,x2,y2);

    int x1,y1;   pixel coordinates of the first endpoint or corner
    int x2,y2;   pixel coordinates of the second endpoint or corner

DESCRIPTION

The `drawline` function draws a line on the screen and the `drawrect` function draws an outline of a rectangle on the screen. Each line is composed of pixels. The line's color is the current color established by the `setcolor` function. You specify each endpoint or corner using a row and column (X,Y) location on the coordinate grid, where (0,0) is at the top left corner of the screen. These functions can be used only in a graphics display mode.

RETURN VALUE

These functions have no return values.

SEE ALSO

    setcolor, fillrect

EXAMPLE

```
/* Draw a line on the screen in a graphics display mode. */

#include <stdio.h>
#include <dos.h>
#include <bios.h>

void
main()
{
int oldmode;
```

drawline, drawrect

```
    oldmode = getvideomode();        /* Save current display mode. */
    setvideomode(4);                 /* Set display to graphics mode. */
    setpalette(BLUE,3);              /* Select palette 3 with blue background. */
    setcolor(2);                     /* Draw line in color 2 - light magenta. */
    drawline(0,0,40,55);             /* Draw a diagonal line. */
    drawline(50,150,75,50);        /* Draw a rhombus. */
    drawline(75,50,200,50);
    drawline(200,50,175,150);
    drawline(175,150,50,150);
    getchar();                       /* Wait for user to type a character. */
    setvideomode(oldmode);           /* Reset display mode. */
}
```

fillrect - Fill a rectangle   **Class: BIOS**

NAME
    `fillrect`   Fill a rectangle.

SYNOPSIS
```
#include <bios.h>

void fillrect(x1,y1,x2,y2);

int x1,y1;    pixel coordinates of the first corner
int x2,y2;    pixel coordinates of the second corner
```

DESCRIPTION
The `fillrect` function draws a filled rectangle on the screen. The color of the filled rectangle is the current color established by the `setcolor` function. You specify each corner using a row and column (X,Y) location on the coordinate grid, where (0,0) is at the top left corner of the screen. This function can be used only in a graphics display mode.

RETURN VALUE
This function has no return value.

SEE ALSO
`drawline`, `setcolor`, `drawrect`

EXAMPLE
See the example under the `setpalette` function.

Chapter 18
Source-Level Debugger for the Student Compiler

Chapter 18

CONTENTS

Introduction 569
The Student Compiler Debugger 569
    Invoking the Debugger for the Student Compiler 571
The User Interface 571
    Debugger Screen 571
    Using the Menu System 574
    Session Menu 574
        Help 575
        Restart 575
        Quit 576
    Display Menu 576
        Variable 577
        String 578
        Where 578
    Break Menu 579
        List 580
        Set/Clear 580
        Clear All 581
    Execute Menu 581
        Once 582
        Trace 583
        Proceed 583
        Go 583
Chapter Summary 584

Introduction

This chapter shows you how to use the Student Compiler's source-level debugger. You can use this debugger to identify programming errors once you have successfully compiled your C language source program. Topics covered include:

- entering the debugger from the Student Compiler's editor
- using the debugger menus and commands to detect errors
- using the editor and compiler to run corrected programs.

Like the Student Compiler's editor, the debugger is menu-driven and very easy to use. Read the next section if you have not used a debugger before. It explains when to use a source-level debugger and how this debugger works. If you have used a source-level debugger in the past, skip to the next section, **Invoking the Debugger**.

The Student Compiler Debugger

You can write a program, have it compile successfully, and then discover that it is not solving the problem or doing the task you expected it to do. It may be syntactically correct, but the outcome is wrong. This is when you need a debugger. You have already run the program (using the Run command in the File menu) at least once to see its results. You may know that part of your program is correct, but that its logic falls apart later or that the values being displayed on the Program Screen are way out of the expected range. To find the problem, you need to watch your C source program as it executes.

Selecting the **Debug command** (instead of the Run command) allows you to compile the program and monitor its execution. The Debug command interrupts the usual *compile then execute* process by pausing after the program has successfully compiled. You then enter any command line arguments (as described in the Debug command, Chapter 14) and press the <enter> key. This puts you into the debugger and begins the program's execution. You can then use the debugger menus and commands to examine every step of your source program as it executes.

The Student Compiler's debugger provides many ways to examine a program, such as allowing you to set **breakpoints** (in the Break menu) in your program. This means that you set points in your program to suspend execution, so you can look at the partial results. For example, you can set a breakpoint at each function call so that you can examine the return values after each call; this may help you in detecting invalid data or unexpected interactions.

You can also use the Trace command to proceed through a program one line at a time during execution; this process is referred to as **single-stepping** through the program. As you step through the program, a **trace program** produces the code's output on a line-by-line basis. This trace output may alert you to a change in the flow of control or to a change in the value of a specific variable.

Chapter 18

Once you have detected errors in your program, you can select the Quit command to return to the Student Compiler's editor in order to modify your source file. You can then use the Run or Debug commands again to run your program. The editor, compiler, and debugger work together, as illustrated in **Figure 18.1**.

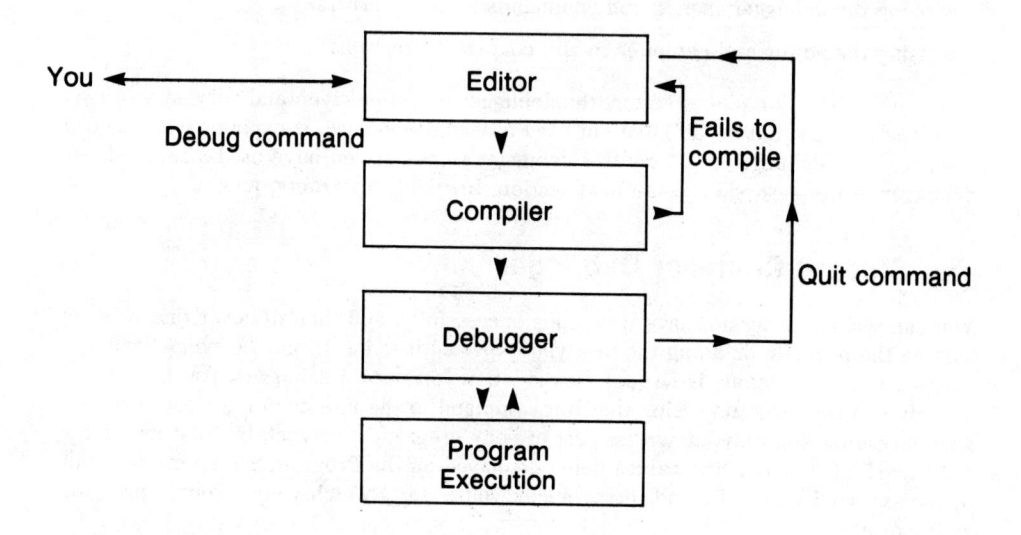

```
You  ←――――――→  Editor  ←―――――┐
       Debug command    ▼      │ Fails to
                              │ compile
                     Compiler ―┘
                        ▼              ↑
                     Debugger ―――――→   │ Quit command
                        ▼▲
                     Program
                     Execution
```

Figure 18.1   Debugging Process

Source-Level Debugger for the Student Compiler

Invoking the Debugger for the Student Compiler

You invoke the debugger by selecting the Debug command from the File menu of the Student Compiler's Editing Screen. To do this, press function key F10 and the letter F to display the File menu. You then move the cursor down to select Debug and press <enter> or type the initial letter D (for Debug). The results of the program's compilation, including any errors, are displayed on the Program Screen. (See Chapter 14 for more information on the Debug command.)

If your PC contains a CGA card but has a monochrome display monitor, you may see some highlighting irregularities when you set the debugger breakpoints. You can remedy this by adding the following line to your AUTOEXEC.BAT file or by typing it from the MS-DOS command line before you invoke the Student Compiler.

```
mode BW80
```

If you add this line to your AUTOEXEC.BAT file, do so before the CTRL-Z sequence. See Chapter 13 for a description of the AUTOEXEC.BAT file.

Note: the debugger cannot be used for screen management or graphics functions.

To exit from the debugger, press function key F4 or select the Quit command in the Session menu. You are returned to the Editing Screen.

The User Interface

The debugger has two major screen displays: the Debugger Screen and the Program Screen.

- Debugger Screen
  allows you to monitor the execution of your C program. Its format is similar to the Editing Screen, except that the Debugger Screen divides the display screen into two windows.

- Program Screen
  displays messages from the compiler and output from your program while they are running. This is the same screen as the one you use with the Editing Screen. You can press the function key F9 to go back and forth between the Debugger Screen and the Program Screen.

Debugger Screen

The Debugger Screen contains a menu bar, source and output windows, an input/status line, and a message line. You will note that it is similar to the Student Compiler's Editing Screen, thus making it easy for you to use. The Debugger Screen is shown in **Screen 18.1**.

Chapter 18

```
┌─────────────────────────────────────────────────────────────────┐
│  Session    Display    Break    Execute      (MENU BAR)         │
│─────────────────────────────────────────────────────────────────│
│ === Top of file ===                                             │
│ #include <stdio.h>            (SOURCE WINDOW)                   │
│                                                                 │
│ main()                                                          │
│   {                                                             │
│   int i;                                                        │
│                                                                 │
│   for (i=0; i<10; i++)                                          │
│     printf("Great job!");                                       │
│   }                                                             │
│                                                                 │
│ === Bottom of file ===                                          │
│─────────────────────────────────────────────────────────────────│
│                                                                 │
│ SAS/C Compiler, Student Edition, Version 1.00                   │
│ Copyright 1988 SAS Institute Inc.                               │
│                                                                 │
│ main() line 4 - entry          (OUTPUT WINDOW)                  │
│                                                                 │
│─────────────────────────────────────────────────────────────────│
│  Line 4                      great.c      (INPUT/STATUS LINE)   │
│ (MESSAGE LINE)..................................................│
└─────────────────────────────────────────────────────────────────┘
```

Screen 18.1 Debugger Screen

Menu Bar The menu bar lists the debugger's pull-down menus along the top of the source window. As with the Editing Screen's menu bar, you can move the cursor along this bar to select a pull-down menu and its commands. The Session menu controls the debugging session. The Display menu displays the contents of your program's data or data structures. The Break menu sets and clears breakpoints, whereas the Execute menu lets you single-step through or execute your program to the next breakpoint.

Source Window The source window is below the menu bar and encompasses about half of your screen. It shows the C code currently being executed, using C code statements from your source file. The next line to be executed is displayed in reverse video; this line may or may not coincide with the current line, that is, the line with the cursor on it. (For simplicity, lines appearing in reverse video are referred to as **highlighted** lines.) Lines at which breakpoints have been set are displayed in high intensity, a kind of on-screen boldface type.

The current cursor position indicates where you are in the source file. As in the Student Compiler's editing window, the cursor's location identifies the current line.

Source-Level Debugger for the Student Compiler

Since this debugger is line oriented, not expression oriented, the cursor is always displayed in column one. It can be moved up or down but not side to side.

You can use the same cursor control keys in the source window as you do in the editing window. The only differences are that all the movement is up or down (because of the debugger's line orientation) and that you cannot enter or modify your source file. Otherwise, you can use the same key assignments to move the cursor.

up arrow	moves the cursor one position upwards. Does not move if the cursor is on the first line of the source file. Scrolls the source file upwards by one line if the cursor is on the first line of the source window.
down arrow	moves the cursor one position downwards. Does not move if the cursor is on the last line of the source file. Scrolls the source file downwards by one line if the cursor is on the last line of the source window.
PgUp	scrolls the source file upwards by one page.
PgDn	scrolls the source file downwards by one page.
CTRL-HOME	moves the cursor to the first line of the source file.
CTRL-END	moves the cursor to the last line of the source file.
CTRL-PgUp	moves the cursor to the first line of the source window.
CTRL-PgDn	moves the cursor to the last line of the source window.

Output Window The output window is directly below the source window and encompasses the second half of your screen. It shows a trace of the C code that is currently being executed and additional information, based on the menu command you have selected.

The output window is only nine lines high, but you can use the keypad's plus and minus keys (+ and −) to review output that has already scrolled out of view.

+ key	scrolls the output window down by one line.
− key	scrolls the output window up by one line.

In the output window, you can scroll up to fifty lines of your program's output. If you exceed this limit, the system discards the oldest lines of output to make room for the most current output.

Status Line The status line is below the source window and tells you which line the cursor is on and the name of the source file being debugged.

Input Line The input line replaces the status line once you begin to type on it. For example, you may input the name of a character pointer in response to a prompt.

Chapter 18

Message Line   The message line is the last line on the screen and it displays all the debugger's messages. Messages are always highlighted.

Using the Menu System

The debugger menu system works in exactly the same way as the editor menu system. A very brief summary of the steps you take to select one of the pull-down menus listed on the debugger menu bar and the commands in that menu follows.

- To select a pull-down menu, press function key F10 and the initial letter of the menu you want to display. The specified menu is then displayed over part of the source window. The debugger does not allow you to use ALT keys to switch between menus.

- To select a command in a pull-down menu, use the arrow keys to move the cursor to the command you want and press the <enter> key or type the initial letter of that command. You can use only the commands listed in that menu.

- If a menu command has a fast path key, you can press it from anywhere in the source window to execute that command, as long as a pull-down menu is not currently being displayed.

For more information on executing these steps, see Chapter 14. As an overview, each debugger menu and its commands and fast path keys are listed in **Table 18.1**.

Table 18.1   Summary of Commands in Each Debugger Menu

Session Menu	Display Menu	Break Menu	Execute Menu
Help (F1)	Variable (F2)	List	Once (F6)
Restart	String (F3)	Set/Clear (F5)	Trace (F7)
Quit (F4)	Where	Clear All	Proceed (F8)
		Go	

Session Menu

The Session menu allows you to request online help, to restart the program at the first line of code, or to quit the debugger. You can access this menu using the methods described earlier in **Using the Menu System**. The Session menu is displayed over part of the source window, as shown below in **Screen 18.2**.

Each command in the Session menu is described following **Screen 18.2**. Remember, if you do not use the fast path key to execute a command, you can use only the commands in the currently displayed menu. If you want to use commands in another menu, you have to select that menu.

Source-Level Debugger for the Student Compiler

```
 Session    Display     Break      Execute
┌─────────┐
│ Help  F1│file ===
│ Restart │tdio.h>
│ Quit  F4│
└─────────┘
    {
      int i;
      for (i=0; i<10; i++)
        printf("Great job!");
    }


    === Bottom of file ===


    main() line 4 - entry




    Line 2                              great.c
```

Screen 18.2 Session Menu

Help The Help command displays information on your screen about two topic areas: the syntax and use of the ANSI Standard, graphics, and screen management functions and explanatory information on the Student Compiler's error messages (accessed by their error number). This is the same Help facility that you invoke from within the compiler's editor.

To invoke the online Help facility, select Help from the Session menu and press the <enter> key. See the Help command description in Chapter 14 for more information.

Fast Path

Function Key: F1

To get Help information, press the function key F1. Note that you cannot have any pull-down menu displayed when you press F1.

Restart The Restart command lets you recompile and execute your C source program from its first line of code. To restart your program, select Restart from the Session menu and press the <enter> key.

This command has no fast path key.

Chapter 18

Quit   The Quit command lets you exit the debugger and return to the Student Compiler's editing window. To do this, select Quit from the Session menu and press the <enter> key.

Fast Path

Function Key: F4

To quit the debugger from anywhere in the source window, press function key F4. Note that you cannot have any pull-down menu displayed when you press F4.

Display Menu

The Display menu contains commands that allow you to examine the contents of your program's data. You can access this menu using the methods described earlier in **Using the Menu System**. The Display menu is displayed over part of the source window, as shown in **Screen 18.3**.

Each command in the Display menu is described following the screen. Remember, if you do not use the fast path key to execute a command, you can use only the commands in the currently displayed menu. If you want to use commands in another menu, you have to select that menu.

```
Session      Display      Break       Execute

=== Top o   Variable    F2
#include    String      F3
            Where

main()
-  {
   int i;
   for (i=0; i<10; i++)
     printf("Great job!");
   }

=== Bottom of file ===

main() line 5 - entry
breakpoint list
main 6
main 7
i = 0



Variable Name: "i"
```

Screen 18.3 Display Menu

576

Source-Level Debugger for the Student Compiler

Variable The Variable command displays your program's variables, data structures, and objects. A variable is an expression in your program that designates an object. It can be either a simple identifier or an expression referring to an array element, structure member, or object pointed to by a pointer. In addition, it may begin with a specification of the form

    function'\'

where *function* is the name of a function in your program. Examples of valid variable names include:

    i
    max
    array[3]
    readfile\length
    mystruct->name[2]
    *cptr
    opnf\count
    opnf\i
    array

When you select Variable from the Display menu and press the <enter> key, you will be prompted to enter the name of the variable whose value you want to display. Type in the variable name between the double quotes of the **Variable Name:** prompt on the input line. Use the backspace key to correct any typing mistakes. Press the <enter> key to display the contents of the variable or press the ESC key to cancel your request. The variable's value is displayed in the output window.

For example, if your program contained an integer and you input the variable **i**, the following is displayed in the output window:

    i = 10

Or, if you want the value of an element in an array and you input the variable and element number **a[7]**, the following is displayed in the output window:

    a[7] = 15

The Variable command works only if you have already reached the variable in your program. If the variable name you input is not valid or refers to a variable that does not exist, the following error message is printed on the message line:

    Invalid variable

Fast Path

Function Key: F2

Press function key F2 to select the Variable command and to display the **Variable Name:** prompt. Then follow the instructions listed above.

577

Chapter 18

String   The String command lets you examine the contents of a null-terminated string via a character pointer. A null-terminated string is a character string constant terminated with a NULL character ('\0'). You can pass an address to the debugger in the form of a C pointer variable: `char *p`, where `p` is a valid string address.

When you select the String command from the Display menu and press the <enter> key, you will be prompted to enter the character pointer variable. Type this variable name between the double quotes of the **String Variable:** prompt on the input line. Use the backspace key to correct any typing mistakes. Press the <enter> key to display the contents of the string or press the ESC key to cancel your request. The string is displayed in the output window.

Take, for example, a program that contained a character pointer `p` that has been initialized to the starting address of the string `"Great job!"` If you input the string `p`, the output window would contain the following:

```
p = "Great job!"
```

If the string address you input is not valid or refers to the address of a variable that does not exist, the following error message is displayed on the message line:

```
Invalid variable
```

Fast Path

Function Key: F3

Press function key F3 to select the String command and to display the **String Variable:** prompt. Then follow the instructions listed above.

Where   The Where command provides you with a **traceback**, which is a list in reverse order of the functions that have executed in your program. The list is displayed in the output window. Each line of the traceback output contains a function name, preceded by the line number at which the function was called. The most recently called function (that is, the currently executing function) is listed first. Each entry in the traceback is listed immediately above the entry for the function that calls it. The last line of the Where output is the `main` function.

For example, if the `main` program called the function `myfunc` which called the function `toto`, the Where output looks as it does in **Screen 18.4**.

```
 Session    Display    Break    Execute
 ─────────────────────────────────────────
 === Top of file ===

 void
 toto()
 {
   printf("toto was called");
 _ }


 void
 myfunc() {

 ─────────────────────────────────────────
 where?
 toto()   line 14 - entry
 myfunc() line 19 - entry
 main()   line 5  - entry



 ─────────────────────────────────────────
    Line 16                      great.c
```

Screen 18.4 Where Command

This command has no fast path key.

Break Menu

The Break menu allows you to set and clear breakpoints in your source file. When you set a breakpoint on a line, you instruct the debugger to stop executing your program when it reaches that line. You can access this menu using the methods described earlier in **Using the Menu System.** The Break menu is displayed over part of the source window, as shown in **Screen 18.5.**

Each command in the Break menu is described following the screen. Remember, if you do not use the fast path key to execute a command, you can use only the commands in the currently displayed menu. If you want to use commands in another menu, you have to select that menu.

Chapter 18

```
 Session   Display    Break      Execute
 === Top of file ===  List
 #include <stdio.h>   Set/Clear  F5
                      Clear All
 main()
 {
   int i;
   for (i=0; i<10; i++)
     printf("Great job!");
 }

 === Bottom of file ===

 main() line 4 - entry
 breakpoint list
 main 5
 main 6




 Line 4                          great.c
```

Screen 18.5 Break Menu

List   The List command displays a list in the output window of all the active breakpoints. To display the breakpoints and their line numbers, select List from the Break menu and press the <enter> key. In **Screen 18.5** above, the list in the output window indicates breakpoints are set on lines 5 and 6 of the source program.

This command has no fast path key.

Set/Clear   The Set/Clear command lets you set or clear a breakpoint on the current line of the source program. To set a breakpoint, move the cursor to the appropriate line, select List from the Break menu, and press the <enter> key. Lines that have breakpoint settings are displayed in high intensity. A maximum of fifty breakpoints is allowed at any one time.

The Set/Clear command acts as a toggle, that is, if the command is executed once, it sets the breakpoint and if the command is executed again, it clears the breakpoint. If the line is displayed in high intensity, the breakpoint is set and otherwise the breakpoint is cleared.

A breakpoint can be set on any valid, executing line of C code. If you set a breakpoint on a blank line, comment, definition statement, or other nonexecuting statement, the following error message is displayed on the message line:

```
Breakpoints can be set only on valid lines of code
```

Fast Path

Function Key: F5

To set a breakpoint, move the cursor to the line that you want to set and press the function key F5. Press F5 again to clear the breakpoint.

Clear All The Clear All command clears all the breakpoints in your source file. To do this, select **Clear All** from the Break menu and press the <enter> key. This command has no fast path key.

Execute Menu

The Execute menu contains commands that let you execute your program until the next breakpoint or to single step through the program. While your program is executing, it displays all of the results and return values on the Program Screen. You can use the function key F9 to go back and forth between the source window and the Program Screen.

You can access this menu using the methods described earlier in **Using the Menu System**. The Execute menu is displayed over part of the source window, as shown in **Screen 18.6**.

Each command in the Execute menu is described following the screen. Remember, if you do not use the fast path key to execute a command, you can use only the commands in the currently displayed menu. If you want to use commands in another menu, you have to select that menu.

Chapter 18

```
 Session   Display    Break    Execute
─────────────────────────────────────────────────
 === Top of file ===        ┌─────────────┐
 #include <stdio.h>         │ Once    F6  │
                            │ Trace   F7  │
                            │ Proceed F8  │
                            │ Go          │
                            └─────────────┘
 main()
─{
   int i;
   for (i=0; i<10; i++)
     printf("Great job!");
   }

 === Bottom of file ===
─────────────────────────────────────────────────
 main() line 6 - entry
 main line 7
 main line 8



─────────────────────────────────────────────────
 Line 6                            great.c
```

Screen 18.6 Execute Menu

Once   The Once command creates a temporary breakpoint on the current line. It executes your program from the highlighted line (that is, the line in reverse video indicating it is to be executed next) until it reaches a line with a breakpoint or the cursor on it. This command is similar to the Go command, except that this command uses the current line as a temporary breakpoint.

To use this command, move the highlighted line to the code line you want to begin on, select Once from the Execute menu, and press the <enter> key. You can move the highlighted line by single-stepping through the program using the Trace or Proceed commands, as described below.

| Fast Path |

Function Key: F6

Press function key F6 to execute your program from the highlighted line until it reaches the current line or a breakpoint.

Source-Level Debugger for the Student Compiler

Trace The Trace command lets you single-step through your program. This means that you proceed through the source program stopping at each line to execute it. You can use the function key F9 to see the results (up to that line in the program) on the Program Screen. To continue stepping through your program, you can re-select Trace for each line of code or you can use the fast path function key F7 to execute each line.

The Trace command steps *into* function calls in your source program. If the current line contains a function call, then the first line of that function is executed and subsequent Trace commands will execute each line within that function. Control returns immediately to the debugger after the function call.

To step through your source program, move the cursor to the line you want to start on, select **Trace** from the Execute menu, and press the <enter> key.

Fast Path

Function Key: F7

Press function key F7 to step through your program, executing each line as you go. Note that you cannot have a pull-down menu displayed when you press F7. See the difference between the Trace and Proceed commands, described below.

Proceed The Proceed command is very similar to the Trace command, except this command always steps *over* function calls. If the current line contains a function call, Proceed executes the function but the debugger resumes on the line after the function call; it does not step through each line *within* the function call. The results on the Program Screen show the function's return value (if any) and not the results or values from each variable within that function call.

To step through your source program, move the cursor to the line you want to start on, select **Proceed** from the Execute menu, and press the <enter> key.

Fast Path

Function Key: F8

Press function key F8 to step through your program, executing each line as you go. See the difference between the Trace and Proceed commands, described above.

Go The Go command executes the program you are debugging. If no breakpoints are set, execution continues until your program terminates normally.

This function is often used with Set/Clear and the commands in the Execute menu to resume execution after you have reviewed the (partial) results of your program's execution on the Program Screen. For example, you can use the Go command to

Chapter 18

continue executing to the next breakpoint or to switch from single-stepping a program (using Trace) to letting it execute until it terminates.

This command has no fast path key.

Chapter Summary

This chapter has shown you how to use the Student Compiler's source-level debugger to identify programming errors. The topics covered included:

- entering the debugger from the Student Compiler's editor
- using the debugger's pull-down menus and commands to detect errors
- using the editor and compiler to run corrected programs.

This is the final chapter in the User's Guide. Appendix 1 lists the Student Compiler's error messages and Appendix 2 is a table of the ASCII character set.

Appendix 1
Error Messages for the Student Compiler

Appendix 1

CONTENTS

Overview **587**
Compiler Operational Errors **587**
Debugger Operational Errors **590**
Compiler Syntax Errors and Warnings **590**
Compiler Internal Errors **598**

Error Messages for the Student Compiler

Overview

This appendix includes the error, warning, and diagnostic messages for the SAS/C Compiler, Student Edition. There are four types of error messages.

Compiler Operational Errors
: indicate that the compiler is having trouble operating correctly because it cannot access required files or cannot obtain enough disk or memory space. These error messages are not available through the online Help facility.

Debugger Operational Errors
: indicate that the source-level debugger is having trouble operating correctly because you have requested information on invalid variables or exceeded debugger limits. These error messages are not available through the online Help facility.

Syntax Errors and Warnings
: indicate that the compiler is having difficulty understanding your C source program. The message includes the source filename and line number identifying the point at which the problem was detected. An error message indicates that the problem prevents the construction of a usable object module and must, therefore, be corrected. A warning message (W) indicates that the compiler detects something unusual but will proceed to make an object module, using appropriate assumptions about what you intend the source code to do. These error messages are available through the online Help facility.

Internal Errors
: indicate that the compiler encountered some internal condition that should not have occurred, that is, a bug. Please report any internal errors to SAS Institute Inc. using the **Your Turn** page in the back of the book. However, before doing so, you should conduct a few experiments with your source code to see if you can make the problem go away. The internal error explanations that follow should provide enough clues. These error messages are not available through the online Help facility.

Compiler Operational Errors

The following error messages are displayed on your screen:

`Can't initialize screen`
: The Student Compiler cannot work on your computer system because it cannot initialize the display screen. If this error occurs when you invoke the compiler, you will be returned to DOS. This error may happen because your computer is not entirely IBM PC-compatible or your computer's display adapter card is not compatible.

Appendix 1

Can't open help library

The compiler was unable to open the help library file. This error usually occurs when the compiler cannot find the `sc.hlp` file. Be sure that this file is in the same directory as the Student Compiler's executable file, `sc.exe`, or in the directory in which you are working.

Can't open source file

The compiler (that is, the editor) was unable to open the source file. This error usually occurs because you have misspelled the filename or did not specify the proper disk drive or directory path.

Can't open source file (file not saved)

The open failed while trying to save your source file. See the Save command description in Chapter 14 for some ways you can work around this situation.

Can't open work file

The compiler was unable to open the work file, `sc1.wrk`, `sc2.wrk`, `sc3.wrk`, or `sc4.wrk`. This error usually occurs if you left the disk drive open.

Can't read source file

The compiler was unable to read the source file. This error usually occurs because of a disk error.

Can't read work file

The compiler was unable to read its work files, `sc1.wrk`, `sc2.wrk`, `sc3.wrk`, or `sc4.wrk`. This error usually occurs when the compiler cannot retrieve the file from the disk, there is a disk failure, or the disk drive is open.

Can't write to work file

The compiler was unable to write to one of its work files, `sc1.wrk`, `sc2.wrk`, `sc3.wrk`, or `sc4.wrk`. This error usually occurs if you have left the write-tab on the diskette, if you left the disk drive open, or you have run out of disk space.

Disk is full (file not saved)

The disk is full, so your file cannot be saved. Try inserting another diskette and saving the file to it. If you do not have another diskette, see the Save command description in Chapter 14 for some ways you can work around this situation.

Editor is out of memory

You cannot add more lines to your source file because the editor is out of memory. You can insert a new diskette and save your source file to it or see the Save command description in Chapter 14 for other alternatives.

Error Messages for the Student Compiler

Fatal operational error

This causes your program to abort. This error usually occurs when your program has altered the compiler's internal data. You should return to DOS and try to save your program from there.

Line is full

The length of the current line is 77 characters (the length limit); no new characters can be added to this line. You can start a new line of code or use the C language continuation character backslash (\) to continue your code onto the next line (after you have deleted a character to make room for it).

Line(s) split

The compiler has split your lines. When reading the source file, some lines whose length exceeded 77 characters were split. The C language continuation character backslash (\) was added to the end of split lines. Splitting usually occurs when opening files that have not been created with the Student Compiler's editor.

Line(s) too long to join

The result of joining the two lines would exceed the maximum line length of 77 characters. You may want to split the second line and then join the shorter segment using the C language continuation character backslash (\) to continue your code onto the next line.

Line(s) too long to replace

Replacing the search string with the replace string would cause a line to exceed the 77 character length limit.

Line(s) too long to shift right

One of the lines in the selected area is too long to shift right.

No functions or data defined

The compiler reached the end of the source file without finding any data or function definitions. One common cause of this error is forgetting a comment terminator (*/) in the first function in the source file. This causes the compiler to treat your program as if it were a comment.

No selected block

You must select a block of lines (one or more) using the Select Line command in order to complete this operation.

Not enough memory

The compiler has used all the available working memory while trying to compile your file.

Not found

The search string cannot be found in this file. This can be due to a typographical error when you entered the search string.

Appendix 1

`Printer error (file not printed)`
> A printer error occurred and the file was not printed. This can happen when the printer is out of paper or if it is not properly hooked up to the PC.

`Selected block already exists`
> You have already selected a block of text using the Select Line command; you can select only one block at a time. You must release your current block (using the Undo Select command) in order to select another block.

`Source and target block conflict`
> You cannot move the selected block of text into the specified area. This error usually occurs when you overlap the source and destination blocks.

Debugger Operational Errors

These error messages are displayed on your screen.

`Breakpoints can be set only on valid lines of code`
> You can set a breakpoint on any valid, executing line of code but not on a blank line, comment, definition statement, or other nonexecutable statement.

`Can't add another breakpoint (maximum exceeded)`
> A maximum of 50 breakpoints can be set at one time.

`Invalid variable`
> The specified variable or string variable is invalid so its value cannot be displayed.

Compiler Syntax Errors and Warnings

Syntax errors and warnings are displayed on your screen via a message in the following format:

> *fff* *nnn* `Error` *xxx*: *mmm*

where

> *fff* is the name of the source file that was being processed when the error occurred
>
> *nnn* is the number of the source file line that was being scanned when the error occurred (source file lines begin at 1, not 0)
>
> *xxx* is the error number, as listed below
>
> *mmm* is the error message, as listed below.

Note that all of these fields are of varying length.

Error Messages for the Student Compiler

All messages indicate fatal errors unless the message number listed below is followed by (W). When a fatal error occurs, the compiler aborts and does not produce a workable program.

A message number followed by (W) indicates a warning. When such a message is displayed, the compiler produces a workable program by making reasonable assumptions about what you intend the source file to do. Nonetheless, it is a good idea to investigate these warnings because the compiler's assumptions can differ from your intentions.

1   This error is generated by a variety of conditions in connection with preprocessor commands, including specifying an unrecognized command, failure to include white space between command elements, or the use of an illegal preprocessor symbol.

2   The end of an input file is encountered when the compiler expects more data. This can occur in an `#include` file or the original source file. In many cases, correcting a previous error eliminates this one.

3   The filename specified in an `#include` command is not found.

4   An unrecognized element is encountered in the input file that cannot be classified as any of the valid lexical constructs (such as an identifier or one of the valid expression operators). This can occur if control characters or other illegal characters are detected in the source file.

5   A preprocessor `#define` macro is used with the wrong number of arguments.

6   Expansion of a `#define` macro causes the compiler's line buffer to overflow. This can occur if more than one lengthy macro appears on a single input line.

7   The maximum extent of `#include` file nesting is exceeded; the compiler supports `#include` nesting to a maximum depth of 4.

8   A cast (type conversion) operator is incorrectly specified in an expression.

9   The named identifier is undefined in the context in which it appears; that is, it has not been previously declared. This message is only generated once; subsequent encounters with the identifier assume that it is of type `int` (which can cause other errors).

10 An error is detected in the expression following the ¢ character (presumably a subscript expression). This can occur if the expression in brackets is null (that is, not present).

11 The length of a string constant exceeds the maximum allowed by the compiler (256 bytes). This occurs if the closing " (double quote) is omitted in specifying the string.

Appendix 1

12 The expression preceding the . (period) or -> structure reference operator is not recognizable by the compiler as a structure or pointer to a structure.

13 An identifier indicating the desired aggregate member is not found following the . (period) or -> operator.

14 The indicated identifier is not a member of the structure or union to which the . (period) or -> refers.

15 The identifier preceding the ((open parenthesis) function call operator is not implicitly or explicitly declared as a function.

16 A function argument expression specified following the ((open parenthesis) function call operator is invalid. This can occur if an argument expression is omitted.

17 During expression evaluation, the end of an expression is encountered, but more than one operand is still waiting for evaluation. This can occur if an expression contains an incorrectly specified operation.

18 During expression evaluation, the end of an expression is encountered, but an operator is still pending evaluation. This can occur if an operand is omitted for a binary operation.

19 The number of opening and closing parentheses in an expression is not equal. This error message can also occur if a macro is poorly specified or improperly used.

20 An expression that does not evaluate to a constant is encountered in a context that requires a constant result. This can occur if one of the operators not valid for constant expressions is present.

21 An identifier declared as a structure or union is encountered in an expression where aggregates are not permitted. Only the direct assignment and conditional operators can be used on aggregates, and explicit or implicit testing of aggregates as a whole is not permitted.

22 (W) An identifier declared as a structure or union appears as a function argument without the preceding & operator. Aggregates can be passed by value, so this is a legal construction.

23 The conditional operator is used erroneously. This can occur if the ? operator is present but the colon (:) is not found when expected.

24 The context of the expression requires an operand to be a pointer. This can occur if the expression following * does not evaluate to a pointer.

25 The context of the expression requires an operand to be an lvalue. This can occur if the expression following & is not an lvalue or if the left side of an assignment expression is not an lvalue.

26 The context of the expression requires an operand to be arithmetic (not a pointer, function, or aggregate).

Error Messages for the Student Compiler

27   The context of the expression requires an operand to be either arithmetic or a pointer. This can occur for the logical OR and logical AND operators.

28   During expression evaluation, the end of an expression is encountered but not enough operands are available for evaluation. This can occur if a binary operation is improperly specified.

29   An operation is specified that is invalid for pointer operands, such as one of the arithmetic operations other than addition.

30 (W)   In an assignment statement that defines a value for a pointer variable, the expression on the right side of the — operator does not evaluate to a pointer of the exact same type as the pointer variable being assigned; that is, it does not point to the same type of object. This warning also occurs when a pointer of any type is assigned to an arithmetic object. Note that the same message can be a fatal error if generated for an initializer expression.

31   The context of an expression requires an operand to be integral (that is, one of the integer types: `char`, `int`, `short`, `unsigned`, or `long`).

32   The expression specifying the type name is invalid for a cast (conversion) operation or a `sizeof` expression.

33   An attempt was made to attach an initializer expression to a structure, union, or array that is declared `auto`. Such initializations are expressly disallowed by the language.

34   The expression used to initialize an object is invalid. This can occur for a variety of reasons, including failing to separate elements in an initializer list with commas or specifying an expression that does not evaluate to a constant. Some experimentation may be required to determine the exact cause of the error.

35   During processing of an initializer list, or a structure or union member declaration list, the compiler expects a closing right brace (}), but does not find it. This can occur if too many elements are specified in an initializer expression list or if a structure member is improperly declared.

36   A statement within the body of a `switch` statement is not preceded by a case or `default` prefix that would allow control to reach that statement. This can occur if a `break` or `return` statement is followed by any other statement without an intervening case or default prefix.

37   The specified statement label was encountered more than once during processing of the current function.

38   In a body of compound statements, the number of opening left braces ({) and closing right braces (}) is not equal. This can occur if the compiler gets out of phase due to a previous error.

Appendix 1

39 One of the C language reserved words appears in an invalid context (for example, as a variable name). Note that the entry is reserved, although it is not implemented in the compiler.

40 A `break` statement is detected that is not within the scope of a `while`, `do`, `for`, or `switch` statement. This can occur due to an error in a preceding statement.

41 A `case` prefix is encountered outside the scope of a `switch` statement. This can occur due to an error in a preceding statement.

42 The expression defining a case value does not evaluate to an `int` constant.

43 A `case` prefix is encountered that defines a constant value already used in a previous case prefix within the same `switch` statement.

44 A `continue` statement is detected that is not within the scope of a `while`, `do`, or `for` loop. This can occur due to an error in a preceding statement.

45 A `default` prefix is encountered outside the scope of a `switch` statement. This can occur due to an error in a preceding statement.

46 A `default` prefix is encountered within the scope of a `switch` statement in which a preceding `default` prefix has already been encountered.

47 Following the body of a `do` statement, the `while` clause is expected but not found. This can occur due to an error within the body of the `do` statement.

48 The expression defining the looping condition in a `while` or `do` loop is null (that is, not present). Indefinite loops must supply the constant 1 if that is what is intended.

49 An `else` keyword is detected that is not within the scope of a preceding `if` statement. This can occur due to an error in a preceding statement.

50 A statement label following the `goto` keyword is expected but not found.

51 The indicated identifier, which appears in a `goto` statement as a statement label, is already defined as a variable within the scope of the current function.

52 The expression following the `if` keyword is null (that is, not present).

53 The expression following the `return` keyword cannot be legally converted to the type of the value returned by the function.

54 The expression defining the value for a `switch` statement does not define an `int` value or a value that can be legally converted to `int`.

55 (W) The statement defining the body of a `switch` statement does not contain at least one case prefix.

Error Messages for the Student Compiler

56   The compiler expected but did not find a colon (:). This error message can be generated if a `case` expression is improperly specified or if the colon is simply omitted following a label or prefix to a statement.

57   The compiler expected a semicolon (;) but did not find one. This error generally means that the compiler completed the processing of an expression but did not find a statement terminator. This can occur if too many closing parentheses are included or if an expression is otherwise incorrectly formed. Because the compiler scans through white space to look for the semicolon, the line number for this error message can be beyond the actual line where a semicolon is needed.

58   A parenthesis required by the syntax of the current statement is expected but is not found (as in a `while` or `for` loop). This can occur if the enclosed expression is incorrectly specified, causing the compiler to end the expression early.

59   In processing declarations, the compiler encounters a storage class invalid for that declaration context (such as `auto` or `register` for external objects). This can occur if, due to preceding errors, the compiler begins processing portions of the body of a function as if they were external definitions.

60   The types of the aggregates involved in an assignment or conditional operation are not exactly the same. This error can also be generated for `enum` objects.

61   The indicated structure or union tag is not previously defined; that is, the members of the aggregate are unknown. Note that a reference to an undefined tag is permitted if the object being declared is a pointer, but not if it is an actual instance of an aggregate. This message can be issued as a warning after the entire source file has been processed if a pointer is declared with a tag that is never defined.

62   A structure or union tag is detected in the opposite usage from which it was originally declared (that is, a tag originally applied to a `struct` has appeared on an aggregate with the union specifier). This compiler defines only one class of identifiers for both structure and union tags.

63   The indicated identifier is declared more than once within the same scope. This error can be generated due to a preceding error but is generally the result of improper declarations.

64   A declaration of the members of a structure or union does not contain at least one member name.

65   An attempt is made to define a function body when the compiler is not processing external definitions. This can occur if a preceding error causes the compiler to get out of phase with respect to declarations in the source file.

66   The expression defining the size of a subscript in an array declaration does not evaluate to a positive `int` constant. This can also occur if a

Appendix 1

zero length is specified for an inner (that is, not the left-most) subscript of an array object.

67 A declaration specifies an illegal object as defined by this version of C. Illegal objects include functions that return arrays and arrays of functions.

68 A structure or union declaration includes an object declared as a function. This is illegal, although an aggregate can contain a pointer to a function.

69 The structure or union (whose declaration was just processed) contains an instance of itself, which is illegal. This can be generated if the `*` is forgotten on a structure pointer declaration or if (due to some intertwining of structure definitions) the structure actually contains an instance of itself.

70 The formal parameter of a function is declared illegally as a function.

71 A variable is declared before the opening left brace ({) of a function, but it does not appear in the list of formal names enclosed in parentheses following the function name.

72 An external item is declared with attributes that conflict with a previous declaration. This can occur if a function is used earlier as an implicit `int` function and is then declared as returning some other kind of value. Functions that return a type other than `int` must be declared before they are used so that the compiler is aware of the type of the function value.

73 In processing the declaration of objects, the compiler expects to find another line of declarations but does not find one. This error can be generated if a preceding error causes the compiler to get out of phase with respect to declarations.

74 (W) A string constant used as an initializer for a `char` array defines more characters than the specified array length. Only as many characters as are needed to define the entire array are taken from the first characters of the string constant.

75 An attempt is made to apply the `sizeof` operator to a bit field, which is illegal.

76 The compiler expects, but does not find, an opening left brace ({) in the current context. This can occur if the opening brace is omitted on a list of initializer expressions for an aggregate.

77 In processing a declaration, the compiler expects to find an identifier that is to be declared. This can occur if the prefixes to an identifier in a declaration (parentheses and asterisks) are improperly specified or if a sequence of declarations is listed incorrectly.

Error Messages for the Student Compiler

78   The indicated statement label is referred to in the most recent function in a `goto` statement, but no definition of the label is found in that function.

79 (W)   More than one identifier within the list for an enumeration type has the same value. While this is not technically an error, it is usually of questionable value.

80   The number of bits specified for a bit field is invalid. Note that the compiler does not accept bit fields that are exactly the length of a machine word (such as 16 on a 16-bit machine); these must be declared as ordinary integer or `unsigned` variables.

81   The current line contains a reference to a preprocessor symbol that is a circular definition.

82   The size of an object exceeds the maximum legal size for objects in its storage class; or, the last object declared causes the total size of declared objects for that storage class to exceed that maximum.

83 (W)   An indirect pointer reference (usually a subscripted expression) uses an address beyond the size of the object used as a base for the address calculation. This generally occurs when an expression makes reference to an element beyond the end of an array.

84 (W)   A `#define` statement is encountered for an already defined symbol. The first definition is pushed, so that an additional `#undef` statement is needed to undefine the symbol.

85 (W)   The expression specifying the value to be returned by a function is not of the same type as the function itself. The value specified is automatically converted to the appropriate type; the warning merely serves as notification of the conversion. The warning can be eliminated by using a cast operator to force the return value to the function type.

This warning is also issued when a return statement with a null expression (that is, no return value) appears in a function that is not declared as type `void`.

86 (W)   The types of the formal parameters declared in the actual definition of a function do not agree with those of a preceding declaration of that function with argument type specifiers.

87 (W)   The number of function arguments supplied to a function do not agree with the number of arguments in its declaration using argument type specifiers.

88 (W)   The type of function argument expression does not agree with its corresponding type declared in the list of argument type specifiers for that function. Note that the compiler does not automatically convert the expression to the specified type; it merely issues this warning.

89 (W)   The type of a constant expression used as a function argument does not agree with its corresponding type declared in the list of argument type

Appendix 1

specifiers for that function. In this case, the compiler does convert the expression to the expected type.

90   The type specifier for an argument type in a function declaration is incorrectly formed. Argument type specifiers are formed according to the rules for type names in cast operators or `sizeof` expressions.

91   One of the operands in an expression is of type `void`; this is expressly disallowed because `void` represents no value.

92 (W)   An expression statement does not cause either an assignment or a function call to take place. Such a statement serves no useful purpose and can be eliminated. This error is usually generated for incorrectly specified expressions in which an assignment operator is omitted or mistyped.

93 (W)   An object with local scope is declared but never referenced within that scope. This warning is provided as a convenience to warn of declarations that are no longer needed (if, for example, the code in which the variable was used was eliminated but the variable's declaration was not). It can also occur if the only use of the object is confined to statements that are not compiled because of conditional compilation directives such as `#ifdef` or `#if`.

94 (W)   An `auto` variable is used in an expression without having been previously initialized by an assignment statement or appearing in a function argument list with a preceding `&` (that is, its address passed to a function). The compiler considers the variable initialized once any statement causes it to be initialized, even though control cannot flow from that statement to other subsequent uses of the variable. Note that this warning is issued if the third expression in a `for` statement uses a variable that has not yet been initialized, which can be incorrect if that variable is initialized inside the body of the `for` statement.

Compiler Internal Errors

These error messages are displayed on your screen via the message

    CXERR: *xx*

where *xx* is the error number. When such a message occurs, compilation is terminated immediately and both the quad module and the object module are probably unusable.

1   Invalid error or warning message code number.

2   The compiler has internally called a function that is not applicable to the current host-target environment.

3   Invalid symbol table access.

4   Declaration chain is broken.

5   An unlink error occurred while processing an `undef` statement.

Error Messages for the Student Compiler

6   The compiler attempted to push back too many tokens.
7   There is no aggregate list for a structure reference.
8   Stack underflow occurred.
9   Invalid attempt to generate the address of a constant.
10   A test value is not a constant.
11   Invalid unary operator.
12   Invalid binary operator.
13   A scaling object is not a pointer or an array.
14   An unexpected end-of-chain occurred while restoring internal context.
15   Invalid quad type.
16   Deletion length is less than two bytes.
17   Insufficient memory.
18   An error occurred when releasing memory.
19   Invalid condition during temporary assignment.
20   Invalid condition while processing program section.
21   Literal pool generation error.
22   Invalid condition while processing data section.
23   Invalid quad file.
24   End-of-file while processing `for` quad.
25   Invalid register number.
26   Temporary save or restore error.
27   Invalid operand size.
28   Invalid storage base.
29   Error during branch folding.
30   Error during control statement processing.
31   Error during special addressing setup.
32   Invalid object description block offset.
33   Too many function parameters.
34   Indirect argument for call-by-reference.
35   Invalid external relocation value.

Appendix 2
ASCII Character Set

Appendix 2

ASCII Character Set

Table A2.1 Decimal, Hexadecimal, and ASCII Values

DEC base$_{10}$	HEX base$_{16}$	ASCII
0	0x00	NUL
1	0x01	SOH
2	0x02	STX
3	0x03	ETX
4	0x04	EOT
5	0x05	ENQ
6	0x06	ACK
7	0x07	BEL
8	0x08	BS
9	0x09	HT
10	0x0A	LF
11	0x0B	VT
12	0x0C	FF
13	0x0D	CR
14	0x0E	SO
15	0x0F	SI
16	0x10	DLE
17	0x11	DC1
18	0x12	DC2
19	0x13	DC3
20	0x14	DC4
21	0x15	NAK
22	0x16	SYN
23	0x17	ETB
24	0x18	CAN
25	0x19	EM

(*continued*)

Appendix 2

Table A2.1 (*continued*)

DEC base$_{10}$	HEX base$_{16}$	ASCII
26	0x1A	SUB
27	0x1B	ESC
28	0x1C	FS
29	0x1D	GS
30	0x1E	RS
31	0x1F	US
32	0x20	SP
33	0x21	!
34	0x22	"
35	0x23	#
36	0x24	$
37	0x25	%
38	0x26	&
39	0x27	'
40	0x28	(
41	0x29	)
42	0x2A	*
43	0x2B	+
44	0x2C	,
45	0x2D	−
46	0x2E	.
47	0x2F	/
48	0x30	0
49	0x31	1
50	0x32	2
51	0x33	3
52	0x34	4
53	0x35	5

(*continued*)

Table A2.1 (*continued*)

DEC base$_{10}$	HEX base$_{16}$	ASCII
54	0x36	6
55	0x37	7
56	0x38	8
57	0x39	9
58	0x3A	:
59	0x3B	;
60	0x3C	<
61	0x3D	=
62	0x3E	>
63	0x3F	?
64	0x40	@
65	0x41	A
66	0x42	B
67	0x43	C
68	0x44	D
69	0x45	E
70	0x46	F
71	0x47	G
72	0x48	H
73	0x49	I
74	0x4A	J
75	0x4B	K
76	0x4C	L
77	0x4D	M
78	0x4E	N
79	0x4F	O
80	0x50	P
81	0x51	Q

(*continued*)

Appendix 2

Table A2.1 (continued)

DEC base$_{10}$	HEX base$_{16}$	ASCII
82	0x52	R
83	0x53	S
84	0x54	T
85	0x55	U
86	0x56	V
87	0x57	W
88	0x58	X
89	0x59	Y
90	0x5A	Z
91	0x5B	[
92	0x5C	\
93	0x5D	]
94	0x5E	^
95	0x5F	_
96	0x60	`
97	0x61	a
98	0x62	b
99	0x63	c
100	0x64	d
101	0x65	e
102	0x66	f
103	0x67	g
104	0x68	h
105	0x69	i
106	0x6A	j
107	0x6B	k
108	0x6C	l
109	0x6D	m
110	0x6E	n
111	0x6F	o

(continued)

Table A2.1 (*continued*)

DEC base$_{10}$	HEX base$_{16}$	ASCII
112	0x70	p
113	0x71	q
114	0x72	r
115	0x73	s
116	0x74	t
117	0x75	u
118	0x76	v
119	0x77	w
120	0x78	x
121	0x79	y
122	0x7A	z
123	0x7B	{
124	0x7C	|
125	0x7D	}
126	0x7E	~
127	0x7F	DEL

Part III: Glossary and References

Glossary

Glossary

This glossary defines common programming terms and concepts. For C language-specific keywords and concepts, see the individual chapters in this book or the C language texts listed in the References. Words and phrases that appear in **boldface** indicate that they are defined elsewhere in the glossary.

Access method

> the way data records are selected from a file one at a time for processing, retrieval, or storage. The technique used to access files depends on how the file is organized (see **File organization**). Common methods of data access are sequential and **random access**.

Address

> See **Memory**.

Algorithm

> a method or approach used to solve a problem. Programs are based on algorithms. Algorithms can be mathematical formulas for solving a problem and, at other times, just a series of steps toward a specific goal.

ANSI Standard

> a set of programming language guidelines determined by the American National Standard for Information Systems. The Standard specifies the form and establishes the interpretation of programs in many languages, including C. The Standard was created to promote **portability**, reliability, maintainability, and the efficient execution of C language programs on a variety of computer systems. The C language Standard is currently in a draft form.

Arithmetic operators

> a set of arithmetic symbols used with variables to make expressions. Their **associativity** is from left to right. Arithmetic operators are evaluated according to the following order of **precedence**:
>
> multiplication (*), division (/), modulus (%)
> addition (+), subtraction (-)
>
> Thus, *, /, and % have equal precedence and will be evaluated before the arithmetic operators + and − , which have the same precedence value. If two operators have the same (equal) precedence, they are executed according to the order in which they occur in the equation or statement.
>
> A **unary minus operator** (−), indicating a negative number, takes precedence over multiplication. For more information on operators, see Chapters 3 and 8, especially the table summary of all the C operators in Chapter 8.
>
> You may use parentheses to group values or to nest arithmetic expressions. Parentheses make expressions easier to read and can also be used to change the precedence of operators. Evaluating expressions with parentheses begins at the deepest level of parenthesis and moves outward. For example, C

evaluates **a+b*c** as **a+(b*c)**, though you could add parentheses to make it evaluate as **(a+b)*c** for a very different result.

ASCII (format)

acronym for the American Standard Code for Information Interchange. ASCII is a standard character encoding scheme made up of 256 different bit patterns. Each bit pattern is composed of an 8-bit code (bit positions 0 through 7) of 0s and 1s. Each character has a binary, decimal, hexadecimal, and octal code assigned to it. For example, an uppercase letter *A* is represented by binary 01000001, decimal 65, hexadecimal 0x41, and octal 101. See Appendix 2 for decimal and hexadecimal values of ASCII characters.

ASCII collating sequence

an ordering of characters (for example, in an index sorting program) that follows the order of the characters in the ASCII set. See **ASCII (format)**.

Assembly language

a programming language that uses symbolic names (instead of binary numbers) to perform operations on the computer. Because there is a one-to-one correspondence between each symbol and machine instruction, an assembly language is called a *low-level* programming language. Each computer system has its own assembly language.

An assembly language is often casually referred to as *assembler*, although the assembler is actually a special program that translates the assembly language program from its symbolic format into the machine instructions (coded in 0s and 1s) acted on by the computer. A **high-level language** like C uses a **compiler** to perform this translation.

Assignment

the assigning of a value on the right side of the equal sign (=) to the variable or object on the left side of the sign. For example, **a=b+c** assigns the sum of **b** and **c** to the variable **a**. The equal sign is an **assignment operator**.

Assignment operators

a set of symbols that can perform an operation and then assign the value to the object or variable on the left side of the sign. Their **associativity** is from right to left. Assignment operators are evaluated in the following order of **precedence:**

```
=
*=    /=    %=
+=    -=    &=
^=    |=
<<=   >>=
```

Thus, = is evaluated before all the other assignment operators. The operators *=, /=, and %= have equal precedence, and any of these will be evaluated before the assignment operators +=, -=, and &=, which have the same precedence, and so on. If two operators have the same (equal) precedence, they are executed according to the order in which they occur in the equation or statement.

For more information on assignment operators, see Chapters 3 and 8 in the Tutorial, especially the table summary of all the C operators in Chapter 8. See **Assignment** above for an example using a simple assignment operator.

When one of the arithmetic symbols is coupled with an equal sign, it means that the arithmetic operation is performed and the result is stored in the lvalue or variable on the left side of the assignment operator. For example, the assignment operator *= means that you multiply the expression on the left by the expression on the right and store the result back in the variable on the left. Therefore

```
array[index]*= 2;
```

is equivalent to

```
array[index] = array[index]* 2;
```

Associativity

the order of (sub)expression grouping for operators of equal precedence, that is, operators having the same **precedence** value, such as *, /, and %. The direction in which the operators associate with the operands in an expression is from left to right or right to left. For example, assignment operators associate from right to left, so that the value of a+b is assigned to c in c=a+b.

Binary operator

an operator that acts on two operands, for example, the addition operator in a+b. See **Unary operator.**

Bit

acronym for binary digit. The smallest unit of information in memory, represented by a 0 or 1. Bits are elements of a positional number system based on two, or a binary number system. A bit is often thought of as a switch that can be turned on (1) or off (0).

Bitwise operators
: a set of symbols that can perform operations on the individual bits in a **byte**. Their **associativity** is from left to right. Bitwise operators are evaluated in the following order of **precedence**:

- `~` one's complement
- `<<` left shift
- `>>` right shift
- `&` bitwise AND
- `^` bitwise XOR
- `|` bitwise OR

Thus, `~` is evaluated before all the other bitwise operators. The operator `<<` has a higher **precedence** value than the bitwise operator `>>` or `&`, and so on. For more information, see Chapter 8 and the table summary of all the C operators in that chapter.

Boolean
: an algebraic system of logic that evaluates expressions for a TRUE or FALSE value. The relationships between and among the expressions are represented using the logical operators AND, OR, and NOT. The **associativity** of NOT (`!`) is from right to left; the associativity of AND (`&&`) and OR (`||`) is from left to right. Logical operators are evaluated in the following order of **precedence**:

NOT (`!`)
AND (`&&`)
OR (`||`)

For more information on logical operators, see Chapters 3 and 8, especially the table summary of all the C operators in Chapter 8.

As with the arithmetic operators, you can use parentheses to clarify or change the logical order of evaluation. For example,

```
if ((age >= 6 && age <= 13) && !(today == "Sat"))
    printf("You must wait to get your allowance.\n");
```

evaluates TRUE if the user is between the ages of six and thirteen AND the day of the week is NOT Saturday. Note that because AND (`&&`) is used, both conditions (in parentheses) must be true for the entire `if` statement to be TRUE.

Breakpoint
: a point set (or *planted*) in a program that suspends its execution so a user can review the partial results. Breakpoints are set during debugging to help locate programming errors. See **Debug, Debugger,** and **Trace program.**

Glossary

Buffer
an area in memory that is used to hold data temporarily. Buffer storage can often be dynamically allocated (created as needed by the user) and then freed at execution. Buffers are most often used in input/output operations. For example, data read at one speed may be stored until they can be written at another speed.

Byte
on most computers a byte is defined as a set of 8 bits. This byte structure provides for 256 possible combinations of 0s and 1s and is used as the basis for encoding characters and numbers. On an IBM personal computer, for example, the bits' positions are represented in the following way: 7 6 5 4 3 2 1 0, where the bit in the seventh position is the leftmost bit. See **Sign bit**.

Case-sensitivity
when a compiler or operating system interprets letters of the alphabet, it does so according to their case, either upper or lower. For example, a compiler may interpret the variable name `MYVAR` as a different variable than `Myvar`. Many compilers are case-*in*sensitive and would interpret these two names as referring to the same variable. The C language is always case-sensitive except for external variable names. Some operating systems are case-insensitive with case-sensitive languages; for example, in MS-DOS you can enter commands or command line arguments (to a C program) in upper- or lowercase.

Character
an element of a character set including a letter of the alphabet, a number, or a punctuation symbol (such as a semicolon or equal sign). A character is composed of several bits; on most computers eight bits make up one byte. A character is the smallest addressable unit of data.

A character can be of any arithmetic data type that can hold the ASCII value of a character: `short`, `char`, `int`, `long`, `float`, or `double`. The `long`, `float`, and `double` may require a cast for the C function library to act on them correctly; however, C makes no distinction between a character and a number. `'A'` is an ASCII (decimal) 65 as far as the C compiler is concerned, as are the values 0x41, 0101, and the statements

```
float x;
x='A';
```

which assign the value 65.0 to `x`.

You can use the ANSI `is-` functions, such as `isalnum`, `isdigit`, `iscntrl`, `isspace`, and so on, to determine the appropriate category for the wide range of characters in C. See Chapter 16 for these function descriptions.

Character array
: a varying-length array of character constants. If the programmer terminates the character array with a null character ('\0'), the array becomes a character string array. For example,

```
char m1[] = { 'G','o','o','d',' ','m','o','r','n','i','n','g','\0' };
```

The compiler counts the number of elements in the array when the array is initialized. As with other arrays, the array's name (m1) is a pointer to the first element of the string array, in this case, the character constant 'G'.

The above character string array is equivalent to this **character string constant:**

```
char m1[] = "Good morning";
```

See Chapter 7 for more information on character string arrays.

Character string constant
: zero or more contiguous characters enclosed within double quotes so that the system interprets them as constant (unchanging) values; this kind of character string is also called a string literal. Any valid character, including escape characters, may be included in a character string. By convention, you should terminate a character string by adding a null character ('\0', also called a null-terminating byte) to the end of it. These strings are often used in the C functions `printf` and `puts`, and in the string functions such as `strcpy`.

The C compiler adds a null character to a string and produces a pointer to the string. See the example above in **Character array**.

Command line
: on most operating systems, the line from which commands and programs are executed. This is usually the line that has the system's prompt on it, such as C > in MS-DOS. Command line arguments are entered from the command line, often upon prompting from a program.

Compile-time
: an action that occurs during or relates to the program while it is compiling. For example, compile-time errors occur during the compilation phase and usually indicate syntactic errors.

Compiler
: a program that translates your source language program's statements into machine-level code so that the computer can perform the program's instructions. This translated file is called an **object module.** A compiler checks your program's language statements for correct syntax, returning error messages for any problems that it finds. See Appendix 1 for a list of the Student Compiler's error messages.

Glossary

Configuration file
: a file containing commands that modify a program or the way the operating system works. On MS-DOS and PC DOS, the CONFIG.SYS file is the configuration file.

Constant
: any literal number or single character that represents itself and no other value. For example, the number 12 is a constant integer and the string

    ```
    "I love programming\n"
    ```

    is a character string constant. A constant is never a placeholder for some other value.

Cursor
: a symbol on a display screen that indicates an active position, such as where the next character will be typed or the <enter> key will be pressed. A cursor usually appears as an underline character (_) or as a small box that is the size of a character. On many systems, especially PCs, the cursor blinks so that you can distinguish it from other characters on the display screen.

Data declaration
: a statement that names and defines the properties of an object in memory but may not actually allocate storage. This statement declares the intent to access an object in memory. See Chapter 2 for more information on data declarations. See also **Data definition** because a declaration can also serve as a definition.

Data definition
: a statement that names and defines the properties of an object (such as a structure, union, or enumerated data type) and also allocates memory to store the object. See **Data declaration** and **Object**.

Data set
: a file on a mainframe operating system, such as IBM's MVS. Data sets are organized by two methods, sequential or partitioned. In sequential order, file records are written in processing sequence, one after another, and are always retrieved in that order. A partitioned data set (PDS) is a **directory** that contains members, where each member is a sequentially organized file. A PDS is often referred to as a **library**. The following is a PDS, where GLOSSARY is the member name: SASUSR.CPROJECT.TEXT(GLOSSARY).

Data space
: an area in computer memory that contains all the data items, including variables and constants, necessary for program execution.

Data structure
: an object consisting of named components, where each component can be of a different data type. In C, a structure can include a list of one or more declarations; one way a structure differs from an array is that an array's elements must all be of the same type. See Chapters 8, 10, and 11 for more information on structures in C and data structures.

Data type
: in C, a way to tell the computer what kind of variable to represent and how much space (in bytes) in memory will be needed to represent it. Simple variable types are `integer, char, float,` and so on.

Debug
: the process of removing **run time** errors (bugs) from a source program. You debug when your source program has compiled and linked correctly, but it does not produce the correct results. Sometimes this term is casually used to refer to any process of removing program errors, regardless of when they occur. See **Debugger.**

Debugger (source-level)
: a program that you can use to enter your source language program after it has compiled and linked successfully but before it begins to execute. Once you have entered the debugger, the program's execution begins. The debugger allows you to follow your program as it executes, often one line at a time, so that you can detect errors, see partial output, and interrupt the execution as you need to. Chapter 18 describes the Student Compiler's debugger. See also **Breakpoints** and **Trace program.**

Directory
: a way of managing files that is often used in operating systems running on mini- and microcomputers, such as UNIX or PC DOS. A directory is a way of organizing files into groups—it often acts as a table of contents to the rest of the files. On most operating systems, users create directories as they need them. Directories are generally of two sorts, nonhierarchical and hierarchical. In a nonhierarchical directory, all the files are on the same level and have a one-to-one relationship with the directory, for example:

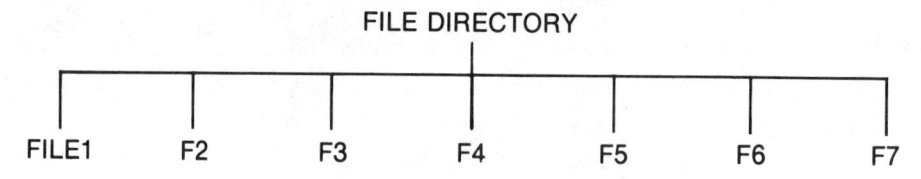

```
                         FILE DIRECTORY
       ┌────────┬────────┬────────┼────────┬────────┬────────┐
     FILE1     F2       F3       F4       F5       F6       F7
```

The structure of a hierarchical directory can look like an upside down tree, where the top directory is the root directory. This type of directory can have files on the same level as well as subdirectories, which in turn may have files

Glossary

and subdirectories, and so on, until it reaches a system-defined limit, for example:

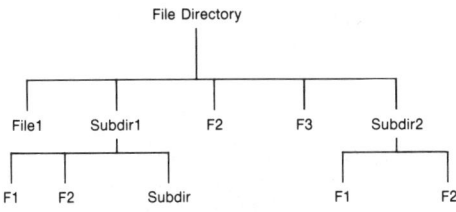

```
                        File Directory
        ┌───────────┬──────┬──────┬───────────┐
      File1      Subdir1   F2     F3       Subdir2
      ┌─┴─┐    ┌───┼────┐                  ┌───┴───┐
      F1  F2   F1  F2  Subdir                F1    F2
```

A directory is also called a file directory.

Disk

a magnetic medium used for storing data. Disks are usually round and vary greatly in size and capability, depending on the computer with which they are used. A disk works with a disk drive, which is a device with read/write heads and other electronic means to store and retrieve data. A disk and its disk drive can be part of a computer, as a hard disk is in a PC, or it can be external to the computer (a peripheral device). A floppy or flexible diskette, which is used with micro- and minicomputers, is often called a *disk* or *floppy* for short.

EBCDIC (format)

acronym for the Extended Binary Coded Decimal Interchange Code. EBCDIC is IBM's standard character encoding scheme that is made up of different bit patterns. Each bit pattern is composed of an 8-bit code (bit positions 7 through 0) of 0s and 1s. EBCDIC is used primarily on the IBM 360-370 series mainframes.

Element

a part or member of a set, such as an element of an array.

ENTER key

a key on the right side of your keyboard that, when pressed, sends information to the operating system. On some keyboards, this key is called RETURN or is represented using an arrow symbol that points down and to the left. For example, to execute the `ls` command in UNIX, you type `ls` at the command line prompt and press the ENTER key; the contents of the current directory are then listed on the screen. In this book, the ENTER key is represented with the symbol <enter>.

Execute

the act of carrying out a program's instructions. This means interpreting the machine language instructions, supplying arguments to parameters, and performing functions and subroutines. To execute a program in MS-DOS, you type the name of the C **executable file** (minus the `.exe` extension) at the command line and press the <enter> key. **Run** is a frequently used term meaning to execute (or sometimes, compile and execute) a source program.

Executable file
: a C language file that has been compiled and linked successfully and is ready to be executed. You execute an *executable* (as it is often called) to see the results of your program.

Expression
: a construction consisting of one or more operators and operands, ranging from the very simple to the complex. Variable names, function calls, constants, literals, lvalues, array names and references, and structure references can all be considered expressions. The following are examples of expressions:

```
a+b    -x    c/d    x=a*b+c    m1[ ]    swap( )
```

An expression's order of evaluation follows the operators' rules of **precedence** and **associativity**. See Chapters 3 and 9 for more information on expressions.

File
: a collection of data or program statements stored on a disk or tape (that is, saved beyond the execution of your program). A file's format, organization, and method to access its data depends on how the file was created and on your operating or computer system. For example, a file may contain a program, numerical information, graphics, or text; its data may be stored in records, which may be accessed in sequential order. See **Access method** and **File organization**.

File organization
: the way data or data records are organized within a file. When files are stored on direct-access storage devices, the file organizations can include sequential, relative, and indexed.

Format (a diskette)
: the process of preparing a diskette to receive and store information. Formatting a previously used diskette wipes out any files or data on that diskette. Under MS-DOS, you format a diskette by putting it in the disk drive, typing the command FORMAT followed by the disk drive letter (for example, A:) and pressing the <enter> key. This formats the diskette in drive A: and displays information about it on the screen.

Function
: in C, a set of code that performs a specific task. You may write your own functions or use the functions that are already included in your compiler's libraries. For example, the library function `sqrt` computes the square root of a floating-point number.

Glossary

Function key
: a specific key on a keyboard that is set or programmed to perform a specific task. For example, if you press key function key F3 in MS-DOS, your previously typed command line is echoed back on the screen. The assigning of a function key to a task is often called *key binding.* Many computer systems allow you to program your keys to fit your own needs. Using a function key can save an experienced user from going through a series of steps to perform the same task, such as saving a file or deleting a line.

Heap
: an area of computer memory where data structures can be allocated and removed. The order of releasing the data structures is random. The heap contains all dynamically allocated memory (memory allocated as needed by the user) used for linked lists, tree structures, and so on.

High-level language
: a programming language that is independent of a machine-specific instruction set. A single high-level language statement can stand for and execute many machine instructions. It is not tied to the computer's architecture by a one-to-one correspondence between a language statement and a machine instruction. Fortran, C, Basic, and Pascal are high-level languages while an **assembly language** is not. A **compiler** translates a high-level language into machine code. See also **Portability**.

Identifier
: a C term referring to the name of an object in storage. An identifier can be a sequence of letters (upper- or lowercase), numbers, and underscores, although it cannot begin with a number. The identifier's length can vary (it is normally up to thirty-two characters), but this number is very compiler-dependent. An identifier cannot be a C language reserved word. Identifiers are usually case-sensitive, depending on the operating system, but it is considered poor style to have two identifiers that differ only by their case, such as `Table_1` and `TABLE_1`.

Initialization of variables
: the process of assigning a starting value to a variable. In the case of a counter, the initial value assigned is often zero.

Installing software
: the process of making a software package **resident** and available for use on your computer system. On a PC, this usually means copying the software from a diskette to the computer's hard disk and, in some cases, configuring it.

Instruction set
: the basic set of operations that a computer system can perform. An instruction describes an operation, specifies its operands, and what the computer is supposed to do with the result. Instructions are accessed using program statements and stored in the (micro)processor's memory.

Interpreter
: a program that analyzes each line of code (that is, your program's statements) and then executes the line of code immediately, rather than translating the code into machine language and then executing the whole program.

Library
: a collection of programs, functions, and so on that have a common organizing theme or purpose. For example, a program library can be one that contains versions of programs for one application that is under development; a library of math functions contains all the functions that perform mathematical calculations. A library can contain loosely related items that are all incorporated when referenced, such as most C compiler function libraries.

Linking
: the process of combining two or more separately compiled object modules into one executable file. Linking ensures that any references between the separate object modules are correct or resolved.

Loop
: a program statement that allows you to execute the same sequence of instructions repetitively, such as a `for` loop. See Chapters 3 and 4 for more information on program loops and control.

Low-level language
: See **Assembly language**.

Machine dependency
: the way memory is allocated, data types or variables declared, and so on depends on the computer's design. For example, an IBM mainframe uses an eight-bit byte while a Honeywell mainframe uses a nine-bit byte. This difference would affect the way data is processed and stored. See also **Portability**.

Machine program
: a version of a source program that the compiler has converted to machine instructions so the computer can understand and execute it. Machine instructions are written in machine code, a series of bytes stored in memory. Each computer has its own machine-level code into which source programs are converted. The terms machine code, machine program, and machine instructions are often used interchangeably.

Memory
: a device or medium that can store information during program execution. Memory is composed of addresses, which are contiguous physical locations that store one piece of information (or data) per address. The addresses are often organized into segments or regions to make the storage and retrieval more efficient. Microcomputers that run under MS-DOS divide memory into segments, where each segment consists of 64 kilobytes of memory. On most computers produced today, memory refers to the (micro)processor's internal storage area. This internal memory can be addressed directly using operating system instructions.

Microprocessor
: in its simplest form, a microprocessor is a semiconductor chip on a printed circuit board (or system board) that controls the computer's central processing unit (CPU). Each microprocessor has an arithmetic logic unit and a control unit; most also have a fixed instruction set. A microprocessor controls a computer's operation, memory addressing (registers, stack, and so on), and input/output facilities, as well as its fundamental data types (for example, an 8-bit byte for a `char`).

    Most IBM personal computers have a 16-bit 8088 or 80286 microprocessor, both of which are in the Intel iAPX86 family of microprocessors. Because these microprocessors are named for their first member (the 8086) and because the 8086 chip is almost identical to the 8088, all the microprocessors in this family are often called 8086 microprocessors.

Module
: another term for a file. Module usually refers to one part of a compiled program that will be linked with other modules to form an **executable file**. See **Object module**.

Null character
: in C, the character ('\0') that terminates a character string; it has a value of zero. The C compiler automatically inserts a null character at the end of a character string. This is called a null byte or null-terminating byte in some C manuals.

Object
: an area of memory used to hold data items, such as variables or structures. This term is often used in C as a more general way of referring to data items in storage because C allows storage to be defined in such a variety of ways.

Object module
: a compiler-generated file that contains the machine (or object) code version of your C source program. An object module is represented by the program's name plus the `.obj` extension, such as `hello.obj`. Object modules are usually linked together into one **executable file**. An object module is also called an object code file or object file.

Operand
: an entity, such as a variable, used with an **operator** to form an **expression**. In the expression a+b, a and b are the operands used with the arithmetic operator + to form an expression. Logical operations can also be performed using operands, as shown in the example under **Boolean**.

Operating system
: software that controls how all the other programs on the computer work. It runs the computer and performs all the functions necessary to control the system operations, such as input/output, debugging, memory allocation, compiling, reporting the system's status, command line operations, interfaces with peripheral devices, and so on. Operating systems are often delivered with the computer itself. Examples of operating systems are AT&T's UNIX, IBM's MVS and PC DOS, Microsoft's MS-DOS, Data General's AOS/VS, and Digital Equipment Corporation's VMS.™

Operators
: a symbol that represents an operation that is to be performed, such as a mathematical operation on two expressions. See the following terms elsewhere in this glossary: **Arithmetic operators, Assignment operators, Binary operator, Bitwise operators, Boolean** (for logical operators), **Expression, Relative operators, Unary operator.** See the table summary of all the C operators in Chapter 8.

Parsing
: during compiling, the process of organizing **tokens** into higher level constructs such as **expressions** or **statements**.

Personal computer (PC)
: a computer designed for individual or small-office use. Specifically, a PC is a microcomputer designed by IBM that contains a **microprocessor** from the Intel iAPX86 family of microprocessors. PC is often casually used for any microcomputer that duplicates the PC's design, that is, a machine that is PC-compatible and can run software designed for the IBM PC.

Pixel
: acronym for picture element. On a computer screen, pixels appear as dots of light that are used to create characters and drawings. The system encodes each pixel with a number of bits that determine the pixel's brightness, color (if any), and other attributes. The number of bits per pixel depends on the computer's display adapter card, a special printed circuit board. See Chapter 17 for more information.

VMS is a trademark of Digital Equipment Corporation.

Glossary

Pointer variable
: the address of a variable (or more generally, an object). For example in C, `int *p` means `p` points to a variable of the type `int`. See Chapter 7 for more on pointers.

Portability
: short for transportability. Writing a program so that it can be run on several operating systems or computers. This is often accomplished by following the accepted guidelines for that language and by keeping **machine-dependent** or operating system-dependent constructs to a minimum. Portability is more often an ideal to aim for rather than an entirely realistic goal, since every machine or system has some dependent characteristics. The C language is more portable than many **high-level languages** because it was designed with portability as a goal.

Precedence (Order of)
: the rules that determine the order in which operations are performed (that is, evaluated) in expressions. In C, precedence applies to all **operators**: arithmetic, assignment, bitwise, logical, relational, and so on. Operators are ranked so that the ones at the top of the ranking (such as an array element reference `[ ]`) are evaluated before operators of lower rank, such as minus (-) or logical AND (`&&`).

Precedence value is the priority assigned to an operator, such as multiplication before addition. If two operators have the same (equal) precedence (as do the arithmetic operators `*` and `/`), they are executed according to the order in which they occur in the equation or statement. See the example under **Boolean** and the table summary of all the C operators in Chapter 8.

Program
: a series of steps, operations, or instructions intended to solve a certain problem or to produce certain results. A program is written in a language, such as C, that can be transformed (using a compiler) so the computer can understand the steps to be taken.

Program space
: an area in computer memory that contains the machine instructions necessary to carry out the program operations.

Pseudocode
: a set of instructions in English that imitates a program's flow and style, so that a user or programmer can understand the steps to take to write the program in a programming language, such as C. Pseudocode lets a programmer examine the semantics of a problem without regard to the syntactic restraints.

Queue

See **Stack**.

Random access

a way of setting the current position in a file, which is the location of the next input or output operation. You can call the ANSI Standard function `fseek` to set a file position; it lets you treat a file (opened with `fopen`) like a single array and move directly to a specific byte. The `ftell` function can be used to obtain the current file position. See Chapter 16 for these functions' descriptions.

Recursion

a process by which a function calls itself repeatedly before returning control to the function that originally called it.

Relational operators

a set of symbols that determines the relationship of one operand to another in an expression. Their **associativity** is from left to right. Relational operators are evaluated in the following order of **precedence**:

    <   less than
    <=   less than or equal to
    >   greater than
    >=   greater than or equal to
    ==   equal to
    !=   not equal to

Thus, < is evaluated before all the other relational operators. The operator <= has a higher **precedence** value than the relational operator > or ==, and so on. See the example under **Boolean**. For more information on relational operators, see Chapter 3 and the table summary of all the C operators in Chapter 8.

Resident

a program that is always present in main memory and not one that is loaded from disk whenever it is needed.

Run

to **execute** a program. In some C compilers, especially those for microcomputers, running a program can also mean *compile then execute* the program in one step.

Run time

an action that occurs during or that relates to a program while it is executing. For example, run time errors occur during the execution phase, not the compilation phase of the process.

Glossary

Scope
: the extent to which an identifier (usually a variable) is known and can be referenced in a program. For example a variable defined inside a function is local, that is, it is known only within that program block. A variable defined outside a function (global) can be known and referenced from its point of definition until the end of the program. See Chapter 9 for a detailed description of scope and its rules.

Semantic analysis
: during compiling, the process of assigning meaning to a construct such as an expression or statement.

Sign bit
: the leftmost bit in a byte or, in an eight-bit byte on a PC, the seventh bit; bits are numbered 7 to 0. The sign bit is used to indicate whether a number is positive or negative in value. See **Bit** and **Byte**.

Software development cycle
: the process of building a working program. The process consists of several steps, some of which may be repeated, until the program performs them correctly. See Chapter 12 for more information on this process.

Source program
: your instructions, written in C or another programming language, of what you want the computer to do to solve a problem or to perform a task. This is often referred to as *source code*.

Source file
: a file containing the original programming language code, such as a file containing C or Fortran code.

Stack
: a special addressless memory structure that is in the form of a linear list. It is often implemented in hardware as memory space for programs and data. Items are accessed, added, or removed from one or both ends of the list. Items can be handled on a *last in first out* (LIFO) basis, also known as a pushdown stack, because an item added to the top of the stack pushes down the item below it.

  Another kind of stack, known as a *queue* or a pushup stack, handles items on a *first in first out* (FIFO) basis, where the first item added is also the first one removed. When items are added or removed from both ends of the queue, it is referred to as a double-queue.

Statement
> in C, an expression (usually an assignment or function call) that is followed by a semicolon (;) or one of the statements defined in the language, such as an `if` statement. Statements can be simple or compound and are introduced in Chapter 3.

String
> See **Character array** and **Character string constant**.

Structure
> See **Data structure**.

Structured programming
> a programming method that simplifies the design, debugging, testing, and documentation of programs. Structured programming uses modules of code and tries to eliminate or minimize the use of `goto` statements. Pascal, ALGOL, and C are structured programming languages.

Text editor
> a program used for adding, changing, and recording data in a file. It usually refers to a program for word processing or one that lets you enter program code. The editor included with the Student Compiler is a text editor.

Toggle
> a switch, command, or key on a keyboard that turns an operation on or off. For example, on many MS-DOS programs, press the INS (insert) key once to type in insert mode, and press it again to return to replace/overwrite mode.

Token
> a fundamental unit of source code. For example, in C, **operators**, separators, **identifiers**, keywords, and **constants** are types of tokens. A token is sometimes referred to as a *lexical* token.

Trace program
> a program within a **debugger** that allows you to stop at and examine each line of C code as it is executing, so that you can see the partial results displayed on the screen. This process is called *single-stepping* through a program. When you detect the errors, you can exit the debugger and return to a **text editor** to correct your source code. The online list of results is sometimes referred to as a traceback or backtrace list.

Transportability
> See **Portability**.

Truth value
> in C, the Boolean value (TRUE or FALSE) assigned to an expression. See **Boolean**.

Glossary

Two's complement arithmetic
: a type of arithmetic based on the binary system. See Chapter 2 for a detailed description.

Unary operator
: an operator that acts on only one operand. For example, the hyphen (-) indicates a negative number and the exclamation point (!) indicates a logical negation. See also **Arithmetic operators.**

Utility programs
: a set of programs that provides a variety of general services, such as command line interpreters, text processing, help (on-line information) services, and so on. Every **operating system** has utility programs.

Variable
: an area in memory that is of a certain data type, such as an integer or character. The name of the variable represents this area in memory and enables your program to save and retrieve data items. A value is associated with a variable and this value can change during program execution. A variable (name) is a placeholder for a value in your program. See also **Constant** and **Scope.**

Word
: the typical unit of memory for a particular computer design. On a **PC**, a word usually equals 16 bits or two bytes; on a mainframe, a word is usually 32 bits or four bytes.

References

Compiler and C Programming References

Aho, Alfred V., Sethi, Ravi, and Ullman, Jeffrey D. (1986), *Compilers: Principles, Techniques, and Tools*, Reading, MA: Addison-Wesley Publishing Company.
Bolsky, M.I. (1985), *The C Programmer's Handbook*, Englewood Cliffs, NJ: Prentice-Hall, Inc.
Brand, Kim Jon (1985), *Common C Functions*, Indianapolis, IN: Que Corporation.
Gehani, Narain (1985), *Advanced C: Food For The Educated Palate*, Rockville, MD: Computer Science Press.
Gehani, Narain (1985), *C: An Advanced Introduction*, Murray Hill, NJ: AT&T Bell Laboratories.
Harbison, Samuel P., and Steele, Guy L., Jr. (1987), *C: A Reference Manual*, Second Edition, Englewood Cliffs, NJ: Prentice-Hall, Inc.
Hogan, Thomas (1984), *The C Programmer's Handbook*, Bowie, MD: Brady Communications Company, Inc.
Hunt, William James (1985), *The C Toolbox*, Reading, MA: Addison-Wesley Publishing Company.
Kernighan, Brian W., and Ritchie, Dennis M. (1978), *The C Programming Language*, Englewood Cliffs, NJ: Prentice-Hall, Inc.
Kochan, Stephen G. (1983), *Programming in C*, Hasbrouck Heights, NJ: Hayden Book Company.
Plum, Thomas, and Brodie, Jim (1985), *Efficient C*, Cardiff, NJ: Plum Hall, Inc.
Plum, Thomas (1983), *Learning to Program in C*, Cardiff, NJ: Plum Hall, Inc.
Purdum, Jack (1983), *C Programming Guide*, Indianapolis, IN: QUE Corporation.
Schustack, Steve (1985), *Variations In C*, Bellevue, WA: Microsoft Press.
Schwaderer, W. David (1985), *C Wizard's Programming Reference*, New York, NY: John Wiley & Sons, Inc.
Sobelman, Gerald E., and Krekelberg, David E. (1985), *Advanced C Techniques & Applications*, Indianapolis, IN: Que Corporation.
Traister, Robert J. (1984), *Programming In C For The Microcomputer User*, Englewood Cliffs, NJ: Prentice-Hall, Inc.

PC DOS and MS-DOS References

IBM Corporation (1987), *Personal Computer Disk Operating System Version 3.3 Reference*, Boca Raton, FL: IBM Corporation.
Microsoft Corporation (1987), *Microsoft MS-DOS Programmer's Reference*, Redmond, WA: Microsoft Corporation.
Norton, Peter (1985), *The Peter Norton Programmer's Guide to the IBM PC*, Bellevue, WA: Microsoft Press.

iAPX86 References

Intel Corporation (1983), *The iAPX86 Programmer's Reference Manual*, Santa Clara, CA: Intel Corporation.

Intel Corporation (1986), *The iAPX86, 88, 186, and 188 User's Manual*, Santa Clara, CA: Intel Corporation.

Palmer, John F., and Morse, Stephen P. (1984), *The 8087 Primer*, New York, NY: John Wiley & Sons, Inc. John Wiley & Sons, Inc.

Function Index

INDEX

Name	Purpose	Class	Page
abort	Abnormally terminate the current process	ANSI	402
abs	Absolute value macro	ANSI	401
access	Test for file accessibility	ANSI	403
acos	Compute the arccosine	ANSI	412
asctime	Convert time to a character string	ANSI	404
asin	Compute arcsine	ANSI	500
atan	Compute the arctangent	ANSI	519
atan2	Compute the arctangent of a quotient	ANSI	519
atof	Convert a string to floating point	ANSI	405
atoi	Convert a string to an integer	ANSI	407
atol	Convert a string to a long integer	ANSI	407
calloc	Allocate and clear memory	ANSI	409
ceil	Round a floating-point number up	ANSI	411
cos	Compute the cosine in radians	ANSI	412
cosh	Compute the hyperbolic cosine	ANSI	412
ctime	Convert a time value to a string	ANSI	414
drawline	Draw a line	BIOS	563
drawrect	Draw an outline of a rectangle	BIOS	563
exit	Terminate execution normally	ANSI	416
exp	Compute the exponential function	ANSI	417
fabs	Floating-point absolute value function	ANSI	418
fclose	Close a standard I/O file	ANSI	420
feof	Check for a standard I/O end-of-file	ANSI	421
ferror	Check for a standard I/O error	ANSI	422
fflush	Flush a standard output buffer	ANSI	423
fgetc	Read a character from a file	ANSI	424
fgets	Read a string from a standard I/O file	ANSI	425
fillrect	Fill a rectangle	BIOS	565
floor	Round a floating-point number down	ANSI	427
fmod	Compute a floating-point modulus	ANSI	428
fopen	Open a standard I/O file	ANSI	429
fprintf	Write formatted print to a file	ANSI	432
fputc	Write a character to a standard I/O file	ANSI	438
fputs	Write a string to a standard I/O file	ANSI	440
fread	Read blocks from a standard I/O file	ANSI	441
free	Free a block of memory	ANSI	443
freopen	Reopen a standard I/O file	ANSI	444

Name	Purpose	Class	Page
frexp	Split a float into a fraction and exponent	ANSI	445
fscanf	Read formatted data from a standard I/O file	ANSI	446
fseek	Set a standard I/O file position	ANSI	450
ftell	Read a standard I/O file position	ANSI	450
fwrite	Write blocks of data to a standard file	ANSI	452
getc	Read a character from a standard file	ANSI	453
getchar	Read a character from the standard input file, stdin	ANSI	453
getcurpos	Get the cursor position	BIOS	542
getcursize	Get the cursor size	BIOS	544
getpixel	Get the color of the pixel	BIOS	561
gets	Read a string from the standard input file, stdin .	ANSI	455
getvideomode	Get the display mode	BIOS	539
gmtime	Separate Greenwich Mean Time into its components	ANSI	457
intdos	Generate a DOS interrupt	MS-DOS	459
intdoss	Generate a DOS interrupt (segments in/out)	MS-DOS	459
intdosx	Generate a DOS interrupt (segments in)	MS-DOS	459
int86	Generate an interrupt	MS-DOS	459
int86s	Generate an interrupt (segments in/out)	MS-DOS	459
int86x	Generate an interrupt (segments in)	MS-DOS	459
isalnum	Test for an alphanumeric character	ANSI	462
isalpha	Test for an alphabetic character	ANSI	462
iscntrl	Test for a control character	ANSI	463
isdigit	Test for a decimal digit	ANSI	464
isgraph	Test for a graphics character	ANSI	465
islower	Test for a lowercase character	ANSI	466
isprint	Test for a printable character	ANSI	468
ispunct	Test for a punctuation character	ANSI	469
isspace	Test for a white space character	ANSI	471
isupper	Test for an uppercase character	ANSI	466
isxdigit	Test for a hexadecimal digit	ANSI	464
labs	Long integer absolute value function	ANSI	472
ldexp	Load an exponent	ANSI	473
localtime	Separate local time into its components	ANSI	474
log	Compute a natural logarithm	ANSI	476
log10	Compute a common logarithm	ANSI	476
longjmp	Perform a nonlocal goto	ANSI	498
malloc	Allocate memory	ANSI	477

Name	Purpose	Class	Page
memchr	Find a character in a memory block	ANSI	480
memcmp	Compare two memory blocks	ANSI	480
memcpy	Copy a memory block	ANSI	480
memset	Set a memory block to a value	ANSI	480
modf	Split a floating-point value	ANSI	483
perror	Map the external variable errno to an error message	ANSI	484
pow	Compute the value of the power function	ANSI	485
printf	Write formatted print to stdout	ANSI	432
putc	Write a character to a standard I/O file	ANSI	486
putchar	Write a character to stdout	ANSI	486
puts	Write a string to the standard output file, stdout	ANSI	487
qsort	Sort a data array	ANSI	488
rand	Generate a random number	ANSI	490
readchar	Read the character and attribute	BIOS	547
realloc	Reallocate memory	ANSI	491
remove	Delete a standard I/O file	ANSI	492
rename	Change a standard I/O filename	ANSI	493
rewind	Reset the file position	ANSI	495
scanf	Read formatted data from the standard input file	ANSI	446
scrolldown	Scroll down the window	BIOS	549
scrollup	Scroll up the window	BIOS	549
setborder	Set the border color	BIOS	551
setbuf	Set buffer mode for a standard I/O file	ANSI	496
setcolor	Set the current color	BIOS	559
setcurpos	Set the cursor position	BIOS	542
setcursize	Set the cursor size	BIOS	544
setjmp	Define a label for a nonlocal goto	ANSI	498
setpalette	Set the color palette	BIOS	553
setpixel	Set the color of the pixel	BIOS	561
setvbuf	Set varying-length buffer for a standard I/O file	ANSI	496
setvideomode	Set the display mode	BIOS	539
sin	Compute sine in radians	ANSI	500
sinh	Compute hyperbolic sine	ANSI	500
sprintf	Write formatted print to storage	ANSI	432
sqrt	Compute the square root	ANSI	502
srand	Set the seed for the rand function	ANSI	503
sscanf	Read formatted data from a string	ANSI	446
strcat	Concatenate two null-terminated strings	ANSI	504

Name	Purpose	Class	Page
strchr	Find the first occurrence of a character in a string	ANSI	**506**
strcmp	Compare two null-terminated strings	ANSI	**507**
strcpy	Copy one null-terminated string to another	ANSI	**509**
strcspn	Measure a span of characters not in a set	ANSI	**511**
strlen	Measure the length of a null-terminated string . . .	ANSI	**513**
strncat	Concatenate two null-terminated strings (limited) .	ANSI	**504**
strncmp	Compare portions of two null-terminated strings .	ANSI	**507**
strncpy	Copy a portion of a null-terminated string	ANSI	**509**
strpbrk	Find the first character of a set in a string	ANSI	**514**
strrchr	Find the last occurrence of a character in a string	ANSI	**506**
strspn	Measure a span of characters in a set	ANSI	**511**
strtok	Get a token	ANSI	**515**
strtol	Convert a string to a long integer	ANSI	**517**
tan	Compute the tangent in radians	ANSI	**519**
tanh	Compute the hyperbolic tangent	ANSI	**519**
time	Get the current time in seconds	ANSI	**522**
tmpnam	Generate a unique filename	ANSI	**523**
tolower	Convert a character to lowercase	ANSI	**524**
toupper	Convert a character to uppercase	ANSI	**524**
ungetc	Undo the effect of getc	ANSI	**525**
writechar	Write the character and attribute	BIOS	**547**

Index

A

access method   613
actual parameters   124
address
  See memory address
address operator   160–162
address-of expressions (& operator)
  lvalues   188
aggregate data types   192
algorithms   613
ALT keys   382
AND operator   47–48
ANSI functions
  See also separate index of functions
  list   401
ANSI standard   613
arguments of functions   124
Arguments prompt
  Debug command   380, 381
  Run command   376–378
arithmetic conversion   201
arithmetic data types   192
arithmetic operators   43, 613
  order of evaluation   53
  precedence   53
array elements
  lvalues   188
array names
  comparison of   314
  lvalues   188
arrays   149–158
  referencing elements beyond end of
    array   308
ASCII
  character set   603
  characters   25
  coding system for characters   25
  collating sequence   614
  format   614
  value   531, 535
assembly language   614
assignment   614
assignment operators   43, 614
assignment statement   34–35
  lvalues   187
associativity   615
  arithmetic operators   53
attribute byte   535, 547
auto storage class   221–222
AUTOEXEC.BAT file   333, 342, 571
  creating   333–334
  editing   334
automatic variables   221–222, 313–314, 393

B

background colors   532, 534–535
  setting   553–554
BACKSPACE key   351
backtrace list   630
base 2 number system   22–26
base 10 number system   22–23
binary file   252
binary number system   22–26
binary operators   44, 615
binary tree   268, 271, 290
bios.h header file   397, 535
bits   21–22, 26, 181, 615
  turning on and off   534–535
bitwise AND operator (&)   185
bitwise exclusive OR operator (^)   185
bitwise negation operator (~)   184
bitwise operations   183
bitwise operators   181, 184–187, 203, 616
  common errors in   312
  hints on use   186–187
bitwise OR operator (|)   185

bitwise shift operators
   left shift (<<) 186
   right shift (>>) 186
block 66
Block menu 343, 344, 355, 356
boldface
   See high intensity lines
Boolean logic 616
branching, using goto statement 83
BREAK command (DOS) 329
Break menu 569, 572, 579–581
break statement
   with loops 75–76
   with switch statement 65–66
breakpoints 569, 579–581, 582, 616
   clearing 580, 581
   listing 580
   setting 580
   temporary 582
brightness 534
buffers 92, 617
bytes 21–22, 26, 617

C

C continuation character (\) 14, 350
%c printf format specifier 38
C-Function template 385
call by reference 126
call by value 125–126
calling functions 124–128
   before they are defined 126–128
calloc function 393
case sensitivity 617
cast 202
central processing unit 625
CGA card 529, 559
char data type 29, 31, 394
character arrays 618
character box 530–531, 535
character constants 35–36
character pointer variables, debugger 578
character strings, debugger 578

character-string arrays 618
character-string constants 618
character-string literals 618
characters 617
Clear All command 581
color attributes 534–535
color numbers 553–556
color palette 553–556
Color/Graphics Adapter (CGA) 529
colors 534–537
comma operator (,) 189
command line 618
command-line arguments 377, 378, 380, 381, 618
commands
   fast path 347–349
   highlighted 345
   selecting in menus 348, 349
comments 309
   in C programs 13
compile time 618
   errors 590–598, 618
compilers 9, 324, 618
compiling programs 9, 10
compound statement 66
computer systems, recommended 329
conditional compilation 235–237
conditional expressions 49
   in while loops 78
conditional operator (?:) 189
conditional statements 49
CONFIG.SYS file 329, 619
configuration file 619
constants 35, 36, 619
   character 35–36
   double 36
   float 36
   integer 35
continue statement
   with loops 76–77
control characters
   escape sequences 13–14, 382, 573
conversion codes for printf 102

conversion operations with printf   39
converting data types   201–203
coordinate system   530
Copy command   358
COPY CON command (DOS)   333
copying Student Compiler diskettes
   floppy disk drive   332
   hard disk drive   330
CPU
   See central processing unit
CTRL keys   349, 351, 382, 383
   compiler   382
   debugger   573
CTRL-BACKSPACE keys   351, 353
CTRL-BREAK keys   378, 383
CTRL-END keys
   compiler   351
   debugger   573
CTRL-HOME keys
   compiler   351, 366
   debugger   573
CTRL-PgDn keys
   compiler   351
   debugger   573
CTRL-PgUp keys
   compiler   351
   debugger   573
CTRL-PrtSc keys   380
CTRL-Z keys   334
ctype.h header file   397
current cursor position
   compiler   342
   debugger   572
current line   342
cursor   619
   compiler   342
   debugger   572
   height   544–545
   size   544–545
   width   545

cursor control keys   350
   compiler   350
   debugger   573
cursor mode   343, 350

D

%d printf format specifier   38
data base operations   264
data bases   259
data declaration   617
data definition   619
data sets   619
data spaces   393, 619
data structures   259, 620
   debugger   577
data types   29–32, 620
   char   29, 31
   characteristics   393–394
   converting   201–202
   creating data-type names   200
   declaring   33–34
   derived   191
   double   29, 32
   float   29, 32
   formats   393–394
   int   29, 30–31
   long   29, 30–31
   short   29, 30–31
   sizes   29, 32
   Student Compiler   393–394
   typedefs   200
debug   620
Debug command   380–382, 569, 571
debugger   567, 569, 571, 574, 620
   exiting   381, 571
   function key F4   381
   function key F9   381
   invoking   571
   returning to editor or Program
     Screen   381
   using the menu system   574
Debugger Screen   571–574
decimal number system   22–23

declaration statement 33–34
declarations 33–34
  function parameter 123
declaring variables 33–34
default commands 345
default menu 345
default statement
  with switch statement 65
#define statement 229–234, 235–237
  preprocessed C code 106–108
defined command
  preprocessed C code 237–238
defining
  functions 121–124
  variables 34
DEL key 351
Delete command 360
Delete Line command 353, 360
destination path 333, 334
differences
  among compilers 11
  from ANSI standard 11
DIR command (DOS) 329
directories 620
  root directory 620
disk drives 621
DISKCOPY command (DOS) 332
diskettes, formatting 331, 332, 622
disks 621
display adapter card 529
display buffer 529–530
Display menu 572, 576–579
display modes 531–534
  choosing the best 534
  color attributes 534–537
  default setting 531
  re-setting 531–533
  setting 531
do while loop 73, 81–83
Do While Loop template 387
DOS commands diskette 332, 333
dos.h header file 397
dot operator (.) 195–196

double constants 36
double data type 29, 32, 394
double-floppy disk drive 329
double-queue 629
down arrow key
  compiler 351
  debugger 573
drawline function 563–564
drawrect function 563–564
dynamic allocation 263

E

%e printf format specifier 39
EBCDIC
  characters 25
  coding system for characters 25
  format 621
Edit menu 343–345, 350, 352
Editing Screen 341–343
editing window 342, 350
editor 8–9
EGA card 529, 559
8086 microprocessor 625
8088 microprocessor 625
80286 microprocessor 625
elements 621
  array 150–151
#elif 237
#else 235–236
else if statement 67
else statement 50
embedded assignment, with getchar in
  while loop 100
END key 351
end of file (EOF) 99
  marker 99
#endif 235, 309
Enhanced Graphics Adapter (EGA) 529
<enter> key 621
enum keyword 193
enum type 193
enum variable 193
enumerations 193, 203

enumerator list   193
enumerator tag   193
Erase to End command   353, 354
errno variable   394–395, 484
error flags, example   183
error messages   15, 394
   compiler   322, 587–590
   debugger   590
   errno variable   394, 484
   MS-DOS   394
   PC DOS   394
   Student Compiler   322
error.h header file   394, 397
ESC key   345
   compiler   344, 345, 383
   help window   373
   return to editing window   343
escape sequences   13–14, 383
executable files   9–10, 324, 622
Execute menu   572, 581–584
executing programs   621
exit condition loop   81
exit function   303
exiting Student Compiler   342
explicit conversion   201
   cast expressions   202
expressions   51, 187, 312, 622
extern storage class   222–224, 393
external declarations   220
   Student compiler   393
external variables   222–224, 311–312

F

%f printf format specifier   38
FALSE value   616
fast path
   Copy command   358, 359
   Delete command   360
   Delete Line command   353, 360
   editing keys   382
   Erase to End command   354
   fast path keys   344–345
   File command   376

First Error command   367
Help command, compiler   373
Help command, debugger   575
Join Line command   354
Left Shift command   362
Move command   359
New File command   379
Next command   366
Once command   582
Proceed command   583
Query Replace command   369, 370
Quit command, compiler   376
Quit command, debugger   576
Right Shift command   363
Run command   378
Save command   375
Search command   365
Select Line command   357
selecting commands   349
selecting menus   347
Set/Clear command   580–581
Split Line command   355
String command   578
Templates menu   383
Trace command   583
Undo Select command   357
Variable command   577
fast path keys   344–345
fclose function   255
fgetc function   95, 96–97, 99
fgets function   95, 101–102
FILE   253
File command   375, 376
File menu   343, 344, 370, 371
files   8–9, 92, 622
   directory   620
   executable   9–10
   header   15
   names   8
   object code   9, 625
   organization   622
   pointers   253
   source   9, 629

fillrect function 565
First Error command 368, 377, 378, 380
float constants 36
float data type 29, 32, 394
float.h header file 397
floating-point overflow 36
floppy disk drive 329
fopen function 253–255
For Loop template 386
for loops 73–75
   infinite loops 75
for statement 73, 307
foreground colors 532, 534–535
formal parameters 124–125
format specifiers for printf 39, 102
formatting diskettes 331, 332, 622
fputc function 95, 96, 99
fputs function 95, 100–102
fread function 255–256
free function 281–282, 393
fseek function 257–258
ftell function 258
function calls 124–128
   debugger 583
function key F4
   quitting compiler 342
   quitting debugger 381, 571
function key F9
   compiler 371
   debugger 571
function key F10 350
   compiler 345
   debugger 571
function keys 382, 623
function libraries
   See also separate index of functions
   ANSI standard 401
   graphics 537
   screen management 537
function names 122–123
   and lvalues 188

function parameters 122–123
   actual 124
   declarations of 123
   formal 124–125
function types 122–123, 311
functions 12, 117, 120, 622
   See also separate index of functions
   arguments 124
   body 123
   definition 121–124
   prototypes 131–132
   structure 120–133

G

getc function 95, 96, 98, 99
getchar function 95, 96–100, 309, 310–311
getcurpos function 542–543
getcursize function 544–546
getpixel function 561–562
gets function 95, 100
getvideomode function 539–541
global variables 128–130, 629
Go command 582, 583
goto statement 83–84
graphics display modes 533–534
graphics functions 529, 537
graphics video mode 530–531, 531
   color attributes 534–535

H

hard disk drive 329–331
hardware requirements, Student Compiler 329
header files 15, 50, 51, 396–397
heap 393, 623
Help command
   compiler 331–332, 371, 373
   debugger 575
Help facility path 331–332
Help On prompt, Help command 372
hexadecimal notation 183
high intensity lines 572

high-level languages   324, 623
high-order bit   24
highlighted commands   345
highlighted lines, debugger   572
HOME key   351

I

I/O
  See input; output
I/O and standard files   94
iAPX86 microprocessor   625
identifiers   27, 623
#if   235–236, 309
if statement   49, 67
  compared to conditional operator
    189
  with switch statement   63
If-Else template   386
#ifdef   236–237, 309
#ifndef   236–237
implicit conversion   201–202
INCLUDE environment variable   333
#include files   393, 396–398
#include statement   15, 50, 51,
    234–235, 315
  preprocessed C code   106
incrementing loop control   71
indirection operator (*)   160–161
  and lvalues   188
information storage   26
initializing
  arrays   152
  loops   71
  variables   34, 623
inline code   397
inorder traversal   300
input line
  compiler   344
  debugger   573
input/output operations   91–94
  header file   398
INS key   351
insert mode   350

installing Student Compiler   329–332
  floppy disk drive   331, 332
  hard disk drive   330, 331
installing software   623
instructions   624
int data type   29, 30–31, 394
integer constants   35
integral data types   192
interpreter   624
invoking Student Compiler   341–342

J

Join Line command   354, 355

K

key binding   623
key combinations   382

L

label, goto statement   83
left arrow key   351
Left Shift command   360–362
lexical tokens   630
libraries   9, 12, 624
limits.h header file   397
#line   238
line continuation character
  See C continuation character
lines, debugger
  high intensity   572
  highlighted   572
  reverse video   572
linked list   267, 269–270, 282
linking   9–10, 624
  Student Compiler   325, 391
List command   580
local variables   311–312, 629
logical expressions, order of
  evaluation   48
logical operators   47, 616
long data type   29, 30–31, 393
long, forcing constants to   35

loop control variable 71
loop counter 71
loop iteration 71
loops 63, 69, 624
   discussion 69–72
   do while loops 73, 81–83
   exit condition loop 81
   for loops 73
   traversing 71
   using ++ and -- 72
   while loops 73
low-level I/O 252
low-level languages 614
lvalues 187–188

M

MA card 529, 537
machine code 624
machine dependency 624
machine instructions 614, 624
machine programs 324, 624
macro expansion 231
macros
   and #define statement 107–108
   defining 230–233
main function 11–13, 117–118
malloc function 280–281, 393
manifest constants 229
math.h header file 397–398
memory 21, 625
   allocating and deallocating 280–282
   dynamic allocation 393
   organization model 391
   Student Compiler 391
memory address 166, 625
memory resident programs 329
menu bar
   compiler 343
   debugger 572
   selecting menus, compiler 346
menu selection 345
menu system, using 344

menus, Student Compiler 343–348
   pull-down 344
   selecting 345
   selecting commands 348
message line 344
   compiler 344
   debugger 574
microprocessor 625
model, memory organization 391
modules 625
modulus operator 44
Monochrome Adapter (MA) 529
Move command 359
MS-DOS 329
multiple statements in a block 66

N

names
   file 8–9
   function 122–123
negative numbers 25, 26, 30
New File command 378, 379
New File prompt, New File command 378
Next command 366, 369
nodes 267
null byte 625
null character 625
NULL pointer 398

O

object code file 9, 625
object module 9, 624, 625
objects 27, 625
   debugger 577
Once command 582
one's complement arithmetic 25, 26
operands 626
operating systems 626
operators 43, 626
   arithmetic 43, 613
   assignment 43, 614

operators *continued*
   binary   44, 615
   bitwise   184-187, 616
   dot   195-196
   logical   47, 616
   relational   46
   structure pointer   196-197
   table of   214-215
   unary   44
OR operator   47-48
order of evaluation   627
   arithmetic operators   53
   expressions   51
   with parentheses   53
order of precedence
   See precedence
output operations   91-94
output window, debugger   573
overflow   36

P

palette   553-556
parameter declarations   123
parameterized macros   231
parameters, function   122-125
   actual   124
   formal   124-125
parentheses
   and arithmetic operators   53
   order of evaluation with   54
parsing   626
partitioned data sets (PDS)   619
PATH command (DOS)   333, 334
path, SC directory   333
PC compatibility   626
PC DOS   329
perror function   396
personal computers (PCs)   626
PgDn key
   compiler   351
   debugger   573

PgUp key
   compiler   351
   debugger   573
pixels   530, 626
   color attributes   534
pointer arithmetic   166
pointer data type   394
pointers   158-170, 316, 627
   and data types   192
   and lvalues   188
   structure pointer operator   196-197
portability   627
positive numbers   24, 26, 30
postfix operator   72
#pragma   238
precedence   52, 53, 627
   arithmetic operators   53
   in expressions   51, 52
precision
   specifying with %e   39
   specifying with %f   38-39
prefix operator   72
preprocessor   105-108, 228
preprocessor commands   228-238
preprocessor directive   228
Print command   379
printf function   13-15, 95, 102-104
   conversion operations   39
   example   12
   format specifiers   38-39
   function of   32, 38
printing
   DOS commands   380
   program input   379
   program output   380
Proceed command   583
Program Screen   341
   compiler   341
   debugger   571
program space   393, 627
Program template   385
programming environment   391

651

programs   323–325, 627
  executing   575, 583–584
  machine   324
  programming languages   323–324
  running   323–324
  source   323, 629
  translating   324
  writing   325
prompts
  Arguments   378, 381
  Help On   372, 373
  New File   378
  Replace String   368
  Save File   366
  Search String   364, 365, 368, 369
  Source   342, 350
  String Variable   578
  Variable Name   577
prototype, function   131–132
pseudocode   69, 627
pull-down menus   344
putc function   95, 96, 98, 99
putchar function   95, 96–97
puts function   95, 100

Q

Query Replace command   368, 369
queue   629
Quit command   376
  compiler   342, 374, 375, 376
  debugger   570, 571, 576
quotes, single
  use with character constants   35–36, 618

R

RAM
  See Random Access Memory (RAM)
random access   450, 628
Random Access Memory (RAM)   329
readchar function   547–548
recursion   282, 293, 628
register storage class   226

relational operators   46, 626
Replace All command   369, 370
replace mode   350
Replace String prompt
  Query Replace command   368
  Replace All command   369
resident programs   329, 628
resolution   530
Restart command   575
return key
  See <enter> key
return statement   123–124
right arrow key   351
Right Shift command   362, 363
root directory   620
rules for naming variables   27–28
Run command   376–378, 569
run time   628
  errors   628
running programs   628

S

Save command   374, 375
scalar data types   192
scalars   149
scientific notation   39
scope   220, 226–227, 629
screen interface   529
screen management functions   529, 537
scrolldown function   549–550
scrollup function   549–550
Search command   364, 365
Search menu   343, 344, 363–364
Search String prompt
  Query Replace command   368, 369
  Replace All command   370
  Search command   364, 365
searching
  search routine for data bases   287
segments   625
Select Line command   356, 357

selecting commands
   debugger 574
   fast path 349
   menu 348–349
selecting menus
   compiler 345
   debugger 574
semantic analysis 629
semicolons (;) 66
   in C statements 12
sequential data sets 619
sequential organization 619
Session menu 572, 574–576
SET command (DOS) 333, 334
Set/Clear command 580–581
setborder function 551–552
setcolor function 531, 534, 555, 559–560
setcurpos function 542–543
setcursize function 544–546
setjmp.h header file 398
setpalette function 531, 534, 553–558, 559
   color number 555
setpixel function 561–562
setvideomode function 531, 532, 533, 534, 539–541
SHIFT TAB key 351
Shift-PrtSc key 380
short data type 29, 30–31, 394
shortcut, selecting commands 348
sign bit 24, 629
signed numbers 24–26, 30
single-stepping 569, 581, 582, 630
   in functions 583
sizeof operator 32
software development cycle 325, 629
source file 9
source programs 323
Source prompt 342
source window, debugger 572, 573
Split Line command 355
splitting a line 342

stack 393, 629
standard files 93
standard function library 398, 401
standard input and output operations 94–105, 252, 398
statement block 66
statement label
   goto statement 83–84
statements 630
static storage class 224–225
static variable 314
status line 343
   debugger 573
stderr file 94–97
stdin file 94–99
stdio.h header file 398
stdlib.h header file 398
stdout file 94–99, 102
storage 21–22
   and declarations 34
   and definitions 34
   how computers store information 26
storage class 220
String command 578
string I/O 100–102
String Variable prompt, String command 578
string.h header file 398
strings
   See character array; character-string constant
struct keyword 194
struct passing 316
structure of C programs 11
structure pointer operator (->) 197
structure tags 194
structured programming 117–118, 630
structures 193–196, 315, 316
   compared to unions 197
   members 194
Student Compiler
   commands 344, 348
   data types 393

Student Compiler *continued*
  debugger 569
  debugging programs 380, 381
  editing programs 350
  Editing Screen 342, 343
  error messages 587–590
  interrupting 329
  memory 391–392
  menus 344, 345
  printing programs 379
  Program Screen 341, 377
  running programs 376–378
subscripts 151
switch statement 63–67, 307
Switch template 386
syntax errors
  warnings 590–598

T

TAB key 350, 351
tab stops 14, 350
Templates menu 383–384
  fast path 383
ternary operator 189
text attributes 534–535
text display modes 532, 547, 556
  setpalette function 556
text editor 630
text files 252
text video mode 530–533, 547
time.h header file 398
toggles 580, 630
tokens 630
Trace command 569, 582, 583
trace program 630
traceback 578, 630
transportabability
  See portability
traversal of a tree 300
traversing loops 71
tree sort 290
  inorder traversal 300

truth values 616, 630
  logical operators 47
  operators 46
  while loops 79
tutorial
  key and type conventions 7
  organization 6–7
  purpose 5
two's complement arithmetic 25, 631
typedefs 200, 203, 315
types
  See data types
typical ranges for C variables on a
    PC 30

U

unary operators 44, 631
#undef 233–234
underscore characters
  in variable names 28
Undo Select command 357
union keyword 197
unions 197–200, 203
  compared to structures 197
units of memory 21–22, 26
unsigned char data type 394
unsigned int data type 394
unsigned long int data type 394
unsigned numbers 24–26, 30
unsigned short int data type 394
unsigned type 309
up arrow key
  compiler 351
  debugger 573
using tutorial with your computer 7
utility programs 631

V

Variable command 577
Variable Name prompt, Variable
    command 577

variables 27
  declaring 34
  global 629
  in debugger 577
  initializing 34, 623
  local 629
  naming 27
video mode 530–531

W

Where command 578–579
While Loop template 387
while loops 73, 77–81
while statement 307
words 26, 631
writechar function 532, 533, 534, 535, 547–548, 553

Special Characters

~ operator 184
>> operator 186
−− operator 72
− operator 44
+ operator 44
\n 310
\0 310
. operator 195–196
<< operator 186
++ operator 80
| operator 185
& operator 185
&& operator 47–48
! operator 47–48
^ operator 185
* operator 44
/ operator 44
|| operator 47–48
, operator 189
% operator 44
?: operator 189

Your Turn

If you have comments or suggestions about this book, please let us know by writing your ideas in the space below. If you include your name and address, we will write to you.

Please return this sheet to the Publications Division, SAS Institute Inc., SAS Circle, Box 8000, Cary, NC 27512-8000.